FREDERICK JACKSON TURNER

a reference guide

A
Reference
Guide
to
Literature

Jack Salzman
Editor

FREDERICK JACKSON TURNER

a reference guide

VERNON E. MATTSON *and* WILLIAM E. MARION

G.K.HALL&CO.

70 LINCOLN STREET, BOSTON, MASS.

Published by G. K. Hall & Co.
A publishing subsidiary of ITT

Library of Congress Cataloging in Publication Data

Marion, William E.
  Frederick Jackson Turner : a reference guide.

  (A Reference guide to literature)
  Bibliography: p.
  Includes index.
  1. Turner, Frederick Jackson, 1861-1932—Bibliography.
2. Frontier thesis—Bibliography. I. Mattson, Vernon E.
II. Title. III. Series.
Z8893.9.M37 1985   016.973'072024   84-25266
[E175.5.T83]
ISBN 0-8161-7997-2

This publication is printed on permanent/durable acid-free paper
MANUFACTURED IN THE UNITED STATES OF AMERICA

Contents

The Authors

William E. Marion is an instructor of English and history at the University of Nevada at Las Vegas. He is currently completing his doctorate for the American and New England Studies Program at Boston University. The title of his dissertation is "Tales of an Un-self Confident Man: Jack Kerouac and the Fictions of Autobiography."

Vernon E. Mattson is an associate professor of history at the University of Nevada at Las Vegas, where he has taught American history since 1969. He did his graduate work in history and psychology at North Texas State University and the University of Kansas. His fields of interest are the role of religion in American history, American intellectual history, and Holocaust studies.

Foreword, by Wilbur R. Jacobs

Those of us immersed in the writing of American history look back with pride and appreciation to the achievements of Frederick Jackson Turner, a native son, a great teacher, and an innovative scholar who, through the lens of frontier history, opened to the world previously obscure vistas of our culture. In his perceptive analyses of our frontier heritage he gave us a sense of self-esteem, and also pride in the manner our forebears built a nation.

We know that though capable of admirable lucidity, even eloquence, in his essays, Turner found writing for publication difficult. His collected papers, research notes, and correspondence show that his approach to history was essentially nonliterary in the sense that he followed a scientific methodology, adopting from the science method of research what history could use. His work lives today though some of the best that came from his pen was composed before 1900. His approach was strikingly modern, following as it did a procedure of massing evidence, sifting facts to reach conclusions, and then formulating hypotheses for theoretical scaffolding. If we examine his method of placing data on maps from thousands of three-by-five cards, we see him as an investigator probing economic, social, political, cultural, and geographical forces. Through this systematic means of working he was able to show evolutionary aspects in the interplay of historical forces in his essays, especially in his brilliant "The Significance of the Frontier in American History," of 1893.

Turner was not expert in depicting the personality of an individual, in giving character to the appearance of a place, or in capturing the mood or excitement of an event. He was not, as he wrote one of his publishers, "competent" in dealing with the "narrative side." "My strength, or weakness," he wrote, lies in interpretation, correlation, elucidation of large tendencies to bring our new points of view and in giving a new setting. . . . I'm not a good saga-man."

Turner's unromantic approach to frontier history, his stress on ideas, the pure intellectual quality of much of his work, may easily challenge his readers because the frontier advance seems to lend itself to dramatic narration. Writing to one of his former students after his retirement from Harvard he made a self-evaluation of his life work:

> My work, whether good or bad, can only be correctly
> judged by noting what American historians and teachers
> of history . . . were doing when I began. . . . The
> attitude toward Western history was at the time
> largely antiquarian or of the romantic narrative type
> devoid of the conception of the "West" as a moving
> process--modifying the East, and involving economic,
> political, and social forces. . . . The "West" with
> which I dealt, was a process rather than a fixed geo-
> graphical region; it began with the Atlantic Coast;
> and it emphasized the way in which the East colonized
> the West. . . . In short, the "frontier" was taken as
> the "thin red line" that recorded the dynamic element
> in American history up to recent times.

By his own description, then, Turner's "West" was not glorious or halcyon, but rather, as near as he was able to portray it, a process involving complexities of change. In one of his unpublished manu-scripts, preserved in the Huntington Library collection of his papers, Turner explained that his analysis of frontier history comprised at least four distinct but interrelated phenomena:

> [1] the spread of settlement westward; and [2] all the
> economic, social, and political changes involved in
> the existence of a belt of free land at the edge of
> settlement; [3] the continual settling of successive
> belts of land; [4] the evolution of these successive
> areas of settlement through various stages of back-
> woods life, ranching, pioneer farming, scientific
> farming, and manufacturing life.

If we examine closely what Turner attempted to do, we can see that he set himself the task of showing westward expansion as a pro-cess that included not only the occupation of the frontier and the parallel evolution of society from a rural pioneer stage to a so-phisticated urban environment, but also something more. He endeavored to show "all the economic, social, and political changes" on the frontier fringe as the various "Wests" underwent a "process" of social evolution. Although a gifted stylist, Turner labored at his writing and encountered perplexing problems in creating history of such density. As his former student Avery Craven once wrote to me about Turner, "the trouble was that his conception of 'what was his-tory' was so complex that neither he nor anyone else could or can do much with it beyond the essay form."

Yet Turner did succeed as a professional historian. Modestly de-clining to assert that he was the founder of a so-called new history, his contribution to it was probably as great as any other scholar of

his generation. When his first book of essays was about to be published in 1919 he declined to have The Frontier in American History,
as the volume was called, to be advertised as "'new history,'" "or
anything of the sort." "What I was dealing with," Turner recalled,
"was the character of American democracy as compared with that of
Europe or of European philosophers." He remembered that before he
had advanced his frontier hypothesis, the West and frontier had often
been explained as merely "annexation of territory."

Considering what he attempted to do, the very complications of
the interdisciplinary, analytic analysis that lay behind his work,
it is amazing that he accomplished as much as he did. It is also
understandable that soon a barrage of critics appeared on the scene
to demonstrate that he tended to overlook or distort such factors as
urban development, conservation, or the significance of Indians, and
black and Mexican Americans.

At the same time, for every critic there appeared a Turner de-
fender. His supporters argued that attacks on the frontier theory
oversimplified Turner's contributions. The frontier theory was
actually a hypothesis linked to his theory of sections, which helped
to explain the growth of our political party system. The frontier
theory was in fact the frontier-sectional theory, which in turn involved principles of multiple causation. The various frontiers,
leaving a terminal moraine of geographical provinces, eventually
evolved into a federation of sections that nourished the American
spirit. Turner, it was argued, forced us to inspect the limits of
our understanding of a new American history.

What makes this Guide to Frederick Jackson Turner's work so fascinating is that it unlocks Turner's career, revealing the tremendous
impact he had upon the writing and interpreting of American history.
The very listing of Turner's writings and examining the niagara of
publications about him and his work are keys in understanding major
shifts in American historical thought. The year-by-year listing of
printed works, along with annotations by the editors, offers a show-
case of what actually took place as Turner made his presence upon the
historical stage.

Turner's own explanation of his theories of frontier-sectional
hypotheses, as well as other numerous publications, appear in the
first section of the Guide. The second part moves us into the historical amphitheater where his theories are debated. In Turner's
lifetime criticism was muted, but after his death in 1932, the wide-
ranging reexamination of his interpretations takes place. The full
slate of books and articles proves that Turner brought a fresh approach to sociopolitical history, historical geography, the origins
of the American character, and the realization of existing interrelationships in the history of agriculture, economics, politics,
westward migration, and urban history. The parade of publications in
the Guide has other themes, such as the role of Turner in the forming

of the American Historical Association and the setting of standards
for its key publication, the Review. Along with the rise of the
association, we can observe the surfacing of Turner's former students,
some of whom were to become distinguished scholars in their own right.
Perhaps the most illustrious of these, writing about their master
teacher, are Carl L. Becker and Merle E. Curti.

This excellent Guide documents how Turner's former students and
disciples not only expounded his theories but gave them special interpretation. Herbert Eugene Bolton and Avery Craven, for instance,
took off from Turner's ideas as a starting point and then went on to
make significant contributions of their own. Merle Curti, gifted
scholar and admirer of Turner, became himself a founding father of
another field, American intellectual history. Later Turnerian
writers, some of whom never knew Turner personally, included Richard
Hofstadter, Norman Harper, and Turner's prize-winning biographer, Ray
Allen Billington. Their articles and critiques, along with a swelling
number of publications on Turner by other writers, became so numerous
that a new field developed, Turnerian bibliography. One of the best
of the early essays summing up Turnerian publications was written by
Gene W. Gressley. The latest, of course, is this fine Guide, giving
us an accounting of the continuous outpouring of scholarship on
Turner.

Turner would be gratified to have this comprehensive new Guide
appear in print. For those of us who have examined his papers at the
Huntington Library there is no question that Turner was concerned
with the impact of his career and historical writings. He wrote his
name on almost every offprint and folder of notes and often left explanatory messages for the use of a future biographer. But the Guide
itself is the kind of tribute that Turner undoubtedly did not antici-
pate. Compiled by talented editors who have a wide knowledge of
Turner's work, the Guide will be indispensable for all future students
of America's frontier history and of the evolution of Turnerian
thought.

Wilbur R. Jacobs
University of California

Preface

Frederick Jackson Turner's seminal essay on "The Significance of the Frontier in American History," since its initial publication in 1893, has been the focal point of a major--if not the major--controversy in American historiography. Few historians have been able to approach the frontier hypothesis and come away feeling neutral, and the vast amount of literature written about Turner documents this fact. This volume is an annotated survey, in chronological form, of the debate surrounding Turner and the frontier thesis. To our knowledge, no attempt has yet been made to provide a comprehensive bibliography of the sort presented here. Everett E. Edwards's bibliography on References on the Significance of the Frontier in American History (see 1935.9) has been helpful in locating some articles, but it is by no means a complete guide and it contains several references that are not central to Turner or the debate. Oscar O. Winther's The Trans-Mississippi West: A Guide to Its Periodical Literature (1942.20), which has been supplemented in 1961 and 1970, contains many entries relevant to the frontier thesis, but these are scattered throughout the volume and there is no specific section on Turner and the frontier. Ray Allen Billington's bibliography in the textbook Westward Expansion: A History of the American Frontier (1949.2) is probably the most in-depth survey of the literature, but it is also incomplete. We do not claim to have found every article or book written on Turner and the frontier hypothesis, but we have aimed for completeness and accuracy.

Because of size limitations, we have limited the scope of this work to those articles and books written in English. The Turner controversy did spread beyond the borders of the North American continent, and a bibliography of non-English sources would be quite valuable and perhaps should constitute a supplemental volume. Neither have we tried to document every instance in which Turner is mentioned or glossed over. It would be nearly impossible to find every textbook that discusses the frontier, and Turner's name appears virtually thousands of times in books and articles that give only a brief, passing treatment. Listings of these sources would provide little scholarly value, except as a means of showing Turner's pervasive influence, and thus we have had to exercise some editorial discretion over which items to include or exclude.

Preface

By the same token, there are several entries that never mention Turner at all, but they are so clearly arguing either in favor of or against Turner's hypothesis that their inclusion has been mandated. Walter Prescott Webb's The Great Frontier (1951.19) and Richard Wade's The Urban Frontier (1951.28) are classic examples. Again, we have aimed at consistency in our policy over inclusion of material, and we have tried to include those sources that figure prominently in the debate.

Along with sources relating to the frontier thesis, we have also included analyses of his other historical contributions. Several critics have argued that Turner's sectional and regional theories are more important and more influential to the understanding of American history. Others have argued that it was not his desire to provide a fully synthesized and systematic interpretation of American development; rather, they view his role as a pathfinder and trailblazer to be the most important aspect of his scholarly contribution. His ability to train other scholars and teachers, along with his ability to probe innovatively into new areas of research, is as important to the field of Turner historiography as is the debate over the frontier thesis.

Similarly, biographical treatments are also vitally important to the realm of Turner scholarship. Turner's life has been nearly as controversial as his theories, and his development as a scholar, his attitudes toward publication and teaching, and his personal life in general reveal much about his stance as a historical theorist. Personal accounts by former students such as Grace Lee Nute, Merle Curti, Thomas P. Abernethy, Louise Phelps Kellogg, and others are rewarding and provocative, and we have tried to include as many of these as we have been able to find.

In addition to sifting through footnotes and bibliographies, our research was assisted by several indexing guides. The most helpful index was the American Historical Association's Writings on American History, which began publication in 1902. Several scattered volumes are missing, most notably the period from 1941 to 1947, but it is hoped that these will reappear. The abstract America: History and Life, beginning in 1964, also proved invaluable in tracking down more recent articles, as did the Social Sciences Citation Index, which began in 1972. Poole's Index, which ended in 1906, and the International Index, which was first published in 1907 and in 1965 became the Social Sciences and Humanities Index, also proved fruitful in tracking down several articles. The Reader's Guide to Periodical Literature, starting in 1901, assisted in locating more popular treatments of the frontier thesis, and it was extremely helpful in locating obituaries. The Essay and General Literature Index, first published in 1900, cited many valuable sources of reprints of articles that otherwise would be difficult for the researcher in a small library to obtain. Finally, the list of dissertations was taken from Dissertation Abstracts and from Warren F. Kuehl's index on Dissertations in History, volumes 1 and 2 (1873-1960 and 1961-1970).

Preface

In regard to our annotation policy, we have tried to be objective and nonjudgemental in our analysis of the item's content. Whenever possible, we have elected to have the authors speak for themselves; this helps lessen, to some extent, our own biases and also helps give the user of this guide a feel for the flavor and the style of the work. In those cases where the work is complex or where the thesis is not clear or direct, we have taken it upon ourselves to codify the material, hoping in the process that we do not do injustice to the article or book. We have also tried to be thorough in providing information about reprints. Reprint information on books, gleaned from the National Union Catalog, is presented at the end of the annotation by year only; reprints of articles are given by year and entry number, which will lead the reader to the appropriate citation. In the case of article reprints, an annotation is provided only with the initial entry. Finally, except for the dissertations noted by an asterisk, we have examined every work cited.

Acknowledgments

The librarians at the University of Nevada, Las Vegas, and the Henry E. Huntington Library and Art Gallery provided invaluable expertise and assistance in the preparation of this guide. We are indebted especially to Bob Ball and Lee Wahrer of the interlibrary loan division of the University of Nevada, Las Vegas, and Virginia Renner at the Huntington Library. Other librarians who were very helpful were Dolores Santa Cruz and Corryn Crosby-Brown. Pat Hudson, Marian Brown, and Margaret Neumann invested considerable energy and expertise in typing, and Anne Marie DiIorio deserves special recognition for having typed the final draft of the manuscript. Iris Jones and Lelia Helgren provided invaluable assistance with the indexing. For their encouragement, support, and advice, we express our appreciation to Catherine Sellmann, Jerry Simich, and Rick Tilman. Our special thanks go to Gertrude J. Mattson, who assisted with typing and who read and critiqued the entire manuscript at three stages of development.

Introduction

Frederick Jackson Turner was born on 14 November 1861 in Portage, Wisconsin, a small trading village nestled between the Fox and Wisconsin rivers some forty miles north of Madison, the state capital. His father, Andrew Jackson Turner, was joint owner-publisher of the Wisconsin State Register and a principal advocate of the town's expansion and growth, and his mother, Mary Hanford Turner, previous to her marriage had been a rural schoolteacher. By the time of Frederick's boyhood, the town of Portage, which Turner's biographer Ray Allen Billington has characterized as a "pseudo-frontier village," was caught between two worlds. On the one hand, it lay on the edge of the Northwest frontier and still felt the influence of the close proximity of a not yet fully subdued wilderness. On the other hand, however, even small rural towns like Portage felt the pressure of the social and technological progress of late-nineteenth-century America, and Frederick watched his town struggle between these two extremes as it fought to make the transition into the modern world. The sense of cultural evolution that manifested itself in Portage's growth left an indelible mark on young Frederick's mind, which, combined with the intellectual curiosity and political awareness inherited from his parents, would provide the foundation for his later perceptions and analyses of American history.

Frederick left Portage in 1880 to attend the University of Wisconsin in nearby Madison, where he received a bachelor's degree in 1884. As an undergraduate, he won fame for his skill in oratory, but more importantly, he was also initiated into the field of history by Professor William Francis Allen. Professor Allen was a scholar trained in the classical, European tradition of history, and he taught Turner the importance of using original source materials for historical interpretation. Allen also taught, however, that the study of history was more than just the study of facts, that it was also the study of cause and effect, progress and growth, and he advocated the use of economic, political, and sociological tools in order to achieve a more complete and balanced understanding of historical development. Turner adopted this interdisciplinary strategy and later molded it into his own historiographical theory, using multiple hypotheses as he sought to uncover the hidden social and economic forces underlying America's historical development.

Introduction

In the spring of 1885, after a year spent as a newspaper reporter, Frederick Turner returned to the University of Wisconsin to teach rhetoric and oratory, and later American history, while pursuing graduate studies. He received a master of arts degree in 1888 and immediately departed for the graduate program in history at Johns Hopkins University. Turner spent a year in Baltimore, where be became a vocal critic of the "germ theory" of the historical development of America. Although his Ph.D. advisor, Herbert Baxter Adams, was the spokesman for this theory, Turner vigorously objected to it because it emphasized the European origins of American institutional development at the expense of the influence of the American environment upon the nation's history. Turner had already explored this dimension in his master's thesis, "The Character and Influence of the Fur Trade in Wisconsin," and Adams, somewhat unwillingly, allowed him to expand the work into a doctoral dissertation. The Turner of graduate-school days already was more impressed with how the American experience differed from its European roots than with how it was similar, and he began focusing on the influence of the American West in order to prove his hypothesis.

Frederick Turner returned to the University of Wisconsin in 1889 and, on 7 November, he married Caroline Mae Sherwood in Chicago. Following the sudden death of Professor Allen in the same year, Turner assumed his mentor's position as an assistant professor of history. He was awarded the doctorate from Johns Hopkins the following year, and he settled down to researching and developing his position regarding the significance of the American West.

Between 1891 and 1893, Turner published three essays ("The Significance of History," "Problems in American History," and his most famous publication, "The Significance of the Frontier in American History") in which he developed his fundamental philosophy of American history. History, said the young scholar, must be relativistic in nature, that is, it must be meaningful to contemporary Americans. He writes in "The Significance of History" that "each age tries to form its own conception of the past. Each age writes the history of the past anew with reference to the conditions uppermost in its own time."[1] Turner argued that the importance of historial inquiry was not merely its ability to record information about the past, but rather, that it uncovers "elements of the present by understanding what came into the present from the past."[2] Thus Turner's primary focus of historical inquiry was an analysis of how present-day political, economic, and social institutions evolved in America, and he turned to the study of past events in order to understand better present American concerns.

Turner argued additionally that historians must identify the underlying forces in the environment that molded American development. The "germ theory" of American history was inadequate because it looked only at the European seeds from which American institutions were spawned, and it denied the ability of those institutions to change once they were transplanted to American soil. Turner embraced the idea that the American experience was unique, and he sought to prove that the environment, particularly the presence of a frontier wilderness, provided a more profound influence upon America's growth than had previously been considered.

On 12 July 1893, at the annual meeting of the American Historical Association in Chicago, site of the World Exposition, Turner delivered an address, "The Significance of the Frontier in American History," which was to provide the foundation for later frontier studies. Turner pointed out the stages of frontier advance and outlined the modifying effect this advance had upon American culture. The importance of this discovery of the significance of the frontier is summed up in a single paragraph; Turner writes:

> In the settlement of America we have to observe how European life entered the continent, and how America modified and developed that life, and reacted on Europe. Our early history is the study of European germs developing in an American environment. Too exclusive attention has been paid by institutional students to the Germanic origins, too little to the American factors. The frontier is the line of most rapid and effective Americanization. The wilderness masters the colonist. It finds him a European in dress, industries, tools, modes of travel, and thought. It takes him from the railroad car and puts him in the birch canoe. It strips off the garments of civilization, and arrays him in the hunting shirt and the moccasin. It puts him in the log cabin of the Cherokee and the Iroquois, and runs an Indian palisade around him. Before long he has gone to planting Indian corn and plowing with a sharp stick; he shouts the war cry and takes the scalp in orthodox Indian fashion. In short, at the frontier the environment is at first too strong for the man. He must accept the conditions which it furnishes, or perish, and so he fits himself into the Indian clearings and follows the Indian trails. Little by little he transforms the wilderness, but the outcome is not the old Europe, not simply the development of Germanic germs, any more than the first phenomenon was a case of reversion to the Germanic mark. The fact is that here is a new product that is American. At first the frontier was the Atlantic coast. It was the frontier of Europe in a very real sense. Moving westward, the frontier became more and more American. As successive terminal moraines result from successive glaciations, so each frontier leaves its traces behind it, and when it becomes a settled area the region still partakes of the frontier characteristics. Thus the advance of the frontier has meant a steady movement away from

the influence of Europe, a steady growth of independence on American lines. And to study this advance,
the men who grew up under these conditions, and the
political, economic, and social results of it, is to
study the really American part of our history.[3]

Turner's philosophy of history, his dissatisfaction with contemporary historiographical methods, and the revolutionary potential of
his thesis are all contained in this brief excerpt. While avoiding a
monocausational explanation of American history, Turner focused his
attention upon the influence of the frontier as one of the important
underlying forces in American development, allowing him to shift the
direction of historical inquiry.

Turner's "frontier thesis" did not make an immediate impact, however, and at first drew little notice. But gradually more and more
historians began to take notice of and incorporate the frontier hypothesis into their own work, and Frederick Jackson Turner rose into
prominence in the American historical profession. By 1896 Turner had
been contacted by his friend from Johns Hopkins days, Woodrow Wilson,
who offered him a chair in American history at Princeton, where
Wilson was currently a professor of history. Turner was likewise
invited to head the Department of History at the University of Chicago
in 1900, and in 1905 he was offered a position at Stanford. Turner
declined these, however, because he was relatively content at the
University of Wisconsin; he was familiar with the research materials
there, and he was concerned about the negative impact moving might
have on his research. During this period he published several articles and, in 1906, completed his first book-length work, The Rise of
the New West, 1819-1829, under the editorial guidance of Albert
Bushnell Hart.

By 1908, however, the regents at the University of Wisconsin began pressuring Turner to spend more time in the classroom and less
time on research. Turner was always conscientious about his students,
and he was highly motivated toward teaching, but he was also dedicated
to scholarly research, so in 1909 he accepted an offer from Harvard
University and in 1910 left Wisconsin to begin teaching there as
professor of history, a post he kept until his retirement in 1924.
The high regard his colleagues held for him was made manifest when,
in 1910, he was elected president of the American Historical Association and, in 1914, he was elected president of the Colonial Society
of Massachusetts.

During his tenure at Harvard, Frederick Turner continued to re-
vise his frontier hypothesis, which culminated in the publication of
The Frontier in American History in 1920. He also continued avidly
working with young scholars, training them in the methods he learned
and used in his historical pursuits, and it was his reputation as a
teacher that brought many students to Harvard to become indoctrinated
into the field of history. At this time Turner also began shifting

perspective in his historical research. By 1914, with the publication of the article "Sectionalism in the United States," Turner began
focusing on the emergence and influence of sections on American development. Always interested in the concept of sections, Turner became concerned with the geographical determinants underlying sectional
evolution and the dynamic interplay of the conflicts and dependencies
that ensued between sections. For Turner an analysis of sections
would, like his frontier theory, contribute to an understanding of
the uniqueness of the American experience, and it was with this in
mind that he published "Sections and the Nation" in the Yale Review
in 1922.

After his retirement from Harvard, Turner spent three years lec-
turing occasionally at the University of Wisconsin and elsewhere, but
he devoted the majority of his time to fishing, his favorite leisurely
pursuit. This leisure would be shortlived, however, for in 1927 he
accepted a position as research associate at the Henry E. Huntington
Library in San Marino, California. Here he continued research on the
importance of sections, but frequent bouts with ill health hampered
his work. Frederick Jackson Turner died in Pasadena, California, on
14 March 1932, but not before the emergence of another major book,
The Significance of Sections in American History, which was published
the same year, and Turner was posthumously awarded the Pulitzer Prize
for history. Frederick Jackson Turner rose from humble beginnings to
become a master of his profession, and he left behind him a rich
legacy of historical creativity and insight that made a permanent
mark on the understanding of American development.

Frederick Jackson Turner's famous "frontier hypothesis," first
advanced in 1893, enjoyed an enthusiastic acceptance and increasing
acclaim until his death in 1932. During this era American historians
accepted Turner's interpretation of the American experience in such
numbers that Ray Billington concluded that the "American Historical
Association during those years" could be "described as one giant
'Turner-verein.'"[4] The only exceptions to this general acceptance
prior to 1932 were a few scholars who were critical of the frontier
thesis in the 1920s. In 1921 Charles A. Beard, while reviewing
Turner's The Frontier in American History, concluded that American
history could be understood best by focusing upon the conflict between labor and capital rather than upon Turner's version of the
frontier process.[5] Implicity, Beard was challenging the prevailing
notion that Turner's thesis was the only convincing interpretation of
the nation's history. In the same year, Clarence W. Alvord faulted
Turner's explanation of the frontier process. But the first major
attack upon Turner's dominant assumptions did not materialize until
1925, when John C. Almack issued a plea for a general reassessemnt of
Turner's entire thesis.[6] Almack expanded upon Beard's earlier brief
warning about the danger of embracing Turner's thesis as the explanation of American history. John C. Parish, the only other scholar who
was critical of Turner's thesis prior to 1932, argued that in his
opinion, Turner and his enthusiastic disciples had erred in their

preachment that there had been only one frontier and that it had closed in the last decade of the nineteenth century.

Although Turner's death in 1932 made it easier for critics to attack his famous thesis, Earl Pomeroy was correct when he asserted that the Great Depression had more to do with the tidal wave of criticism that emerged in the 1930s and 1940s than did the death of its author.[7] The economic crisis of the 1930s altered the intellectual climate of the United States. Ray A. Billington captured the essence of this shift in scholarly interest and its relationship to Turner's frontier thesis. "An interpretation of the American past that stressed agrarianism rather than industrialism, rugged individualism rather than state planning; and optimistic nationalism rather than political internationalism seemed out-moded in a economic cataclysm."[8] The critics of the frontier thesis singled out Turner's emphasis upon the positive contribution of America's agrarian past as an example of how useless the frontier thesis was for those who wished to understand American history from the perspective of the 1930s. Marxists faulted Turner's stress upon geographical forces at the expense of class conflict. Liberal scholars disliked his celebration of the rugged individualism of the frontier because they saw governmental planning and intervention as a necessity if the United States were to have a promising future. Collectively the critics of the 1930s and 1940s faulted Turner's methodology, his dependence upon symbols at the expense of social science language, his unsupported generalizations, and, above all, his definition of terms such as "frontier." Scholars of this era heaped scorn upon Turner for allegedly making contradictory claims for the frontier's influence upon American development. How was it possible, asked the critics, for the frontier heritage at the same time to cause rugged individualism and community building, sectional divisions and national unity, and the advancement of civilization while it provided an avenue of escape from civilization?[9] Turner was also accused of having embraced a monocausational interpretation of American history.[10] Historians of the 1930s and 1940s spent considerable energy criticizing Turner's failure to appreciate the influence of the European heritage upon the development of American culture.[11] By overemphasizing the uniqueness of the American experience, historians of the frontier school of historiography had allegedly reinforced the undesirable tendency on the part of Americans to celebrate their independence from international influences.[12] Other scholars underscored Turner's inability to recognize the significance of urbanization in the American development.[13] Although Turner himself had not emphasized the "safety-valve" concept, his critics attributed the doctrine to Turner and attempted to discredit it as a valid explanation of the relationship between the migration of eastern laborers and the frontier. Carter Goodrich and Sol Davison launched the attack by arguing that workers in eastern cities did not move to the frontier during periods of economic difficulty as Turner had suggested because they lacked the capital to undertake such a costly adventure.[14] Other scholars followed the lead of Goodrich and

Davison by showing that Turner was wrong when he suggested that the Homestead Act made the West attractive to eastern urban workers.[15]

A cardinal characteristic of the heated debate regarding the validity of Turner's frontier thesis during the 1930s and 1940s was the division of historians into two camps: Turner's defenders and Turner's critics. Both failed to emulate Turner's refusal to make extravagant claims for his frontier thesis. As Ray A. Billington has observed, Turner's defenders in the 1930s and 1940s viewed Turner's hypothesis as the "Divine Word, utterly unassailable."[16] The response of the critics to what they viewed as an irrational glorification of Turner's thesis was as heated and one-sided as the approach of Turner's defenders, although during the 1930s and 1940s the flow of scholarship was overwhelmingly anti-Turnerian.

Turner's defenders underscored their hero's positive influence upon American historiography. "Frederick Jackson Turner wrote less and influenced his own generation more," said Avery Craven in 1937, "than any other important historian."[17] According to Craven and other enthusiasts of this era, Turner's influence was a result of the "wealth of suggestive ideas"[18] that were communicated in brief, interpretive essays. Turner's "stimulating personality which stirred students"[19] was identified by his champions as a key to his influence within the historical profession. His defenders attempted to reaffirm the Turnerian faith in the promise of American democracy, the uniqueness of the American experience, the import of geographical conditions upon American development, the rejuvenating influence of the frontier, the dynamism of American nationalism and, above all, the positive contribution of the frontier experience upon the development of the United States. Yet the writings generated by Turner's defenders were dedicated to answering specific criticisms of his detractors rather than to celebrating Turner's frontier truths. The frontier thesis and its champions were clearly on the defensive in the 1930s and 1940s.

The massive criticisms of the 1930s and 1940s failed to deal a death blow to Turner's frontier thesis, however. Collectively these critics were unable to discredit the essential appeal of Turner's interpretation of American history. The sheer volume of articles and books dealing with the frontier thesis remained as high in the 1950s and 1960s as it had been in the previous two decades. In the 1950s and 1960s a third generation of Turnerian scholarship emerged, characterized by a renewed interest in the frontier thesis itself combined with a willingness to suspend final judgment about the validity of the thesis. This new generation of scholars viewed the critics of the 1930s and 1940s as having been given to overstatement and faulty methodology.

No work did more to stimulate interest in Turner's frontier hypothesis than Henry Nash Smith's <u>Virgin Land: The American West as Symbol and Myth</u> (1950). By tracing the development of myths associated with the West throughout our nation's history, Smith attempted to place Turner's version of our frontier history within the context of what he called the "myth of the garden."[20] For Smith, Turner's frontier thesis was important because it was a vital part of a much older and encompassing agrarian myth, which was deeply rooted in our national folklore. Turner's assumptions about our frontier experience were not to be viewed as objective truth about our frontier past but rather as the "main ideas in an intellectual tradition" that could be characterized best as the "American West as symbol and myth."[21] Smith expanded frontier studies to include our literary and intellectual history.

During the 1950s and 1960s scholars spent considerable energy attempting to assess what was still salvageable in the frontier thesis in the aftermath of the massive attack on it in the 1930s and 1940s. Central to this reassessment was an attempt by scholars to do what Turner himself had failed to do, define the word "frontier." Scholars of the 1950s and 1960s faulted Turner for having used the term, "frontier" and "West" as synonyms.[22] Ray A. Billington concluded that the scholarship of these two decades had helped students of the frontier understand that "two definitions" were "necessary, one of the frontier as a geographical area, and the other of the frontier as a process."[23]

Scholars of the 1950s and 1960s spent almost as much time finding fault with Turner's critics as with a reassessment of his thesis itself. The continued debate about the frontier as a safety valve illustrated this aspect of the frontier historiography of the 1950s and 1960s. Every scholar who reexamined Turner's safety-valve concept after 1950 felt obligated to reassess and, in some cases, even discredit, the extant secondary literature on the subject. The net yield of this reexamination of the safety valve was a reaffirmation of the essential soundness of Turner's general point regarding the frontier as a safety valve and a massive documentation of the inherent flaws of the methodology of those scholars who had been critical of the safety-valve concept during the 1930s and 1940s. As a result of the massive effort of scholars of the post-1905 era, Turner's original simple concept of the frontier as a safety valve was developed into an extremely complex social science concept with numerous intricate complexities and nuances. One of Turner's original simple symbols, which depicted the West as a release for the dangerous pressures created by the urbanization of the East, was expanded by the scholars of the post-1950 era into a labyrinth involving "indirect safety valves," "migration flows," "wage scales," "slabs of western resources," "sociopsychological safety valves," "upward mobility," and even "economic escalators."[24] To a lesser degree, all aspects of Turner's original thesis were reexamined with this kind of social science methodology in the post-1950 era of frontier studies.

Fortunately the safety-valve controversy, which first erupted in the 1930s and 1940s and came to a climax in the 1950s and 1960s, yielded more than a social science version of Turner's original

safety-valve concept. At least four distinct safety valves were
identified and explained in the massive literature on the subject.
In addition to Turner's direct safety valve, which provided a western
escape for unemployed eastern workers, students of the subject identified an escape mechanism that involved eastern farmers who responded
to competition with western farmers by becoming western farmers themselves. A third western safety valve documented by scholars of the
1950s and 1960s involved western resources, which allegedly provided
lucrative jobs for eastern workers. The last safety valve identified
by recent scholarship on the subject can be characterized as psychological in nature; eastern workers, according to scholars of this
orientation, were less inclined to become involved in radical protests
against the American capitalistic system because they believed the
West was an avenue of escape if conditions in the urban East became
too unbearable.

What Richard C. Wade called the "Urban Frontier" was an example
of how scholars of the 1950s and 1960s expanded frontier studies in
an effort to deal with important aspects of the frontier neglected by
Turner. Wade and other scholars argued that the "towns were the
spearheads of the frontier."[25] Scholars of the urban school of
thought challenged Turner's thesis at its agrarian base. The frontier
was not, said they, simply a study of America's agrarian past; the
growth of cities in the West was the dominant force in the development of western life.

In the post-1950 era of Turnerian scholarship a number of Turner's
concepts were amplified. Few subjects attracted more attention than
Turner's ideas regarding the influence of the frontier upon the
development of American institutions and cultural characteristics.
A heated debate arose as to whether or not the frontier contributed
to the growth of American democracy. This debate centered on a number of questions. Did American democracy predate the frontier experience? Did the East contribute more to American democracy than the
West? Did liberalism emerge in the West or in the East? Was the
West more open to political, social, and economic experimentation
than the established East, or was the West an imitation of the established East? How can studies of other frontier nations shed light
upon the frontier experience of the American people? What was the
relationship between the emergence of American nationalism and the
frontier experience? Did the frontier process produce a culture that
underscored the value of individualism, or did the frontier teach
Americans the need for cooperation and community effort? Did Americans become a more inventive people as a result of their frontier
experience? Was the frontier more important as a source of material
abundance than as a source of democracy as Turner argued? Was Turner
correct when he claimed that the frontier was the major source of
economic and social upward mobility? Was the frontiersman more ideal-
istic than his eastern counterpart? Did the frontier make Americans
restless? Is the frontier tradition relevant to the problems that
the United States is facing in the twentieth century? Does the

Introduction

United States have new frontiers to replace the frontier that Turner
said closed in the late nineteenth century? Has the Turner thesis
served to rationalize and defend a provincial, pro-American interpretation of American history? Questions of this nature constituted
the thrust of post-1950 debate about the validity of the frontier
thesis, and frontier historians of this period also began questioning
the Turnerian assumption that the American environment transformed
the European heritage into a totally unique American culture.

During the 1970s scholars faulted the Turnerian interpretation of
America for its failure to deal with very important aspects of the
American experience. Professor Wilbur Jacobs and others explored the
relationship between the Turnerian interpretation of American history
and the failure of American historians to acknowledge the contribution
of the native Americans to the development of American culture. In
Professor Jacobs's words, frontier historians of the Turnerian tradition have treated native Americans "as if they were some kind of
geographical obstacle to the westward movement of whites."[26] Other
scholars faulted the Turnerian school of historiography for having
celebrated the power of the American environment to mold the immigrants
into a new composite whole at the expense of the contribution of
ethnic influences to the formation of American culture. Critics have
also faulted Turner's view of the West for having ignored the role of
black Americans in frontier development.

But despite these criticisms, interest and concern in Turnerian
historiography has remained high. The rhetoric of the frontier hypothesis, for example, was studied in depth by scholars in communication studies, and Ronald H. Carpenter concluded his study of Turner
by attributing his unparalleled influence to his rhetorical skill.
During the 1970s specialists in the new field of environmental history, while criticizing Turner's alleged environmentalism, generally
acknowledged their indebtedness to Turnerian studies as they attempted
to establish their specialty in college curricula. Turner's influence upon other distinguished scholars in western history is also
evident in the secondary literature of the 1970s, and interest in
Turner the man reached an apex in the monumental biography authored
by Ray Allen Billington, which was received with wide acclaim.
Interest in Turner's life, his frontier thesis, and the mass of
secondary literature that has emerged since his death in 1932 remained as high in the 1970s as it had been in previous decades, and
it is clear that Turnerian studies are vibrant and alive in the 1980s.

Notes
    1. Frederick Jackson Turner, "The Significance of History," in
The Early Writings of Frederick Jackson Turner, ed. Everett Edwards
(Madison, 1938), p. 52.
    2. Ibid.
    3. Frederick Jackson Turner, "The Significance of the Frontier in
American History," in The Early Writings of Frederick Jackson Turner,
ed. Everett Edwards (Madison, 1938), pp. 188-89.

4. Ray Allen Billington, The American Frontier Thesis: Attack and Defense (Washington, D.C., 1958), p. 5.
5. Charles A. Beard, "The Frontier in American History," New Republic 25 (16 February 1921):349-50.
6. John C. Almack, "The Shibboleth of the Frontier," Historical Outlook 16 (May 1925):197-202.
7. Earl Pomeroy, "The Changing West" in Higham, Reconstruction of American History, pp. 63-81.
8. Ray A. Billington, America's Frontier Heritage (New York, 1966), p. 15.
9. George W. Pierson, "The Frontier and Frontiersmen of Turner's Essays," Pennsylvania Magazine of History and Biography 64 (October 1940):449-78, and "The Frontier and American Institutions. A Criticism of the Turner Theory," New England Quarterly 15 (June 1942):224-25.
10. Louis M. Hacker, "Sections--or Classes," Nation, 26 July 1933, pp. 108-10.
11. Carlton J. H. Hayes, "The American Frontier--Frontier of What?" American Historical Review 51 (1945-46):199-216.
12. Ibid.
13. Arthur M. Schlesinger, "The City in American Civilization," Mississippi Valley Historical Review 27 (June 1940):43-67.
14. Carter Goodrich and Sol Davison, "The Wage-Earner in the Westward Movement," Political Science Quarterly 50 (June 1935):161-85, and 51 (March 1936):61-116.
15. Fred A. Shannon, "The Homestead Act and Labor Surplus," American Historical Review 41 (July 1936):637-51.
16. Ray A. Billington, Introduction to The Frontier Thesis: Valid Interpretation of American History? (New York 1966), p. 3.
17. Avery Craven, "Frederick Jackson Turner," in The Marcus W. Jernegan Essays in American Historiography (Chicago, 1937), p. 252.
18. Ibid.
19. Ibid.
20. Henry Nash Smith, Virgin Land: The American West as Symbol and Myth (Cambridge, 1950), pp. 1-11.
21. Ibid., p. 251.
22. The following works are examples of this search for a definition of the word "frontier." Fulmer Mood, "Studies in the History of American Settled Areas and Frontier Lines: 1625-1790," Agricultural History 26 (1952):16-34; Jack D. Forbes, "Frontiers in American History," Journal of the West 1 (1962-63):63-73; T.M. Pearce, "The 'Other' Frontiers of the American West," Arizona and the West 4 (1962):105-12; Ray A. Billington, "The Frontier in American Thought and Character," in A.R. Lewis and T.F. McGann, eds., The New World Looks at Its History (Austin, 1963), pp. 77-94.
23. Billington, American Frontier Thesis, p. 19.
24. Norman J. Simler, "The Safety-Valve Doctrine Re-Examined," Agricultural History 32 (1958):250-57; George G.S. Murphy and Arnold Zellner, "Sequential Growth, the Labor-Safety-Valve Doctrine and the Development of American Unionism," Journal of Economic History 19 (1959):402-21; Ellen Von Nardroff, "The American Frontier as Safety-Valve--The Life, Death and Reincarnation and Justification of a

Theory," <u>Agricultural History</u> 36 (1962):123–42; Henry M. Littlefield,
"Has the Safety Valve Come Back to Life?" <u>Agricultural History</u> 38
(1964):47–49.

    25. Richard C. Wade, <u>The Urban Frontier: Pioneer Life in Early
Pittsburgh, Cincinnati, Lexington, Louisville, and St. Louis</u> (Chicago,
1959), p. 1.

    26. Wilbur R. Jacobs, "The Fatal Confrontation," <u>Pacific Historical
Review</u> 40 (1971):283–309.

Writings by Frederick Jackson Turner

"History of the 'Grignon Tract' on the Portage of the Fox and the Wisconsin Rivers." State Register (Portage, Wis.), 23 June 1883.

Outline Studies in the History of the Northwest. Chicago: C.H. Kerr & Co., 1888.

"Wisconsin." In Encyclopaedia Britannica. 9th ed. 24:616–19. New York: Charles Scribner's Sons, 1888.

"The Character and Influence of the Fur Trade in Wisconsin." Wisconsin State Historical Society Proceedings 36 (1889):52–98.

"The Significance of History." Wisconsin Journal of Education 21 (October and November 1891):230–34, 253–56.

Syllabus of a University Extension Course of Six Lectures on the Colonization of North America. Madison, Wis.: Tracy, Gibbs & Co., 1891.

"The Extension Work of the University of Wisconsin." University Extension: A Monthly Devoted to the Interests of Popular Education 1 (April 1892):311–24.

"Problem in American History." Aegis 7 (4 November 1892):48–52.

The Colonization of North America from the Earliest Times to 1763: Syllabus of a Course of Six Lectures. Madison, Wis.: Tracy, Gibbs & Co., 1893.

"The Significance of the Frontier in American History." American Historical Association, Annual Report (Washington, D.C., 1893), pp. 199–227 (originally read before the ninth annual meeting of the American Historical Association at Chicago).

"Frontier." In Johnson's Universal Cyclopedia. 3:606–7. New York: A.J. Johnson Co., 1894.

Writings by Turner

A Half Century of American Politics, 1789–1840: Syllabus of a
Course of Six Lectures. Madison, Wis.: Tracy, Gibbs & Co.,
1894.

American Development, 1789–1829: Syllabus of a Course of Six Lectures. Madison, Wis.: Tracy, Gibbs & Co., 1895.

"Western State-making in the Revolutionary Era." American Historical
Review 1 (October 1895):70–87, and (January 1896):251–69.

"The Problem of the West." Atlantic Monthly 78 (September 1896):
289–97.

"The Rise and Fall of New France." Chatauquan 24 (October 1896):31–
34, and (December 1896):295–300.

"The West as a Field for Historical Study." American Historical
Association, Annual Report (Washington, D.C., 1897), pp. 281–87.

"Carondelet on the Defense of Louisiana, 1794." American Historical
Association 2 (April 1897):474–505.

"Dominant Forces in Western Life." Atlantic Monthly 79 (April 1897):
433–43.

"The Mangouit Correspondence in Respect to Genet's Projected Attack
upon the Floridas, 1793–97." American Historical Association,
Annual Report (Washington, D.C., 1898), pp. 569–679.

"Documents on the Relations of France to Louisiana, 1792–1795."
American Historical Review 3 (April 1898):490–516.

"Jefferson to George Rogers Clark, 1783." American Historical Review
3 (July 1898):672–73.

"The Origin of Genet's Projected Attack on Louisiana and the
Floridas." American Historical Review 3 (July 1898):650–71.

"The Middle West." International Monthly 4 (December 1901):794–820.

Suggestive Outlines for the Study of the History of the Middle West,
Kentucky, and Tennessee. State Historical Society of Wisconsin
Bulletin of Information, 1901.

"English Policy toward America in 1790–1791." American Historical
Review 7 (July 1902):706–35, and 8 (October 1902):78–86.

"Contributions of the West to American Democracy." Atlantic Monthly
91 (January 1903):83–96.

Writings by Turner

"The Democratic Education of the Middle West." <u>World's Work</u> 6
    (August 1903):3754-59.

"George Rogers Clark and the Kaskaskia Campaign, 1777-1778." <u>American
    Historical Review</u> 8 (April 1903):491-506.

"The Significance of the Louisiana Purchase." <u>American Monthly Re-
    views</u> 27 (May 1903):578-84.

"The Diplomatic Contest for the Mississippi Valley." <u>Atlantic
    Monthly</u> 93 (May 1904):676-91, and (June 1904):807-17.

"Documents on the Blount Conspiracy, 1795-1797." <u>American Historical
    Review</u> 10 (April 1905):574-606.

"Geographical Interpretations of American History." <u>Journal of
    Geography</u> 4 (January 1905):34-37.

"The Policy of France toward the Mississippi Valley in the Period of
    Washington and Adams." <u>American Historical Review</u> 10 (January
    1905):249-79.

"The Colonization of the West, 1820-1830." <u>American Historical Re-
    view</u> 11 (January 1906):303-27.

"Problems in American History." In <u>International Congress of Arts
    and Science, University Exposition, St. Louis, 1904</u>. Edited by
    Howard J. Rogers. Boston and New York: Houghton Mifflin Co.,
    1906.

<u>The American Nation: A History</u>. . . . Edited by A.B. Hart. Vol.
    14, <u>Rise of the New West, 1819-1829</u>. New York and London:
    Harper & Brothers, 1906.

"The South, 1820-1830." <u>American Historical Review</u> 11 (April 1906):
    559-73.

"Report of the Conference on the Relation of Geography and History."
    <u>American Historical Association Annual Report, 1907</u> (Washington,
    D.C., 1908), 1:45-48.

"The Development of American Society." <u>Alumni Quarterly of the Uni-
    versity of Illinois</u> 2 (July 1908):120-36.

"Is Sectionalism in America Dying?" <u>American Journal of Sociology</u>
    13 (March 1908):661-75.

"The Old West." <u>Wisconsin State Historical Society, Proceedings</u> 56
    (1908):184-233.

"Pioneer Ideals and the State University." Indiana University Bulletin 8 (June 1910):6-29.

List of References on the History of the West: 1911. List of References in History 17: History of the West. Cambridge, Mass.: Harvard University Press, 1911.

"The Place of the Ohio Valley in American History." Ohio Archeological and Historical Quarterly 20 (January 1911):32-47, and History Teacher's Magazine 2 (March 1911):147-52.

"The Significance of the Mississippi Valley in American History." Mississippi Valley Historical Association, Proceedings, 1909-1910 3 (1911):159-84.

"Social Forces in American History." American Historical Review 16 (January 1911):217-33.

Guide to the Study and Reading of American History. Coauthored with Edward Channing and Albert Bushnell Hart. Boston and London: Ginn & Co., 1912.

"The Harvard Commission on Western History." Harvard Graduates' Magazine 20 (June 1912):606-11, and History Teacher's Magazine 3 (September 1912):146-47.

"The Territorial Development of the United States." In The Harvard Classics University Extension Course I, History, section 5, pp. 35-40. Cambridge, Mass., 1913.

"Frontier in American Development." In Cyclopedia of American Government. 2:61-64. Edited by Andrew C. McLaughlin and Albert Bushnell Hart. New York and London: D. Appleton & Co., 1914.

"Geographical Influences in American Political History." American Geographical Society Bulletin 46 (August 1914):591-95.

"Sectionalism in the United States." In Cyclopedia of American Government. 3:280-85. Edited by Andrew C. McLaughlin and Albert Bushnell Hart. New York and London: D. Appleton & Co., 1914.

"The West and American Ideals." Washington Historical Quarterly 5 (October 1914):243-57.

"West as a Factor in American Politics." In Cyclopedia of American Government. 3:668-75. Edited by Andrew C. McLaughlin and Albert Bushnell Hart. New York and London: D. Appleton & Co., 1914.

"The First Official Frontier of the Massachusetts Bay." Colonial
    Society of Massachusetts, Publications. 17:250-71. Boston:
    The Society, 1915.

"Greater New England in the Middle of the Nineteenth Century."
    American Antiquarian Society, Proceedings 29 (October 1919):222-
    41.

"Middle Western Pioneer Democracy." Minnesota History Bulletin 3
    (August 1920):393-414.

The Frontier in American History. New York: Henry Holt & Co., 1920.

"Sections and Nation." Yale Review 12 (October 1922):1-21.

"Since the Foundation." Clark University Library, Publications 7
    (February 1924):9-29.

"The Significance of the Section in American History." Wisconsin
    Magazine of History 8 (March 1925):255-80.

"The Children of the Pioneers." Yale Review 15 (July 1926):645-70.

"Geographical Sectionalism in American History." Association of
    American Geographers, Annals 16 (June 1926):85-93.

"The West-1876 and 1926: Its Progress in a Half-Century." World's
    Work 52 (July 1926):391-27.

"New England, 1830-1850." Huntington Library Bulletin 1 (May 1931):
    153-98.

The Significance of Sections in American History. New York: Henry
    Holt & Co., 1932.

The United States, 1830-1850: The Nation and Its Sections. New
    York: Henry Holt & Co., 1935 (published posthumously).

Writings about Frederick Jackson Turner 1895-1982

1 WILSON, WOODROW. "The Proper Perspective of American History."
  Forum 19 (July):544-59.
      Claims Turner influenced him to single out the frontier as
"the central and determining fact of our national history" and to
attribute many of the weaknesses of "our history" to its having
been "written in the East." Generalizes in a true Turnerian
tone: "The 'West' is the great word of our history." Believes,
like Turner, that "we have lost our frontier."

1 WILSON, WOODROW. "The Making of the Nation." Atlantic
  Monthly 80 (July):1-14.
      Embraces a sectional interpretation of American history and
acknowledges Turner as the key spokesman for this approach.

1 LEGLER, HENRY E. Leading Events of Wisconsin History: The
  Story of the State. Milwaukee, Wis.: Sentinel Company,
  p. viii, 156.
      Cites Turner as an expert on the Wisconsin fur trade. Re-
printed: 1901.

2 VINCENT, GEORGE E. "The Retarded Frontier." American Journal
  of Sociology 4 (July):1-20.
      Utilizes Turner's thesis as a theoretical framework for
analyzing the Kentucky frontier.

1900

1 SHAMBAUGH, BENJAMIN F. "Frontier Land Clubs, or Claim Associations." <u>American Historical Association, Annual Report</u>, pp. 69-84.
Places the frontier land clubs within a Turnerian framework: they were a "product of frontier life," and they support Turner's claim "that there has been a 'recurrence of the process of evolution in each Western area reached in the process of expansion.'"

1902

1 NORRIS, FRANK. "The Frontier Gone at Last." <u>World's Work</u> 3 (February):1728-31.
Although the frontier had been declared closed by Turner, in actuality the American push westward had simply extended the frontier to the Orient, thereby giving the United States frontier an international scope.

2 _____. "A Neglected Epic." <u>World's Work</u> 5 (December):2904-6.
Rejects Turner's thesis; depicts the West as a place subdued by eastern civilization rather than as an environmental incubator for a uniquely American civilization.

3 STEPHENS, HENRY MORSE. "Some Living American Historians." <u>World's Work</u> 4 (July):2316-27.
Turner is included among "five contemporary American writers of history, who meet all the canons of the severest expert criticism." Credits Turner's "The Significance of the Frontier in American History" with contributing in a major way to the quest for an "understanding of the character of the American people."

1903

1 SEMPLE, ELLEN CHURCHILL. <u>American History and Its Geographic Conditions</u>. Boston: Houghton Mifflin, 466 pp., passim.
Quotes and draws upon Turner's "The Significance of the Frontier in American History," and comes to the conclusion that the "presence of the new West reacted . . . upon the East" in a significant manner. "The stimulating effect of inexhaustible opportunity . . . and the democratic spirit of the . . . frontier fostered the spirit of democracy and youth in the whole nation." Reprinted: 1933; revised by Clarence Field Jones, 1963 and reprinted, 1968.

1907

2 YOUNG, F.G. "The Lewis and Clark Centennial." Oregon Historical Society Quarterly 4 (March):1-20.
    Turner is cited as "the highest authority on western history."

1904

1 REED, HENRY E. "Great West and the Two Easts." North American Review 178:512-26.
    Does not mention Turner, but argues in a similar vein that "the West, instead of proving the destroyer of the nation, has proved its savior."

1906

1 GARRISON, GEORGE P. The American Nation: A History. Vol. 17, Westward Extension, 1841-1850. New York: Harper, 366 pp., passim.
    A survey of frontier history that depends heavily upon the writings and views of Turner and his students. Reprinted: 1907, 1968, 1969.

2 HART, ALBERT BUSHNELL, ed. Introduction to The American Nation: A History. Vol. 14, Rise of the New West, 1819-1829, by Frederick Jackson Turner. New York: Harper, pp. xii-xvi.
    Turner is presented as the leading expert on western history whose "point of view is that the west and east were always interdependent."

3 SHAW, ALBERT. "Our Legacy from a Century of Pioneers." South Atlantic Quarterly 5 (October):311-33.
    Suggests that industrialism is the new frontier, which will translate the "pioneering . . . spirit of individuality" into twentieth-century reality.

1907

1 PAXSON, FREDERIC L. "The Pacific Railroads and the Disappearance of the Frontier in America." American Historical Association, Annual Report, pp. 107-18.
    Accepts Turner's views regarding the frontier's influence upon American character and identifies the development of national railroads as the cause of Turner's closed frontier. Reprinted: 1914.14.

1908

1 POOLEY, WILLIAM VIPOND. "The Causes for the Settlement of Illinois," in The Settlement of Illinois from 1830 to 1850. Bulletin of the University of Wisconsin, no. 220 (History series, vol. 1, no. 4), pp. 330-51.
   Utilizes Turner's safety-valve doctrine as the major explanation of why easterners settled Illinois in the early nineteenth century.

2 SPARKS, EDWIN ERLE. "Report on the Conference on the Relations of Geography to History." American Historical Asssociation, Annual Report, pp. 57-61.
   Turner is reported to have called for "the necessity of analyzing the various divisions of America in order to see of what economic sections they are composed."

1909

1 BOWEN, CLARENCE WINTHROP. "Congress of American Scholars." Harper's Weekly 8 (25 December):24-25.
   Turner is cited as one of the prominent leaders in the evolution of the American Historical Association. Portraits (including Turner's) of the most famous leaders surround the article.

2 CROLY, HERBERT DAVID. "What Is the Promise of American Life?" In The Promise of American Life. New York: Macmillan, pp. 1-26.
   "All the conditions of American Life have tended to encourage an easy, generous, and irresponsible optimism. As compared to Europeans, Americans have been much favored by circumstances. Had it not been for the Atlantic Ocean and the virgin wilderness, the United States would never have been the Land of Promise." Explains America's "greatness" in a vein similar to Turner's.

3 LAUT, AGNES C. "The Last Trek to the Last Frontier: The American Settler in the Canadian Northwest." Century Magazine, n.s. 56 (May):99-110.
   The frontier was not closed as Turner had suggested in 1893. Half a million American settlers migrated to the Canadian Northwest in the first six years of the twentieth century.

4 MATHEWS, LOIS K. The Expansion of New England: The Spread of New England Settlement and Institutions to the Mississippi River, 1620-1865. Cambridge: Houghton Mifflin, 303 pp., passim.
   Opens with the Turnerian generalization that the "history

of the spread of settlement in the United States is the story of
an ever-retreating wilderness, an ever-advancing frontier" and
proceeds to write the history of New England development within a
Turnerian framework. Reprinted: 1962.

5 MEANY, EDMOND S. "The Towns of the Pacific Northwest Were Not
   Founded on the Fur Trade." American Historical Association,
   Annual Report, pp. 165-72.
      "While conceding the full value and validity of the thesis
[Turner's] as applied to that portion of the United States lying
east of the Rocky Mountains, it is the purpose of this . . .
paper to demonstrate that west of those mountains, is the Pacific
Northwest. . . . The evolution of civilization did not follow the
lines so successfully elaborated by Professor Turner."

1910

1 BECKER, CARL. "Kansas." In Essays in American History Dedicated to Frederick Jackson Turner. Edited by Guy Stanton Ford.
   New York: Holt, pp. 85-111.
      Depicts Kansas frontiersmen in Turnerian terms: they were
"individualists" who insisted that "everything" be "done by the
individual and nothing by organized society." They learned the
"endurance of extreme adversity," which often was translated into
a "tendency to conform," and they were "men of faith" who envisioned a better future.

2 FORD, GUY STANTON, ed. Essays in American History Dedicated
   to Frederick Jackson Turner. New York: Holt, 293 pp.
      Collection of ten essays written by Turner's former students
in honor of his election to the presidency of the American Historical Association.

3 MATHEWS, LOIS KIMBALL. "The American Frontier." Nantucket
   Historical Association, Proceedings 16 (20 July):34-42.
      Analyzes the American frontier from a Turnerian perspective.
Praises Turner's revolutionizing ideas.

4 PAXSON, FREDERIC LOGAN. The Last American Frontier. New
   York: Macmillan, 402 pp., passim.
      The first book to attempt to synthesize the growing volume
of articles and books in the Turnerian school into a general
treatment of the West. Reprinted: 1911, 1918, 1924, 1937; New
York: Cooper Square Publishers, 1970.

5 PAXSON, FREDERIC L. "The West and the Growth of the National
   Ideal." Illinois State Historical Society, Transactions, pp.
   24-33.

1910

Turnerian in tone. Specifically: "What the United States became, it became by growth and development," which is simply another way of describing "what is already known to most of you, through the labors of the greatest of our western historians, Turner."

6 ROSS, EDWARD ALSWORTH. "The Study of the Present as an Aid to the Interpretation of the Past." Mississippi Valley Historical Association, Proceedings 11 (1908-1909):128-36.
    Observes that "in the course of a decade there has come about a wide acceptance of Professor Turner's generalization that in America the democratic spirit grew up in . . . the frontier." Uses Turner's frontier thesis to illustrate that "one cannot comprehend the past save by study of the present."

7 VAN DER ZEE, J. Review of The Last Frontier, by Frederic Logan Paxson. Iowa Journal of History and Politics 8 (July): 423-24.
    "The importance of western history is gaining recognition year by year and the author justly gives most of the credit to Professor Frederick J. Turner."

1911

1 SEMPLE, ELLEN CHURCHILL. "Geographical Boundaries." In Influences of Geographic Environment. New York: Holt, pp. 204-41.
    Turner's point of view is evident throughout the article, especially in her definition of the "frontier" as a place where the spirit of freedom, enterprise, and self-reliance reigns. Reprinted: 1925, 1927, 1930; New York: Russell & Russell, 1968.

2 SIMONS, ALGIE MARTIN. Social Forces in American History. New York: Macmillan, 325 pp., passim.
    In a personal letter to Turner (attached to the cover of Turner's autographed copy at the Huntington Library) the author acknowledges that "your teachings were at the bottom of" this "little book."

1912

1 COMAN, KATHERINE. Economic Beginnings of the Far West. 2 vols. New York: Macmillan, 1:417 pp.; 2:450 pp., passim.
    Traces the development of the West from a Turnerian point of view. Reprinted: Fairfield, N.J.: Kelley, 1969.

2 WEYL, WALTER E. "Can a Democracy Endure?" In The New Democracy: An Essay on Certain Political and Economic Tendencies
   in The United States. New York: Macmillan, pp. 348-57.
       Asserts that "our conquest of the Continent, though essen-
   tial to national expansion, . . . did not aid" in the creation of
   a "socialized democracy." The frontier experience generated an
   "excess of individualism," which in turn caused twentieth-century
   Americans to be overly concerned about individual freedom. "Much
   of our complaint about the restriction of Liberty is an echo from
   the forest, a belated cry from the old pioneer period." Disagrees
   with Turner's assumption that the frontier produced American
   democracy. Revised: 1914; reprinted: New York: Harper & Row,
   1964.

3 _____. "The Conquest of the Continent." In The New Democracy:
   An Essay on Certain Political and Economic Tendencies in the
   United States, New York: Macmillan, pp. 23-35.
       Does not view the froniter as the source of a desirable
   form of democracy as did Turner; sees it, instead, as a source of
   a tradition that makes a desired "socialized democracy" difficult
   to achieve. The frontier experience had "made America atomic."
   Believes like Turner that "what our land is, what our state is,
   what we are, our present problems and our present hopes are
   largely traceable to the hasty occupation of the continent." But
   unlike Turner, does not think the frontier past offers any promise
   for the future. Revised: 1914; reprinted: New York: Harper &
   Row, 1964.

4 _____. "The Individualistic Spirit of America." In The New
   Democracy: An Essay on Certain Political and Economic Tendencies in the United States. New York: Macmillan, pp. 36-50.
       Rejects Turner's emphasis upon the uniqueness of the Ameri-
   can experience and acknowledges the European influences upon the
   formulation of American culture. Agrees with Turner that the
   frontier had a powerful influence, but unlike Turner, views the
   frontier heritage as dysfunctional in the twentieth century. Revised: 1914; reprinted: New York: Harper & Row, 1964.

1913

1 BECKER, CARL. "Some Aspects of the Influence of Social Problems and Ideas upon the Study and Writing of History." American Journal of Sociology 18 (March):641-75.
       Analyzes the various historical methods and examines the
   difficulty in defining what history should do. Explores the influence of social problems on both the method and the content of
   historical writing. Notes that all histories, however, are

1913

"inspired by a common motive, the desire, namely, to appropriate
out of the past something which may serve the ideal of social
programs. . . ."

2 RAMSDELL, CHARLES W. Review of Guide to the Study and Reading
of American History, by Edward Channing, Albert Bushnell Hart,
and Frederick Jackson Turner. Southwestern Historical Quarterly 16 (January):334.
    "The present volume is a great improvement over the first
edition" largely because "Turner, who was not connected with the
earlier edition, has contributed many valuable references to
writings on Western history."

3 THOMPSON, JAMES WESTFALL. "Profitable Fields of Investigation
in Medieval History." American Historical Review 18 (April):
490-504.
    "With scarcely more than a change of dates and proper names
many of the paragraphs in Professor Turner's essay may be applied
to German medieval history. . . . The stages of transition are
identical--from cattle-raising and swine-herding to farming, to
commerce, to manufacturing." Is confident that "the American
medievalist has an advantage over his European confrere, because
. . . in 1893, in his memorable paper upon 'The Significance of
the Frontier in American History,' Professor Turner quoted the
words of the Italian economist Loria: 'America has the key to
the historical enigma which Europe has sought for centuries in
vain." Enlarged: 1915.7.

1914

1 TRIMBLE, WILLIAM J. "Influence of the Passing of the Public
Lands." Atlantic Monthly 113 (June):755-67.
    Uncritically accepts Turner's thesis. "The first great
chapter of the nation's history is closing with the passing of
public lands" and the country must as a result face a "period of
fundamental readjustment. . . . The purpose of the present essay
is to call attention to the fundamental nature of the process
through which we are passing, and try to discern . . . its . . .
consequences."

1915

1 ANON. "The New Pioneer." New Republic 3 (19 June):165.
    Rejects the Turnerian view of the West as place and process
of new beginnings.

2 CHASE, L.A. "The Last American Frontier." <u>History Teacher's</u>
   <u>Magazine</u> 6 (February):37-40.
       Draws upon the Turner thesis to explain the migration of
   Americans to the "Canadian northwest."

3 FINLEY, JOHN. "The Valley of the New Democracy." In <u>The</u>
   <u>French in the Heart of America</u>. New York: Scribner's, pp.
   291-308.
       Applies Turner's frontier thesis to the Mississippi Valley.
   Agrees that American democracy is the outcome of the American
   people in dealing with the West. Reprinted: 1918.

4 MILLSPAUGH, ARTHUR C. "Points of Emphasis in Teaching of
   Government in the West." <u>History Teacher's Magazine</u> 6
   (February):40-44.
       Accepts Turner's view that "the most constantly potent sec-
   tion has been the West." Agrees with his emphasis upon the fron-
   tier as a source of democracy, individualism, and "all that is
   American."

5 PAXSON, FREDERIC L. "A Constitution of Democracy--Wisconsin,
   1847." <u>Mississippi Valley Historical Review</u> 2 (June):3-24.
       Turner's concepts regarding the frontier as a source of
   democracy are used as theoretical constructs in the analysis of
   the formation of Wisconsin's first constitution. Reprinted:
   1918.4.

6 _____. "The New American History." <u>Quarterly Review</u> 223
   (January):159-81.
       Identifies Turner as "the leader in forcing upon American
   historians the importance of economic history and the significance
   of the frontier," and concludes that "no one is to-day combating
   his generalization that the influence of the frontier was the
   most important single factor in the first century of American
   history."

7 THOMPSON, JAMES WESTFALL. "East German Colonization in the
   Middle Ages." <u>American Historical Association, Annual Report</u>,
   pp. 125-50.
       Enlarged version of 1913.3.

8 WILLIAMS, MARY W. "A Fragment of the Passing Frontier."
   <u>History Teacher's Magazine</u> 6 (February):33-37.
       Bases her observations on Turner's writings and ideas and
   argues that "certain universal characteristics determine the
   classification of a region a frontier."

1916

1916

1 ALVORD, CLARENCE W. "Virginia and the West: An Interpretation." Mississippi Valley Historical Review 3 (June):20-38.
      Discusses the conflict between Virginia land speculators
and the prohibitions of western settlement imposed by the British
government. This conflict, along with the "famous expedition of
George Rogers Clark," led to the cession of western lands by the
British after the Revolutionary war.

1917

1 ANON. "Frontier American." Nation 104 (January):66-67.
      Celebrates the Turnerian frontier.

2 BOLTON, HERBERT E. "The Mission as a Frontier Institution in
   the Spanish-American Colonies." American Historical Review 33
   (October):42-61.
      "Turner has devoted his life to a study of the Anglo-
American frontier, and rich has been the reward . . . and for him
who interprets, with Turner's insights, the methods and the significance of the Spanish-American frontier, there awaits a recognition not less marked."

3 FISH, CARL RUSSELL. "The Frontier a World Problem." Wisconsin
   Magazine of History 1 (December):121-41.
      Just as "the striking feature in the history of Wisconsin
has been the transformation within a lifetime of a virgin forest
into a civilized area" which in turn was "a part of the American
frontier movement," so the cutting edge of world history can be
located on the many frontiers that can be identified as a central
part of the life of most modern nations. Although the author
never referes to Turner by name, his indebtedness to Turner for
his approach to world history is clear. Reprinted: 1961.12.

1918

1 BOUCHER, CHAUNCEY S. "The Eleventh Annual Meeting of the
   Mississippi Valley Historical Association." Mississippi
   Valley Historical Association, Proceedings 9 (May):335-48.
      Report of an address delivered by Frederick Jackson Turner
entitled "Middle Western Pioneer Democracy," which was "stimulating and suggestive, as are all the writings of the revered dean
of the students of western history."

2 COMMONS, JOHN R. Introduction to <u>History of Labor in the</u>
   <u>United States</u>, by John R. Commons et al. Vol. 1. New York:
   Macmillan, pp. 3-21.
       "Labor movements in America have arisen from peculiar
   American conditions" and "the condition which seems to distinguish
   most clearly the history of labor in America from its history in
   other countries is the wide expanse of land." Reprinted: 1921,
   1926, 1936, 1940; Fairfield, N.J.: Kelley, 1966.

3 KUTTNER, ALFRED BOOTH. "A Study of American Intolerance."
   <u>Dial</u> 64 (March):223-25.
       Attributed American intolerance to the frontier experience.
   Instead of viewing the frontier as the source of Turner's desirable
   characteristics, it is depicted as the basic source of one of our
   most undesirable tendencies.

4 PAXSON, FREDERIC L. "Wisconsin: A Constitution of Democracy."
   In <u>The Movement for Statehood</u>. Edited by Milo M. Quaife.
   Madison: State Historical Society of Wisconsin, pp. 30-53.
       Reprint of 1915.5.

                              <u>1919</u>

1 GARLAND, HAMLIN. "The Passing of the Frontier." <u>Dial</u> 17 (4
   October):285-86.
       Turnerian view of the closing of the frontier.

2 IGLEHART, JOHN E. "The Spirit of the Ohio Valley." <u>Indiana</u>
   <u>Magazine of History</u> 15 (June):144-49.
       Laments the pro-New England bias of the last generation of
   historians and heralds the growing influence of the Turnerian
   approach. Embraces Turner's ideas.

3 MacKINDER, HALFORD J. <u>Democratic Ideals and Reality</u>. New
   York: Holt, 266 pp., passim.
       Applies Turner's closed frontier thesis to the global fron-
   tier of the western world. Reprinted: 1942, 1944; New York:
   Norton, 1962.

4 SHEPHERD, WILLIAM R. "The Expansion of Europe." <u>Political</u>
   <u>Science Quarterly</u> 34 (March):43-60; 34 (June):210-25; 34
   (September):392-412.
       Broadens Turner's frontier thesis to include western
   European expansion in general. Emphasizes, in Turnerian fashion,
   the impact of frontier expansion upon the home base of that ex-
   pansion--in this case Europe.

1919

5 USHER, ELLIS B. "Cyrus Woodman: A Character Sketch." Wisconsin Magazine of History 2 (June):397.
      Turner is cited as the authoritative source of the idea "that 'the frontier' is a social and not a geographical condition."

1920

1 BECKER, CARL. "The American Frontier." Nation 3 (10 November):536.
      A review of The Frontier in American History in which Turner's thesis is summarized by "one who has long been under" the "spell" of Professor Turner. Concludes that "Turner's original paper on the frontier was to prove an epoch-making event in the investigation of American History" and "time has not diminished the validity of it."

2 _____. The United States: An Experiment in Democracy. New York: Harper, 332 pp., passim.
      Utilizes Turner's frontier thesis to trace the development of American democracy. Reprinted: 1927.3.

3 EMERSON, GUY. The New Frontier: A Study of American Liberal Spirit, Its Frontier Origin, and Its Application to Modern Problems. New York: Holt, 314 pp., passim.
      Turnerian in approach, assumptions, and conclusions.

4 HENDERSON, ARCHIBALD. The Conquest of the Old Southwest. New York: Century, 395 pp., passim.
      Dedicated "to the historian of OLD WEST and NEW WEST, FREDERICK JACKSON TURNER with admiration and regard." Turner's influence is reflected in the emphasis upon the democratic impact of the frontier, the frontier as the source of desirable American cultural characteristics and the "series of frontiers." Reprinted: Spartanburg, S.C.: Reprint Co., 1974.

1921

1 ALVORD, CLARENCE W. Review of The Frontier in American History. Mississippi Valley Historical Review 7 (March):403-7.
      To Turner "belongs the honor of founding the scientific school of western history." Praises Turner as much as his book; asserts that his "special genius lies in synthesis" and "no one since Bancroft has so completely redirected the course of historical research."

2 ANON. "Frederick Jackson Turner: The Frontier in American
   History." Times (London) Literary Supplement 25 (August) : 538.
      Summarizes Turner's Frontier in American History and
   stresses the relationship of the frontier to the development of
   "American democracy." Reprinted: 1954.1.

3 BEARD, CHARLES. "The Frontier in American History." New
   Republic 25 (16 February):349-50.
      Criticizes Turner's thesis for being "too broad and sweep-
   ing." Furthermore, "it is certainly questionable whether . . .
   the frontier" has "exercised a more profound influence on American
   development than either the industrialism of the East or the semi-
   feudal plantation system of the South."

4 CHANNING, EDWARD. "Notes: Bibliography." In A History of
   the United States. Vol. 5. New York: Macmillan, p. 67.
      Turner "broke away from the ordinary path of American his-
   torical endeavor and with his students organized the study of
   'the West.'" Reprinted: 1926, 1936, 1949.

5 FULLER, GEORGE N. Review of The Frontier in American History.
   Michigan History Magazine 5 (July-October):322-23.
      "Turner . . . brings together for the first time under one
   cover the materials essential to a correct understanding of the
   meaning of our westward expansion" in a work "'inspirational'
   rather than properly historical."

6 IGLEHART, JOHN E. "American Methodism and American Democracy."
   Indiana Magazine of History 17 (June):138-41.
      Traces the increasing acceptance of Turner's views and sum-
   marizes them.

7 JOHNSON, ALLEN. Review of The Frontier in American History.
   American Historical Review 26 (April):542-43.
      Although Turner's frontier thesis in 1893 "was then a fresh
   and exceedingly suggestive interpretation of our history" it has
   now "come to be almost a commonplace in American historiography."
   The younger historians have made this point of view their own.

8 MEANY, EDMOND S. Review of The Frontier in American History.
   Washington Historical Quarterly 12 (January):73.
      Calls Turner "one of the best loved" American historians.

9 PAXSON, FREDERIC L. "Influence of Frontier Life on the
   Development of American Law." State Bar Association of Wisconsin, Proceedings 13 (23-25 June):477-89.
      Discusses the influence of the frontier on the development
   and evolution of the political structures in the United States.

1921

Argues in Turnerian fashion that the "frontier process . . . may be regarded as our American great first cause."

10 _____ . Recent History of the United States, 1865 to the
   Present. New York: Houghton Mifflin, pp. 33-34, 116-18.
      "Frederick Jackson Turner produced . . . in 1893 his essay
on the Significance of the Frontier in American History with such
compelling logic as to force a complete restatement of the facts
in American history." Reprinted: 1925; revised: 1937.12.

11 SCHLESINGER, ARTHUR M. "The Influence of Immigration on
   American History." American Journal of Sociology 27 (July):
   71-85.
      Suggests that immigration has been as responsible for the
development of American culture as has Turner's frontier environment. Reprinted: 1922.4, 1928.10.

                                1922

1 ANON. "Corresponding Members." Geographical Review 12
   (April):297-98.
      Underscores the significance of Turner's writings because
they "are especially distinguished by the appreciation of geo-
grpahical science to historical research."

2 DEWEY, JOHN. "The American Intellectual Frontier." New Republic 30 (May):303-5.
      Traces the things he most disliked about the American cul-
ture of his day--especially paranoia about science, anti-intellec-
tualism, evangelicalism, William Jennings Bryan, and excessive
emotionalism--to the nineteenth-century frontier experience. Reprinted: 1929.2.

3 SCHAFER, JOSEPH. "The Yankee and the Teuton in Wisconsin."
   Wisconsin Magazine of History 6 (December):125-45.
      Modifies Turner's assumption that the spirit of nationalism
generated on the frontier caused a rapid fusion of ethnic immigrants. Shows, instead, that frontier nationalism was not as
powerful a force in this regard as Turner had suggested. Continued: 1923.7.

4 SCHLESINGER, ARTHUR M. New View Points in American History.
   New York: Macmillan, pp. 1-22, 23-46, 69-71 passim.
      Presents Turner as the "first historian who perceived the
importance of economic influence in American history" and stimulated "students who sought to apply his viewpoint to particular
periods or aspects of American History." Accepts and elaborates

                                14

upon Turner's ideas regarding the influence of geographical
forces upon the development of American cultural characteristics
such as individualism, love of freedom, intense nationalism, and
democracy. Pp. 1-22 reprint of 1921.1. Reprinted: 1928.10.

1923

1 ADAMS, JAMES TRUSLOW. History of New England. Vol. 2,
   Revolutionary New England, 1761-1776. Boston: Atlantic
   Monthly, 469 pp., passim.
      One of the first eastern scholars to accept and apply
   Turner's ideas concerning frontier influences upon American
   democracy and character. Reprinted: 1927, 1941; New York:
   Cooper Square Publishers, 1968.

2 ANON. Review of List of References on the History of the
   West, by Frederick Jackson Turner and Frederick Merk. Wisconsin Magazine of History 7 (September):122.
      Recommended as an assigned book for college courses on
   western history.

3 BELAUNDE, VICTOR A. "The Frontier in Hispanic America." Rice
   Institute Pamphlet 10 (April):202-13.
      "The dynamic element par excellence in the development of
   Anglo-Saxon America has been the frontier." We owe this genial
   idea to Professor Turner." Concludes that a study of "Hispanic
   America" reveals an "absence of frontier, in the sense that
   Professor Turner gave the word."

4 GARLAND, HAMLIN. "Pioneer and City Dwellers." Bookman 58
   (December):369-72.
      Questions Turner's assumption that Americans would migrate
   to the frontier if it were still open by suggesting that large
   cities are more attractive than any frontier.

5 IGLEHART, JOHN E. "The Environment of Abraham Lincoln: The
   Frontier." Indiana Historical Society Publications 8, no. 1:
   148-55.
      Borrows Turner's ideas regarding the influence of the fron-
   tier environment to explain the formation of Lincoln's character.
   Lengthy summary of the growing support for Turner's ideas.

6 MODE, PETER G. The Frontier Spirit in American Christianity.
   New York: Macmillan, 196 pp., passim.
      Although "it is more than a quarter of a century since
   Professor Frederick J. Turner called attention to the significance
   of the Frontier in American History, there does not exist an

1923

"interpretation of American Christianity" that takes "cognizance
of the influence of the frontier in giving it its distinctive
characteristics." Responds to this perceived need.

7 SCHAFER, JOSEPH. "The Yankee and the Teuton in Wisconsin."
   Wisconsin Magazine of History 6 (March):261-79; 6 (June):286-
   302; 7 (September):3-19; and 7 (December):148-71.
       Continuation of 1922.3.

8 STEVENS, WAYNE E. "Shortridge: A Typical Frontier." Minnesota History Bulletin 5 (February):48-52.
       Review of a master's thesis by William P. Shortridge en-
   titled "The Transition of a Typical Frontier with Illustrations
   from the Life of Henry Hastings Sibley," which concludes that it
   attempts "to illustrate Turner's interpretation of the significance of the frontier as a 'laboratory specimen.'"

                              1924

1 ANON. "Exit Frontier Morality." New Republic 37 (2 January):
   137-38.
       Reviews the past influence of the agrarian frontier on the
   national character and suggests the new frontiers lie before
   Americans which will mold American character as much as the frontier of the past. Critical of the morality of Turner's frontier
   while simultaneously excited about the emerging one.

2 BUCK, SOLON J. "News and Comment." Minnesota History Bulletin
   5 (August):512-19.
       Credits "Turner and his disciples" with having established
   a national trend in historiography that encourages the study of
   local history.

3 COULTER, E. MERTON. "Early Frontier Democracy in the First
   Kentucky Constitution." Political Science Quarterly 39
   (December):665-77.
       Kentucky frontiersmen, as a result of frontier conditions,
   developed "a spirit of independent initiative" and had "little
   patience for control from any authority east of the mountains."
   Entire article is based upon Turnerian assumptions.

4 HAYNES, FREDERICK E. Social Politics in the United States.
   Boston: Houghton Mifflin, 414 pp., passim.
       Turner's frontier thesis serves as the intellectual frame-
   work for the entire volume. One section is significantly titled
   "Significance of the Frontier in American History."

1925

5 HIBBARD, BENJAMIN H. History of the Public Land Policies.
   Land Economics Series, edited by Richard T. Ely. New York:
   Macmillan, 91 pp., passim.
       Dedicated to "Frederick Jackson Turner: an inspiring
   teacher who has made the study of the conquest of the West more
   fascinating than fiction." Turner's influence is evident throughout. Reprinted: 1939; University of Wisconsin Press, 1965.

6 HICKS, JOHN D. "The People's Party in Minnesota." Minnesota
   History Bulletin 5 (November):531-60.
       States that the People's party of Minnesota understood that,
   "as Mr. Turner puts it, 'the defenses of the pioneer democrat'
   had shifted 'from free land to legislation, from the ideal of
   individualism to the ideal of social control through regulation
   by law." Abridged: 1970.16.

7 PAXSON, FREDERIC L. History of the American Frontier, 1763-
   1893. Boston: Houghton Mifflin, 598 pp., passim.
       Acknowledges that when he began his research "Turner had
   already pointed out the significance of the frontier in our history." This book is a "synthesis, in which an attempt is made to
   show the proportions of the whole story of the frontier first
   interpreted by Frederick Jackson Turner." Reprinted: 1924.8;
   Dunwoody, Ga.: N.S. Berg, 1967.

8 _____. History of the American Frontier, 1763-1893. Students
   edition. Boston and New York: Houghton Mifflin, 598 pp.
       Reprint of 1924.7.

9 ROWE, HENRY KALLOCH. History of Religion in the United States.
   New York: Macmillan, 213 pp., passim.
       Attempts to do for American religious history what Turner
   did for American secular history. Reprinted: 1928.

                              1925

1 ALMACK, JOHN C. "The Shibboleth of the Frontier." Historical
   Outlook 16 (May):197-202.
       Examines the frontier thesis and concludes that Turner's
   adulation is unwarranted. Agrees that the frontier has been an
   important factor in American life, but "it has not been an important agency of progress." Claims that in terms of intellectual
   contribution, economic organization, moral and social conditions,
   and political progress, the frontier fell far short of the standards set by the older eastern states. Concludes that "proofs of
   frontier shortcomings" may also be found [in] the same regions
   today."

1925

2 HUBBELL, JAY B. "The Frontier in American Literature."
   Southwest Review 10 (January):84-92.
       Argues that a literary history of the frontier is needed
   for the study of American Literature. Praises Turner's thesis
   and claims that the frontier contributed new material, new backgrounds, new types of characters, and a new point of view. "The
   frontier furnished the chief nationalizing influence in a literature which is too often considered only a minor branch of English
   literature."

3 LARSON, LAURENCE. "The Changing West." Journal of the Illinois
   State Historical Society 17 (January):551-64.
       Asks: "Why have . . . our social and institution systems
   . . . changed?" and finds his answer in the influence of Turner
   and his thinking. "Rarely has a new doctrine in the field of
   history found such ready acceptance. . . . If the historical
   profession . . . has its prophets Professor Turner belongs to the
   major group."

4 MacDONALD, WILLIAM. "Some Observations on the Spirit and Influence of the American Frontier." Colonial Society of
   Massachusetts, Transactions 26:165-80.
       Credits Turner with establishing "the importance of the
   frontier in American history" and generalizes that Turner provided "a new point of view from which the history of the United
   States must thenceforth be written." Criticizes Turner for emphasizing "politics at the expense of other social forces."
   Attempts to correct this alleged imbalance by studying the degree
   to which "characteristics of the older communities" were "modified"
   by frontier "conditions."

5 McDOUGALL, WILLIAM. The Indestructible Union: Rudiments of
   Political Science for the American Citizen. Boston: Little,
   Brown, pp. 114-17, 171-74.
       Presents Turner's views regarding the frontier as the most
   convincing interpretation of the significance of the frontier.
   Subscribes to Turner's interpretation of the closing of the frontier in the discussion of individualism in the American experience.

6 STRUNSKY, SIMEON. "About Books, More or Less: Frontiers and
   Limits." New York Times Book Review, 5 July, p. 4.
       Credits the frontier hypothesis, first stated by Frederick
   Jackson Turner, for opening new doors to the study of America.
   Suggests that "there are so many truths" to it that the frontier
   is "on its way to expanding into a philosophical system." Emphatically warns, however, that "the frontier . . . should be
   used with caution."

7 THOMAS, FRANKLIN. "Critics of Geographical Determinism." In
   The Environmental Basis of Society, A Study in the History of
   Sociological Theory. New York: Century, pp. 255-306.
       An analysis of critiques of geographical determinism like
   that implied in Turner's thesis. Reprinted: Boulder: Johnson
   Reprint Co., 1965.

                              1926

1 ANON. "Geographical News: Twenty-second Annual Meeting of
   the Association of American Geographers." Geographical Review
   16 (April):330-32.
       Review of Turner's "Geographic Sectionalism in American
   History," in which he is credited with demonstrating, with a
   "striking series of maps, the development within the United
   States of sections of more or less political homogeneity."

2 DONDORE, DOROTHY ANNE. The Prairie and the Making of Middle
   America. Cedar Rapids, Iowa: Torch Press, 472 pp., passim.
       Attempts to do for the study of American literature what
   Turner did for the study of American history. Reprinted: New
   York: Antiquarian Press, 1961.

3 FOERSTER, NORMAN. "American Literature." Saturday Review of
   Literature 2 (3 April):677-79.
       Urges literary scholars to awaken to the "very special
   opportunity . . . owing to the work of recent American historians
   . . . like Turner." Turner had provided literary scholars with
   "a new vision of the forces dominant in our past."

4 MUMFORD, LEWIS. "The Romanticism of the Pioneer." In The
   Golden Day: A Study in American Experience and Culture. New
   York: Boni & Liveright, pp. 47-81.
       Rejected Turner's assumption that the pioneer was a product
   of the American environment. "The truth is that he [the pioneer]
   existed in the European mind before he made his appearance here."
   Stresses the European and literary origin of frontier ideas. Reprinted: New York: Norton, 1933; Dover, 1968.

5 PARISH, JOHN C. "The Persistence of the Westward Movement."
   Yale Review 15 (April):461-77.
       Accepts the validity of Turner's thesis and argues that the
   frontier "did not cease in 1890 but has been a persistent factor
   in our national life, still tending to distinguish the American
   people from the people of Europe." After 1890 new frontiers
   emerged to supersede Turner's closed frontier. "These were frontiers of intensive farming, of conservation . . . , of adequate

1926

banking facilities, of manufacturing industries, of colleges . . .
and . . . frontiers of convenience and comfort." Reprinted:
1943.12.

6 THOMAS, JOHN M. "Influence of Frontier Life on American
   Christianity." New Jersey Historical Society, Proceedings 19
   (January):1-18.
       "It is the great service of Professor Frederick J. Turner
to have pointed out the significance of the frontier in American
history" and his thesis can be utilized to explain the uniqueness
of American religion.

7 WOODBURN, JAMES A. "Western Radicalism in American Politics."
   Mississippi Valley Historical Review 13 (September):143-68.
       The advance of democracy in America "has been the result of
radical opinion, radical action, and radical leadership." Claims
that "Professor Turner in his Frontier in American History has
revealed this once and for all. . . ."

8 WRIGHT, C.W. "[The Significance of the Disappearance of Free
   Land in Our Economic Development.]" American Economic Review,
   Supplement 16 (March):265-71.
       Argues in a Turnerian fashion that the "vast supply of
relatively free and undeveloped land" in the West was the predominant factor in shaping American political, economic, and
soical history. Notes that with the end of the frontier and the
end of free lands, economic development necessarily changes.
Examines these changes in the fields of agriculture, manufacturing,
foreign trade, and finance.

                              1927

1 BAKER, RAY STANNARD. Woodrow Wilson: Life and Letters,
   Princeton 1890-1910. Garden City, N.Y.: Doubleday, pp. 43,
   120-25.
       Documents Wilson's attempt "to persuade Professor Frederick
J. Turner to come to Princeton." Turner's willingness to share
his personal struggles with Wilson and Wilson's indebtedness to
Turner's frontier thesis are discussed. Reprinted: 1946; Westport, Conn.: Greenwood Press, 1968.

2 BECKER, CARL. "Frederick Jackson Turner." In American
   Masters of Social Science. Edited by Howard W. Odum. New
   York: Holt, pp. 273-318.
       Presents recollections of Turner as an undergraduate pro-
fessor. Turner the master teacher is in the spotlight throughout
the first half of the article while Turner's frontier thesis is

the focal point of the remainder. Provides insights into the way
Turner's mind worked and conveys a feeling for Turner the human
being. Reprinted: 1935.2, 1941.2, 1946.4.

3 _____. Our Great Experiment in Democracy. New York: Harper,
   332 pp.
      Reprint of 1920.2.

4 BOWMAN, ISAIAH. "The Pioneer Fringe." Foreign Affairs 6
   (October):49-66.
      Explores the question of "whether the pioneer spirit as
manifested in the westward spread of settlers in the United
States still exists" by studying the frontiers of the Canadian
Northwest, Rhodesia, and West Australia in a Turnerian approach.

5 COMMAGER, HENRY. "The Literature of the Pioneer West."
   Minnesota History 8 (December):319-28.
      Although historians like Turner "have given us their evalua-
tions of the physical processes and institutions of the frontier
and of the westward movement," they have failed to understand
that "the significance . . . of the frontier for the development
of American character" can best be discovered in the "psychological
experiences of the individuals and communities that participated
in the great enterprise." Writers like O.E. Rölvaag have had the
most to offer in this broader interpretation of the frontier experience."

6 FOX, DIXON RYAN. "Civilization in Transit." American Historical Review 32 (July):753-68.
      Traces the main characteristics of American culture back to
European origins, thereby rejecting Turner's central assumption
that American culture was a by-product of the frontier. "Civilization . . . declines when it strikes the frontier" rather than
being revitalized as Turner claimed.

7 GRAS, A.S.B. "The Rise and Development of Economic History."
   Economic History Review, 1st ser. 1 (January):12-34.
      Investigates the history of economic history. Finds that
although Turner was not an economic historian, he did influence
the writing of economic history in America by turning the focus
of investigation from European to indigenously American values
and influences.

8 HAZARD, LUCY LOCKWOOD. The Frontier in American Literature.
   New York: Barnes & Noble, pp. xv, xvi, xvii, 25, 34, 149,
   163, 183, 206, 207, 211, 245, 246, 248, 249, 258, 281, 285.
      Acknowledges that "within the last quarter of a century we
have had a redefinition of the significance of American

1927

history. . . . Professor Turner" with his "'Significance of the Frontier'" has "revolutionized the treatment of United States History." Hazard attempts to do for the interpretation of American literature what Turner did for history.

9   HOWLAND, CHARLES P.   "America's Coming of Age." Survey 53
    (August):437-40.
        Accepts Turner's view that the closing of the frontier marked a major turning point in American history, but rejects his assumption that the closing of the frontier places America's future in jeopardy.

10 HUBBELL, JAY B.   "The Decay of the Provinces: A Study of
    Nationalism and Sectionalism in American Literature." Sewanee
    Review 35 (October-December):473-87.
        Uses the sectional analysis of Frederick Jackson Turner to interpret the writing of literature in America. Also notes that the national characteristics of American literature have three major influences: (1) the influence of social differences among immigrants, (2) the frontier, and (3) the economic or industrial revolution. States that "we who teach American literature have much to learn from Turner, Beard and Robinson."

11 HUNTINGTON, ELLSWORTH.   "Why the American Woman Is Unique."
    Nation 125 (3 August):105-7.
        Argues that natural selection stemming from migration, geographic and environmental conditions, and the stimulating envrionment in America has led to the ambitious, progressive, and adaptable temperament of Americans.

12 JONES, HOWARD MUMFORD.   America and French Culture, 1750-1848.
    Chapel Hill: University of North Carolina Press, 615 pp.,
    passim.
        Argues that the eastern "cosmopolitan spirit" combined with French influences and the frontier spirit as defined by Turner were dynamically interacting during the period under study with the former proving to be the dominant influence. Turner's view of the frontier prevails throughout the volume while his conclusions regarding the frontier's influences are challenged. Reprinted: 1965, 1973.

13 ODUM, HOWARD W.   "Pioneers and Masters of Social Science." In
    American Masters of Social Science: An Approach to the Study
    of the Social Sciences through a Neglected Field of Biography.
    New York: Henry Holt, pp. 3-20.
        Turner is identified as one of the "master minds" among American social scientists.

1928

14 RÖLVAAG, OLE E. Giants in the Earth. Harper's Modern Classics. New York: Harper, 405 pp., passim.
    A literary synthesis of the westward movement in which the author challenges Turner's emphasis upon the impact of the physical frontier environment and resulting boundless optimism by underscoring the psychological and spiritual impact of the westward movement upon the frontiersmen. Instead of depicting the frontier as generating a high civilization, Rölvaag characterizes the environment as wresting civilization from man. The frontier is pictured as a place of human suffering and even death rather than as a source of all that is laudable in American experience as depicted in Turner's writings. Reprinted numerous times.

15 TAYLOR, LYON G. "Southern Rule." Tyler's Quarterly Historical and Genealogical Magazine 9 (October):79-82.
    A critique of Turner's "The South 1820-1830" in which Tyler challenges Turner's assertion that "the Southerners for a long time ruled the nation, but when they found that they had lost their hold upon the government they adopted . . . secession."

1928

1 BEARD, CHARLES A. "The City's Place in Civilization." American City 39 (November):101-3.
    Claims that urbanism, the culture of the city, will dominate the future instead of the culture of the country. The machine age is taking precedence over the agrarian age, and its beauty and influence should be nurtured and mastered. Does not lament the passing of the frontier, but instead looks forward to the changes brought on because of the rise of the city.

2 _____. "Culture and Agriculture." Saturday Review of Literature 5 (20 October):272-73.
    Praises Turner as "the outstanding scholar of his generation, almost the only one who did not devote himself to rehashing rehash." Argues, however, that research needs to be expanded beyond the frontier thesis to incorporate "the contributions of capitalism, industrial labor, and the old plantation system" in order to understand contemporary America. Turner's "agrarian thesis is inadequate" because it ignores some of the "powerful economic forces" which have molded American society.

3 DOBBS, CHARLES. "A Changing Viewpoint of Pioneer Development." Filson Club History Quarterly 2 (July):145-56.
    Argues that too many historians have been forsaking reality for romance. Proposes using a method of "multiple hypothesis" similar to that of Turner. Finds, however, that "even such

1928

scholars as Turner and Schlesinger are found repeatedly failing
to distinguish between fond hopes and hard facts."

4 MacLEOD, WILLIAM C. The American Indian Frontier. New York:
   Alfred A. Knopf, 598 pp., passim.
        Critical of Turner for having failed to recognize that
"every frontier has two sides. . . . This volume represents the
first attempt at an analysis of American frontier history . . .
from the viewpoint of the Indian side of the frontier development." Reprinted: Chicago: Argonaut, 1968; London: Dawsons,
1968.

5 MILLER, PERRY G. "Contemporary Observations of American Frontier Political Attitudes." Ethics 39 (October):80-92.
        Describes frontier politics and frontier courts and finds
"traditional institutions being modified in incredible directions
by the new environment, being compelled, will they nill they, to
suffer sea changes as the frontier tidal wave swept over them."

6 PAINE, GREGORY. "The Frontier in American Literature."
   Sewanee Review 36 (April-June):225-36.
        Praises Turner's thesis and argues that the significance
of the frontier on American literature needs to be delved into
more completely. Several attempts at such a study are reviewed,
but most gloss over the issue. Elaborates on the prerequisites
necessary for a thorough analysis.

7 RANSOM, JOHN CROWE. "The South--Old or New?" Sewanee Review
   35 (April):139-47.
        "This is the thesis:--That the South in its history to date
has exhibited . . . a culture based on European principles which
has lasted as long as a century." Turner's thesis does not apply
to the South.

8 RUSSEL, ROBERT R. "A Revaluation of the Period before the
   Civil War: Railroads." Mississippi Valley Historical Review
   15 (December):341-54.
        Rejects the Turnerian assumption that the frontier had a
greater influence on the industrial East than vice versa. Cites
the railroad as a prime example of how eastern technology "revolutionized the character of the new frontier."

9 SAGE, WALTER N. "Some Aspects of the Frontier in Canadian
   History." Canadian Historical Association, Report of the
   Annual Meeting, 1928, pp. 62-72.
        Stresses the "obvious parallels which may be drawn between
. . . the westward movement in the United States . . . and the
development of the Canadian frontier," and calls for more

comparative studies of this sort. Accepts Turner's thesis and
suggests that its only limitation was a result of Turner's failure
to include Canada in his scheme of frontier advance.

10 SCHLESINGER, ARTHUR M. New View Points in American History.
    New York: Macmillan, pp. 1–22, 23–46, 69–71, passim.
        Reprint of 1922.4; pp. 1–22 reprint of 1921.11.

11 STEPHENSON, NATHANIEL W. "An Illustration of the Frontier as
    Seed Bed." American Historical Association, Pacific Coast
    Branch, Proceedings, pp. 56–66.
        In discussing the frontier, most historians describe the
    movement from the North to the West, and too little attention is
    directed to the parallel southern movement. An explanation of
    this "is the key to a great deal of history."

12 VAN DOREN, MARK. "The Repudiation of the Pioneer." English
    Journal (college edition) 17 (October):616–23.
        Celebrates the fact that there are "no more physical worlds
    to subdue" because, contrary to the Turnerian tradition, the
    frontier experience had prevented Americans from becoming
    civilized.

1929

1 ANON. "Turner, Frederick Jackson." Encyclopaedia Britannica.
   14th ed. 22:626.
       Brief summary of Turner's career.

2 DEWEY, JOHN. "The American Intellectual Frontier." In Characters and Events: Popular Essays in Social and Political
   Philosophy. Vol. 2. Edited by Joseph Ratner. New York:
   Holt, pp. 447–52.
       Reprint of 1922.2; reprinted: New York: Octagon Books,
1970.

3 GABRIEL, RALPH HENRY. The Pageant of America: A Pictorial
   History of the United States. Edited by Ralph Henry Gabriel.
   Vol. 2, The Lure of the Frontier: A Story of Race Conflict.
   New Haven: Yale University Press, 327 pp., passim.
       "Frederick Jackson Turner, in July 1893, addressed a small
   group of scholars. 'What the Mediterranean Sea was to the
   Greeks, breaking the bond of customs, offering new experiences,
   calling out new institutions and activities, that, and more, the
   ever retreating frontier has been to the United States.' . . .
   Many phases of the march of the frontier across the continent lie
   within the province of other volumes in this series. Within the

1929

pages at hand an effort has been made to chronicle only the work
of exploration which preceded the advance of civilization."
Develops this thesis within a Turnerian framework.

4 HEATON, HERBERT. "The Development of New Countries--Some Com-
    parisons." Minnesota History 10 (March):3-25.
       Accepts Turner's assumptions regarding the frontier origins
of democracy and the frontier as a safety valve.

5 McDOUGALL, JOHN L. "The Frontier School and Canadian History."
    Canadian Historical Association, Report of the Annual Meeting,
    pp. 121-25.
       Contains a "statement of . . . Turner's position" and a
critique of his thesis. If Turner were correct "we ought . . .
to expect similar frontiers in other sections of the globe to
produce corresponding results." French Canada, although a frontier area, is significantly different from Turner's American
frontier and so similar to France that it serves to discredit
Turner's frontier thesis. Reprinted: 1970.23.

7 NEVINS, ALLEN. "Recent Progress of American Social History."
    Journal of Economic and Business History 1 (May):365-83.
       Asserts that "for a generation the chief prophet of the
creed that the controlling forces of our history are sound and
economic was Frederick J. Turner." Furthermore, his "'Significance of the Frontier'" . . . possessed a seminal power of the
profoundest kind."

8 NIXON, HERMAN CLARENCE. "Precursors of Turner in the Inter-
    pretation of the American Frontier." South Atlantic Quarterly
    28 (January):83-89.
       Develops the thesis that Turner "not only marked a turning
point in American historical research, but also furnished a
synthesis and climax for ideas envisaged by different observers
of American social forces in the preceding half century."

9 PAXSON, FREDERIC L. "The American Frontier." Encyclopaedia
    Britannica. 14th ed. 1:769-73.
       Turnerian summary of the significance of the frontier.
Stresses Turner's stages of frontier development and frontier
characteristics.

10 PHILLIPS, ULRICH B. "The Central Theme of Southern History."
    American Historical Review 34 (October):30-43.
       The "Southern scheme of life and thought" was a result of
neither Turner's frontier nor European influence. Racism rather
than the frontier gave the South its uniqueness according to
Phillips.

26

1930

1 ADAMS, JAMES TRUSLOW. "Our Deep-Rooted Lawlessness." New York Times Magazine, 9 March, pp. 1-2.
"Throughout our entire history, from the first settlements in Virginia and New England to the official closing of the frontier in 1890, our attitude toward law has been highly colored by the influence of the wilderness." Laments that this attitude is one of disrespect and disregard.

2 BIZZILLI, P. "Geopolitical Conditions of the Evolution of Russian Nationality." Journal of Modern History 2 (March):27-36.
Examines similarities in Russian and American colonization. "We are struck afresh by the analogy between Russia and America, especially by the analogous role played in the history of the two countries by the zone of the 'moving frontier.'" Both frontiers helped form the respective national characteristics by serving as "melting pots."

3 BOYNTON, PERCY H. "The Conquest of the Frontier." In The Trans-Mississippi West. Edited by James F. Willard and Colin B. Goodykoontz. Boulder: University of Colorado Press, pp. 163-74.
"The Turnerian thesis of the frontier, none too rapid in spreading among the historians themselves, was slower still in penetrating the thickish skins of the literarians." Examines the Turnerian assumptions reflected in the writings of Willa Cather.

4 BRADLEY, HAROLD WHITMAN. "American Frontier in Hawaii." American Historical Association, Pacific Coast Branch, Proceedings, pp. 135-50.
Concludes that because of the "similarity of the principal actors, of their natures and of the results," America's involvement in the Hawaiian Islands was "in reality the farthest extension of the American frontier" as outlined by Turner.

5 BRANCH, EDWARD DOUGLAS. Westward: The Romance of the American Frontier. New York and London: D. Appleton, 627 pp., passim.
Treats the stages of frontier development within in a Turnerian framework. Reprinted: 1936; New York: Cooper Square Publishers, 1969.

6 EDWARDS, EVERETT E. A Bibliography of the History of Agriculture in the United States. Washington, D.C.: Government Printing Office (U.S. Dept. of Agriculture, no. 24), pp. 4-6, 40-43, 60-63, 440-42, 478-82 passim.
An extensive bibliography of secondary books and articles of the frontier. Reprinted: New York: B. Franklin, 1970.

1930

7 GREEN, FLETCHER M. "Constitutional Trends, 1776-1860." In
Constitutional Development in the South Atlantic States, 1776-
1860: A Study in the Evolution of Democracy. University of
North Carolina Social Study Series. Chapel Hill: University
of North Carolina Press, pp. 297-304.
Challenges Turner's assumptions regarding the democratic
influence of the frontier. Reprinted: New York: Norton, 1966.

8 HARRIS, J. ARTHUR. "Frontiers." Scientific Monthly 30
(January-June):19-32.
Accepts Turner's view that "geographically, our western
frontier has passed into history" as well as his belief that the
frontier experience "developed our national character." Calls
for a new "moral equivalent for the old frontier" and identifies
"the frontier of science" as the most promising "new . . . frontier." These "new frontiers of research" are more promising than
Turner's geographical frontier because they are not limited by
geographical boundaries.

9 JAMES, ALFRED P. "The First English-Speaking Trans-Appalachian
Frontier." Mississippi Valley Historical Review 17 (June):55-
77.
Corrects the mistaken impression that the first American
frontier was in Kentucky and Tennessee. Argues that the oldest
frontier was west of the Appalachians in the Monongahela country.
Also argues that the majority of frontier settlers in this region
were English, not Scotch-Irish as previously supposed.

10 LACHER, J.H.A. "Francis A. Hoffmann of Illinois and Hans
Buschbauer of Wisconsin." Wisconsin Magazine of History 13
(June):327-55.
Turner is cited as "that high authority" on matters referring
to frontier settlement patterns.

11 LOWER, A.R.M. "The Origins of Democracy in Canada." Canadian
Historical Association, Report of the Annual Meeting, pp. 18-
39.
Calls for the formulation of a "modified . . . version of
the [Turner] thesis which can be fitted to Canada." Reprinted:
1970.22.

12 PARISH, JOHN CARL. "Reflections on the Nature of the Westward
Movement." American Historical Association, Pacific Coast
Branch, Proceedings, pp. 98-112.
Presents a Turnerian analysis of the westward movement.
Discusses the American nature of the movement, the inward and out-
ward pressures affecting the process, the stages of advance, and
the significance of the frontier. States that in interpreting

the frontier, "no one has gone beyond the vision of Professor
Turner a generation ago. His finely interpretive mind envisaged
the whole movement in time and space and quality." Reprinted:
1930.13, 1943.13.

13 _____. Reflections on the Nature of the Westward Movement.
Los Angeles: McBride Printing Co., 15 pp.
   Reprint of 1930.12.

14 PAXSON, FREDERIC L. "Finance and the Frontier." In The Trans-
Mississippi West. Edited by James F. Willard and Colin B.
Goodykoontz. Boulder: University of Colorado Press, pp. 257-
66.
   "In spite of all the diligence of western historians since
Frederick Jackson Turner pointed out its significance, the field
of the frontier has not been more than reconnoitered in a pre-
liminary way." Reviews the Turnerian reasons for studying frontier history and calls for a massive study of the "repetition of
the frontier process in every county and every state" with a
special emphasis on economic factors.

15 _____. When the West Is Gone. New York: Holt, 137 pp.,
passim.
   Turner's influence is evident in the emphasis upon "a
knowable past that . . . made . . . American civilization a
unique thing," the frontier as "a process as well as a region,"
the westerner as a "new type of American," the frontier as a
creator of "opportunity," and the frontier as a place "to democ-
ratize the American character." In characteristically Turnerian
language, generalizes that "given an environment . . . in which
the normal restrictions of society are relaxed" the "emphasis
is . . . upon . . . personal strength, courage and endurance. . . .
The American was more than a mere native of America. He was a
survivor of a process of relentless selection." Presents a
militant defense of Turner's ideas. Reprinted: 1941.

16 PRYDE, GEORGE S. "The Scots in East New Jersey." New Jersey
Historical Society, Proceedings, n.s. 15 (January):1-39.
   Acknowledges in an explanatory footnote that all of the
points concerning the influence of the frontier upon the European
heritage are "lucidly expounded in the works of F.J. Turner."

17 RIEGEL, ROBERT E. America Moves West. New York: Henry Holt,
595 pp., passim.
   A survey of American frontier history written from a
Turnerian perspective. Includes a chapter entitled "The Historian
Discovers the West" in which Turner is credited with launching
"the real beginning of the modern history of the West." Further-

1930

more, the "influence of Turner grew rapidly, so that within a
generation the Turner ideas had become thoroughly embedded, not
only in historical writing, but in other fields of research and
even in general literature." Revised: 1947, 1956, 1964.

18 SAUER, CARL O. "Historical Geography and the Western Frontier."
     In The Trans-Mississippi West. Edited by James F. Willard and
     Colin B. Goodykoontz. Boulder: University of Colorado Press,
     pp. 267-89.
        Analyzes Turner's ideas regarding the influence of the
frontier environment upon American development from the point of
view of contemporary scholarship in geography.

19 SWEET, WILLIAM WARREN. Story of Religion in America. New
     York and London: Harper, 571 pp., passim.
        Underscores the democratizing effect of the frontier.
Draws upon Turner's frontier thesis throughout the volume. Reprinted: 1931; revised: 1939; reprinted: 1950.

20 WALKER, ERIC A. The Frontier Tradition in South Africa.
     London: Oxford University Press, 24 pp.
        Accepts the frontier "definition given by Turner, the his-
torian of the United States frontiers" as valid and treats his
subject from a Turnerian perspective.

21 WRIGHT, BENJAMIN F., Jr. "American Democracy and the Frontier."
     Yale Review 22 (December):349-65.
        After acknowledging that Turner's "'The Significance of the
Frontier in American History'" had "become the most widely read
and probably the most influential one ever written upon American
History," proceeds to criticize Turner's thesis. It tended to
"isolate . . . American democracy from the general course of
Western Civilization," equate democracy with the frontier, and
attribute American greatness to environmental determinism.
Challenges Turner's theory that democracy was a by-product of the
frontier by demonstrating that many frontier political practices
were imported from the East.

<u>1931</u>

1 ADAMS, JAMES TRUSLOW. The Epic of America. Boston: Little,
    Brown & Co., 433 pp., passim.
       An interpretation of the American experience that is
Turnerian in conception, assumptions, and conclusions. In a
chapter entitled "The End of the Frontier" (pp. 270-306) the
significance of the closing of the frontier is expressed in
Turnerian phraseology. The controlling idea in the monograph is

the assumption that American history can best be explained in
light of the frontier process. Concludes that the "idea of the
frontier as first given to us by Professor Frederick J.
Turner . . . , with the possible exception of the economic interpretation of all history, has caused more reconsideration of
American development than any other single suggestion." Reprinted:
numerous times.

2 BEARD, CHARLES A. "The Myth of Rugged American Individualism."
   Harper's Magazine 164 (December):13-22.
        Analyzes the controversy of government interference in
   business affairs. Concludes that "the cold truth is that the
   individualist creed of everybody for himself and the devil take
   the hindmost is principally responsible for the distress in which
   Western civilization finds itself. . . ."

3 BOWMAN, ISAIAH. *The Pioneer Fringe*. American Geographical
   Society Bulletin, Special Publication no. 13. Edited by G.M.
   Wrigley. New York: American Geographical Society, 361 pp.,
   passim.
        Implies that Turner's thesis is not relevant to the twenti-
   eth century. "Pioneering today does not conform to the American
   frontier traditions of the nineteenth century. . . . It is the
   purpose of this book to sketch the outlines of a 'science of
   settlement' to set forth the ideas that have moved men to take
   such diverse paths. . . . The tools of conquest no less than new
   fields of conquest are now in the mind of the enterprising
   settler." Includes a treatment of international frontiers. Reprinted: Freeport, N.J.: Books for Libraries Press, 1970.

4 BOYNTON, PERCY HOLMES. *The Rediscovery of the Frontier*.
   Chicago: University of Chicago Press, 185 pp., passim.
        Accepts Turner's thesis and calls it the "most exciting
   single idea that has ever been injected into the study of American
   history." Applies this concept of the frontier to a study of
   fiction and literary criticism. Like Turner, finds that the
   frontier "holds out a promise for the future of America." Literature reveals, as does history, that this promise has not been
   fulfilled, but at best, the pioneer "was stronger for the ordeal.
   He learned to endure and to attempt the impossible and never to
   lose hope. In him and the sterner of his offspring is the capacity for a new vision, and perhaps for finding a new America
   within himself." Reprinted: Westport, Conn.: Greenwood Press,
   1968; New York: Cooper Square Publishers, 1970; Darby, Pa.:
   Folcroft Library Editions, 1974.

5 BREBNER, J. BARTLET. "Canadian and North American History."
   Canadian Historical Association, Report of the Annual Meeting,
   pp. 37-48.

1931

After treating Canadian expansion as a manifestation of Turner's frontier environmental determinism, Brebner points out that "the enthusiastic elaboration of Professor F.J. Turner's reasonable suggestions, obviously will not serve" when historians attempt to explain specific aspects of Canada's frontier experience.

6 CURTI, MERLE. "The Sections and the Frontier in American History: The Methodological Concepts of Frederick Jackson Turner." In Methods in Social Science. Edited by Stuart Rice. Chicago: University of Chicago Press, pp. 353-67.
    Discusses Turner's evolutionary methodolgy and examines the various modes of inquiry he employed including historical criticism, the natural sciences, environmental factors, economic history, and political and cultural behavior. Refutes critics who argue that Turner's view was limited. Turner was interested in how all interacting forces contributed to the development of the society.

7 JOSEPHSON, MATTHEW. "The Frontier and Literature." New Republic 68 (2 September):78.
    Argues that the "environment of the Frontier . . . created no social philosophy other than the anarchic individualism of the jungle." The combination of frontier values and industrial capitalism resulted in an exploitive society and created a climate of opinion hostile to artistic production. Turner's glorified frontier must be purged from the nation's awareness before there can be any hope of establishing a national literature.

8 McWILLIAMS, CAREY. "Myths of the West." North American Review 232 (November):424-32.
    In examining the myth of the West, comments that ever since Turner announced the closing of the frontier, "funeral laments" and "obsequies" have arisen over its demise. "This dolorous mood has resulted in an enormous and incredible renascence of the Western myth."

9 MARCHANT, ERNEST. "Emerson and the Frontier." American Literature 3 (May):149-74.
    Depicts Emerson as a precursor of Turner; Turner's ideas regarding the relationship between the frontier and American individualism, democracy, progress, etc., were "clearly recognized by Emerson eighty-five years ago."

10 OLIVER, JOHN W. "The Twenty-fourth Annual Meeting of the Mississippi Valley Historical Association." Mississippi Valley Historical Review 18 (September):213-31.
    Pages 218-20 report a discussion of Turner's frontier thesis

presented at the annual meeting. Frederic Paxson, John D. Hicks,
and Solon J. Buck applauded Turner's creativity. A synopsis of
each of their discussions is given.

11 PAXSON, FREDERIC L. "Frontier." Encyclopaedia of the Social
    Sciences. Edited by Edwin R.A. Seligman. New York:
    Macmillan, 6:500-503.
    A Turnerian summary of the importance of the frontier in
American history. Includes a bibliography reflecting the
Turnerian orientation.

12 SCHAFER, JOSEPH. "The Author of the 'Frontier Hypothesis.'"
    Wisconsin Magazine of History 15 (September):86-103.
    Laudatory tribute to Turner in which his oratorical skills
and effectiveness as a teacher are stressed.

13 _____. Review of New England, 1830-1850. Wisconsin Magazine
    of History 15 (December):256-57.
    Although "Turner publishes only intermittently," his pub-
lications are greeted by fellow scholars with enthusiasm because
they set a "standard of achievement in historical writing."

14 VANCE, RUPERT B. "Frontier--Geographical and Social Aspects."
    Encyclopaedia of the Social Sciences. Edited by Edwin R.A.
    Seligman. New York: Macmillan, 6:503-5.
    A Turnerian treatment of the geographical and sociological
dimensions of frontier development. Includes a brief bibliography.

15 WEBB, WALTER PRESCOTT. The Great Plains. Boston: Ginn, 525
    pp., passim.
    Disagrees with Turner's depiction of the frontier pattern
as monolithic by showing that the frontier experience has manifested itself in various nations in a wide variety of different
patterns. Reprinted: 1959; New York: Grosset & Dunlap, 1931,
1957; Boston: Houghton Mifflin, 1936.

16 WILSON, CHARLES MORROW. "The Surviving American Frontier."
    Current History 34 (May):189-92.
    Rejects the Turnerian assertion that the frontier had
closed, and quotes Turner to prove that "American democracy may
continue, since both the forest and the frontier remain."

1932

1 ABERNETHY, THOMAS P. From Frontier to Plantation in Tennessee:
   A Study in Frontier Democracy. Chapel Hill: University of
   North Carolina Press, 392 pp., passim.

1932

Abernethy, a former student of Turner, argues that the
Tennessee frontier does not verify Turner's frontier thesis.
Describes the Tennessee frontier as dominated by exploitive,
grasping, antidemocratic land speculators. Dedicated to Turner.
Reprinted: Memphis State College Press, 1955; University of
Alabama Press, 1965.

2 ALBION, ROBERT G. "The Communication Revolution." American
Historical Review 37 (July):718-20.
"The turnpikes, canals, steamboats, and railroads were
knitting the country together and pushing the frontier westward
quite irrespective of the growth of American cotton mills or iron
foundries."

3 ANON. "April Meeting." Colonial Society of Massachusetts,
Transactions, 1930-1933 28 (April):252.
Turner's death reported.

4 ANON. "Dr. F.J. Turner Dies: Noted as Historian." New York
Times, 16 March, 21:1.
Briefly chronicles his life and contributions.

5 ANON. "Frederick Jackson Turner." Current History 36 (May):
213.
Obituary notice.

6 ANON. "Frederick Jackson Turner." Geographical Review 22
(July):499.
Obituary notice. "In Professor Turner was the rare com-
bination of historical originality with geographical insight.
His death is or was no less severe to American geography than to
the study of American History."

7 ANON. "Frederick Jackson Turner." Publishers Weekly 121 (19
March):1395.
Obituary notice.

8 ANON. "Frederick Jackson Turner." Washington Historical
Quarterly 23 (April):158-59.
Obituary. Turner's "industrious search for fundamental
sources and his elucidation of them when found have given his
work a status that will attract other historians for untold time."

9 ANON. "The Man of the Portage." New York Times, 17 March,
20:3.
"Turner was like the portage path between the East and the
West--holding the frontier West ever in memory of the East."

1932

10 ANON. "News and Comment." Western Pennsylvania Historical
    Magazine 15 (May):181.
        Announcement of Turner's death in which his contribution to
    the study of "regional, state, and local history" is cited as his
    major achievement.

11 ANON. "News and Comment: Miscellaneous." Oregon Historical
    Quarterly 33 (June):179-80.
        Announcement of Turner's death in which he is referred to
    as a "recognized authority on the history of westward expansion."

12 ANON. [Obituary Notice]. Canadian Historical Review 13
    (September):343.
        Claims the frontier thesis will have a "profound effect" on
    the writing of Canadian history just as it has had on American
    history.

13 ANON. [Obituary Notice]. Nation 134 (30 March):355.
        Turner was "one of the best American historians as well as
    one of the most modest." He was a pioneer.

14 ANON. [Obituary Notice]. Pacific Historical Review 1 (June):
    267-68.
        Presents a brief biographical sketch and emphasizes Turner's
    ability as a scholar and as a teacher.

15 ANON. [Obituary Notice]. School and Society 35 (26 March):
    424.

16 ANON. "Personal." Agricultural History 6 (April):102.
        Announcement of Turner's death.

17 ANON. "Report of the Council." Colonial Society of Massachu-
    setts, Transactions, 1930-1933 28 (November):273.
        Eulogy in which Turner is credited with having established
    the "full significance" of the West and having given "a new turn
    to historical writing . . . in the United States."

18 ANON. "Report of the Council." Massachusetts Historical
    Society, Proceedings 64 (April):449.
        Turner's death announced.

19 BEZANSON, ANNE. "Some Historical Aspects of Labor Turnover."
    In Facts and Factors in Economic History. Edited by Arthur H.
    Cole, A.L. Dunham and N.S.B. Gras. Cambridge, Mass.: Harvard
    University Press, pp. 692-708.
        Challenges Turner's safety-valve theory.

1932

20 BOGART, ERNEST LUDLOW. "Pushing Back the Frontiers." American
    Economic Review 22 (March):1-9.
        Agrees with the statement of the Superintendent of the Cen-
    sus in 1890 that the frontier closed, and finds evidence for this
    in the spread of material achievement, cultural values, and educa-
    tion over the entire country. Economic science has since become
    "a new frontier," and if there is to be continued material and
    cultural advance, "the unsolved economic problems which constitute
    the frontier of our science" must be overcome.

21 BOWMAN, ISAIAH. "The Pioneering Process." Science 75 (20
    May):521-28.
        Suggests that pioneer movement into the frontier is not
    made by individuals or "by twos and threes"; rather, "the advance
    is made by communities, by groups of people. . . ." Discusses
    some of the complexities of the pioneering process.

22 BRIGHAM, CLARENCE S. "Frederick Jackson Turner." American
    Antiquarian Society, Proceedings, n.s. 42, no. 1:14-16.
        Obituary. Though his literary output was not large, his
    concepts of the frontier and the section are "of far reaching
    importance in the interpretation of history."

23 BROWN, E. FRANCIS. "Frederick Jackson Turner." Current His-
    tory 34 (May):213.
        Obituary. Through his emphasis upon the influence of the
    frontier in American history Turner "altered the direction of
    the interpretation of American History" and became "one of the
    nation's great historical scholars."

24 BURT, A.L. "Our Dynamic Society." Minnesota History 13
    (March):3-23.
        Writes about the development of American society in a com-
    pletely Turnerian tone: "The restless energy, the driving power,
    the practical resourcefulness, the buoyancy, and the exuberance
    of the westerner leavened the whole lump of America." Argues
    that the frontier shaped American character into a form different
    from Europe, and points out that "the frontier was the corner
    stone of our democracy, the perennial preserver of our freedom."
    In the twentieth century, America is losing its dynamic quality
    and is becoming more static, but looks forward to the development
    of "new and positive virtues," which will enhance "a real growth,
    a native growth" in American culture.

25 CLARK, ROBERT CARLTON. "Why History Needs to Be Rewritten."
    Oregon Historical Quarterly 33 (December):295-310.
        "When a historian in his . . . cognitions brings forth a
    new idea that illuminates the past, not only does he assure

himself of immortality, but he causes as well a great deal of history rewriting. No American historian . . . has earned greater fame for himself or been more responsible for more revamping of United States history than the late Frederick Jackson Turner."

26 FARRAND, MAX. Introduction to The Significance of Sections in American History, by Frederick Jackson Turner. New York: Holt, pp. iii-v.
    Explains the procedure followed in the posthumous publication of this manuscript, which Turner left unfinished at his death. Reprinted: 1950, 1959.

27 JAMES, ALFRED P. Review of America Moves West, by Robert E. Riegel. Western Pennsylvania Historical Magazine 15 (May): 161-62.
    "Like so many . . . of the now numerous accounts of the westward movement . . . this book . . . comes out of the Frederick Jackson Turner School of Historiography." However, the "volume shows little of the masterful philosophical and speculative interpretations of . . . Turner."

28 KELLOGG, LOUISE PHELPS. "The Passing of a Great Teacher--Frederick Jackson Turner." Historical Outlook 23 (October): 270-72.
    "Turner was always a great teacher." He was a "stimulating, inspiring, and delightful instructor." "There was never anything formal in Turner's classes, never anything repetitious or methodical. Only one description is appropriate, the class was inspirational." Turner's behavior in the classroom is described, and the author's own interaction with Turner is discussed.

29 MEANY, EDMOND S. "Frederick Jackson Turner." Washington Historical Quarterly 23 (April):158-59.
    Announcement of Turner's death and a summary of his accomplishments.

30 MERK, FREDERICK. [Obituary Notice]. American Historical Review 37 (July):823-25.
    Turner is recognized as an influential historian and as a penetrating, magnetic teacher.

31 NUTE, GRACE LEE. "Frederick Jackson Turner." Minnesota History 13 (June):159-61.
    Obituary. Emphasizes that Turner's primary concern was not an economic interpretation of history; rather, he was more interested in human relations and social history. "It was never an abstract frontier, never an abstract section that he was

1932

describing--it was toiling, thinking, loving, hating human beings
of whom he was thinking." Comments on her own growth as a student under Turner's direction.

32 PAULIN, CHARLES O. Atlas of the Historical Geography of the
United States. Edited by John K. Wright. Washington, D.C.
and New York: published jointly by the Carnegie Institution
of Washington and the American Geographical Society of New
York, no. 401, 162 pp., passim.
       The influence of Turner and his school of historiography is
evident throughout the work.

33 PAXSON, FREDERIC L. Review of The Great Plains, by Walter
Prescott Webb. American Historical Review 37 (January):359-60.
       The frontier hypothesis has "never permitted itself to be
classified." Comments that "Turner is as much the economist
working along historical lines, as the historian working among
economic provinces."

34 PHILLIPS, ULRICH B. "Memorial to Frederick Jackson Turner."
American Historical Association, Annual Report, p. 55.
       Assessment of Turner's contribution to the historical
profession.

35 ROBINSON, EDGAR E. "Frederick Jackson Turner." North Dakota
Historical Quarterly 6 (July):259-61.
       Tribute to Turner by a former student. Turner's ability to
inspire others to learn and write history is underscored.

36 ROOSEVELT, FRANKLIN DELANO. "Text of Governor Roosevelt's
Speech at Commonwealth Club, San Francisco." New York Times,
24 September, p. 6.
       Accepts Turner's assumption that American greatness had
been generated by the frontier experience and that its closing
had created a crisis. Suggests that the New Deal would help
formulate a new frontier of opportunity to replace the closed
physical one.

37 SCHAFER, JOSEPH. "Death of Professor Turner." Wisconsin
Magazine of History 15 (June):495-99.
       Eulogy and obituary by a former student and lifetime ad-
mirer.

38 SHIPP, RALPH. "Frontier and American Political Life." Aerend:
A Kansas Quarterly 3 (Fall):195-203.
       The factors of "equality, self-confidence and individuality"
on the frontier were instrumental in causing political change in
the areas of suffrage, nationalism, banking, education, and political reform.

39 WRIGHT, JOHN K. "Sections and National Growth: An Atlas of
    the Historical Geography of the United States." Geographical
    Review 22 (July):353-60.
        Quotes and elaborates upon Turner's concepts about section-
    alism, the relationship between geography and politics, and the
    general impact of the frontier upon American culture.

40 _____. "Voting Habits in the United States: A Note on Two
    Maps." Geographical Review 22 (October):666-72.
        The insights of "Professor Turner show clearly that party
    politics are often deeply rooted in the facts of geography."
    Acknowledges Turner's inspiration.

                            1933

1   ANON. "Historical News." North Carolina Review 10 (October):
    342.
        "The Pulitzer Prize for History has been awarded post-
    humously to Frederick Jackson Turner for his book, The Signifi-
    cance of Sections in American History."

2   ANON. "Winners of the Pulitzer Prize in Literature." New
    York Times, 5 May, 13:1.
        Notes that the late Frederick Jackson Turner was post-
    humously awarded the Pulitzer Prize for his collection of essays
    on The Significance of Sections in American History.

3   BAILEY, THOMAS A. "The West and Radical Legislation, 1890-
    1930." American Journal of Sociology 38 (January):603-11.
        Attempts to identify "qualities" in twentieth-century
    America that demonstrate that "the West of which Professor Turner
    wrote" is still the major influence upon American culture in
    general and American reform in particular.

4   BOLTON, HERBERT. "Epic of Greater America." American Histori-
    cal Review 38 (April):448-74.
        Expands Turner's frontier thesis to include the entire
    Western Hemisphere.

5   BUCK, SOLON J. Review of "The Significance of Sections in
    American History." Western Pennsylvania Historical Magazine
    16 (August):205-7.
        Generalizes that the "contributions of the late Frederick
    J. Turner to the interpretation of American history" are "now
    generally recognized as more influential than those of any other
    single individual." Concludes that his "interpretations and con-
    clusions are still valid."

1933

6 COMMAGER, HENRY STEELE. "Farewell to Laissez-Faire." Current History 38 (August):513-20.
       The Roosevelt administration's "abandonment of laissez-
   faire" was a result of its awareness that "laissez-faire . . .
   was born of the American wilderness and of the boundless resources
   of the American Continent." With the frontier closed, the "old
   theories of individualism and laissez-faire were no longer applicable."

7 CURTI, MERLE. Review of The Significance of Sections in American History. American Journal of Sociology 39 (September):
   265-66.
       This book shows that "the concept of the section was . . .
   even more important in Turner's thinking" than the frontier.
   Turner identified class conflict with sectional conflicts, and
   though "there is a substantial measure of truth in this identification," more needs to be studied about class difference conflicts
   within sections and subsections. "Turner would have welcomed
   such analysis. . . ."

8 DAVIDSON, DONALD. "Sectionalism in the United States." Hound
   and Horn 6 (July-September):561-89.
       States that Turner "has at last altered the old false per-
   spective [concerning sectionalism in our national development]
   and has drawn the outline of a thesis which must inevitably raise
   the sections to a new level of importance." Defends and elaborates
   upon Turner's ideas concerning sectionalism.

9 FARRAND, MAX. "Frederick Jackson Turner at the Huntington
   Library." Huntington Library Bulletin, no. 3 (February):157-
   64.
       Explains that Turner's limited number of publications is
   directly related to his pioneer spirit: "he liked to open new
   trails. He was willing to break ground, but like so many of the
   pioneers he then moved on to fresh endeavors, leaving the fields
   for his followers to cultivate." He achieved his purpose through
   teaching rather than through publication. Describes Turner's
   tenure at the Huntington Library in light of this fact.

10 HACKER, LOUIS M. "Sections-or Classes?" Nation 137 (26
    July):108-10.
        A review of Turner's The Significance of Sections in Amer-
    ican History. "The perverted reading of Turner gave to American
    history in his insistence upon the uniqueness of American experi-
    ence" is pointed to as Turner's greatest weakness. Reprinted:
    1949.8.

11 HILL, FRANK ERNEST. "Frontier." In What Is American? New
    York: John Day, pp. 34-52.
        Accepts Turner's thesis as valid and treats the frontier
    influence upon American culture from a Turnerian perspective.
    Reprinted: 1935.

12 HOWE, M.A. DeWOLFE. "Memoir of Frederick Jackson Turner."
    Colonial Society of Massachusetts, Transactions, 1930-1933 28
    (April):494-502.
        Observes that Turner's "place among historians had not been
    won, in 1910, by any impressive output of books. Indeed, there
    was only one." However, his influence is great, and implies that
    this influence rested upon his ability as a teacher of graduate
    students.

13 KELLOGG, LOUISE PHELPS. Review of The Significance of Sections
    in American History. Wisconsin Magazine of History 16 (June):
    470.
        Underscores Turner's contribution to frontier studies.

14 MORRISON, SAMUEL ELIOT. "Frederick Jackson Turner (1861-
    1932)." American Academy of Arts and Sciences, Proceedings
    68 (December):685-86.
        Turner's writing has been "profound"; his "Significance of
    the Frontier in American History" is "the most influential
    [paper] ever written on American History."

15 NEVINS, ALLEN. "Historical Scholarship in America." Minne-
    sota History 14 (March):88-90.
        Review of Historical Scholarship in America: Needs and
    Opportunities declaring it to be a "disappointing work" because
    of its failure to identify the real opportunities in the histori-
    cal profession. Points to "the late Frederick Jackson Turner,"
    who "looms up like a giant" in the search for a history that will
    meet the needs of people outside the academic community.

16 PAXSON, FREDERIC L. "A Generation of the Frontier Hypothesis:
    1893-1932." Pacific Historical Review 2, no. 1:34-51.
        The significance of Turner's contribution is found in his
    devotion of "himself . . . 'to the task of understanding and ex-
    plaining the United States.'" After reviewing Turner's ideas
    with acceptance and admiration, asserts that the "Turner hypoth-
    esis stands today as easily to be accepted as it was when
    launched." Reprinted: 1941.12.

17 _____. Review of The Significance of Sections in American
    History. American Academy of Political and Social Science,
    Annals 167 (May):237.

1933

This volume "indicates the broadening of Turner's interest" in his later years.

18 ROBBINS, ROY M. "Horace Greeley: Land Reform and Unemployment." Agricultural History 7 (January):18-41.
    Argues that during the Panic of 1837 Greeley embraced a concept very similar to Turner's safety-valve theory.

19 ROOSEVELT, FRANKLIN D. "Reappraisal of Values." In Looking Forward. New York: John Day, pp. 15-36.
    Borrows Turner's assumptions. In the nineteenth century "the frontier land was substantially free" and when depressions hit, urban easterners could climb "into a covered wagon" and move West. "In retrospect we can now see that the turn of the tide came with the turn of the century. We were reaching our last frontier then; there was no more free land . . . there is no safety valve in the form of Western prairie." Reprinted: 1973.

20 SCHAFER, JOSEPH. Review of The Significance of Sections in American History. Wisconsin Magazine of History 16 (June):470.
    Lists the essays contained in this volume.

21 _____. "Turner's Frontier Philosophy." Wisconsin Magazine of History 16 (June):451-69.
    Although the America of 1933 was very different from the America of 1893, when Turner first advanced his thesis, "Turner's historical interpretation" had stood the test of time so well that his contemporaries had to acknowledge their "inability thus far either to supplement it fundamentally, or to weaken it by criticism." Turner is pictured as the first historian to "interpret the general movement" of the American drama. Turner and his ideas are defended in the face of emerging criticism within the historical profession. Reprinted: 1961.24.

22 SCHLESINGER, ARTHUR M. A History of American Life. Vol. 10, The Rise of the City, 1878-1898. New York: Macmillan, 494 pp., passim.
    Challenges Turner's frontier thesis by advancing an urban interpretation of the American experience. Reprinted: 1944, 1946, 1957.

23 STEPHENSON, GEORGE M. "Turner: Significance of Sections." Minnesota History 14 (September):316-18.
    Review of Turner's The Significance of Sections in American History in which the focus is as much upon Turner the man and his great influence upon the historical profession as upon this particular book.

1934

24 STOLBERG, BENJAMIN. "Turner, Marx, and the A.F. of L."
    Nation 137 (13 September):302-3
        Defends "Turnerism" in the face of Louis M. Hacker's attack
    (see Nation, 26 July 1933) and concludes that "without Turner's
    key to the frontier the abnormality of the American class struggle
    remains a mystery" and the "American dream" unexplained.

25 WEEKS, O. DOUGLAS. Review of The Significance of Sections in
    American History. South-Western Social Science Quarterly 14
    (December):386-87.
        Uncritical summary of Turner's major points concerning
    "sectional interests in American history."

26 WRIGHT, BENJAMIN F., Jr. Review of The Significance of Sec-
    tions in American History. New England Quarterly 6 (September):
    630-34.
        "Certainly no man has influenced American historians of the
    past generation so deeply as did Turner. . . . Turner, more than
    any other man, turned the study of America inward." Comments
    positively on this book, especially its scholarship and its
    scope.

<u>1934</u>

1   CRAVEN, AVERY. "The Advance of Civilization into the Middle
    West in the Period of Settlement." In Sources of Culture in
    the Middle West: Backgrounds versus Frontier. Edited by
    Dixon Ryan Fox. New York: Appleton-Century, pp. 39-71.
        Turner's greatest insight was that the "occupation of new
    areas by the American pioneer was but the first step in an ex-
    tended process" that eventually resulted in the elimination of
    the "wilderness" and the erection in its place of "that complexity
    called 'civilization.'" The American frontier was "not entirely
    unique"; "Turner lifted" the frontier story "into dignity of
    world history" and demonstrated that the American pioneer "was
    one with the men of Western Europe." Reprinted: New York:
    Russell & Russell, 1964.

2   DAVIDSON, DONALD. "Where Regionalism and Sectionalism Meet."
    Social Forces 13 (October):23-31.
        Accepts Turner's definition of sections and calls upon
    those who support the validity of "the New Regionalism" to seek
    common ground with those like "the late F.J. Turner" who view
    America as a nation of sections.

3   DeVOTO, BERNARD. "The West: A Plundered Province." Harper's
    Magazine 169 (August):355-64.

1934

Analyzes the exploitation of the West by eastern "manipula-
tors." "Looted, betrayed, sold out, the Westerner is a man whose
history has been just a series of large-scale jokes." The East
has bled the resources of the West, making it "the one section of
the country in which bankruptcy, both actuarial and absolute, has
been the determining condition from the start." Concludes, however, in a tone reminiscent of Turner, that the westerner "is
the first American who has worked out a communal adaptation to
his country," and "the long pull may show--history has precedents--
that the dispossessed have the laugh on their conquerors."

4 FOX, DIXON R. "Editor's Explanation." In Sources of Culture
   in the Middle West, Background versus Frontier. New York:
   Appleton-Century, pp. 3-14.
       Introduces the articles in this volume, all of which deal
with some aspect of the Turner tradition, by suggesting that such
a study of Turner was needed because "over forty years" had
elapsed "since . . . Turner, in the most famous and most influential paper in American historiography" had "forged a key for
the understanding of America's development." Reprinted: New
York: Russell & Russell, 1964.

5 HANSEN, MARCUS L. "Remarks." In Sources of Culture in the
   Middle West, Backgrounds versus Frontier. Edited by Dixon
   Ryan Fox. New York: Appleton-Century, pp. 103-10.
       Critical of those who parrot Turner's ideas in lieu of ad-
vancing fresh interpretations themselves. Suggests instead that
the Turnerian approach to the study of American history has resulted in a failure to study European origins of American culture
as well as a failure to develop comparative approaches. Reprinted: New York: Russell & Russell, 1964.

6 HAWKINS, GLENN B. Review of The Greater Southwest by Rupert
   N. Richardson and Carl C. Rister. Chronicles of Oklahoma 12
   (December):481.
       "Every year since the last decade of the nineteenth century
when the late Professor Frederick Jackson Turner began preaching
the 'spirit of the frontier,' both in and out of the classroom,
an ever increasing demand has existed for such a work."

7 HEATON, HERBERT. "Migration and Cheap Land--The End of Two
   Chapters." Sociological Review, o.s. 26 (July):231-48.
       Argues, almost as a corollary to Turner's thesis, that the
age of migration is over. With the end of cheap or free land and
with the closing of immigration doors, "man must stay where he
is." This problem is international in scope, but the cases of
North America and Australia as places of movement are more
closely examined.

8 HICKS, JOHN. "The Development of Civilization in the Middle
   West, 1860-1900." In Sources of Culture in the Middle West,
   Backgrounds versus Frontier. Edited by Dixon Ryan Fox. New
   York: Appleton-Century, pp. 73-101.
      Turner's greatest contribution was his assertion that "the
   most American part of America" was "the West" with its "frontier
   experience," which constituted "the most profound of all influences that went into the shaping of the American character."
   Hicks refers to himself as "a reasonably orthodox Turnerian" who
   wishes to take the "middle ground" in the debate regarding Turner.
   Modifies Turner's thesis by minimizing the uniqueness of the West
   and emphasizing the interdependence of the East and West in the
   formulation of American culture. Reprinted: New York: Russell
   & Russell, 1964.

9 HINTZE, HEDWIG. "Regionalism." Encylopaedia of the Social
   Sciences. Edited by Edwin R.A. Selgiman. New York: Macmillan,
   13:208-18.
      Frederick Jackson Turner's "sectionalism is in effect a
   regionalist approach," and although he envisioned a future time
   when "sectional self-consciousness . . . is likely to be increased . . . , there has been but slight substantiation of
   Turner's prediction."

10 KNAPLUND, PAUL. "Editorial Comment." Wisconsin Magazine of
    History 18 (September):97.
       Identifies Turner's theory on the significance of the fron-
    tier as one of the two most influential theories in the last
    forty years.

11 McBRIDE, GEORGE M. Review of The Significance of Sections in
    American History. Pacific Historical Review 3, no. 4:451-52.
       Regrets that this volume does not include several of
    Turner's papers that focus on the subject of sections and American
    history. Praises Turner for "the emphasis he placed upon the im-
    portance of taking regional differences into account. . . ."

12 MICHENER, DWIGHT W. "'Economic Repercussions' from the 'Pass-
    ing of the American Frontier.'" Annalist 44 (21 December):
    853-54.
       A critical analysis of the Turnerian assumptions underlying
    the philosophy and policies of the New Deal of the 1930s.

13 NETTELS, CURTIS. "Frederick Jackson Turner and the New Deal."
    Wisconsin Magazine of History 17 (March):257-65.
       Thesis: although "there is not an historian in the brain
    trust," it was nevertheless true that "a strong current running
    through the philosophy of the New Deal may be traced directly to

1934

the interpretation of American Society developed" by Turner.
"The engineers of the New Deal" viewed the closing of the frontier as the passing of the "automatic adjustor" of the nation's
economic ills and therefore "something must be put in its place,"
and that "something" was the New Deal. Reprinted: 1961.20.

14 ODUM, HOWARD W. "Regionalism versus Sectionalism in the
    South's Place in the National Economy." Social Forces 12
    (March):338-54.
        Warns that the "common confusion of Turner's sectionalism
with the newer prospects of regionalism . . . is of crucial importance," and proceeds to explore why this is the case.

15 PAXSON, FREDERIC L. "Frederick Jackson Turner." Encyclopaedia
    of the Social Sciences. Edited by Edwin R.A. Seligman. New
    York: Macmillan, 15:132-33.
        Generalizes that "American history" has been "reorganized
around Turner's frontier hypothesis" and summarizes his views.

16 PETERSEN, WILLIAM J. "Population Advance to the Upper Mis-
    sissippi Valley, 1830-1860." Iowa Journal of History and
    Politics 32 (October):312-53.
        Accepts Turner's general thesis, but directly challenges
Turner's assumption regarding the frontier as safety valve by
arguing that westward migrations were greatest during times of
prosperity and seriously curtailed during times of depression.

17 PIQUET, JOHN A. "Our Unconquered Frontier." Scribner's
    Magazine 96 (December):354-58.
        Argues that people are flocking to the cities from the
rural areas in such large numbers that "the frontier is returning."
Finds, however, that resettlement is occurring--first to the "sun-
shine states" and then broader to encompass entire regions. Concludes that "the frontier still howls around us, but we are
finding out how to make it smile and help us."

18 SCHAFER, JOSEPH. "Editorial Comment: A Literary Symposium."
    Wisconsin Magazine of History 18 (September):85-97.
        Contains comments by several scholars of the Madison
Literary Club in response to Schafer's paper "Turner's America"
(see 1934). Curtis Nettles examines the principle criticism,
points to recognition of Turner's work by European scholars, and
discusses the relationship between Turner's thesis and Roosevelt's
New Deal. George C. Sellery comments that Turner "was a social
philosopher . . . searching down deep in the very depths of the
life of the people." Edward A. Birge posits the "greatness" and
"genius" of Turner's achievement.

19 _____. "Turner's America." Wisconsin Magazine of History 17
   (June):447-65.
   Compares Turner's method as a historian with Darwin's scientific method: both shared "the urge to be constantly making
and testing hypotheses." Turner was not biased by any single
position; rather, he borrowed from every method applicable to
history: social, economic, urban, geographic, etc. Discusses
Turner's attitude toward sectionalism.

20 WALLACE, HENRY A. New Frontiers. New York: Reynal &
   Hitchcock, pp. 249-62, 269-87.
   Because "we are no longer a pioneer nation with free lands"
or a country "where individualism and free enterprise prove to be
mutually beneficial, Turner's view of America is not relevant in
the Twentieth Century." Calls for a "new frontier"--characterized
by "cooperative achievement" and labeled the "New Deal." Reprinted: Westport, Conn.: Greenwood Press, 1969.

21 WRIGHT, BENJAMIN F., Jr. "Political Institutions and the
   Frontier." In Sources of Culture in the Middle West, Backgrounds versus Frontier. Edited by Dixon R. Fox. New York:
   Appleton-Century, pp. 15-38.
   Challenges Turner's generalization that the political
arrangements and practices of the western states were different
and more democratic than those of their eastern counterparts by
pointing out the dependency of the new western states upon the
eastern models. Attacks Turner's attempt to explain American
democracy as a product of the frontier and concludes that "the
conception of the 'transforming influence' of the frontier, as
it appears in Turner's essays, is largely a myth." Reprinted:
New York: Russell & Russell, 1964; article reprinted: 1949.23.

                              1935

1 BARNHART, JOHN D. Review of The United States, 1838-1850:
   The Nation and Its Sections. Journal of Southern History 1
   (November):525-27.
   Though this book does not devote itself to the frontier, it
is clear that Turner did not modify his thesis to suit his
critics. This work "was not given the usual finishing polish and
revision," yet, "it is a remarkable monument to his career."

2 BECKER, CARL. "Frederick Jackson Turner." In Everyman His
   Own Historian: Essays on History and Politics. New York:
   Appleton-Century-Crofts, pp. 191-232.
   Reprint of 1927.2; reprinted: El Paso, Tex.: Academic Re-
prints, 1959; New York: Quadrangle Books, 1966.

1935

3 BELLOT, H. HALE. Review of Sources of Culture in the Middle
   West: Backgrounds versus Frontier. Edited by Dixon Ryan Fox.
   Minnesota History 16 (June):196-97.
        "'Neo-Turnerism'" is declared to be the tide of future
   scholarship. Predicts the future subsidence of criticisms against
   Turner.

4 BROGAN, D.W. "The Rise and the Decline of the American
   Agricultural Interest." Economic History Review 5 (April):
   1-23.
        Considers Turner's "'The Significance of the Frontier in
   American History'" to have been the "most important of all the
   communications which have been made . . . to the American Historical Association" because it not only signaled the closing of
   the frontier but the demise of American agriculture.

5 BURT, A.L. "Trotter: Canadian History." Minnesota History
   16 (March):83-85.
        Review of Canadian History: A Syllabus and Guide to Read-
   ing by Reginald George Trotter in which critics of the "Turnerian
   School of American History" lectured on evidence that the frontier remained open after 1890: "It . . . simply shifted across
   the line to the Canadian prairie."

6 CATE, WIRT ARMISTEAD. "Lamar and the Frontier Hypothesis."
   Journal of Southern History 1 (November):497-501.
        The credit for first stating the theory of the West belongs
   to Lucius Q.C. Lamar, and Turner is indebted to Lamar for laying
   the groundwork for his frontier hypothesis. Lamar had been
   neglected for too long and deserves to be "accorded a position of
   increasing importance" by historians and students of history.

7 _____. Preface to Lucius Q.C. Lamar: Secession and Reunion.
   Chapel Hill: University of North Carolina Press, pp. vii-x.
        Lamar rather than Turner should be viewed as the originator
   of the frontier thesis. Reprinted: 1969.

8 CRAVEN, AVERY. Introduction to The United States, 1830-1850:
   The Nation and Its Sections, by Frederick Jackson Turner. New
   York: Holt, pp. v-ix.
        Explores some of the possible reasons that Turner published
   so little and explains the reason for this posthumous volume.
   Reprinted: 1950.

9 EDWARDS, EVERETT E. References on the Significance of the
   Frontier in American History. Washington, D.C.: United
   States Department of Agriculture Library, Bibliographical Con-
   tributions, no. 25, 63 pp.

An annotated bibliography of the secondary literature
dealing with "the influence of the historical interpretation
known as the frontier hypothesis." Includes eighty-nine annotated
entries and a four-page preface underscoring the "active intellectual force this [Turner's] explanation of America's development"
had sustained. Enlarged: 1939.9.

10 FARRAND, MAX. Frederick Jackson Turner: A Memoir. Boston:
    N.p., 11 pp.
        Reprint of 1935.11.

11 _____. "Frederick Jackson Turner: A Memoir." Massachusetts
    Historical Society. Boston. Proceedings 65 (May):432-40.
        Briefly summarizes Turner's basic ideas and intellectual
development. Attributes his great influence more to his teaching
ability than to his publication record. Reprinted: 1935.10.

12 FOX, DIXON RYAN. Ideas in Motion. Appleton-Century Essays.
    Edited by William E. Lingelbach. New York: Appleton-Century,
    126 pp., passim.
        Reverses Turner's fundamental assumption that 'the West in-
fluenced the East by arguing that our most desirable institutions
and ideas were transported to the frontier in the heads of immigrants rather than generated by the frontier experience.

13 GOODRICH, CARTER, and SOL DAVISON. "The Wage-Earner in the
    Westward Movement I." Political Science Quarterly 50 (June):
    161-85.
        "When Turner referred to 'the undeveloped West' as a 'safety
valve' for industrial discontent" he was advancing a theory which
is invalid because of a "sheer absence of direct evidence in its
support." Entire article is a refutation of Turner's safety-
valve theory. Continued: 1936.3; reprinted: 1966.16.

14 LEYBURN, JAMES G. Frontier Folkways. New Haven: Yale Univer-
    sity Press, pp. i, 5-6, 187-88, 231-37.
        Rejects Turner's generalization that "America began with
aristocracy and changed to democracy because of free land" as
being too "simple." Concludes that in "reality there was more of
the primitive in frontier American government than there was of
progress toward some [democratic ideal]." Reprinted: Hamden,
Conn.: Archon Books, 1970.

15 MALIN, JAMES C. "The Turnover of Farm Population in Kansas."
    Kansas Historical Quarterly 4 (November):339-72.
        In Kansas "economic depression was usually associated with
declining numbers of farm operators during the frontier . . .
stage of development." This fact has "an important bearing on

1935

the so-called safety-valve theory of the frontier hypothesis. It
has been rather generally assumed by the followers of F.J. Turner
that unfavorable conditions in the East or older regions resulted
in the flow of population westwards to free and cheap land. . . .
The data in the study does not seem to bear out such a theory."

16   NICHOLS, ROY F. Review of Sources of Culture in the Middle
     West: Background versus Frontier, edited by Dixon Ryan Fox.
     Western Pennsylvania Historical Magazine 18 (June):150-51.
        "Ever since it was first suggested in 1893, American his-
     torians have been debating the significance of" Turner's "frontier
     thesis." This volume is simply the most recent evidence that the
     debate still rages.

17   OWSLEY, FRANK L. "The Historical Philosophy of Frederick
     Jackson Turner." American Review 4 (Summer):368-75.
        Summarizes "Turner's main concepts" and reviews The United
     States, 1830-1850 in a supportive, uncritical manner.

18   PAXSON, FREDERIC L. "The New Frontier and the Old American
     Habit." Pacific Historical Review 4, no. 4:309-27.
        Discusses the emergence of new political parties in America
     and relates them to the moving line of the frontier. The four
     major parties (the Whigs, the Jeffersonian Democrats, the Jackson-
     ian Democrats, and Lincoln's Republicans) were directly related
     to the frontier. Applies this concept to Roosevelt's New Deal
     and tries to anticipate its success, especially in relation to
     the potentiality of the middle class, "which lies along the new
     frontier of class." Reprinted: 1941.13.

19   ROBBINS, ROY M. Review of The United States, 1830-1850: The
     Nation and Its Sections. Mississippi Valley Historical Review
     22 (September):295-97.
        Comments that the work is an "outstanding contribution" to
     American historical scholarship, and calls it the "capstone" of
     Turner's career; "Had it been finished it undoubtably would have
     been the masterpiece."

20   SHIELS, W. EUGENE. "The Frontier Hypothesis: A Corollary."
     Mid-America 17 (January):3-9.
        Because the "focus of historical thought in the United
     States had been, is, and will continue to be the 'frontier hy-
     pothesis' of Frederick Jackson Turner," the role of religion in
     general and more particularly "the significance of the mission in
     the frontier story" have been ignored.

21   SKINNER, CONSTANCE LINDSAY. "Notes Concerning My Correspon-
     dence with Frederick Jackson Turner." Wisconsin Magazine of

History 19 (September):91-95.
    Asserts that Turner's "literary talent has its origin . . .
in his frontier childhood." Compares Turner's sectionalism with
her own view of the importance of rivers in the development of
American democracy. Turner's autobiographical letter follows.
Reprinted: 1961.25.

22 STEPHENSON, GEORGE M. Review of The United States, 1830-1850:
    The Nation and Its Section. Minnesota History 16 (September):
    325-27.
        Turner is assessed as "the most distinguished interpreter
of American history." This posthumous volume is summarized as "a
synthesis based on thirty years of research and teaching."

23 TUGWELL, REXFORD G. "No More Frontiers." Today 4 (22 June):
    3-4, 21.
        Undersecretary of Agriculture Tugwell argues that the Home-
stead Act of 1862 and the American land policy "signed the death
warrant of the prudent use of our land use." Discusses problems
that have already emerged and outlines a policy of conservation
and control.

                        1936

1 EZEKIEL, MORDECAI. $2500 a Year: From Scarcity to Abundance.
   New York: Harcourt, Brace, p. 37.
       Accepts Turner's safety-valve concept. Reprinted: 1973.

2 GATES, PAUL WALLACE. "The Homestead Law in an Incongruous
   Land System." American Historical Review 41 (July):652-81.
       Depicts the Homestead Law as a relatively unsuccessful
means of attracting settlers to the frontier, thereby challenging
one of Turner's basic assumptions.

3 GOODRICH, CARTER, and SOL DAVISON. "The Wage-Earner in the
   Westward Movement, II." Political Science Quarterly 51
   (March):61-116.
       Continuation of 1935.13; reprinted: 1966.16.

4 HAYTER, EARL W. "Sources of Early Illinois Culture." Illinois
   State Historical Society, Transactions 1, no. 43:81-96.
       Challenges Turner's thesis by arguing that "the sources of
culture . . . of early Illinois . . . lay mainly in eastern and
European states." Faults the Turner thesis for having "failed to
take cognizance of the essential unity of American and European
history." Acknowledges, however, that "probably no school of
writers has had a greater influence than the frontier historians."

1936

5   HICKS, JOHN D.   Review of The United States, 1830-1850: The
    Nation and Its Sections. American Historical Review 41 (Jan-
    uary):354-57.
        Laments the fact that "young scholars can think of no
better way to make reputations for themselves than by attacking
or defending the views" of Turner.

6   HUGH-JONES, E.M., and E.A. RADICE.   "The United States."   In
    An American Experiment. London: Oxford University Press, pp.
    1-32.
        The "main feature" of the United States has been the in-
fluence of the frontier, for "it has . . . played a tremendously
important part in American History." Turner's frontier was "the
cause of many of the most distinctive American characteristics."
Cites many of Turner's ideas.

7   LOWER, A.R.M.   Settlement and the Forest Frontier in Eastern
    Canada. Canadian Frontiers of Settlement, edited by W.A.
    Mackintosh and W.L.G. Joerg, vol. 9. Toronto: Macmillan Co.
    of Canada, 166 pp., passim.
        Concludes that "Turner's classic analysis" depicting the
frontier as "a steadily westward-moving Line," while verified by
the reality of American history, is not supported by the Canadian
experience. But the Canadian frontier experience does demonstrate
the international relevance of Turner's views regarding the impact of the frontier upon the "frontiersman" and the general
culture. Reprinted: Millwodd, N.Y.: Krause Reprints, 1974.

8   McMURRAY, DONALD L.   "The Ghost of the Frontier." Middle
    States Association of History and Social Science Teachers,
    Proceedings, no. 34:1-16.
        Summarizes "the Chief propositions of the frontier inter-
pretation," and attempts to answer the questions: "How seriously
are they [the followers of Turner] to be taken?" and "Are there
any other equally valid explanations of the qualities that have
been attributed to the frontier?"

9   NUTE, GRACE LEE.   Review of References on the Significance of
    the Frontier in American History, by Everett E. Edwards.
    Minnesota History 17 (June):198-99.
        This "List of commentators on the Turner idea" demonstrates
"its almost complete acceptance by all classes of thinkers."

10 ODUM, HOWARD W.   "A New Regional Analysis: Southern Regions
    in the National Picture." In Southern Regions of the United
    States. Chapel Hill: University of North Carolina Press, pp.
    245-90.
        Draws a distinction between "Turner's . . . authentic,

1936

historical, political and economic sectionalism within the whole
nation" and "regionalism" as defined by the author. Views
Turner's sectionalism as incompatible with nationalism. Reprinted: 1943; New York: Agathon Press, 1969.

11 PARK, ROBERT. "Succession, an Ecological Concept." American
Sociological Review 1 (April):171-79.
      Describes the process of succession using several different
examples, one of which is the frontier. The analysis here is
similar to Turner's: the first wave was comprised of "explorers,
trappers, Indian traders, and prospectors"; the next groups were
"land seekers, squatters, and frontier farmers"; and these were
followed by "the lawyers, politicians, and newspapermen." These
are not examined in any detail, but merely presented as a case of
succession.

12 P[AXSON], F[REDERIC] L. "Frederick Jackson Turner." In Dictionary of American Biography. Edited by Dumas Malone. New
York: Scribners, 19:62-64.
      Summary of Turner's career and contribution to historiog-
raphy.

13 QUINN, ARTHUR HOBSON. "New Frontiers of Research." Scribner's
Magazine 99 (February):95-97.
      "Although the geographical frontiers of the United States
have been closed" since Turner stressed the fact in the 1890s
"national decay can set in only when limits are set to that restless spirit" which was generated by the frontier experience.

14 SCHAFER, JOSEPH. "Some Facts Bearing on the Safety-Valve
Theory." Wisconsin Magazine of History 20 (December):216-32.
      Critiques recent articles dealing with the safety-valve
theory and rejects the tendency in this scholarship to depict
Turner as the father of this theory. Goes on to discuss the
kinds of sources which would be helpful in documenting the safety-
valve theory. Reprinted: 1961.23.

15 SHANNON, FRED A. "Homestead Act and Labor Surplus." American
Historical Review 41 (July):637-51.
      Dispels the myth that by 1890, when the frontier was de-
clared to be closed, all of the free land in the West had been
homesteaded. Charges further that the Homestead Act did not turn
the frontier into a safety valve for the poor working class of
the East because of expense, and only rarely was there any migration from the urban, industrial areas to the frontier farms.

1937

1 ABERNETHY, THOMAS PERKINS. Western Lands and the American Revolution. New York: Appleton-Century, University of Virginia Institute for Research in the Social Sciences, no. 25, 413 pp., passim.

Qualifies Turner's assumptions regarding the relationship between the frontier and democracy, the frontier as a safety valve and the impact of the frontier upon American culture. Reprinted: 1959, 1964.

2 CLARK, DAN ELBERT. The West in American History. New York: Thomas Y. Crowell, 628 pp., passim.

A history of three centuries of westward American expansion within a Turnerian framework. Comes to a Turnerian conclusion in the last section of the book entitled "The Disappearance of the Frontier." Reprinted: 1943, 1948, 1950.

3 CRAVEN, AVERY. "Frederick Jackson Turner." In The Marcus W. Jernegan Essays in American Historiography. Edited by William T. Hutchinson. Chicago: University of Chicago Press, pp. 252-70.

"Turner wrote less and influenced his own generation more than any other important historian. . . . The explanation is simple. It is found in a wealth of suggestive ideas packed into short essays which interpret rather than narrate, and in a stimulating personality which stirred students to curiosity and inspired them to independent research. Turner was both a 'first-class mind' and a great teacher." His "basic idea" was that America's "chief characteristic is expansion" and its "chief peculiarity of institutions, constant readjustment." Summarizes Turner's thesis. Reprinted: New York: Russell & Russell, 1958; Freeport, N.Y.: Books for Libraries Press, 1972.

4 ELLISON, J.W. Review of The West in American History, by Dan Elbert Clark. Oregon Historical Quarterly 38 (June):232-34.

As a result of Turner's influence, "historians have considered the frontier as the most characteristic and most vital phase of American history." All existing surveys of western history are "based on Turner's thesis."

5 HAMILTON, J.G. DeROULHAC. Introduction to Truth in History and Other Essays, by William A. Dunning. Edited by J.G. DeRoulhac Hamilton. New York: Columbia University Press, pp. xi-xxviii.

In his attempt to document Dunning's significant contribution to historiography, Hamilton generalizes that in terms of "intellectual descendents," Dunning shares "a rare distinction"

with Frederick Jackson Turner. Reprinted: Port Washington, N.Y.:
Kennikat Press, 1965.

6 HUTCHINSON, WILLIAM T., ed. Marcus W. Jernegan Essays in
   American Historiography. Chicago: University of Chicago
   Press, pp. 59, 139, 177-78, 235, 252-70, 300, 304, 326-27,
   357, 359-60, 366.
     Turner's relationship with other major historians is in-
vestigated in several of the essays included in this volume.
Includes an article by Avery Craven entitled "Frederick Jackson
Turner" which capsulizes Turner's career. Reprinted: New York:
Russell & Russell, 1958; Freeport, N.Y.: Books for Libraries
Press, 1972.

7 KRAUS, MICHAEL. "The Frontier and Sectional Historians." In
   A History of American History. New York: Farrar & Rinehart,
   pp. 492-545.
     Discusses western, New England, and southern historians.
Describes Turner's life and work, and points out the influence
and range of Turner's analysis. Revised: 1953.13.

8 LINGELBACH, WILLIAM E. "American Democracy and European
   Interpreters." Pennsylvania Magazine of History and Biography
   61 (January):1-25.
     Concludes that "contemporary European observers of American
democracy" were in agreement with Turner's views regarding the
importance of the frontier when interpreting twentieth-century
American history.

9 LOBB, JOHN. "Frontier Adjustment in South Africa." In
   Studies in the Science of Society. Edited by George Peter
   Murdoch. New Haven: Yale University Press, pp. 395-411.
     Accepts Turner's thesis for American frontier development,
but finds that it does not apply to the South African frontier.
Many of the conditions present in America were present in South
Africa, but South African society remained static and relatively
unadjusting. Reprinted: Freeport, N.Y.: Books for Libraries
Press, 1969.

10 MOOD, FULMER. "An Unfamiliar Essay by Frederick Jackson
   Turner." Minnesota History 18 (December):381-83.
     Introduction to a reprint of one of Turner's early and less
well known essays entitled "The Rise and Fall of New France."
The significance of the essay is underscored.

11 PAXSON, FREDERIC L. Recent History of the United States,
   1865 to the Present. New York: Houghton Mifflin, pp. 62-63,
   149-75, passim.

1937

Revised and enlarged version of 1921.10. Surveys frontier development from a Turnerian point of view.

12 SCHAFER, JOSEPH. "Beginnings of Civilization in the Old Northwest." Wisconsin Magazine of History 21 (December): 211-36.
    Reviews the historiography of the area Turner "called 'The Old West'" from a Turnerian point of view.

13 _____. "Concerning the Frontier as Safety Valve." Political Science Quarterly 52 (September):407-20.
    Defends Turner's safety-valve concept in the face of Goodrich's and Davison's (see 1935 and 1936) criticism and rejection of the concept by attempting to demonstrate that influential leaders including Franklin, Hamilton, and Jefferson embraced the concept long before Turner popularized it.

14 _____. "Was the West a Safety Valve for Labor?" Mississippi Valley Historical Review 24 (December):299-314.
    Focuses upon nineteenth-century American history and presents data and generalizations that support Turner's safety-valve concept.

15 SHIPTON, CLIFFORD K. "The New England Frontier." New England Quarterly 10 (March):25-36.
    New England is a "striking . . . corollary" to the frontier hypothesis because the New England culture owes more to its European heritage than it does to environmental influences. The influence of European ideals on church, education, and government represent "the successful transplanting of cultural ideas to a new environment."

16 WEBB, WALTER PRESCOTT. "Crisis of a Frontierless Democracy." In Divided We Stand: The Crisis of a Frontierless Democracy. New York: Farrar & Rinehart, pp. 152-216.
    "The historians Turner and his disciples have not yet seemed to realize that it the frontier was a dominant force until 1890, the absence of the frontier has been just as dominant since 1890. They have accepted the thesis [Turner's] that the frontier shaped American life, but they have not so readily accepted the corollary that the absence of the frontier must change the shape." This argument is developed at length. Revised: 1944; reprinted: Manchaca, Tex.: Chapparral Press, 1947; Ann Arbor, Mich.: University Microfilms, 1973.

1938

1 ABERNETHY, THOMAS P. "Democracy and the Southern Frontier."
   Journal of Southern History 4 (February):3-13.
      Turner's safety-valve concept is "only partially correct."
Turner's frontier experience must share the limelight with other
major forces in any attempt to explain the origins of American
democracy.

2 ANON. "News and Comment." Illinois State Historical Society,
   Journal 31 (December):500-501.
      "In modern historical writing the most influential name, by
long odds, is Frederick Jackson Turner" even though he "was not
a prolific writer, and most of his contributions appeared in
periodicals now difficult to find."

3 BELLOT, H. HALE. "Turner: Early Writings." Minnesota History
   19 (December):432-34.
      A review of The Early Writings of Frederick Jackson Turner
(1938). Summarizes the content of the volume and calls for a
revision of Turner's thesis.

4 BROWN, GEORGE W. "Some Recent Books on the History of the
   United States." Canadian Historical Review 19 (December):
   411-14.
      "One cannot but be struck with the emphasis given to
Turner's influence in contemporary discussions of American historical writing." Although there has been "a re-appraisal of
the Turner thesis . . . the importance of Turner remains, and
historians are still frequently judged by the degree in which
they appear to have been affected by Turner's influence."

5 DAVIDSON, DONALD. The Attack on Leviathan: Regionalism and
   Nationalism in the United States. Chapel Hill: University
   of North Carolina Press, 368 pp., passim.
      In chapter one, "The Diversity of America," Davidson argues
that the complete formation of the theory of the sections and
their integral place in national history was . . . mainly the
work of one man, the late Frederick Jackson Turner." In chapter
two, "Two Interpretations of American History," Turner's analysis
of American history is contrasted with that of Charles A. Beard.
"Turner would seem to represent . . . an American and democratic
interpretation of American history" while "Beard . . . represents
a late-European, anti-traditional view of all society, including
the American." The entire volume deals with Turner's ideas regarding sectionalism and nationalism. Reprinted: 1962.

1938

6 EDWARDS, EVERETT E. The Early Writings of Frederick Jackson
   Turner, With a List of All His Works. Madison: University of
   Wisconsin Press, 316 pp.
        Collection of four of Turner's more obscure early essays
   with a preface by Louise P. Kellogg and an article entitled
   "Turner's Formative Period" by Fulmer Mood. Includes a "Comparison of Differing Versions of 'The Significance of the Frontier'"
   and a chronologically arranged bibliography of Turner's writings
   as well as a list of "References on His Life and Work."

7 ELY, RICHARD T. Ground Under Our Feet, An Autobiography. New
   York: Macmillan, pp. 179, 181-84, 196-98, 227-30.
        This internationally known American economist credits
   Turner with having been influential in arranging his move from
   Johns Hopkins to the University of Wisconsin. Concludes that
   "Turner's book on the 'Frontier' was an important contribution to
   the interpretation of American economic history." Documents
   Turner's contribution to the development of the University of
   Wisconsin.

8 GOODRICH, CARTER, and SOL DAVISON. "The Frontier as Safety
   Valve: A Rejoinder." Political Science Quarterly 53 (June):
   268-71.
        An answer to Schafer's "Concerning the Safety Valve" (see
   1937), which dealt with the author's earlier article on Turner's
   safety-valve concept.

9 HANSEN, MARCUS L. The Problem of the Third Generation Immigrant. Augustana Historical Society. Publication no. 8, pt.
   1. Rock Island, Ill.: Augustana Historical Society, 24 pp.,
   passim.
        Challenges the originality of Turner's frontier thesis.
   "Turner or no Turner, the frontier hypothesis was bound to come
   and to appear in the very decade during which he wrote his famous
   essay. In fact, the hypothesis may be distilled from the con-
   glomerate mass of conformation and theory jumbled together in the
   ten volumes of Scotch-Irish Proceedings. . . . It is quite possible
   that Turner . . . drew upon the frontier interests that the
   Scotch-Irish were arousing by their studies of the part that the
   Ulstermen took in the movement . . . into the West."

10 HOLT, W. STULL, ed. Historical Scholarship in the United
   States, 1876-1901: As Revealed in the Correspondence of
   Herbert B. Adams. Baltimore, Md.: Johns Hopkins Press, pp.
   119-20, 123, 136-37, 139, 144-45, 151, 156-61, 163-64, 168-69,
   173-76, 212, 273, 276, 282.
        Documents the voluminous correspondence between Adams and
   Turner; Adams interacted with Turner more than any other historian. Reprinted: University of Washington Press, 1967.

1938

11 KELLOGG, LOUISE PHELPS. Preface to The Early Writings of
    Frederick Jackson Turner, With a List of All His Works.
    Edited by Everett E. Edwards. Madison: University of Wiscon-
    sin Press, pp. v-ix.
        This volume containing four of Turner's essays is important
    because it "presents an opportunity for a restudy of the early
    writings of one who has had a great influence in reshaping Ameri-
    can historiography."

12 _____. "Wisconsin's Eminence." Wisconsin Magazine of History
    21 (June):397-404.
        Turner is cited as an example of Wisconsin's production of
    leaders in the "academic field."

13 MOOD, FULMER. "Turner's Formative Period." In The Early
    Writings of Frederick Jackson Turner, With a List of All His
    Works. Edited by Everett E. Edwards. Madison: University
    of Wisconsin Press, pp. 3-39.
        Begins by asserting that "Turner was unquestionably orig-
    inal." Traces his intellectual development in an attempt to ex-
    plain "how Turner came upon his influential doctrine."

14 ODUM, HOWARD W., and HARRY E. MOORE. American Regionalism: A
    Cultural-Historical Approach to National Integration. New
    York: Holt, pp. 25-51, 520-49, passim.
        Draws a sharp distinction between Turner's "sectionalism"
    and what the authors mean by "regionalism." Argues, however,
    that "the Southeast qualifies admirably as an example of Frederick
    Jackson Turner's sectionalism and of his historical frontier
    Americanism." Reprinted: Gloucester, Mass.: Peter Smith, 1966.

15 SCHAFER, JOSEPH. "Turner's Early Writings." Wisconsin Maga-
    zine of History 22 (December):213-31.
        Includes a review of The Early Writings of Frederick
    Jackson Turner, With a List of All His Works edited by Everett E.
    Edwards, but the primary focus is upon an internal and external
    analysis of Turner's writings. Turner the master teacher is dis-
    cussed. Views Turner's "Significance of the Frontier" as an
    attempt to break the "Eastern monopoly" upon the interpretation
    of American history and in the process established "a new his-
    toriography in which the West" was prominent.

16 STAVRIANOS, L.S. "Is the Frontier Theory Applicable to the
    Canadian Rebellions of 1837-1838?" Michigan History Magazine
    22 (Summer):326-37.
        "The purpose of this study . . . is to estimate to what
    extent, if at all, the Turner hypothesis is applicable to the
    Canadian rebellions." Concludes that it is partially relevant.
    Reprinted: 1970.31.

<u>1939</u>

1 BEARD, CHARLES A. "'The Frontier in American History.'" <u>New</u>
   <u>Republic</u> 97 (1 February):359-62.
       Ascribes to Turner's "'The Significance of the Frontier in
   American History' . . . a more profound influence on thought
   about American history than any other essay or volume ever written
   on the subject." Breaks Turner's "conception of American history"
   into "twelve major elements" and criticizes some of his assumptions.

2 _____. "Turner's 'The Frontier in American History.'" In
   <u>Books That Changed Our Minds</u>. Edited by Malcolm Cowley and
   Bernard Smith. New York: Doubleday, pp. 61-71.
       Briefly recounts Turner's life. Outlines the frontier
   thesis and comments on the safety-valve theory and on western
   individualism, doubting the validity of the former and arguing
   that there was more cooperation than radical individualism on the
   frontier. Concludes that Turner's frontier does not "'explain'
   American development" but it has opened up an abundance of "rich
   treasures" for American historians.

3 BRADERMAN, EUGENE M. "Early Kentucky: Its Virginia Heritage."
   <u>South Atlantic Quarterly</u> 18 (October):449-61.
       Challenges those historians who depict Kentucky as simply a
   carbon copy of Virginia by utilizing certain aspects of "Turner's
   Statement."

4 BUCK, SOLON J., and ELIZABETH HAWTHORN BUCK. <u>Planting of</u>
   <u>Civilization in Western Pennsylvania</u>. Pittsburgh: University
   of Pittsburgh Press, 555 pp., passim.
       The last three chapters, entitled "Frontier Radicalism and
   Rebellion," "Jeffersonian Democracy," and "The Pattern of Culture," are Turnerian in approach and conclusions. The section in
   the bibliography entitled "History of the West" documents the
   author's heavy dependence upon the Turnerian school of historiography. Reprinted: 1967.

5 CRAVEN, AVERY. Review of <u>The Early Writings of Frederick</u>
   <u>Jackson Turner</u>. <u>Mississippi Valley Historical Review</u> 25
   (March):567-69.
       "This volume, while not of major importance, will be of use
   to those interested in Turner's work." Notes that Turner's
   "Significance of the Frontier" underwent only minor revisions between 1893 and 1920, a fact that is significant in light of "recent criticisms" of the Turner thesis.

6 _____. "The 'Turner Theories' and the South." Journal of
Southern History 5 (August):291-314.
   The South's westward advance in the period from 1830 to
1860 "had all the characteristics . . . ascribed to the westward
movement" by Turner and his disciples. Concludes that "the
Turner approach has a considerably wider application to the antebellum South than has usually been suggested."

7 DALE, EDWARD EVERETT. Review of The Early Writings of
Frederick Jackson Turner, With a List of All His Works, edited
by Everett E. Edwards. Southwestern Historical Quarterly 43
(October):265-66.
   "It is safe to say that every former student of Turner's as
well as the thousands of others who have known and admired this
great scholar will be deeply grateful for this book . . . and the
excellent picture of Professor Turner . . . adds much to the
attractive volume."

8 DAVENPORT, F. GARVIN. "Culture versus Frontier in Tennessee,
1825-1850." Journal of Southern History 5 (February):18-33.
   Examines frontier life from the perspective of Philip
Lindsley, a transplanted easterner who became president of
Cumberland College (later to become the University of Nashville).
Lindsley despised the crude habits of frontier individuals, and
he sought to raise the cultural educational level of the frontier.
The frontier mind was "a negative force in Tennessee's social and
cultural development." The influences of frontier self-sufficiency
and frontier religion are examined in this regard.

9 EDWARDS, EVERETT E. References on the Significance of the
Frontier in American History. Washington, D.C.: United
States Department of Agriculture Library, Bibliographical Contributions, no. 25 (edition 2), 99 pp.
   Revised and expanded reprint of 1935. Includes 124 annotated entries and also has citations of review articles. Enlarged version of 1935.9.

10 JOHNSON, T. WALTER. "Peter Akers: Methodist Circuit Rider
and Educator (1790-1886)." Illinois State Historical Society,
Journal 32 (December):417-41.
   "As Frederick Jackson Turner" has shown, "the pioneer . . .
developed an individualism, and with it a sense of equality and
self-reliance. . . . Peter Akers is an excellent example" of
Turner's thesis.

11 LOWER, A.R.M. "Geographical Determinants in Canadian History."
In Essays in Canadian History. Edited by R. Flenley. Toronto:
Macmillan Co. of Canada, pp. 229-52.

1939

Although Turner is not specifically mentioned, his ideas regarding the environmental influence of the frontier are borrowed to explain Canadian national development.

12 LYNCH, WILLIAM O. "The Mississippi Valley and Its History." Mississippi Valley Historical Review 26 (June):3-20.
Attempts to answer the question: "To what degree has the hope and belief of Turner that the people of the Mississippi Valley would be able to devise ways . . . to preserve democracy been vindicated to date?"

13 SHRYOCK, RICHARD H. "Cultural Factors in the History of the South." Journal of Southern History 5 (August):333-46.
Comments on Turner's "geographical determinism" and briefly shows its relationship to Southern history.

14 SHURTLEFF, HAROLD R. The Log Cabin Myth: A Study of the Early Dwellings of the English Colonies in North America. Cambridge, Mass.: Harvard University Press, 243 pp., passim.
Critical of Turner's environmentalism. Reprinted: 1967.

15 TROTHER, REGINALD G. "The Appalachian Barrier in Canadian History." Canadian Historical Association, Annual Report, pp. 5-21.
Explores in a Turnerian fashion some of the "factors of environment" on the frontier that have shaped Canadian national development. The differences between the Canadian and the American frontiers are best explained "by peculiarities of environment."

16 WITTKE, CARL. We Who Build America: The Saga of the Immigrant. New York: Prentice Hall, 547 pp., passim.
Implicity challenges Turner's thesis by attempting to show that American culture was transmitted from Europe to America by the immigrants rather than generated by the frontier. Reprinted: 1945, 1946, 1948; Press of Case Western Reserve, 1964, 1967.

17 WOESTEMEYER, INA FAYE. "Notes on the Literature of the Westward Movement." In The Westward Movement: A Book of Readings on Our Changing Frontiers. New York: Appleton-Century, pp. 477-84.
This is an annotated "bibliography of suggestions for further readings" on "the best material on . . . the precise nature and scope and comparative importance of the frontier influence in the making of our civilization . . . , including the classic essay of F.J. Turner and some of the writings of his best interpreters and chief critics."

1940

1 ABERNETHY, THOMAS PERKINS. Three Virginia Frontiers. University: Louisiana State University Press, 96 pp., passim.
   Interprets the Virginia frontiers in a Turnerian scheme: the frontier holds the key to an understanding of "our national habits and institutions"; the West was a source of free or cheap land, and the frontier environment was the primary source of American democracy. Reprinted: Gloucester, Mass.: Peter Smith, 1962.

2 AUMANN, FRANCIS R. "Conflicting Views Concerning the Nature of Colonial Law." In The Changing American Legal System: Some Selected Phases. Graduate School Series: Contributions in History and Political Science, no. 16. Columbus: Ohio State University Press, pp. 3-18.
   Accepts the Turnerian interpretation of the influence of the frontier upon legal practices in the West.

3 BURT, A.L. "The Frontier in the History of New France." Canadian Historical Association, Report of the Annual Meeting, pp. 93-99.
   Applies Turner's thesis to "New France" and concludes that the impact of the frontier experience generated a "real democracy" that "conformed to the familiar (Turnerian) North American Type."

4 FARRAND, MAX. "Frederick Jackson Turner, A Memoir." Massachusetts Historical Society, Proceedings 65:432-40.
   "The name of Frederick Jackson Turner seems destined to remain forever linked with the frontier." Attributes his influence as much to his ability as a teacher as to the influence of his writings.

5 GABRIEL, RALPH HENRY. "The Significance of the Frontier and of the Law of Entropy." In The Course of American Democratic Thought. New York: Ronald Press, pp. 315-33.
   "Two historians, Frederick Jackson Turner and Henry Adams, have been chosen to illustrate trends in the thinking of American historians at the end of the century about the democratic faith." In the development of this thesis, Gabriel briefly traces Turner's development as an historian, outlines his ideas regarding American history, and underscores his belief in America's uniqueness. Concludes that "before his death Turner had become a prophet among historians. Since his passing his fame has mounted." Reprinted: 1945, 1956.

1940

6 GOLDMAN, ERIC F. "Democratic Bifocalism: A Romantic Idea and
   American Historiography." In Romanticism in America. Edited
   by George Boas. Baltimore: Johns Hopkins Press, pp. 1–11.
       Defines "democratic bifocalism" as the romantic tendency to
   glorify the individual and an abstract people simultaneously.
   When popular revolt was repellent to the romantics, "the people
   became persons" and their actions could always be called "an in-
   fringement of the liberties of the individual." The concepts of
   "the people and the individual," however, "contained little feeling for ordinary men." This bifocalism is evident in the historical writings of George Bancroft, the Teutophiles, and
   Frederick Jackson Turner. As far as Turner was concerned, "When
   the West acted with the approbation of Turner, the West was a
   people. . . . When Turner disapproved, the West atomized into
   persons." Reprinted: New York: Russell & Russell, 1961.

7 HANCOCK, W.K. Problems of Economic Policy, 1918–1939. Survey
   of British Commonwealth Affairs, vol. 2, part 1. London, New
   York, and Toronto: Oxford University Press, 374 pp., passim.
       Contrasts and compares Turner's concept of the frontier
   with the dominant European meaning of the term "frontier."

8 HANSEN, MARCUS L. "Immigration and Expansion." In The Immigrant in American History. Cambridge, Mass.: Harvard University Press, pp. 53–76.
       Turner's "followers extended and confirmed the thesis; and
   as they assumed positions of authority in the academic world,
   instruction in the frontier theory became a part of every orthodox
   course in American history." Furthermore, "without Turner's frontier theory, the New Deal would have been politically much more
   difficult to achieve." Reprinted: New York: Harper & Row, 1964.

9 HANSEN, MARCUS L., and JOHN BARTLET BREBNER. The Mingling of
   the Canadian and American Peoples. Toronto: Ryerson Press;
   New Haven: Yale University Press, 274 pp., passim.
       Treats Canadian settlement as a part of the larger process
   of expansion across the North American continent. Turnerian in
   approach: "A good deal of the story which Professor Hansen and
   Professor Brebner tell in these pages is an expansion of the
   great theme of American history which Professor Frederick Turner
   opened up in his studies of the Westward Movement." Reprinted:
   New York: Russell & Russell, 1970.

10 JOHNSON, T. WALTER. "Charles Reynolds Matheny: Pioneer
   Settler of Illinois (1786–1839)." Illinois State Historical
   Society, Journal 33 (December):438–68.
       Turner's frontier thesis is exemplified in the career of
   Charles R. Matheny for he "illustrates the fluidity of American

life, the expansion westward, and the return to primitive conditions of an advancing frontier line."

11 KANE, MURRAY. "Some Considerations on the Frontier Concept of
    Frederick Jackson Turner." Mississippi Valley Historical Re-
    view 27 (December):379-400.
        "It is the purpose of this paper to extend the criticism of
    the Turner hypothesis beyond that of the safety-valve doctrine."
    Criticizes Turner and his disciples for not being "scientific in
    method," for utilizing faulty economic and geographic analysis,
    and for using an unsound "statistical method."

12 KURATH, HANS. "Dialect Areas, Settlement Areas, and Cultural
    Areas." In The Cultural Approach to History. Edited by
    Caroline F. Ware. New York: Columbia University Press, pp.
    331-51.
        Concludes that the "determination of the relation of dialect
    areas to settlement areas, trade areas, and culture areas has
    been made possible through the work of F.J. Turner and his school
    of historians . . . and geographers." Reprinted: Port Washing-
    ton, N.Y.: Kennikat Press, 1965; New York: Gordon Press, 1974.

13 MALIN, JAMES C. "Local Historical Studies and Population
    Problems." In The Cultural Approach to History. Edited by
    Caroline F. Ware. New York: Columbia University Press, pp.
    300-307.
        Studies of migration patterns in Kansas do not confirm
    Turner's "simple formulas." Reprinted: Port Washington, N.Y.:
    Kennikat Press, 1965; New York: Gordon Press, 1974.

14 MOOD, FULMER. "Little Known Fragments of Turner's Writings."
    Wisconsin Magazine of History 23 (March):328-41.
        Designed to make available for "those interested in the
    literary output of the master" two little-known essays not in-
    cluded in The Early Writings of Frederick Jackson Turner. The
    first, entitled "Wisconsin," was published in the Encyclopaedia
    Britannica in 1888 and the second, entitled "Frontier," was pub-
    lished in Johnson's Universal Cyclopaedia in 1894. Includes a
    three-page introduction. Reprinted: 1961.19.

15 PIERSON, GEORGE WILSON. "The Frontier and Frontiersmen of
    Turner's Essays: A Scrutiny of the Foundations of the Middle
    Western Tradition." Pennsylvania Magazine of History and
    Biography 64 (October):449-78.
        This critic acknowledges that by 1920 Turner's ideas had
    become so popular that he could claim a "nation wide influence
    and a whole army of faithful followers." By 1940 it was accurate
    to say that never "before . . . has any single historian, or so

1940

slight a body of published work, so . . . influenced the thinking
habits of American historians." But recent claims that "Turner's
inspiration" was so "brilliant" that "no one has been able to
find serious fault with it" serve to "illustrate . . . the parti-
san and, in part, sectional bias of the more convinced of the
'frontier historians.'" Calls for a major "overhauling" of the
Turner thesis because in its unrevised form it is "no longer a
safe guide to the student." Final two-thirds of this article
are reprinted: 1966.28.

16 PRESTON, WHEELER. American Biographies. New York and London:
    Harper & Brothers, p. 1034.
        Brief sketch of Turner's career.

17 SCHLESINGER, ARTHUR M. "The City in American History."
    Mississippi Valley Historical Review 27 (June):43-66.
        Calls for "a reconsideration of American history from the
    urban point of view" in order to correct the Turnerian interpre-
    tation of American history, which has ignored the influence of
    urbanization.

18 SHANNON, FRED A. "An Appraisal of Walter Prescott Webb's The
    Great Plains: A Study in Institutions and Environment." In
    Critiques of Research in the Social Sciences. Vol. 3. Edited
    by Arthur M. Schlesinger. New York: Social Science Research
    Council, pp. 3-112.
        Critique of Webb's treatise, which some scholars view as an
    extension of the Turner thesis applied to the broader interna-
    tional sphere.

19 _____. "Homestead and Other Grants to Individuals." In
    America's Economic Growth. New York: Macmillan, pp. 368-70.
        This book is a revision of Economic History of the People
    of the United States. Develops the argument that it "is no
    longer seriously believed that the Western lands relieved labor
    congestion and acted as a safety valve for labor."

20 SHRYOCK, RICHARD H. "Philadelphia and the Flowering of New
    England: An Editorial." Pennsylvania Magazine of History and
    Biography 64 (July):305-13.
        The Turnerian tradition in American historiography estab-
    lished a "Middle Western slant on our national past" that attrib-
    uted the uniqueness and greatness of our nation to westward ex-
    pansion. Laments that the "'Middle Atlantic' tradition in Amer-
    ican history" has been overshadowed by traditions like the "fron-
    tier interpretation."

21 STANLEY, GEORGE F. "Western Canada and the Frontier Thesis."
    Canadian Historical Association, Report of the Annual Meeting,
    pp. 18-31.
        Acknowledges that Turner's "essay became one of the most
widely read and . . . most influential ever written in North
America" and attributes its popularity to its emphasis upon
"significance" and the endorsement of many eminent scholars.
Critiques and rejects Turner's thesis as not helpful for a study
of Canadian history. Includes the response of seven discussants.

22 TUCKER, RUFUS S. "The Frontier as an Outlet for Surplus
    Labor." Southern Economic Journal 7 (October):158-86.
        Attributes the "pessimism existing at present concerning
the future growth of prosperity in this country" to "a belated
recognition . . . that the free land frontier has disappeared,"
which was "most clearly stated by Frederick Jackson Turner." By
drawing upon census reports, Tucker attempts to "drive some nails"
into the coffin of Turner's safety-valve theory.

23 TURNER, RALPH E. "The Industrial City: Center of Cultural
    Change." In The Cultural Approach to History. Edited by
    Caroline F. Ware. New York: Columbia University Press, pp.
    228-42.
        Documents Turner's contribution to the formation of the
"concept of culture" approach as a method of social-science
analysis. Reprinted: Port Washington, N.Y.: Kennikat Press,
1965; New York: Gordon Press, 1974.

                            1941

1 BARNHART, JOHN D. "Frontiersmen and Planters in the Formation
   of Kentucky." Journal of Southern History 7 (February):17-36.
       Argues that the Kentucky frontier experience confirms
Turner's thesis.

2 BECKER, CARL. "Frederick Jackson Turner." In What College
   Offers. Edited by Frank H. McClosky et al. New York: F.S.
   Crofts, pp. 155-72.
       Reprint of 1927.2.

3 BOATRIGHT, MODY C. "The Myth of Frontier Individualism."
   Southwestern Social Science Quarterly 22 (June):14-32.
       The man who is "chiefly responsible" for the acceptance of
the myth "that rugged individualism is or has been the way of
American life . . . is Frederick Jackson Turner. . . ." Argues
against this myth by showing that pioneers "regulated private
enterprise" when it suited their interests and also worked

1941

together under a system of voluntary enterprise. The pioneer
"was perhaps more self-reliant. But all this is not to say that
he was individualistic in the sense that he eschewed collective
action. . . ." Reprinted: 1968.7.

4 BROEK, JAN O.M. "The Relations between History and Geography."
Pacific Historical Review 10 (September):321–25.
Laments that the critics of Turner and his disciples assume,
without scientific evidence, that any "collaboration between . . .
history and geography" will of necessity result in a doctrine of
"environmental determinism."

5 CRAVEN, AVERY. "The West and Democracy." In Democracy in
American Life: A Historical View. Chicago: University of
Chicago Press, pp. 38–67.
Credits Turner with having "pointed out the significance of
the frontier in American history" and summarizes his ideas re-
garding American democracy.

6 DANHOF, CLARENCE H. "Economic Validity of the Safety–Valve
Doctrine." Journal of Economic History, Supplement 1:96–106.
Begins with the generalization that "the validity of the
safety-valve doctrine is still an unsettled historical problem."
Identifies the underlying assumptions involved in Turner's theory
and challenges their validity. Reverses Turner's safety–valve
theory by concluding that eastern workers were able to move West
only during favorable economic conditions in the East."

7 _____. "Farm–Making Costs and the 'Safety Valve': 1850–60."
Journal of Political Economy 49 (June):317–59.
Examines the assumption of the safety–valve theory that
wage laborers could participate "with little difficulty" in the
settling and exploitation of available western lands. Finds that
the costs of western farming were prohibitive, and without the
necessary capital at the outset, the eastern wage earner would be
unable to enter the western migration. Consequently, "it is
clearly an error to consider western farm–making opportunities as
determinate of the status of eastern wage labor."

8 GARRAGHAN, GILBERT J. "Non–Economic Factors in the Frontier
Movement." Mid–America 23 (October):263–71.
Argues that "Turner was not bent on interpreting history
. . . from an exclusively economic point of view." He utilized
a multiple–hypothesis approach that included social as well as
economic forces. Argues that Turner was neither a materialist
nor a determinist. Concludes with a brief discussion of the influence of religion on the frontier and criticizes Turner for
having ignored this factor.

1941

9 HICKS, JOHN D. "The 'Ecology' of the Middle-Western Historians." Wisconsin Magazine of History 24 (June):377-84.
      Discusses the regional influence on frontier historians and
   examines the way historians incorporate their environment into
   their history. Critics of Turner who argue that industrializa-
   tion is the dominant factor in explaining American history are
   similarly influenced by their own environment. Historians of the
   future "will not try to industrialize the frontier period or to
   frontierize the industrial period." They will recognize the
   validity of Turner's thesis: "people did go West, there was a
   frontier, and it made a difference," and they will recognize that
   "hard on the heels of the frontier came an era of intense indus-
   trialization" which also "made a difference." Reprinted: 1955.11.

10 LOKKEN, RAY L. "The Turner Thesis: Criticism and Defense."
   Social Studies 32 (December):350-65.
      Focuses primarily upon the critics of the Turner thesis.

11 MARTIN, ASA E. "Beyond the Pale of the Law on the American
   Frontier." Social Studies 32 (November):306-15.
      Uncritically accepts Turner's assumptions regarding the
   influence of the frontier environment, the safety-valve role of
   the frontier, and the frontier's ability to generate "individualism, self-reliance" and the love of freedom.

12 PAXSON, FREDERIC L. "A Generation of the Frontier Hypothesis."
   In The Great Demobilization and Other Essays. Madison: University of Wisconsin Press, pp. 23-41.
      Reprint of 1933.16.

13 _____. "The New Frontier and the Old American Habit." In The
   Great Demobilization and Other Essays. Madison: University
   of Wisconsin, pp. 138-56.
      Reprint of 1935.18.

14 _____. "The Pacific Railroads and the Disappearance of the
   Frontier." In The Great Demobilization and Other Essays.
   Madison: University of Wisconsin Press, pp. 62-75.
      Reprint of 1907.1.

15 SAUER, CARL O. "Forward to Historical Geography." Association
   of American Geographers, Annals 31 (March):1-24.
      Challenges Turner's view that the American frontier ad-
   vanced through "an identical series of stages" of development.

16 STILL, BAYARD. "Patterns of Mid-Nineteenth Century Urbanization in the Middle West." Mississippi Valley Historical Review 28 (September):187-206.
      Critical of the Turnerian interpretation of American history

1941

for its "persistent preoccupation with the agrarian aspects of the westward march of American settlement." This theory has "obscured the fact that the prospect of future towns and cities as well as the promise of broad and fertile acres lured settlers to . . . the West."

17 TURNER, RALPH. "The Cultural Setting of American Agricultural Problems." In Yearbook of Agriculture: Farmers in a Changing World. Washington, D.C.: Government Printing Office, United States Department of Agriculture, pp. 1003-32.
    Discusses the character of American life and American agriculture since the closing of the frontier. Examines cultural factors, the conflict between urban and rural cultures, and European influences in this regard, and analyzes the problems associated with economic control, production, standard of living, and population.

1942

1 ABERNETHY, THOMAS PERKINS. Review of The Great Demobilization and Other Essays, by Frederic Logan Paxson. North Carolina Historical Review 19 (April):226-27.
    Associates Paxson with a "group of scholars which has undertaken to follow the trail of frontier history . . . blazed by Frederick Jackson Turner."

2 ALEXANDER, FRANZ. "New Frontiers." In Our Age of Unreason: A Study of the Irrational Forces in Social Life. Philadelphia: J.B. Lippincott, pp. 262-71.
    Whereas the nineteenth century was a century of individualism as described by Turner, the twentieth century is characterized by organization and centralization. In Turner's century, material acquisition was an appropriate preoccupation, but in the present century it is inappropriate behavior. The values generated by Turner's frontier serve Americans poorly in the twentieth century. Revised: 1951.

3 _____. "The Tradition of the Frontier." In Our Age of Unreason: A Study of the Irrational in Social Life. Philadelphia: J.B. Lippincott, pp. 247-52.
    Accepts Turner's basic ideas and suggests that social psychologists could benefit from Turner's insights regarding American civilization. Antisocial behavior can be explained as a result of frontier individualism. "The American criminal of our day represents a . . . caricature of this individualistic spirit of the part." Revised: 1951.

1942

4 BARKER, EUGENE C. "Three Types of Historical Interpretation."
   Southwestern Historical Quarterly 45 (April):323-34.
      Critical of the contemporary use of Turner's views to
   justify the need for President Roosevelt's New Deal.

5 BEARD, CHARLES A., and MARY R. BEARD. The American Spirit: A
   Study of the Idea of Civilization in the United States. The
   Rise of American Civilization. New York: Macmillan, pp. 357,
   360-64.
      Credits Turner with having "shifted the emphasis in American
   historiography from the sea board to the continent as a whole."
   Analyzes Turner's contribution to the historigraphical emphasis
   upon individualism as "the driving force in American civilization."
   Reprinted: New York: Collier Books, 1962.

6 CLARK, SAMUEL D. The Social Development of Canada: An Introductory Study with Selected Documents. Toronto: University
   of Toronto Press, 484 pp., passim.
      A sociological study in which Turner's approach and ideas
   are used to study the relationship between the frontier and social problems in Canadian development. Reprinted: New York:
   AMS Press, 1976.

7 CRAVEN, AVERY. "Frederick Jackson Turner, Historian." Wisconsin Magazine of History 25 (June):408-24.
      Asserts that Turner's "conception of the American historian's
   task is all-important in any appraisal of . . . his work" and
   attempts to show how "it determined the form, the character, and
   even the quantity of what he wrote." The breadth, interdisciplinary implications, mature environmentalism, and pioneering dimensions of Turner's contribution are explored in light of Turner's
   basic vision of historiography. Turner's famous essay on the
   frontier was significant as a source of "stimulation and suggestion" rather than as a source of specific truths regarding the
   frontier. Reprinted: 1961.8.

8 DERLETH, AUGUST. "Frontiersman in History." In The Wisconsin
   River of a Thousand Isles. New York: Farrar & Rinehart, pp.
   289-92.
      Turner was a product of the Wisconsin frontier and a founder
   of "a school of historiography."

9 DIAMOND, WILLIAM. "American Sectionalism and World Organization, by Frederick Jackson Turner." American Historical Review 47 (April):545-51.
      One of Turner's previously unpublished papers entitled
   "International Political Parties in a Durable League of Nations"
   is presented here.

1942

10 _____. "Introduction to a Manuscript by Turner Entitled 'International Political Parties in a Durable League of Nations.'" American Historical Review 47 (April):545-47.
    Assets that "this document is an effort by one of America's most distinguished and stimulating historians to put historical knowledge to work for society."

11 DODGE, STANLEY D. "The Frontier of New England in the Seventeenth and Eighteenth Centuries and Its Significance in American History." Michigan Academy of Science, Arts, and Letters, Papers 28:435-39.
    Concludes that "the Appalachian barrier was a barrier in appearance only," and that the advance of settlement across the frontier was halted more by the pressure of the French in the interior of North America rather than the pressure of natural barriers.

12 EDWARDS, EVERETT. "Rural Communities and the American Pattern." In The Quest for Political Unity in World History. Edited by Stanley Pargellis. Vol. 3 of the Annual Report of the American Historical Association, pp. 353-59.
    Asserts that a study of rural communities "would . . . provide the realities of what Frederick Jackson Turner termed 'the vital forces' that called institutions into life."

13 GATES, PAUL W. "The Role of the Land Speculator in Western Development." Pennsylvania Magazine of History and Biography 66 (July):314-33.
    Depicts the frontier as an area dominated by land speculators where eastern money was invested rather than as a source of free land as Turner suggested. Furthermore, the movement to the frontier surged during boom times and subsided during depressions—just the opposite of the Turnerian view.

14 MOOD, FULMER. "Pacific Coast Influences and Historical Writing." Pacific Historical Review 11 (June):201-12.
    Credits Turner and the University of Wisconsin with having had a profound influence upon the direction of historical research on the Pacific Coast. As a result, all western historians have been influenced by "the frontier point of view as propounded by Turner."

15 NEVINS, ALLAN, and HENRY STEELE COMMAGER. America: The Story of a Free People. Boston: Little, Brown, 507 pp., passim.
    Attempts to modify Turner's thesis by emphasizing the interaction between expanding Europe and the American frontier: "The story of America is the story of the impact of an old culture upon a wilderness environment" in which "the New World was never

merely an extension of the Old . . . for the unconquered wilderness, confronting the pioneer . . . profoundly modified inherited institutions." Reprinted: 1966; New York: Oxford University Press, 1976.

16 PIERSON, GEORGE W. "American Historians and the Frontier Hypothesis in 1941." Wisconsin Magazine of History 26 (September):36-60.

Explores the question "What do American historians now think of the great frontier hypothesis of Frederick Jackson Turner?" by sending a questionnaire to 220 "critics and defenders" of Turner's theory. The questionnaire contained a "condensed . . . statement of what the Frontier Hypothesis . . . appears to contain; . . . a listing of . . . criticisms . . . that have been leveled against the hypothesis; and . . . arguments . . . in its defense." The 106 responses to the questionnaire are discussed at length. The major criticisms of Turner's thesis were that it "is too simple and all-inclusive; . . . the definition of 'frontier' is too vague" and Turner and his supporters were overly influenced by "cultural, regional and patriotic preferences." Continued: 1942.17; reprinted: 1961.21.

17 _____. "American Historians and the Frontier Hypothesis in 1941." Wisconsin Magazine of History 26 (December):170-85.

Second part of a study (1942.16) dedicated to assessing the status of Turner's ideas. The study demonstrated that "critics and champions alike.. . . generally" agreed that Turner was more influential in the classroom than he was in print. After reviewing the major criticisms of Turner's ideas revealed in his questionnaire, Pierson concludes that "the champions and believers still clearly outnumber the critics." Pierson tries to explain Turner's popularity by maintaining that he "was a sort of American Treitschke, a patriot," who wrote a history which was "100 percent America." Continuation of 1942.16; reprinted: 1961.21.

18 _____. "The Frontier and American Institutions: A Criticism of the Turner Theory." New England Quarterly 16 (June):224-55.

Complains that the Turner thesis needs to be revised. It is not an adequate explanation for much of American culture, and where it is adequate, it is overused. Finds that Turner's thesis is invalidated on two major counts; it is internally inconsistent and it ignores major economic, social, and comparative approaches. Meticulously analyzes Turner's thesis in this light. Reprinted: 1949.15, 1968.40.

19 ROBBINS, ROY M. Our Landed Heritage: The Public Domain, 1776-1936. Princeton: Princeton University Press, pp. 427-33.

1942

Attempts to "integrate American land history" into the
Turner thesis. Reprinted: 1976; Gloucester, Mass.: Peter Smith,
1950; University of Nebraska Press, 1962, 1969, 1976.

20 WINTHER, OSCAR OSBOURN. The Trans-Mississippi West: A Guide
to Its Periodical Literature (1811-1938). Indiana University
Publications, Social Science Series. Bloomington: Indiana
University Press, 263 pp., passim.
Topical guide to scholarly articles on the West published
in state, regional, and national professional journals. Includes
a one-page section on the "Frontier" but does not have a specific
section on Turner or the frontier thesis. Articles relevant to
the frontier thesis are scattered throughout the guide. Revised:
1961.32.

1943

1 ALEXANDER, EDWARD P. Review of "The Development of Frederick
Jackson Turner as a Historical Thinker," by Fulmer Mood.
Minnesota History 24 (December):336-37.
Reviews Turner's career.

2 ANDERSON, RUSSEL H. "Advancing Across the Eastern Mississippi
Valley." Agricultural History 17 (April):97-104.
Analyzes one phase of the frontier experience within a
Turnerian framework.

3 CLARK, DAN ELBERT. "Introduction: John Carl Parish, Historian." In The Persistence of the Westward Movement and Other
Essays, by John Carl Parish. Berkeley: University of California Press, pp. xiii-xxii.
Parish "gave his full approval to the Turner thesis when
accepted in accord with the meaning of its author." Reprinted:
Freeport, N.Y.: Books for Libraries Press, 1968.

4 DALE, EDWARD EVERETT. "Memories of Frederick Jackson Turner."
Mississippi Valley Historical Review 30 (December):339-58.
Laudatory reminiscences of Turner the man, teacher, and
scholar by a former student. Includes five letters which Turner
wrote to Dale from 1923 to 1930. Reprinted: 1943.5, 1975.9.

5 _____. Memories of Frederick Jackson Turner. Cedar Rapids,
Iowa: Torch Press, 20 pp.
Reprint of 1943.4.

6 DICK, EVERETT. "Going Beyond the Ninety-fifth Meridian."
Agricultural History 17 (April):105-12.

1943

Treats the struggle to transform the "Great American Desert" into a farming area within a Turnerian framework.

7 LOEHR, RODNEY C. "Moving Back from the Atlantic Seaboard." Agricultural History 17 (April):90-96.
    Observes that the last word on "the Westward movement remains Frederick Jackson Turner's." Entire article reflects a dependence upon Turner.

8 MALIN, JAMES C. "Mobility and History: Reflections on the Agricultural Policies of the United States in Relation to a Mechanized World." Agricultural History 17 (October):177-91.
    Rejects the conclusion of the New Deal leadership that Turner's frontier thesis was no longer relevant. The "free raw material" still so abundant in the United States would provide "opportunity for the industrial urbanism" in the same way that Turner's frontier supplied "free land . . . to agriculture" in the nineteenth century.

9 MOOD, FULMER. "The Development of Frederick Jackson Turner as a Historical Thinker." Colonial Society of Massachusetts, Transactions 34:283-352.
    Examines Turner's early life and educational experience at the University of Wisconsin and at Johns Hopkins University in an attempt to understand the source of his basic ideas and convictions as well as the acquisition of his skills. Includes a detailed treatment of the courses he took as a student and the scholars with whom he worked. Turner's dissertation and early publications are treated. Turner's indebtedness to Scribner's Statistical Atlas of 1885 is documented; from it he developed a "taste for statistical and sociological data."

10 _____. "The Historiographic Setting of Turner's Frontier Essay: Comments on the Occasion of Its Fiftieth Anniversary." Agricultural History 17 (July):153-55.
    Makes a distinction between "historians" and "historical thinkers." Those in the latter category have "a fertile mind, evolving new interpretations and ideas." Turner was just such a rare "historical thinker."

11 MOOD, FULMER, and EVERETT E. EDWARDS, eds. "Frederick Jackson Turner's 'History of the Grignon Tract on the Portage of the Fox and Wisconsin Rivers.'" Agricultural History 17 (April): 113-20.
    One of Turner's earliest attempts to write history with a brief introduction by the editors.

1943

12 PARISH, JOHN CARL. "The Persistence of the Westward Movement."
    In The Persistence of the Westward Movement and Other Essays.
    Berkeley: University of California Press, pp. 1-23.
        Modifies Turner's thesis by suggesting that "it seems perti-
    nent to ask if we have not become so engrossed in the task of
    writing the obituary of a single frontier--that of settlement--
    that we have shut our eyes to the fact that the westward movement
    in its larger sense, with its succession of many kinds of fron-
    tiers . . . , did not cease in 1890 but has been a persistent
    factor in our national life, which still tends to distinguish the
    American people from the people of European nations." Reprint of
    1926.5; reprinted: Freeport, N.Y.: Books for Libraries Press,
    1968.

13 _____. "Reflections on the Nature of the Westward Movement."
    In The Persistence of the Westward Movement and Other Essays.
    Berkeley: University of California Press, pp. 25-45.
        "With respect to the importance of our national expansion
    in its relation . . . to political, economic, and social life,
    and in its effects upon American characteristics, no one has gone
    beyond the vision of Professor Turner." Calls for research to
    fill in the "broad lines of his basic interpretation." Reprint
    of 1930.12; reprinted: Freeport, N.Y.: Books for Libraries
    Press, 1968.

14 _____. "The West." In The Persistence of the Westward Move-
    ment and Other Essays. Berkeley: University of California
    Press, pp. 183-87.
        Draws a distinction between the "Westward Movement" as de-
    fined by Turner and "The West"; the latter "was the sum total . . .
    of the various zones of advance." Furthermore, "the West . . .
    did not disappear with the frontier" and therefore, in spite of
    the "development of a new industrial order . . . the earlier
    transforming forces" of the West "have not been erased." Re-
    printed: Freeport, N.Y.: Books for Libraries Press, 1968.

15 PLAISTED, THAIS M. "The Unpublished Papers of Frederick
    Jackson Turner." Social Studies 34 (May):220-21.
        An enthusiastic report by one of Turner's former students
    on the value of Turner's unpublished papers housed at the Henry
    E. Huntington Library.

16 SCHLESINGER, ARTHUR M. "What Then Is the American, This New
    Man?" American Historical Review 48 (January):225-44.
        Calls for a modification of the part of Turner's thesis
    that explained the development of America as a result of the
    West's influence upon the East. "The American . . . is the
    product of the interplay of his Old World heritage and New World
    conditions."

1944

17 SELLERY, G.C. Review of "The Development of Frederick Jackson
    Turner as an Historical Thinker," by Fulmer Mood. Wisconsin
    Magazine of History 27 (December):229-31.
        Praises Mood's article as "a fine performance" and goes on
    to assess Turner's significance rather than review this particular
    article. Refers approvingly to the fact that recently "a wit
    spoke of the American Historical Association as 'one big Turner.'"

18 SUMNER, BENEDICT H. "The Frontier." In A Short History of
    Russia. New York: Reynal & Hitchcock, pp. 1-48.
        Attaches great significance to the frontier in Russia's
    development. Draws a comparison between Russia and the United
    States and cites Turner as an authoritative source: "Russia like
    American development exhibits 'not merely an advance along a
    single line, but a return to primitive conditions on a continually
    advancing frontier." Published in England under the title Survey
    of Russian History (see 1944.10). Revised: 1949.

19 WILSON, WOODROW. "Woodrow Wilson's Opinion of Professor
    Turner." Facsim. Wisconsin Magazine of History 26 (June):
    470-71.
        Copy of letter dated "30 January 1902" to J.B. Gilden of
    New York City, which asserts that Turner is "the coming man in
    American history. . . . Both in knowledge and in the gift of ex-
    pression he is already in the first class."

1944

1 ANON. "Ten Great Badgers." Wisconsin Magazine of History 27
   (March):257-62.
       Turner is the only scholar included in a list of "Wiscon-
   sin's ten greatest persons." He was selected because, although
   "not many original theories have appeared in American thought,
   . . . Turner with his emphasis on the frontier . . . and sectional
   controversy as explanations for the development of America is
   known to every American scholar."

2 DESTLER, CHESTER McARTHUR. "Western Radicalism, 1865-1901:
   Concepts and Origins." Mississippi Valley Historical Review
   31 (December):335-68.
       Historians of the Turnerian school have failed to discover
   radical thought in the West because they have been "insulated by
   the continued influence of the frontier hypothesis from the
   records of . . . urban movements within or without the region."
   The Turner approach to western history failed to identify a radical tradition because of its "conviction that radicalism in the
   American West was exclusively the product of repetitive sociological

1944

and economic processes at work on the frontier." Shows how radical ideas influenced the western region through "effective inter-
course between the rural West and the urban world, whether inside
or outside the region."

3 HESSELTINE, WILLIAM B. "Regions, Classes, Sections in American
   History." Journal of Land and Public Utility 20 (February):
   35-44.
      Credits Turner with having been the first historian to em-
phasize the significance of sectionalism in American history.

4 MALIN, JAMES C. "The Farmer's Alliance Subtreasury Plan and
   European Precedents." Mississippi Valley Historical Review
   31 (September):255-60.
      Comments that Turner's influence has led to a "provincialism
of outlook" among American historians. Argues that "the assumption of American originality, and particularly the uniqueness of
the frontier influence, must be revised." Only through a broader
outlook can problems such as the one under consideration here,
the Farmer's Alliance Subtreasury Plan, be understood.

5 _____. "Space and History: Reflections on the Closed-Space
   Doctrines of Turner and Mackinder and the Challenge of Those
   Ideas by the Air Age, Part 1." Agricultural History 18
   (April):65-74.
      Examines Turner's thesis regarding the significance of the
closing of the American frontier in its international setting and
concludes that "it would be a mistake to assume that the idea of
closed space was original with . . . Turner. It was 'in the air'
during the last two decades of the nineteenth century." Malin
views Turner's thesis as narrowly nationalistic. In an attempt
to correct this error, Turner's ideas are compared with those of
the British geographer Halford J. Mackinder. Continued: 1944.6.

6 _____. "Space and History: Reflections on the Closed-Space
   Doctrines of Turner and Mackinder and the Challenge of Those
   Ideas by the Air Age, Part 2." Agricultural History 18 (July):
   107-26.
      The age of "air communications--radio, television, and air-
craft" was reopening the "closed space" Turner announced to his
age. "The air age opens again a new world of possibilities, and
some revival of hope after . . . a half century under the shadow
of the idea of [Turner's] closed space." Continuation of 1944.5.

7 NICHOLS, ROY F. Review of "American Historians and the Fron-
   tier Hypothesis in 1941," by George W. Pierson, and "The
   Development of Frederick Jackson Turner as a Historical
   Thinker," by Fulmer Mood. Geographical Review 34 (July):510-11.

1945

Explains Turner's influence as a result of his having been "so great a teacher" and concludes that there remains a "general interest in Turner and his ideas." Furthermore, "so great was the teacher, so numerous and devoted the disciples, and so vague and varied the doctrine that there is bound to be much more controversy" in the future.

8 _____. Review of "The Development of Frederick Jackson Turner as a Historical Thinker," by Fulmer Mood. Pennsylvania Magazine of History and Biography 68 (April):207-8.
   "The essential fact of the situation is that Frederick Jackson Turner was born with the capacity to be a great teacher. . . . Therefore he was bound to draw young people to him."

9 RANEY, WILLIAM F. "The Peopling of the Land." In The Culture of the Middle West. Edited by Howard T. Taylor. Lawrence College Lecture Series. Appleton, Wis.: Lawrence College Press, pp. 13-24.
   Challenges Turner's emphasis upon the frontier process as the key to understanding American culture. Underscores the influence of immigration upon the formulation of American civilization.

10 SUMNER, BENEDICT H. "The Frontier." In Survey of Russian History. London: Duckworth, pp. 1-48.
   Reprint of 1943.18; revised: 1947.

11 WILLIAMS, SAMUEL C. "The Clarksville Compact of 1785." Tennessee Historical Quarterly 3 (September):237-47.
   Accepts "Turner as a master in the field of the history of the West and . . . the greatest historian in that field of American history, even down to the present." Presents the "Clarksville Compact" in 1895 as an example of Turner's voluntary democracy in the West.

1945

1 ANON. "Chats with the Editor." Wisconsin Magazine of History 28 (March):388.
   An announcement that the Wisconsin Historical Society had commissioned the writing of a biography of Turner as a part of the state's centennial celebration.

2 BILLINGTON, RAY ALLEN. "The Origin of the Land Speculator as a Frontier Type." Agricultural History 19 (October):204-12.
   "When Frederick Jackson Turner pictured the westward movement of the American people in terms of a succession of pioneer

1945

types . . . he omitted one individual who played a major role in the march of civilization, namely the land speculator." Attempts to show how important the speculator was in the frontier environment.

3   BREBNER, JOHN BARTLET. "Pioneers and Democrats (1815-1850)." In North Atlantic Triangle: The Interplay of Canada, the United States and Great Britain. New Haven: Yale University Press, pp. 124-45.
        Suggests that the raging debate in response to Turner's assertion that the "frontier provided . . . an all-embracing formula for explaining the history of American life" could be resolved if the "whole of the Americas is examined instead of merely the United States." Reprinted: Columbia University Press, 1958; Toronto: McClelland & Stewart, 1966; New York: Russell & Russell, 1970.

4   FREUND, RUDOLF. "Turner's Theory of Social Evolution." Agricultural History 19 (April):78-87.
        For Turner, "American history became an example of social evolution" and he "found the basic character as well as the stages of this evolution clearly revealed in the story of the American West." Explains that "Turner molded a certain set of demographic and historical facts into an example of . . . a universal occurrence--namely, of the process of social evolution."

5   HOCKETT, HOMER CAREY, and ARTHUR M. SCHLESINGER, eds. Land of the Free: A Short History of the American People. New York: Macmillan, pp. 26, 212, 364, 441.
        Turnerian interpretation of the frontier and its importance in American History.

6   KIENITZ, JOHN FABIAN. "Fifty-two Years of Frank Lloyd Wright's Progressivism, 1893-1945." Wisconsin Magazine of History 27 (September):68.
        Compares Wright to Turner; both emphasized the importance of frontier influences in determining the character of the American people. In addition, "each man gave the frontier . . . another aspect and dimension."

7   MOOD, FULMER. "A British Statistician of 1854 Analyzes the Westward Movement in the United States." Agricultural History 19 (July):142-51.
        The "Seventh Census" of 1850 and its analyses by British scholars reveal that the growing tendency "to think of the immigration to the West in a conceptual way" antedated Turner's frontier hypothesis of 1893.

1945

8 _____. "The Concept of the Frontier, 1871-1898: Comments on
a Select List of Source Documents." Agricultural History 19
(January):24-30.
    Annotated bibliography of twenty books and articles on
United States Census Office data of the period. These studies
demonstrate that the "Census scholars . . . anticipated . . .
Turner" for "they were the . . . formulators of the [frontier]
concept in its statistical form."

9 PHILLIPS, ULRICH BONNELL. "The Traits and Contributions of
Frederick Jackson Turner." Agricultural History 19 (January):
21-23.
    An appraisal of Turner the teacher by a former student,
colleague, and close friend.

10 SABINE, GEORGE H. Introduction to Freedom and Responsibility
in the American Way of Life, by Carl L. Becker. New York:
Alfred A. Knopf, pp. vii-xiii.
    Carl Becker was influenced by Turner more than by any other
scholar.

11 SCHLESINGER, ARTHUR M., Jr. The Age of Jackson. Boston:
Little, Brown, 577 pp., passim.
    Challenges Turner's view that American democratic ideals
and practices originated in the West by arguing that in the
Jacksonian era, American democracy derived much of its ideology
and leadership from the eastern urban proletariat and intellectual
leaders. Reprinted: 1946, 1950, 1953, 1968; abridged: New
York: New American Library, 1962.

12 SHANNON, FRED A. "The City as a Safety Valve for Rural Discontent." In The Farmer's Last Frontier: Agriculture, 1860-
1879. Vol. 5 of The Economic History of the United States.
Edited by Henry David et al. New York: Farrar & Rinehart,
pp. 356-59.
    Challenges Turner's safety-valve theory by demonstrating
that "from 1850 to the end of the century" migration "was pre-
ponderatingly from the farm to the city, rather than the reverse"
as Turner had suggested. Reprinted: 1963, 1966, 1968; Armonk,
N.Y.: M.E. Sharpe, 1970, 1977.

13 _____. "Disposing of the Public Domain." In The Farmer's
Last Frontier: Agriculture, 1860-1867. Vol. 5 of The Economic
History of the United States. Edited by Henry David et al.
New York: Farrar & Rinehart, pp. 51-75.
    Turner was incorrect when he depicted the frontier as a
haven of opportunity "for needy people from congested parts of
the country" because the Homestead Act benefited speculators and

1945

monopolists more than it did individual farmers. Reprinted:
1963, 1966, 1968; Armonk, N.Y.: M.E. Sharpe, 1970, 1977.

14 _____. "A Post Mortem on the Labor-Safety-Valve Theory."
Agricultural History 19 (January):31-37.
      Rejects Turner's safety-valve theory on the basis of nine-
teenth-century census data and argues that "the safety valve that
actually existed worked in entirely the opposite direction."
Urbanization and industrial expansion "provided a release from
surplus farm population." Reprinted: 1949.20, 1966.33, 1968.45.

15 STEPHENSON, WENDELL H., ed. "The Influence of Woodrow Wilson
on Frederick Jackson Turner." Agricultural History 19
(October):249-53.
      A series of letters and other documentary evidence suggest-
ing that Woodrow Wilson the scholar had influenced Turner's
thinking while he was a graduate student at Johns Hopkins University.

                              1946

1 ADAIR, DOUGLAS. "The New Thomas Jefferson." William and Mary
Quarterly, 3d ser., no. 3 (January):125-33.
      Asserts that together Frederick Jackson Turner and Charles
Beard "succeeded in making 'Jeffersonianism' intellectually re-
spectable for the first time since the Civil War."

2 ALEXANDER, EDWARD P. "Let's Study the Local History of
Illinois." Illinois State Historical Society, Journal 39
(March):7-20.
      Credits Turner and his disciples with having been more sup-
portive of the study of local history than any other school of
historiography.

3 BEALE, HOWARD K.. "What Historians Have Said About the Causes
of the Civil War." In Theory and Practice in Historical Study:
A Report of the Committee on Historiography. Social Science
Reserch Council, bulletin 54. New York: Social Science Research Council, pp. 53-102.
      Comments on Turner's direct and indirect influences on
Civil War historiography, especially in relation to geographic
history and sectional history.

4 BECKER, CARL LOTUS. "Wisconsin Historian." In Great Teachers,
Portrayed by Those Who Studied Under Them. Edited by Houston
Peterson. New Brunswick: Rutgers University Press, pp. 231-
50.
      Reprint of 1927.2.

1946

5 BERGE, WENDELL. Foreword to his Economic Freedom for the West.
   Lincoln: University of Nebraska Press, pp. ix-xiv.
      Turnerians were wrong when they "assumed that the passing
   of the geographic frontier also meant the disappearance of broad
   opportunities for economic development."

6 HAYES, CARLTON J.H. "The American Frontier--Frontier of
   What?" American Historical Review 51 (January):199-216.
      Criticizes the narrow, nationalistic approach implicit in
   Turner's thesis. The Turner interpretation depicts the "American
   way of life" as "something entirely indigenous, something wholly
   new, and something vastly superior to any other nation's."
   Stresses European sources and influences in the development of
   American culture, and defines the American frontier "as part of a
   larger Atlantic community." Reprinted: 1949.9, 1958.15.

7 HEATON, HERBERT. "Other Wests Than Ours." Journal of Economic
   History, Supplement 6:50-62.
      Makes a "plea for the abandonment of that academic isola-
   tionism that marks" the study of the frontier phenomenon. Argues
   for a comparative approach to frontier studies. Underscores the
   shared characteristics of all frontiers in the western world.

8 LERNER, MAX. "America--A Young Civilization?" Antioch Review
   6 (Fall):368-75.
      Observes that the extended debate among scholars has centered
   "too much on the validity of the Turner thesis and too little on
   the implications to be drawn from it." Proceeds to "extend the
   Turner analysis" to include the "industrial and capitalist revolution taking place at the same time as the frontier settlement"
   and thereby demonstrates that the American frontier experience
   was "not a genesis which began and closed . . . but a continued
   genesis."

9 LOWER, ARTHUR R.M. "The Spirit of the New World." In Colony
   to Nation: A History of Canada. Toronto, London, and New
   York: Longmans, Green & Co., pp. 47-50.
      Modifies Turner's thesis in order to emphasize the European
   origins of the development of the heterogenous civilization of
   the North American continent. Reprinted: 1957, 1964; Toronto:
   McClelland & Stewart, 1977.

10 MALIN, JAMES C. "N.S. Shaler on the Frontier Concept and the
   Grassland." In Essays on Historiography. Lawrence, Kans.:
   James C. Malin, pp. 45-92.
      Builds a case for the need to reexamine "Turner's concepts"
   in light of Nathaniel Shaler's scholarship in the field of geography.

1946

11 _____. "The Turner-Mackinder Space Concept of History." In
Essays on Historiography. Lawrence, Kans.: James C. Malin,
pp. 1-44.
    The sense of space is central to the theories of Frederick
Jackson Turner as an historian and Halford J. Mackinder as a
geographer. "As applied to history, there were three aspects of
the space concept: migration; expansion, or the frontier; and
closed space, or the passing of the frontier." Turner's thesis
and his methodology are analyzed. Notes that there are several
significant themes which are absent, for example, the themes of
science and technology, communication, and the city. Concludes
that "the historian must free himself not only from the space
theory of history, but from all forms of single factor interpretations."

12 MOOD, FULMER. "The Rise of Official Statistical Cartography
in Austria, Prussia, and the United States, 1855-1872."
Agricultural History 20 (October):209-25.
    Argues that the "frontier interpretation of United States
history, as expounded by Frederick Jackson Turner and his suc-
cessors, rests upon census maps showing frontier lines of population."

13 RANDALL, JOHN HERMAN, Jr., and GEORGE HAINES, IV. "Controlling
Assumptions in the Practice of American Historians." In
Theory and Practice in Historical Study: A Report of the Committee on Historiography. Social Science Research Council,
bulletin 54. New York: Social Science Research Council, pp.
15-52.
    Turner's conception of history was not narrowly prescribed
by the frontier thesis as many critics have argued; rather, his
conception was broad, both in terms of space and time, and he
utilized various approaches. Analyzes Turner as a social evolu-
tionist and as a multiple theorist.

14 RIEGEL, ROBERT E. "The Frontier and the West." In The Study
and Teaching of American History. Edited by Richard E.
Thursfield. Seventeenth yearbook of the National Council for
the Social Sciences. Washington, D.C.: National Council for
the Social Sciences, pp. 133-42.
    Attributes the popularity of western history to "the call
of Frederick Jackson Turner" for a serious study of the West.
Summarizes Turner's views as well as those of his critics.

15 ROSS, EARLE D. "A Generation of Prairie Historiography."
Mississippi Valley Historical Review 33 (December):391-410.
    Credits Turner with having done more than any other scholar
to stimulate interest in regional history. Furthermore, Turner's

hypothesis . . . was in fact predicated largely upon the unique conditions of the Prairie West," and as a result encouraged a study of the area.

1947

1 ADAMS, FREDERICK B., Jr., and THOMAS W. STREETER. One Hundred Influential American Books Printed Before 1900. Edited by Carroll A. Wilson. New York: Grolier Club, pp. 125-26.
Turner's paper "The Significance of the Frontier in American History" is included in a list of "One Hundred American Books Printed before 1900, chosen on the basis of their influence on the life and culture" of the American people.

2 ALEXANDER, FRED. Moving Frontiers: An American Theme and Its Application to Australian History. Victoria, Australia: Melbourne University Press, 48 pp., passim.
Restates "Turner's theme," considers "the consequences of the closing of the American frontier," and explores "the applicability of a similar frontier theme to the interpretation . . . of Australian history." Reprinted: Port Washington, N.Y.: Kennikat Press, 1969.

3 BAKER, JOSEPH E. "The Midwestern Origins of America." American Scholar 17 (Winter):58-68.
Identifies the Turnerian school of historiography as the reason historians have failed to "look at the development of America from the point of view of the Middle West."

4 BILLINGTON, RAY A. "The Historians of the Northwest Ordinance." Illinois State Historical Society, Journal 40 (December):397-413.
Identifies "Turner, the historian of the frontier" as the first scholar to call "attention to the western influences" in the formulation of the Northwest Ordinance.

5 BRIGGS, HAROLD E. "An Appraisal of Historial Writings in the Great Plains Region since 1920." Mississippi Valley Historical Review 34 (June):83-100.
Theorizes that "regionalism is implied in the sections of Frederick Jackson Turner and constitutes a logical development of his frontier hypothesis." Uses Turner's concept of "region" in his analysis of the literature dealing with the Great Plains.

6 BURKHART, J.A. "The Turner Thesis: A Historian's Controversy." Wisconsin Magazine of History 31 (September):70-83.
Reviews the evolution of the debate (which he believes

1947

started with the publication of J.C. Almack's article in 1925)
among historians regarding Turner's ideas. Reprinted: 1961.6.

7 CAUGHEY, JOHN M. "The Mosaic of Western History." Mississippi
   Valley Historical Review 33 (March):595-606.
     A guide to the periodical literature of the West that under-
scores the dominant influence of the Turnerian interpretation in
western historiography.

8 FITZPATRICK, BRIAN. "The Big Man's Frontier and Australian
   Farming." Agricultural History 21 (January):8-12.
     Differences in frontier settlement between Australia and
America are "attributable in large part" to the contrasting land
policies of their respective governments. In America, the Homestead Act catered to the small, independent farmer. In Australia,
however, land legislation was geared to the large financier
rather than to the crop farmer.

9 FROST, JAMES. "The Frontier Influence--a Perspective."
   Social Education 11 (December):361-63.
     Reviews the historiography of Turner's thesis with an em-
phasis upon the criticism that emerged after 1930. Cites nine
"important interpretations that are valid today" as proof that
the attacks "have not entirely destroyed the Turner thesis."

10 JOHNSON, THOMAS H. "America as Frontier." In One Hundred
   Influential American Books Printed Before 1900. Edited by
   Carroll A. Wilson. New York: Grolier Club, pp. 23-36.
     On the basis of his study of a "list . . . of One Hundred
Influential American Books Before 1900" (as selected by the
Grolier Club), Johnson cites Turner as the one historian most
responsible for emphasizing the frontier.

11 PAUL, RODMAN. California Gold: The Beginning of Mining in
   the Far West. Lincoln: University of Nebraska Press, 380
   pp., passim.
     Demonstrates that Turner's contention that the frontier
experience was normative cannot be verified in the mining camps
of California. The frontier was a scene of paradoxes, collective
versus individualism, petty capitalism versus corporate capitalism,
etc., rather than set patterns of development outlined by Turner.
Reprinted: 1965.

12 PERKINS, DEXTER. "Geographical Influences in American History."
   Geographical Journal 109, no. 1-3:26-39.
     The purpose of this study is to reveal "how geography
shaped the destiny of the United States"; disclaims any originality by acknowledging that he is building upon the foundation laid

by "Frederick Jackson Turner . . . in one of the greatest essays ever written in American history." Accepts Turner's frontier interpretation of American character.

13 PIERSON, GEORGE W. "Recent Studies of Turner and the Frontier Doctrine." Mississippi Valley Historical Review 34 (December): 453-58.
    Identifies five primary questions associated with the Turner thesis: (1) what was Turner like "as writer, teacher, pathfinder"; (2) what is the frontier theory; (3) how much of the theory is usable; (4) "How, or from whom, did Turner derive his ideas"; (5) what made this doctrine possible? Analyzes recent critical articles (1945) published in Agricultural History in light of these questions.

14 SHARP, PAUL F. "The American Farmer and the 'Last Best West.'" Agricultural History 21 (April):65-75.
    Suggests that the "year 1890 and the 'passing of the frontier' . . . are seen in a somewhat different perspective when a continental viewpoint is adopted." Turner and his disciples were wrong when they announced that the North American frontier was closed in 1890. "The first two decades of the twentieth century were marked by one of the greatest land rushes in North American history" and it included "over a million Americans."

15 TOYNBEE, ARNOLD J. "Encounters Between Civilizations." Harper's Magazine 194 (April):289-94.
    American culture, instead of being a unique result of frontier experience as Turner argued, has always been an inalienable part of western European culture.

16 WECTOR, DIXON. "Instruments of Culture on the Frontier." Yale Review n.s. 36 (Winter):242-56.
    Discusses the cultural advancement of the frontier West through an analysis of the building of schools, colleges, and free libraries. Modifies one of Turner's basic assumptions by arguing that the imported eastern culture "was destined to transform the frontier" and have as much influence as the frontier condition itself.

1948

1 BOWMAN, ROBERT G. "A Walkabout Down Under: Recent Geographical Literature on Australia and New Zealand." Geographical Review 38 (April):250-70.
    Considers recent attempts by students of Australian history to use Turner's thesis.

1948

2 BROWN, RALPH H. "Frontiers of the Seaboard States and the St. Lawrence Valley." In Historical Geography of the United States. New York: Harcourt, Brace, pp. 173-91.
     Acknowledges that Turner's "teachings and writings in the field of frontier history have become classic" and deals with his subject within a Turnerian framework.

3 CARELESS, J.M.S. "The Toronto Globe and Agrarian Radicalism, 1850-67." Canadian Historical Review 39 (March):14-39.
     Argues that the Toronto Globe was not molded by its agrarian environment as the Turner school of historiography would suggest. The Globe was actually controlled by "wealthy farmers" and the business elite of distant Toronto. Reprinted: 1970.8.

4 CREIGHTON, D.G. "Sir John MacDonald and Canadian Historians." Canadian Historial Review 29 (March):1-13.
     Critical of the influence of the Turner school of historiography upon the writing of Canadian history. Rejects the "simple-minded environmentalism" of Turner's approach.

5 FISHER, ESTELLE. "Documents: Frederick Jackson Turner Letters." Wisconsin Magazine of History 31 (March):339-45.
     Includes an introduction and two letters; in one of the letters, Turner accepts an invitation to deliver his famous paper "The Significance of the Frontier in American History."

6 HERRING, PENDLETON. "A Political Scientist Considers the Question." Pennsylvania Magazine of History and Biography 72 (April):118-36.
     Argues that the "most penetrating thinkers are partly the exponents of their own times and . . . the sensitive reactors to their environment." The key to Turner's influence was that he "hit upon a hypothesis which gave fresh relevance in the 1890s for all that had transpired in the preceding century."

7 HOLT, W. STULL. "Hegel, the Turner Hypothesis, and the Safety-Valve Theory." Agricultural History 22 (July):175-76.
     Scholars have failed to note that "Turner's Frontier hypothesis and . . . safety-valve theory" can be found in "Hegel's Philosophie der Goschichte." The relevant passage is cited in German and in English translation. "Although evidence is lacking to prove that Turner knew about this work by Hegel it would be extraordinary if he had not read it."

8 MOOD, FULMER. "Notes on the History of the Word Frontier." Agricultural History 22 (April):78-83.
     Traces the derivation of the word "frontier" through three centuries of English and American history. Concludes that

1948

Turner's writings did not have much influence upon the definition
and use of the term until after the publication of his influential
The Frontier in American History in 1920.

9 PAGE, EVELYN. "The First Frontier--The Swedes and the Dutch."
   Pennsylvania History 15 (October):276-304.
       "In belief that Frederick Jackson Turner's much debated
   'frontier theory' is still in need of such documentary examination as Turner himself suggested, . . . this essay professes to
   discuss it in relation to the history of the Dutch and Swedish
   colonies." Attempts to "compare Turner's frontier theory and
   historical fact." The findings confirm Turner's general theory.

10 RUGG, HAROLD. "The Spirit of the Frontier." In Wellsprings
   of the American Spirit: A Series of Addresses. Edited by F.
   Ernest Johnson. Religion and Civilization Series. New York:
   Institute for Religious and Social Studies; distributed by
   Harper & Brothers, pp. 97-115.
       Borrows Turner's frontier "traits, beliefs and values" in
   an attempt to prepare Americans to face the challenge of contemporary frontiers.

11 SAVETH, EDWARD N. "Frontier and Urban Melting Pots." In
   American Historians and European Immigrants, 1875-1925.
   Studies in History, Economics and Public Law. New York:
   Columbia University Press, pp. 122-49.
       Contains sections on Frederick Jackson Turner and Woodrow
   Wilson. Notes that Turner was "cognizant of a number of valid
   approaches to the immigration problem." Personally, Turner re-
   spected the German and Anglo immigrants because they contributed
   to the frontier values he lauded. Turner did not respond as
   favorably to southeastern European immigrants because they were
   urban oriented and were a "'loss to the social organism of the
   United States.'" Discusses Turner's views on the "melting pot."
   Reprinted: New York: Russell & Russell, 1965.

12 SHARP, PAUL F. "The Last West." In The Agrarian Revolt in
   Western Canada: A Survey Showing American Parallels. Minneapolis: University of Minnesota Press, pp. 1-20.
       Accepts Turner's assumptions regarding the closing of the
   American frontier, the frontier influences upon the growth of
   democracy, and the West's impact upon the established East. Reprinted: New York: Octagon Books, 1971.

13 WERTENBAKER, THOMAS J. "The Molding of the Middle West."
   American Historical Review 53 (January):223-34.
       Challenges Turner's thesis by arguing that the development
   of the American West can be best explained as an extension of

1948

the "Atlantic seaboard" the "source . . . out of which it [the West] sprang." It is not "true that American democracy was born on the Frontier. American democracy was born in Westminster Hall." Rejects the Turner thesis as invalid.

14 WRIGHT, LOUIS B. "The Westward Advance of the Atlantic Frontier." Huntington Library Quarterly 11 (May):261-75.
   Forcefully argues that eastern civilization was extended to the West without being dramatically transformed by the frontier environment. Observes that since Turner, writers on the frontier West "have been inclined to romanticize the rebelliousness of the West against the 'effete East'" and to "magnify the political liberalism, the independence, the originality, and the 'progressiveness' of the settlers in the . . . frontier."

15 ZASLOW, MORRIS. "The Frontier Hypothesis in Recent Historiography." Canadian Historical Review 29 (June):153-67.
   Explains the frontier hypothesis as a "product of a given environment." Summarizes Turner's views and evaluates the major attacks upon them, and explores Turner's influence upon Canadian and Russian historiography. Concludes that "it is readily apparent that Canadian historiography of today is being influenced, to a considerable degree, by the frontier hypothesis."

1949

1 BALDWIN, LELAND D. Review of Westward Expansion: A History of the American Frontier, by Ray Allen Billington. Pennsylvania Magazine of History and Biography 73 (October):522-23.
   The "value of the text would have been enhanced by a bolder critique of the ideas . . . of Turner."

2 BILLINGTON, RAY ALLEN. Westward Expansion: A History of the American Frontier. New York: Macmillan, 933 pp., passim.
   This standard college textbook is built around a Turnerian framework. Includes an annotated bibliography with a section entitled "The Frontier Hypothesis." Reprinted: 1957; 2d edition printed 1960; 3d edition printed 1967; and 4th edition printed 1974.

3 CRAVEN, AVERY. "Frederick Jackson Turner." In The Turner Thesis: Concerning the Role of the Frontier in American History. Edited by George Rogers Taylor. Problems in American Civilization Series. Boston: D.C. Heath, pp. 94-104.
   Reprint of 1937.3; reprinted: 1956, 1972.

1949

4 CURTI, MERLE. Frederick Jackson Turner. Mexico City:
   Instituto Panamericano de Geografía e Historia, Publicación
   no. 96, 38 pp.
      Biographical treatment of Turner and his ideas. Contends
   that "in originality and influence, Turner has thus far had no
   superior if he has had any peer." Reprinted: 1955.6, 1961.10.

5 CURTI, MERLE, and VERNON CARSTENSEN. The University of Wis-
   consin, 1848-1924. 2 vols. Madison: University of Wisconsin
   Press, vol. 1:739 pp.; vol. 2:608 pp., passim.
      A thorough assessment of Turner's contribution to the
   University of Wisconsin.

6 DANHOF, CLARENCE H. "American Evaluations of European Agriculture." Journal of Economic History, Supplement 9:61-71.
      Embraces a Turnerian assumption: the differences between
   "the development of American agricultural techniques in the
   period prior to 1800" and developments in European agriculture as
   a result of "forced changes" were caused by "the moving frontier,"
   which "required adjustment."

7 DILLARD, IRVING. Review of Westward Expansion: A History of
   the American Frontier, by Ray Allen Billington. Illinois
   State Historical Society, Journal 42 (December):472-73.
      "A good case could be made for the proposition that no
   single piece of historical writing has had such an influence on
   American historical investigation as the late Frederick Jackson
   Turner's The Significance of the American Frontier."

8 HACKER, LOUIS M. "Sections--or Classes?" In The Turner
   Thesis: Concerning the Role of the Frontier in American His-
   tory. Edited by George Rogers Taylor. Problems in American
   Civilization Series. Boston: D.C. Heath, pp. 61-64.
      Reprint of 1933.10; reprinted: 1956, 1972.

9 HAYES, CARLTON J.H. "The American Frontier--Frontier of
   What?" In The Turner Thesis: Concerning the Role of the
   Frontier in American History. Edited by George Rogers Taylor.
   Problems in American Civilization Series. Boston: D.C. Heath,
   pp. 84-93.
      Reprint of 1946.6. Reprinted: 1956, 1972.

10 HICKS, JOHN D. "Frederick Jackson Turner." In The American
   Nation: A History of the United States from 1865 to the Present. 2d edition. New York: Houghton Mifflin, pp. 280-83.
      Presents Turner as the most influential historian of the
   early twentieth century. Includes a full-page portrait of Turner.
   Revised: 1955; reprinted: 1963, 1971.

1949

11 HOFSTADTER, RICHARD. "Turner and the Frontier Myth." American
    Scholar 18 (Autumn):433-43.
        Observes that "the frontier thesis . . . has embodied the
    predominant American view of the American past." Explains why
    Turner's thesis became so popular and reviews the "more important
    arguments . . . of Turner's critics." Reprinted: 1966.19,
    1970.18.

12 JOHANSEN, DOROTHY O. "A Tentative Appraisal of Territorial
    Government in Oregon." Pacific Historical Review 18 (Novem-
    ber):483-99.
        The influence of "Frederick Jackson Turner's essays" with
    their emphasis upon the economic and social aspects of the fron-
    tier has resulted in a neglect of "the political framework within
    which this [frontier] society existed." Turner and his disciples
    have ignored the degree to which territorial governments were
    dominant on the frontier and served to transmit eastern influ-
    ence to the West.

13 LERNER, MAX. "History and American Greatness." American
    Quarterly 1 (Fall):209-17.
        Credits the "famous Turner theory of the moving frontier"
    with having been "a crucial link between the theories that ex-
    plain American greatness in terms of individualism and those that
    explain it in terms of American uniqueness and the nations'
    separation from world forces." Explains Turner's great popularity
    as a result of his glorification of American uniqueness, indi-
    vidualism, and laissez-faire capitalism.

14 PAXSON, FREDERIC L. "When the West Was New." In The Turner
    Thesis: Concerning the Role of the Frontier in American His-
    tory. Edited by George Rogers Taylor. Problems in American
    Civilization Series. Boston: D.C. Heath, pp. 34-41.
        Excerpt from 1930.15.

15 PIERSON, GEORGE WILSON. "The Frontier and American Institu-
    tions: A Criticism of the Turner Theory." In The Turner
    Thesis: Concerning the Role of the Frontier in American His-
    tory. Edited by George Rogers Taylor. Problems in American
    Civilization Series. Boston: D.C. Heath, pp. 65-83.
        Reprint of 1942.18; reprinted: 1956, 1972.

16 RIEGEL, ROBERT E. "The West." In Young America, 1830-1840.
    Norman: University of Oklahoma Press, pp. 52-66.
        "The frontier was not a safety valve to release the pres-
    sure of industrial discontent during periods of depression" as
    Turner and his early disciples argued, for "men went West in good
    times rather than bad." Reprinted: 1973.

17 SAVELLE, MAX. "Imperial School of American Colonial Histo-
    rians." Indiana Magazine of History 45 (June):123-34.
        Discusses those historians of Colonial America before 1783
    who argue that their history should be studied as part of the
    history of the British Empire. Notes, however, that many of the
    historians of this group share some of Turner's positions on the
    influence of the frontier in the modification and alteration of
    Old World ideology.

18 SCHLESINGER, ARTHUR M. "The City in American Civilization."
    In Paths to the Present. New York: Macmillan, pp. 210-33.
        In Turner's zeal to overcome historical problems by empha-
    sizing the frontier, he overlooked another major force, the city.
    "A true understanding of America's past demands this balanced
    view--an appreciation of the significance of both frontier and
    city." Revised: Boston: Houghton Mifflin, 1964.

19 _____. "The Role of the Immigrant." In Paths to the Present.
    New York: Macmillan, pp. 51-76.
        Revised version of 1921.11; revised: Boston: Houghton
    Mifflin, 1964.

20 SHANNON, FRED A. "A Post Mortem on the Labor-Safety-Valve
    Theory." In The Turner Thesis: Concerning the Role of the
    Frontier in American History. Edited by George Rogers Taylor.
    Problems in American Civilization Series. Boston: D.C.
    Heath, pp. 51-60.
        Reprint of 1945.14.

21 TAYLOR, GEORGE ROGERS. Introduction to The Turner Thesis:
    Concerning the Role of the Frontier in American History.
    Problems in American Civilization Series. Boston: D.C. Heath,
    pp. v-vii.
        Gives a brief background of the Turner thesis and the en-
    suing controversy and introduces the essays that follow. Presents
    "Suggestions for Additional Reading" at the end of the volume
    (pp. 105-6). Revised: 1956, 1972.

22 VAN ALSTYNE, RICHARD W. "The Significance of the Mississippi
    Valley in American Diplomatic History, 1686-1890." Mississippi
    Valley Historical Review 36 (September):215-38.
        Asserts that "Turner was thinking beyond his celebrated
    frontier hypothesis into an area in which the history of the
    United States could be placed in a genuine world setting."
    Addresses this issue by exploring the influence of the Mississippi
    Valley in the realm of the United States' international affairs.

1949

23 WRIGHT, BENJAMIN F., Jr. "Political Institutions and the
    Frontier." In The Turner Thesis: Concerning the Role of the
    Frontier in American History. Edited by George Rogers Taylor.
    Problems in American Civilization Series. Boston: D.C. Heath,
    pp. 42-50.
        Reprint of 1934.21; reprinted: 1956, 1972.

                                1950

1 AUSUBEL, HERMAN. Historians and Their Craft: A Study of the
   Presidential Addresses of the American Historical Association,
   1884-1945. Studies in History, Economics, and Public Law.
   New York: Columbia University Press, 373 pp., passim.
       Analyzes and synthesizes the presidential addresses of the
American Historical Society. Turner spoke in 1910 on "Social
Forces in American History." Comments on Turner's interdisciplin-
ary scope and calls him the "first president of the Association
to back wholeheartedly cooperation with allied investigators."
Reprinted: New York: Russell & Russell, 1965.

2 BENSON, LEE. "Achille Loria's Influence on American Economic
   Thought: Including His Contributions to the Frontier Hypothesis." Agricultural History 24 (October):182-99.
       Turner was markedly influenced by Loria, the famous Italian
economist. Turner's assertion that the "'ever retreating frontier of free land is the key to American development'" can be
traced directly to Loria's writings. Turner was also indebted
to Loria for his ideas regarding the "rebirth of American life."
Reprinted: 1960.2.

3 BILLINGTON, RAY A. "The Frontier in Illinois History."
   Illinois State Historical Society Journal 43 (April):28-45.
       Utilizes Turner's emphasis upon "imported traits and the
environmental influences operating upon" frontiersmen in order to
understand the Illinois frontier. Concludes that in "few areas
were the two ingredients sufficiently balanced to create a completely typical result" as was the case in Illinois.

4 BREBNER, J.B. Review of Westward Expansion: A History of the
   American Frontier, by Ray Allen Billington. Geographical Review 40 (April):341-43.
       Billington treats Turner with a "grand filial piety. . . .
It is as though he had detected the beginning of a return swing
of the pendulum in Turner's favor and had been unable to resist
adding a push."

94

5   BURT, A.L. "Broad Horizons." <u>Canadian Historical Association</u>
    <u>Report, 1949-1950</u>, pp. 1-10.
        Makes a plea for the usefulness of a Turnerian type of en-
    vironmentalism in the writing of Canadian history.

6   COMMAGER, HENRY STEELE. "Innovators in Historical Interpreta-
    tion: Turner, Parrington, Beard." In <u>The American Mind</u>. New
    Haven: Yale University Press, pp. 293-309.
        Of these three historians, Turner "remains in many respects
    the most influential." Claims that "Turner was not the historian
    of the frontier--that he left to others--but the historian of
    America, who took his vantage point along the frontier." Briefly
    analyzes the frontier thesis. Reprinted: 1959, 1967.

7   HOFSTADTER, RICHARD. Review of <u>Virgin Land: The American</u>
    <u>West as Symbol and Myth</u>, by Henry Nash Smith. <u>American Quar-</u>
    <u>terly</u> 2 (Fall):279-82.
        "Mr. Smith," although "no Turnerian, has gone far to re-
    assert the importance of the West in more moderate, acceptable,
    and intellectually sophisticated terms, on the ground of its
    mythic symbolic role." In addition, his book "suggests how far
    out . . . scholarship has advanced from the simple formulas of
    Turner's generation."

8   LE DUC, THOMAS. "The Disposal of the Public Domain on the
    Trans-Mississippi Plains: Some Opportunities for Investiga-
    tion." <u>Agricultural History</u> 24 (October):199-204.
        Outlines major areas of study in the dispersal of public
    lands, indicating the type of work that needs to be done in the
    field. Deals with geographic and economic approaches similar to
    Turner's.

9   MALIN, JAMES C. "Ecology and History." <u>Scientific Monthly</u>
    70 (May):295-98.
        Argues that "an ecological methodology applied to history"
    in "one stroke . . . renders the Turner . . . doctrine of 'closed
    space' meaningless."

10 MOOD, FULMER. "Frederick Jackson Turner and the Milwaukee
    Sentinel, 1884." <u>Wisconsin Magazine of History</u> 34 (Autumn):
    21-28.
        Deals with "Turner the young newspaper reporter . . . during
    some months in 1884 and 1885." A brief biographical sketch re-
    counts Turner's search for a career.

11 MOOD, FULMER, ed. "Radisson and Groseilliers: A Newly Re-
    covered Historical Essay by Frederick J. Turner." <u>Wisconsin</u>
    <u>Magazine of History</u> 33 (March):318-26.

1950

Includes a four-page introduction to a previously unknown
"popular account of Radisson and Groseilliers," which Turner sent
to the "Milwaukee Sentinel with the notion of earning a little
extra money."

12 NUTE, GRACE LEE. "Late Frontier." American Heritage 1
    (Winter):2-5, 73-75.
    "Northern Minnesota has been a frontier--or a succession of
frontiers" and has "followed the customary pattern of American
frontiers" as outlined by Turner.

13 ROSTOW, W.W. "The National Style." In The American Style:
    Essays in Value and Performance. Edited by Elting E. Morison.
    New York: Harper & Brothers, pp. 246-313.
    Draws upon Turner's ideas to explain the development of
what he calls "The National Style."

14 SHARP, PAUL F. "When Our West Moved North." American Histori-
    cal Review 55 (January):286-300.
    "The theory of the passing of the Frontier in 1890, like
other broad generalizations, does not stand the test of close
examination." The "last frontier was the Canadian West," which
remained open for "nearly three decades after 1890." Emphasizes
the significance of the Canadian frontier during the first three
decades of the twentieth century. "Frederick Jackson Turner
interpreted the frontier as a past phenomenon, but, even as he
wrote, thousands of his fellow countrymen were seeking in Canada
the economic and social opportunities he described as characteristic of a frontier society."

15 SMITH, HENRY NASH. Virgin Land: The American West as Symbol
    and Myth. Cambridge, Mass.: Harvard University Press, 305
    pp., passim.
    Study of the impact upon the awareness of nineteenth-
century Americans of the unknown, nearly unoccupied West.
Stresses the idea of the American West rather than the physical
environment of the West as did Turner. While acknowledging that
Turner's thesis had achieved widespread acceptance among historians, Smith attempts to prove that even though "brilliant and
persuasive," the Turner thesis "could hardly have attained such
universal acceptance if it had not found an echo in ideas and
attitudes already current." It was not so much that Turner's
thesis explained American development, but rather that the American mind was predisposed to accept Turner's ideas. Without what
Smith calls the "myth of the garden," Turner's thesis would have
never been popular. Reprinted: 1957, 1971.

1951

1 ANON. Review of <u>The Significance of Sections in American His-</u>
   <u>tory</u>. <u>Georgia Historical Quarterly</u> 35 (March):97.
      "An important contribution to American history" by a his-
   torian who "greatly influenced the interpretations which have
   been applied to the facts of the American past."

2 BENSON, LEE. "The Historical Background of Turner's Frontier
   Essay." <u>Agricultural History</u> 25 (April):59-82.
      Studies the historical setting of Turner's frontier thesis
   and argues that the theory was a product of this setting. Explores "some of the sources from which Turner drew inspiration,
   and attempts to clarify further the meaning of his concepts and
   terminology." Also examines "the powerful forces at work tending
   both to produce the frontier thesis and to insure its rapid and
   widespread acceptance." Reprinted: 1960.2, 1973.2.

3 BENTON, THOMAS HART. "American Regionalism: A Personal History of the Movement." <u>University of Kansas City Review</u> 18
   (Autumn):41-75.
      This famous painter of western landscapes acknowledges his
   "indebtedness to Turner" and agrees with those who characterize
   his work as "a sort of Turner in paint."

4 BINKLEY, WILLIAM C. "The South and the West." <u>Journal of</u>
   <u>Southern History</u> 17 (February):5-22.
      "Although it has been more than half a century since
   Frederick Jackson Turner made us conscious of the importance of
   the West in American development, one still looks in vain for a
   systematic study of the part which the South may have played in
   determining the character of the West." Calls for a use of
   Turner's thesis in the study of southern history.

5 BOWMAN, ISAIAH. "Settlement by the Modern Pioneer." In
   <u>Geography in the Twentieth Century: A Study of Growth, Fields,</u>
   <u>Techniques, Aims, and Trends</u>. Edited by Griffith Taylor. New
   York: Philosophic Library, pp. 248-66.
      Disagrees with Turner's assumption that the frontier closed
   in the 1890s but agrees with his contention that the frontier
   environment greatly modified the invading culture. Revised:
   1953, 1957.

6 BYRD, PRATT. "The Kentucky Frontier in 1792." <u>Filson Club</u>
   <u>History Quarterly</u> 25 (July):181-203; 286-94.
      Opens with the observation that "Turner's position as dean
   of American historians is now well assured" but goes on to argue
   that "Turner's thesis and its disciples . . . do not provide

1951

completely adequate answers to the questions raised by the study
of the frontier in Kentucky." Includes a brief summary of
Turner's assumptions.

7   COMMAGER, HENRY STEELE. Introduction to Turner's "The Sig-
    nificance of the Frontier." In Living Ideas in America.
    Edited by Henry Steele Commager. New York: Harper &
    Brothers, pp. 72-73.
       Places Turner's famous work in its historiographical set-
    ting. Enlarged: 1964.

8   CRAVEN, AVERY. "Frederick Jackson Turner and the Frontier
    Approach." University of Kansas City Review 18 (Autumn):3-17.
       Turner's "The Significance of the Frontier in American His-
    tory" ushered in "the birth of a new era in the study and writing
    of American History." Summarizes Turner's ideas and those of his
    major interpreters. Concludes that "the approach which he
    took stimulated more interest in American history and produced
    more good research in the field than did that of any of his con-
    temporaries."

9   CRAVEN, AVERY; WALTER JOHNSON; and F. ROGER DUNN. Introduction
    to Turner's "The Significance of the Frontier in American His-
    tory." In A Documentary History of the American People.
    Edited by Avery Craven, Walter Johnson, and F. Roger Dunn.
    Boston: Ginn, p. 242.
       Evaluates Turner's contribution and significance.

10 DALE, E.E. "Turner--The Man and Teacher." University of
    Kansas City Review 18 (Autumn):18-28.
       Turner had "far more influence upon the study and interpre-
    tation of American history than did any other man of his genera-
    tion." Explores "the secret of Turner's power and influence"
    and finds it in the "great man" and the "great teacher." Includes
    personal recollections about his former mentor as well as personal
    correspondence with Turner.

11 FINE, SIDNEY. "Richard T. Ely, Forerunner of Progressivism,
    1880-1901." Mississippi Valley Historical Review 37 (March):
    599-624.
       A biography of Richard Ely, noted economist and social re-
    former. Comments that Turner was "among the Ely 'gallery'" as a
    graduate student at Johns Hopkins University.

12 HARPER, NORMAN D. "Turner the Historian: 'Hypothesis' or
    'Process'? With Special Reference to Frontier Society in
    Australia." University of Kansas City Review 18 (Autumn):76-
    86.

Turner "was concerned primarily with the process of western expansion" rather than "with the end results." This emphasis made his approach useful in the study of other frontier nations for Turner's "process . . . could be a universal one." Suggests that Turner's thesis provides an excellent model for the study of the Australian frontier.

13 MOOD, FULMER. "The Origin, Evolution, and Application of the Sectional Concept, 1750-1900." In Regionalism in America. Edited by Merrill Jensen. Madison: University of Wisconsin Press, pp. 5-98.

Concludes that "Turner's own thinking on sections as historical phenomena represents the apex of development in the field [sectional studies of American history] during the time covered by this study. From Turner's classroom at Madison the study of sectionalism, historically considered, now spread outward by degrees, so that more and more its influence came to be felt in the study of history and the social sciences in general." Includes a lengthy letter by Turner in which he discusses the concept of sectionalism in the study of American history.

14 ____. Review of The United States, 1830-1850: The Nation and Its Sections. 1950 edition. Wisconsin Magazine of History 35 (Winter):149-50.

Compares this volume with Turner's earlier works in order to demonstrate that "Turner had . . . moved away from the simple sectional scheme of his young manhood."

15 MORRISEY, RICHARD J. "The Shaping of Two Frontiers." Americas 3 (January):3-6, 41-42.

Compares the Spanish-American frontier and the Anglo-American frontier. The similarities can be traced to the environment and geographic factors and the dissimilarities result from cultural differences. Concludes that "in the meeting of the two frontiers was the key to the conquest of the Far West."

16 MORTON, W.L. "The Significance of Site in the Settlement of the American and Canadian Wests." Agricultural History 25 (July):97-104.

Discusses the factor of "site" in the movement toward the frontier, and indicates its importance in "the various stages of frontier history." Argues against the frontier thesis by showing that the "Americanization" and "Democracy" which emerged were "products of the total environment," including metropolitan social controls as well as factors peculiar to the frontier.

17 SMITH, HENRY NASH. "The West as an Image of the American Past." University of Kansas City Review 18 (Autumn):29-40.

1951

Suggests that "the influence of the West on American thought at the level of unsystematic popular ideology" is a "parody of Turner's Frontier Hypothesis: a statement in vulgarized terms of ideas which Turner advanced as a general interpretation of American history." Explores the "puzzling" question of why the "cultural image of the frontier in . . . the Turner Hypothesis . . . has attained such a wide currency in the world of scholarship." Concludes that "its influence on historical scholarship has been unfortunate."

18 WEBB, WALTER PRESCOTT. "Ended: Four Hundred Year Boom: Reflections on the Age of the Frontier." Harper's Magazine 203 (October):25-33.
    Credits Turner's thesis with being "the most influential single piece of historical writing ever done in the United States." Reinterprets the frontier thesis by suggesting that "what happened in America was but a detail in a much greater phenomenon, the interaction between European civilization and the vast raw lands into which it moved." Europe's frontier predated the American frontier and "was much greater than that of the United States." Furthermore, "the frontier of Europe was almost . . . as important in determining the life and institutions of modern Europe as the frontier of America was in shaping the course of American history." Since the "frontier is gone" Americans now must address "the problems now facing a frontierless society." Reprinted: 1956.16.

19 ____. The Great Frontier. Austin: University of Texas Press, 434 pp., passim.
    Critical of Turnerian historiography for having "treated the frontier as if it were something exclusively American, as if the United States were the only nation that had felt the powerful influence of access to vacant land." This volume is Webb's response to his conviction that the "American frontier concept. . . needs to be lifted out of its present national setting and applied on a much larger scale to all western civilization in modern times." Reprinted: 1964, 1979.

20 ____. "Windfalls of the Frontier." Harper's Magazine 203 (November):71-77.
    Applies Turner's frontier concepts to all the frontiers of western Europe and to expansionistic capitalism. Generalizes the "the Great Frontier came to western Europe as a windfall and capitalism was the method devised for appropriating . . . it."

1952

1 BARDOLPH, RICHARD. Review of The United States, 1830-1850:
The Nation and Its Sections. North Carolina Historical Review
29 (January):140-42.
    "This [book] is the matured Turner . . . still in search of
hypotheses but subjecting them to increasingly rigorous tests"
and "in the last of his book the critic looks in vain for over-
simplifications. . . . It seems unlikely that it will ever be
quite superseded."

2 BELLOT, HUGH HALE. "Some Aspects of the Recent History of
American Historiography." In American History and American
Historians: A Review of Recent Contributions to the Interpretation of the History of the United States. Norman: University of Oklahoma Press, pp. 1-40.
    Identifies Turner as the historian most responsible for the
founding of the "middle western school" of historiography. Reprinted: Westport, Conn.: Greenwood Press, 1974.

3 BLAKE, NELSON MANFRED. "The Frontier Tradition." In A Short
History of American Life. New York: McGraw-Hill, pp. 397-
400.
    Places the Turner theory within the broader framework of
the general history of the West in the late nineteenth century.

4 CAUGHEY, JOHN WALTON. "Historians' Choice: Results of a Poll
on Recently Published American History and Biography."
Mississippi Valley Historical Review 39 (September):289-302.
    Turner's "The Frontier in American History" placed second
in a poll of "Preferred Works in American History, 1920-1935."

5 CURTI, MERLE. "The Democratic Theme in American Historical
Literature." Mississippi Valley Historical Review 39 (June):
3-28.
    Discusses major historians' views on American democracy.
Compares and contrasts Turner's evaluation of democracy with
those of Henry Adams and Charles Beard. Turner is identified as
the most famous contributor to the celebration of democracy American style. Reprinted: 1955.5.

6 FRYKMAN, GEORGE A. "Regionalism, Nationalism, Localism: The
Pacific Northwest in American History." Pacific Northwest
Quarterly 43 (October):251-61.
    "At the end of the nineteenth century . . . another great
historian, Frederick Jackson Turner, challenged . . . the German-
inspired theories of the European origin of American culture, in
his frontier and sectional thesis. The theoretical inspiration
for contemporary regionalism comes, in part, from Turner."

1952

7 HARPER, NORMAN D. "Revision Article--Frontier and Section: A
   Turner 'Myth.'" Historical Studies; Australia and New Zealand
   5 (May): 135-53.
        "A reassessment of Turner" that summarizes his views in
   light of the historiography of the Turner thesis. Concludes that
   Turner's "fundamental contribution lay in his enlargement of the
   field of history . . . and the development of a new methodology."
   Based on research in the Turner Papers at the Henry E. Huntington
   Library.

8 HESSELTINE, WILLIAM B. "Lyman Copeland Draper, 1815-1891."
   Wisconsin Magazine of History 35 (Spring):163-66, 231-34.
        In spite of a legend that claims that young Turner refused
   even to talk to Professor Draper because he was an "'old dilet-
   tante,'" Hesseltine attempts to prove that Draper was actually
   Turner's "intellectual grandfather." Draper "gathered the
   materials . . . out of which the architect Turner would build the
   house of an important historical theory."

9 HOWARD, JOSEPH KINSEY. "New Concepts of Plains History."
   Montana Magazine of History 2 (October):16-23.
        Sees "the so-called 'semi-popular'" western historians as
   practicing Turner's "ideal" when they write history which is characterized by "synthesis and social judgement within a frame of
   reference which" makes "history's significance readily intelli-
   gible."

10 KAPLAN, LAWRENCE S. "Frederick Jackson Turner and Imperialism."
    Social Science 27 (January):12-16.
        "Although fifty-five years have passed since the American
    historian Frederick Jackson Turner first drew the attention of
    America to himself and to his native Middle West, the magic of
    his personality has not yet worn off." Futhermore, "despite the
    attacks upon the 'Turnerian school' in the last fifteen years,
    Turner the man has emerged above the heat of partisan debate over
    the merits of his ideas as the most important writer of American
    History in the last two generations." Argues that Turner, be-
    cause of his intense nationalism, "may have been seized by the
    . . . expansionist fever of his day--fever that can only be diag-
    nosed as imperialism." The imperialists of the day found in
    Turner's ideas "what they still lacked, namely, the historical
    justification of imperialism."

11 MOOD, FULMER. "Frederick Jackson Turner and the Chicago Inte-
    Occar, 1885." Wisconsin Magazine of History 35 (Spring):188-
    94, 210-17.
        Examines Turner's brief experience as political staff cor-
    respondent; attempts to show how this experience served "him well

102

when later on he undertook this historical study of American
politics." Includes a selection of Turner's dispatches conveying
Turner's journalistic style.

12   _____. "Studies in the History of American Settled Areas and
      Frontier Lines: Settled Areas and Frontier Lines, 1625-1790."
      Agricultural History 26 (January):16-36.
      Attempts to "call into question the popularly received
opinion of the unity on the one-ness of the Frontier Line."
Turner is depicted as having slavishly depended upon Francis
Walker's census maps published in 1874. By studying the frontier
from 1607-1790, Mood concludes "that the common notion [Turner's]
that there was one Frontier Line during this period is groundless.
The truth is that . . . a pluarility of frontier lines . . .
existed."

13   _____. "The Theory of the History of an American Section and
      the Practice of R. Carlyle Buley." Indiana Magazine of History
      18 (March):1-22.
      F.J. Turner not only first focused the attention of histo-
rians upon "the history of the Section," but he also rallied
"young writers to undertake sectional study."

14   RABINOWITZ, ISADORE. "Turner's Safety-Valve Theory." Journal
      of Social Studies 8 (Winter):66-70.
      Rejects Turner's safety-valve theory as "invalid" and
"specious." Argues that Turner's evidence is weak and that his
theory is inconsistent and contradictory. Hopes that with the
elimination of the frontier theory, "geographical determinism
will never again receive a serious hearing by American historians."

15   RIEGEL, ROBERT E. "Current Ideas of the Significance of the
      United States Frontier." Revista de Historia de America 33
      (June):25-43.
      From a sympathetic point of view, summarizes a cross section
of the secondary literature on Turner and his ideas. Attempts to
trace the evolution of the Turnerian tradition in American historiography. Concludes that although friends and foes alike have
demonstrated that Turner's views must be modified, his thesis is
still valid.

16   SWEET, WILLIAM WARREN. Religion in the Development of American
      Culture, 1765-1840. New York: Scribner, 338 pp., passim.
      Accepts, with modifications, the Turner thesis that the
moving frontier "should be the central theme in American history,"
but argues that economic determinism should not be the sole cri-
terion. Turner did not belittle the influence of religion as a
factor in American development, but he did pass over religion

1952

"because he did not have sufficient knowledge of it to put it in
its rightful place." Religious development during the period
1765-1840 played a significant role in the evolution of American
culture. Reprinted: Gloucester, Mass.: Peter Smith, 1963.

17 TREADGOLD, DONALD D. "Russian Expansion in the Light of
   Turner's Study of the American Frontier." Agricultural History 26 (October):147-51.
   Accepts Turner's frontier thesis as valid and builds upon
Turner's "suggestion that 'if with our own methods of the occupation of the Frontier, we should compare those of other countries
which have dealt with similar problems--such as Russia.'" The
author's aim is "to show that in relation to the problem of Russian history," Turner's call for comparative research "has
validity." Expanded: 1957.24.

1953

1 ANON. Report on the Fourth Newberry Library Conference on
   American Studies. Newberry Library Bulletin 3 (October):127-
   35.
   Turnerian scholars in attendance at the conference defended
Turner's definition of the frontier in response to a paper presented by Professor Arthur E. Bestor, which in tone and substance
expressed "marked disapproval" of Turner's famous thesis.

2 BARNHART, JOHN D. Valley of Democracy: The Frontier versus
   the Plantation in the Ohio Valley, 1775-1818. Bloomington:
   Indiana University Press, 338 pp., passim.
   As a former student of Turner, the author attempts to test
"the Turner interpretation" by studying "the development of democracy in the Ohio Valley" in light of "the writings of Turner and
his critics." Finds that "the history of the Valley supports the
writings of Turner" while it demonstrates that the "interpretation" of "his critics . . . , particularly when it deviated from
Turner, was not so dependable nor so accurate as his." Reprinted:
1966.2.

3 BEALE, HOWARD K. "The Professional Historian: His Theory and
   His Practice." Pacific Historical Review 22 (August):227-55.
   "History is fast losing the place of importance it once
held" because of the failure of professional historians "to choose
research subjects that have significance." Urges his profession
to inspire students to recognize "the significance of things as
did Turner."

4 BESTOR, ARTHUR. "Patent Office Models of the Good Society:
   Some Relationships between Social Reform and Westward Expansion." American Historical Review 58 (April):505-26.
      If the frontier is defined in the way Turner used the term,
as an "outer margin of the 'settled area,' . . . then a close
relationship between the frontier and communitarianism is hard to
find." Reprinted: 1969.3.

5 BILLINGTON, RAY ALLEN. Review of The Great Frontier, by Walter
   Prescott Webb. Mississippi Valley Historical Review 40 (June):
   107-8.
      Argues that Webb's book is not merely an "overextension of
the Turner thesis" as several critics have complained.

6 CAUGHEY, JOHN WALTON. "Herbert Eugene Bolton." Pacific Historical Review 22 (May):109-12.
      Eulogy in which Turner is credited with profoundly influ-
encing Bolton; Bolton's thesis regarding the Spanish borderlands
was an expansion of Turner's frontier thesis.

7 DAVIS, HAROLD E. "Three Interpretations of America in History."
   Americas 10 (October):131-39.
      Credits Turner with authoring one of the most influential
theories of history and explores the common ground he shared with
two well-known Latin American scholars--Euclydes da Cunha and
Domingo F. Sarmiento. All three scholars "agreed in recognizing
the influence of land and environment . . . as basic to the historical process in the New World." Observes that Herbert Eugene
Bolton, the famous historian of the frontiers of the Americas,
was "greatly influenced by Turner."

8 HAMMOND, GEORGE P. "In Memoriam: Herbert Eugene Bolton."
   Americas 9 (April):391-98.
      Underscores the fact that at "the University of Wisconsin,
Bolton came under the influence of several professors who helped
shape his career, notably Frederick Jackson Turner."

9 HEIMERT, ALAN. "Puritanism, the Wilderness, and the Frontier."
   New England Quarterly 26 (September):361-82.
      Rejects Turner's interpretation of Cotton Mather's views of
the western frontier. Claims that Turner's treatment of the
Puritan's response to their environment was far too simplistic.

10 HESSELTINE, WILLIAM B. "Lyman Draper and the South." Journal
    of Southern History 19 (February):20-31.
      Credits Draper with having "established a climate of opinion
from which Frederick Jackson Turner eventually extracted the
frontier hypothesis."

1953

11 HICKS, JOHN D. "The American Tradition of Democracy." <u>Utah</u>
<u>Historical Quarterly</u> 21 (January):25-41.
Dismisses those who "scoff at Frederick Jackson Turner and
his emphasis upon the significance of the frontier" as simply
"bright young men . . . fanatically eager to prove that Turner
was wrong." Reprinted: 1955.10.

12 HOLT, W. STULL. "Some Consequences of the Urban Movement in
American History." <u>Pacific Historical Review</u> 22 (August):337-
51.
As a result of "contemplating the achievement of Frederick
Jackson Turner," the author asks "if another hypothesis could not
be found to give meaning to otherwise unrelated facts and to give
a reputation to its originator." Finds a new hypothesis in the
"significance of the urban movement."

13 KRAUS, MICHAEL. "Frontier and Sectional Historians." In
<u>Writings of American History</u>. Norman: University of Oklahoma
Press, pp. 271-314.
Revised and enlarged version of 1937.7; reprinted: 1963.

14 LOKKEN, ROY. "Frederick Jackson Turner's Letters to Edmond S.
Meany." <u>Pacific Northwest Quarterly</u> 44 (January):30-39.
Correspondence from Turner to Meany "preserved in the University of Washington's Pacific Northwest Collection . . . affords
a glimpse into the mind and the heart of one of America's really
great teachers. . . ." Also helps to "clarify or elaborate upon
Turner's ideas concerning the frontier."

15 MEAD, SIDNEY E. "Prof. Sweet's Religion and Culture in America." <u>Church History</u> 22 (March):33-49.
Examines Sweet in relation to the Turner thesis and to the
historical writing of John Bach McMaster. Argues that "Professor
Sweet has always worn a Turner mantle over a McMaster frame."

16 SHERA, JESSE HAUK. "Regionalism." In <u>Historians, Books and</u>
<u>Libraries: A Survey of Historical Scholarship in Relation to</u>
<u>Library Resources, Organizations and Services</u>. Cleveland:
Press of Western Reserve University, pp. 75-76.
"Partly because he was an inspiring teacher and partly because of the importance of his interpretation he [Turner] has
achieved a wider influence than any other historian of recent
years." Summarizes his contribution to the concept of regionalism
in American development.

17 STEVENS, HARRY R. "Cross Section and Frontier." <u>South</u>
<u>Atlantic Quarterly</u> 52 (July):445-63.
Presents Turner as the father of the "Frontier School" of

historiography; attempts to explain origins of the school, traces
its growth and includes a list of Turner's most famous students.
The last third of the article is a bibliography essay on secondary
works within the frontier school and a detailed review of Bernard
DeVoto's The Course of Empire and Walter Prescott Webb's Great
Frontier.

18 WILLIAMSON, W.L. "A Sidelight on the Frontier Thesis: A New
    Turner Letter." Newberry Library Bulletin 3 (April):46-49.
        Turner's "Frontier Essay . . . was perhaps the most influ-
    ential single pronouncement in American historiography" and the
    letter first printed here "indicates that if Turner's wishes had
    been followed, he would not have read his paper" when he did.

                              1954

1 ANON. "The American Frontier." In American Writing Today.
   Edited by Allan Angoff. London: Times Publishing Company,
   pp. 348-51.
       Reprint of 1921.2; reprinted: 1957.

2 BARRACLOUGH, G. "Metropolis and Macrocosm: Europe and the
   Wider World, 1492-1939." Past and Present, no. 5 (May):77-93.
       A review of Walter Prescott Webb's The Great Frontier in
   which the author concludes that Webb's "debt to Turner's famous
   'frontier concept' is obvious."

3 BERTHRONG, DONALD J. "Andrew Jackson Turner, 'Work Horse of
   the Republican Party.'" Wisconsin Magazine of History 38
   (Winter):77-86.
       The political figure under study can be best identified as
   "the father of Frederick Jackson Turner."

4 BILLINGTON, RAY ALLEN. The American Frontiersman: A Case-
   Study in Reversion to the Primitive. London: Clarendon Press,
   23 pp.
       An eloquent summary statement of the "'Americanization' of
   both men and society" from a neo-Turnerian point of view. The
   emphasis is upon the frontier "environment, which reshaped the
   transplanted civilization of the Old World into the distinctive
   cultural patterns of the United States." Reprinted: 1977.2.

5 BLACKWOOD, GEORGE D. "Frederick Jackson Turner and John
   Rogers Commons--Complimentary Thinkers." Mississippi Valley
   Historical Review 41 (December):471-88.
       Notes major similarities in the methods of the historian
   and the economist: "Turner and Commons were working at a time

1954

when the tendency was to split the various fields, and in some ways . . . they contributed to the splitting. But in a more vital way they were integrating materials of the social sciences into a meaningful whole." These similarities are based on four core concepts: (1) historical relativism, (2) evolution of distinctively American institutions, (3) the concept of balance between contesting forces, and (4) the "multiple-pole" approach to the social sciences.

6 BOLTON, HERBERT EUGENE. "Turner, As I Remember Him." Edited by Wilbur R. Jacobs. Mid-America 36 (January):54-61.
    A former student discusses Turner's classroom technique, personality, and influence. Bolton's indebtedness to Turner is explored by Jacobs, and the selections by Bolton provide an "excellent word-picture of Turner as a professor."

7 CARELESS, J.M.S. "Frontierism, Metropolitanism, and Canadian History." Canadian Historical Review 35 (March):1-21.
    Turner's frontier thesis "broadly affected the thinking of a number of distinguished Canadian historians." Canadian historiography has been heavily influenced by "the North American-environmentalist view . . . which stemmed originally from Turner's frontier thesis." Describes the Turnerian approach to history as a form of "environmental determinism." Traces and assesses the impact of Turner's thesis upon Canadian historiography.

8 CARTER, CLARENCE E. "The Transit of Law to the Frontier: A Review Article." Journal of Mississippi History 16 (July): 183-92.
    Suggests that Turner errored when he made all frontiers appear to be alike and when he ignored the role which "law . . . of Anglo-American origin" played on the frontier.

9 ELKINS, STANLEY M., and ERIC L. McKITRICK. "A Meaning for Turner's Frontier, Part I: Democracy in the Old Northwest." Political Science Quarterly 69 (September):321-53.
    Observes that although Turner's critics have been able to "demonstrate the absurdities of Turner's internal logic," they have not been able to discredit Turner's basic point: "That some relation . . . does exist between our history and our frontier." By utilizing a "conceptual framework" borrowed from social science, the authors try to verify Turner's "undeniable fact--that an organic connection exists between American democracy and the American frontier." The "establishment of new communities" in the "Old Northwest, the southwest frontier in Alabama and Mississippi, and the . . . frontier in Massachusetts Bay" are the specific areas studied. Continued: 1954.10; reprinted: 1956.3, 1964.7, 1968.9, 1970.12, 1970.13.

1954

10 _____. "A Meaning for Turner's Frontier, Part II: The Southwest Frontier and New England." Political Science Quarterly
69 (December):565-602.
    Concludes that Turner's "insight," although "crude in form,
. . . has remained the closest thing that we have had to a seminal
contribution to the theory of American history." The exciting
prospect is that "a host of [contemporary] problems may be
examined with fresh interest if we put in testable terms facts
which he [Turner] knew by instinct." Continuation of 1954.9.

11 FERGUSON, RUSSELL. Review of The Valley of Democracy: The
Frontier versus the Plantation in the Ohio Valley, 1775-1818,
by John D. Barnhart. Pennsylvania Magazine of History and
Biography 78 (July):379-81.
    "Professor . . . Barnhart in this volume has reopened the
controversy over the validity of the well-known 'Turner thesis.'"

12 GLASER, WILLIAM A. "Algie Martin Simons and Marxism in America." Mississippi Valley Historical Review 41 (December):419-
34.
    Briefly comments on Turner's influence upon Simons, and dis-
cusses how Simons used the frontier thesis in examining the differences between American and European radicalism.

13 HARDIN, BAYLESS E. Review of Valley of Democracy, The Frontier
versus the Plantation in the Ohio Valley, 1775-1818, by John
D. Barnhart. Filson Club History Quarterly 28 (April):186-87.
    Views Barnhart's book as one contribution to "completing
Turner's work rather than in trying to refute it."

14 JACOBS, WILBUR R. "Frederick Jackson Turner--Master Teacher."
Pacific Historical Review 23 (February):49-50.
    Tribute to Turner as a great teacher. "Only by giving
proper balance to Turner the teacher and Turner the writer can
his correct place in American historiography be ascertained."

15 _____. "Wilson's First Battle at Princeton: The Chair for
Turner." Harvard Library Bulletin 8 (Winter):74-87.
    Explores the "abiding friendship" between Turner and
Woodrow Wilson, "Wilson's longtime ambition . . . to have Turner
with him on the same faculty," and Turner's influence upon
Wilson's writings.

16 KEYES, NELSON BEECHER. The American Frontier: Our Unique
Heritage. Garden City, N.Y.: Hanover House, 384 pp., passim.
    Claims that the frontier thesis is as relevant for the
America of the 1950s as it was in Turner's day.

1954

17 LONDON, LENA. "The Initial Homestead Exemption in Texas."
    Southwestern Historical Quarterly 17 (April):432-53.
        The "Homestead Exemption, so proudly hailed as an innovation
    of the genius of American frontiersmen, and often cited to sup-
    port the Turner thesis . . . was first incorporated into . . .
    law in Texas." Concludes that "Turner's thesis is valid in so
    far as it concerns homestead exemption."

18 MOOR, DEAN. "The Paxton Boys: Parkman's Frontier Hypothesis."
    Mid-America 36 (October):211-19.
        Briefly describes the implications of Turner's frontier hy-
    pothesis. Analyzes Francis Parkman's vision of history, making
    special references to his description of the Paxton conflict,
    showing that, like Turner after him, "Parkman was an evolutionist"
    who looked to the environment as a primary influencing factor.

19 NICHOLS, ROY F. "The Territories: Seedbeds of Democracy."
    Nebraska History 35 (September):159-72.
        Accepts Turner's belief that the frontier was a source of
    "self-renewal" and that "American democracy derives its strength
    from the fact that . . . the people" have experienced "over and
    over again the art of creating their own government." Also
    agrees with Turner that the closing of the frontier marked a
    major turning point in our nation's history.

20 PIERSON, GEORGE W. "The Moving American." Yale Review 44
    (Autumn):99-112.
        Argues that the typical American is a "Moving American";
    this cardinal characteristic of American culture in fact can be
    explained as a by-product of the frontier experience.

21 POTTER, DAVID M. "Abundance and the Frontier Hypothesis." In
    People of Plenty. Chicago: University of Chicago Press, pp.
    142-65.
        Discusses the relationship between the theories of abundance
    and of the frontier. By confining his explanation of American
    development to the frontier stages, Turner implies that "nothing
    distinctly American would be left, except as a residue, after the
    pioneer stage had been passed." Turner cuts himself off from the
    factors of technological advance, urban growth, and the higher
    standard of living, "all of which have contributed quite as much
    as the frontier to the fluidity and facility for change in Ameri-
    can life." Reprinted: 1958, 1965, 1966, 1973.27; pp. 154-60
    reprinted: 1966.30.

22 SAVETH, EDWARD N. "Historical Understanding in Democractic
    America." In Understanding the American Past. Boston: Little,
    Brown, pp. 3-64, passim.

1955

Discusses several approaches to American history, one of which (pp. 15-18) is "The Frontier Hypothesis." Turner, "shared some of the ideas of the Teutonists," but he rebelled against the notion that "the forces of race and historic continuity" were responsible for the development of our political institutions, and he stressed, instead, "changing environmental conditions." Also comments that "the implications of the Turner thesis were Jeffersonian and Jacksonian, not Marxian." Reprinted: 1965.

23 ULLMAN, EDWARD L. "Amenities as a Factor in Regional Growth." Geographical Review 44 (January):119-32.
    "The new 'frontier' of America is . . . a frontier of comfort, in contrast with the traditional frontier of hardship." Extends the Turner thesis by arguing that this factor of pleasant living conditions is perhaps the greatest stimulant to present regional growth.

1955

1 ANDERSON, JOHN M. "The Journey West: An American Orientation." In The Individual and the New World: A Study of Man's Existence Based Upon American Life and Thought. State College, Penn.: Bald Eagle Press, pp. 15-27.
    Like Turner, Anderson argues that for Americans the frontier experience "became a symbol of release from the repressive forms of the 'old' society of the Atlantic Coast" and a source of "new life." The author rejects Turner's environmentalism.

2 ANON. "The Sixth Newberry Library Conference on American Studies." Newberry Library Bulletin 3 (August):274-82.
    The transcript of a discussion of a paper by Merle Curti designed "to test empirically, within a small area which had undergone the transition from wilderness to settled community, Frederick Jackson Turner's thesis that democracy in America was the product of frontier experience." More than twenty eminent historians were involved in the dialogue.

3 BABCOCK, C. MERTON. Introduction to The American Frontier: A Social and Literary Record. Edited by C. Merton Babcock. New York: Holt, pp. 1-19.
    Approaches the subject of the frontier from a Turnerian point of view. Turner's "The Significance of the Frontier in American History" is included in the volume.

1955

4 BARKER, CHARLES ALBRO. "Before the World: <u>Progress and Poverty</u>." In <u>Henry George</u>. New York: Oxford University Press, pp. 265-304.
    Argues that Henry George "anticipated" Turner's frontier thesis.

5 CURTI, MERLE. "The Democratic Theme in American Historical Literature." In <u>Probing Our Past</u>. New York: Harper, pp. 3-31.
    Reprint of 1952.5; reprinted: 1962.

6 _____. "Frederick Jackson Turner, 1861-1932." In <u>Probing Our Past</u>. New York: Harper & Brothers, pp. 32-55.
    Reprint of 1949.4; reprinted: Gloucester, Mass.: Peter Smith, 1962.

7 _____. "Intellectuals and Other People." <u>American Historical Review</u> 60 (January):259-82.
    Discusses the trend of anti-intellectualism in America. Proposes that the frontier sentiment has been one of the factors contributing to the suspicion of intellectualism. The utilitarian cast of the frontier experience stands in opposition to "book learning." "The intellectual represents specialization and re-flection: the frontier cherished versatility and action."

8 DEGLER, CARL N. "The West as a Solution to Urban Unemploy-ment." <u>New York History</u> 36 (January):63-85.
    Argues that a Turnerian-type safety valve served to relieve the mounting social pressures created within New York City as a result of the economic difficulties of the 1850s.

9 GORER, GEOFFREY. Review of <u>People of Plenty: Economic Abundance and the American Character</u>, by David Potter. <u>American Quarterly</u> 7 (Summer):182-86.
    "The main section of . . . Potter's book is an examination of the impact of the idea and fact of economic abundance on various American institutions; and the key of this section is the re-evaluation of F.J. Turner's epoch-making <u>Significance of the Frontier in American History</u>."

10 HICKS, JOHN D. "The American Tradition of Democracy." In <u>The American Tradition</u>. Boston: Houghton Mifflin, pp. 1-18.
    Reprint of 1953.11; reprinted: Westport, Conn.: Greenwood Press, 1973.

11 _____. "The 'Ecology' of Middle-Western Historians." In <u>The American Tradition</u>. Boston: Houghton Mifflin, pp. 59-66.
    Reprint of 1941.9; reprinted: Westport, Conn.: Greenwood Press, 1973.

12 _____. "State and Local History." In <u>The American Tradition</u>.
   Boston: Houghton Mifflin, pp. 93–108.
      Reprint of 1955.13; reprinted: Westport, Conn.: Greenwood
   Press, 1973.

13 _____. "State and Local History." <u>Wisconsin Magazine of His-</u>
   <u>tory</u> 39 (Winter):130–37.
      Turner's "genius was perhaps best manifest in his ability
   to inspire others to write." Reprinted: 1955.12.

14 HOCKETT, HOMER CAREY. <u>The Critical Method in Historical Re-</u>
   <u>search and Writing</u>. New York: Macmillan, pp. vii–xv passim,
   and 225, 231, 234–38.
      Evaluates Turner's contribution to the writing of history
   and concludes that "it may be doubted whether any other scholar
   of the present century has equaled his influence." Revised:
   1963.

15 HOFSTADTER, RICHARD. "The Frontier or the Market?" In <u>The</u>
   <u>Age of Reform: From Bryan to F.D.R</u>. New York: Alfred A.
   Knopf, pp. 46–59.
      Challenges the "conclusion that it was the West, the fron-
   tier spirit, that produced American democracy, and that Populism
   was the logical product of this spirit. . . ." Claims that this
   belief "is a deceptive influence from the Turnerian school." Rejects Turner's safety-valve formula on the grounds that urbanites
   could not get free land in the West. Reprinted: 1961, 1963,
   1972, 1977.

16 JOHANNSEN, ROBERT W. Preface to <u>Frontier Politics on the Eve</u>
   <u>of the Civil War</u>. Seattle: University of Washington Press,
   pp. vii–ix.
      "American historiography of the last half century has been
   characterized by a preoccupation with the American frontier" because of the influence of "Turner's provocative essay of 1893."

17 MALIN, JAMES C. "Exploited Interpretation." In <u>The Contriving</u>
   <u>Brain and the Skillful Hand in the United States</u>. Lawrence,
   Kans.: James C. Malin, pp. 1–2.
      Argues that "the cult of the West, or the frontier inter-
   pretation of United States history . . . under the inspiration of
   Frederick Jackson Turner" did not result in a major reorientation
   of the historiography of the mid-nineteenth century as is commonly
   assumed. Reprinted: 1959.

18 _____. "Geographical Space Concept: Anglo-American New-land
   Version." In <u>The Contriving Brain and the Skillful Hand</u>.
   Lawrence, Kans.: James C. Malin, pp. 338–436.

1955

Critical of Turner's alleged environmental determinism for
its "logical contradiction. . . . If the geographical factor of
. . . the open frontier . . . had determined the character of
American society, logically . . . [the] closed frontier . . .
should deprive the United States of the same features." Acknowledges that "after sixty-odd years . . . of the stereotyped Turner
frontier hypothesis" its influence is "so pervasive" that even
critics are not able to avoid its influence. Reprinted: 1959.

19 MARSHALL, PETER. "The Great Frontier." Past and Present, no.
    7 (April):55-62.
        Places Walter Prescott Webb's The Great Frontier "within a
firmly established tradition, that of the 'frontier hypothesis.'"
Attempts to document the degree to which Webb's "ideas originate
directly from Turner's" writings.

20 NETTLES, CURTIS P. "History Out of Wisconsin." Wisconsin
    Magazine of History 39 (Winter):113-25.
        Credits Turner with contributing to the establishment of
the State Historical Society of Wisconsin and making one of
the outstanding state journals in the nation. But hastens to add
that "without . . . the large, unified, and accessible collection"
of the Society, "Turner's work could not have been done." Observes that "Turner became eminent because he was the foremost
interpreter of the United States."

21 POMEROY, EARL. "Toward a Reorientation of Western History:
    Continuity and Environment." Mississippi Valley Historical
    Review 41 (March):579-600.
        "To Turner the frontier was a cause that acted ultimately
on the East; but now the effects that he thought he saw seem to
have other causes, if they exist at all." After elaborating upon
this theme, Pomeroy comes to the conclusion that the "Westerner
has been fundamentally imitator rather than innovator and . . .
his culture was Western European rather than aboriginal. He was
often the most ardent of conformists." The West was influenced
by the East more than vice-versa. Reprinted (with omissions):
1966.29.

22 SHARP, PAUL F. "Three Frontiers: Some Comparative Studies of
    Canadian, American, and Australian Settlement." Pacific His-
    torical Review 24 (November):369-77.
        A response to "Turner's challenge" that "'we should compare
those'" frontiers of "'other countries which have dealt with
similar problems,'" thereby availing ourselves of "an opportunity
to explore in detail the differences that mark the expansion of
western civilization into . . . sparsely settled areas as well as
to investigate the similarities." Abridged version reprinted:
1970.26.

1956

23 SHARP, PAUL. Whoop-up Country: The Canadian-American West,
    1865-1885. Minneapolis: University of Minnesota Press, 347
    pp., passim.
        Focuses upon the influence of the frontier environment on
    institutional development in both Canadian and American develop-
    ment. Turnerian in approach and assumptions. Reprinted: His-
    torical Society of Montana, 1960; University of Oklahoma Press,
    1973.

24 SORENSON, LLOYD R. "Historical Currents in America." American
    Quarterly 7 (Fall):234-46.
        Traces the rise of "scientific history." Turner opposed
    the scientific school by denying the germ theory and by criticizing
    the "historiographical foundation on which that theory rested."
    Turner argues that unless historians used a "multiple hypothesis"
    method, they could not be writing scientific history.

25 WILLIAMS, WILLIAM APPLEMAN. "The Frontier Thesis: An Ameri-
    can Foreign Policy." Pacific Historical Review 24 (November):
    379-95.
        "The argument here . . . is that a set of ideas, first pro-
    mulgated in the 1890s, became the world view of subsequent genera-
    tions of Americans and is an important clue to understanding
    America's imperial expansion in the twentieth century. One idea
    is . . . Turner's concept that America's unique and true democ-
    racy was the product of an expanding frontier." The objective of
    the article is to "gauge the nature and extent of the impact which
    his [Turner's] frontier thesis had on American foreign policy."
    Concludes that Turner "was the apostle of a revival movement that
    restored the faith of the conquerors of North America and made
    them international crusaders." Reprinted: 1973.35.

26 WRIGHT, LOUIS B. "The Colonial Struggle Against Barbarism."
    In Culture on the Moving Frontier. Bloomington: Indiana
    University Press, pp. 11-45, passim.
        Critical of Turner for having overlooked the eastern
    "minority of cultural bearers" who transplanted "elements of
    traditional civilization on each successive frontier." Points to
    eastern and European sources to explain the development of Amer-
    ican culture and by implication rejects Turner's frontier explana-
    tion, which underscored the uniqueness of American culture. Re-
    printed: 1966; New York: Harper & Row, 1961.

1956

1   ANDERSON, PER SVEAAS. Westward Is the Course of Empire; A
    Study in the Shaping of an American Idea; Frederick Jackson

1956

Turner's Frontier. Oslo, Norway: Oslo University Press, 133 pp., passim.
"The subject matter of this thesis is the genesis . . . of a great idea," namely, Turner's concept that the American frontier was "an omnipresent and omnipotent force" in American history. Three chapters, entitled "The American Frontier, Its Historian, and His Critics," "The Frontier Theory," and "Frederick Jackson Turner, His Times and Circumstances, a Biographical Postscript," reflect the Turnerian approach of this monograph.

2 DOWD, DOUGLAS F. "A Comparative Analysis of Economic Development in the American West and South." Journal of Economic History 16 (December):558-74.
Challenges Turner's ideas by showing how national economic institutions impacted the American West. Rejects the Turnerian assumption, as expressed by Walter Prescott Webb, that the West "bent and molded Anglo-American life, . . . destroyed traditions, and . . . influenced institutions in a most singular manner." Economically "western development was ancillary to that taking place to the east of it."

3 ELKINS, STANLEY, and ERIC McKITRICK. "A Meaning for Turner's Frontier, Democracy in the Old Northwest." In The Turner Thesis: Concerning the Role of the Frontier in American History. Rev. ed. Edited by George Rogers Clark. Problems in American Civilization series. Boston: D.C. Heath, pp. 96-107.
Reprint of 1954.9; reprinted: 1972.

4 FOWKE, VERNON C. "National Policy and Western Development in North America." Journal of Economic History 16 (December): 461-79.
Theories such as Turner's regarding the West lend "credence to a hypothesis . . . that history is comprised of the examination of a succession of conceptual anachronisms devised in each case by the historian's generation for the solution of contemporary problems and applied as an afterthought to the reconstruction of the past." Thus, "Turner advanced the frontier thesis as a tool of analysis of the past at a time when major concern was arising over the frontier's disappearance."

5 GREEN, FLETCHER MELVIN. "Resurgent Southern Sectionalism, 1933-1955." North Carolina Historical Review 33 (April):222-40.
Observes that "sectionalism which, as Frederick Jackson Turner so interestingly pointed out in his Significance of Sections in American History, has lain dormant but may, under sufficient provocation, gain vitality at any time." Views the South of the mid-twentieth century as a prime example of the reoccuring vitality of a Turnerian type of sectionalism. Reprinted: 1969.12.

1956

6 HICKS, JOHN D. "Our Pioneer Heritage: A Reconsideration."
   Prairie Schooner 30 (Winter):359-61.
      Acknowledges that as a young historian he was "under the
   spell of Frederick Jackson Turner's frontier thesis" and as a result tried to make it explain "far more than Turner meant it to
   explain." Cites specific weaknesses of his earlier pro-Turner
   history.

7 KEMMERER, DONALD L. "The Changing Pattern of American Economic
   Development." Journal of Economic History 16 (December):575-
   89.
      Argues that "the United States has in less than two cen-
   turies passed out of an era of cheap land, to one of cheap labor,
   and then to one of cheap capital." Notes that during the process
   of settlement, "it was the prospect of acquiring one's own land,
   and cheaply too, that attracted Europeans here and that pulled
   settlers westward."

8 MILLER, PERRY. Errand into the Wilderness. Cambridge, Mass.:
   Belknap Press, pp. 1-2.
      Turner has done "so much to confuse as to clarify" the
   issue of the wilderness. He is the "foremost . . . victim of his
   fallacy, rather than the master of it." Emphasizes European
   determinants of American culture. Reprinted: 1964, 1978.

9 NORTH, DOUGLASS C. "International Capital Flows and the
   Development of the American West." Journal of Economic History
   16 (December):493-505.
      Deals with "the pace of westward development and the influ-
   ence of the international economy . . . upon that development in
   the years from 1820 to 1860." Challenges one aspect of Turner's
   thesis by suggesting that the "demand for certain staple com-
   modities in the European . . . market" influenced westward expansion as much as the appeal of the West itself.

10 OSBORN, GEORGE C. "Woodrow Wilson and Frederick Jackson
   Turner." New Jersey Historical Society, Proceedings 74
   (July):208-29.
      Explores the close relationship between Turner and Wilson
   based upon their shared experiences at Johns Hopkins and their
   correspondence from 1889 to 1902.

11 PARKER, EDITH H. "William Graham Sumner and the Frontier."
   Southwest Review 41 (Autumn):357-65.
      William Graham Sumner "anticipated by several years"
   Turner's frontier thesis. "I would conclude that by 1893 [the
   date Turner read his now famous paper on the frontier] Sumner had
   evolved in pretty complete form his philosophy of the Frontier,

117

1956

and that within his writings can be found the most important
ideas set forth by Turner." Does not claim that Turner was aware
of Sumner's views or was directly influenced by him.

12 RIEGEL, ROBERT E. "American Frontier Theory." Journal of
World History 3, no. 2:356-80.
      Thorough treatment of the historiography of Turner's fron-
tier theory with an emphasis upon the ebb and flow of its influences and popularity. Focuses upon the ways in which Turner's
views have been modified or rejected. Concludes that the "frontier theory remains today a direct result of the imaginative
thinking of Frederick Jackson Turner, who was one of the few historians of his day to make a . . . permanent contribution to historical thought." In spite of the massive criticism of Turner's
ideas, critics have failed to offer a "new set of generalizations"
that shed as much light on American history as those of Turner.

13 _____. "The Historian and the American Frontier." Montana:
The Magazine of Western History 6 (April):16-21.
      "The greatest popularizer of the frontier for the historian
was Frederick Jackson Turner" and "his ideas were accepted rather
rapidly and apparently seemed to many . . . as divinely inspired."
Assesses Turner's impact upon the writing of western history.

14 SMITH, CHARLOTTE WATKINS. Carl Becker: On History and the
Climate of Opinion. Ithaca, N.Y.: Cornell University Press,
pp. 1, 6, 9, 15, 17, 19-20, 45, 47-48, 65-66, 197.
      Explores Turner's contribution to the intellectual develop-
ment of the famous historian Carl Becker. Reprinted: Southern
Illinois University Press, 1973.

15 STERN, FRITZ. "An American Definition of History: Turner."
In The Varieties of History from Voltaire to the Present.
Edited by Fritz Stern. New York: Meridian Books, pp. 197-208.
      Turner's "The Significance of History" is introduced with
the assertion that the "work of Frederick Jackson Turner . . .
opened a new era in American historiography." Reprinted: 1965,
1970, 1973.

16 WEBB, WALTER PRESCOTT. "The Frontier and the 400 Year Boom."
In The Turner Thesis: Concerning the Role of the Frontier in
American History. Rev. ed. Edited by George Rogers Clark.
Problems in American Civilization Series. Boston: D.C. Heath,
pp. 87-95.
      Reprint of 1951.18; reprinted: 1972.

17 YOUNGER, RICHARD D. "The Grand Jury on the Frontier." <u>Wisconsin Magazine of History</u> 40 (Autumn):3-8, 56.
    Examines the use of the grand jury in frontier societies. Argues that "few imported institutions were as adaptable to the spirit of the frontier as was the grand jury."

<u>1957</u>

1 ABERNETHY, THOMAS PERKINS. "The Southern Frontier, An Interpretation." In <u>The Frontier in Perspective</u>. Edited by Walker D. Wyman and Clifton B. Kroeber. Madison: University of Wisconsin Press, pp. 129-42.
   The first phase of the southern frontier was very different from Turner's description of the frontier in America. The first settlers modeled the English forms and they were far from being self-sufficient. As the boundary of the frontier advanced, however, it became more and more "truly approximated [to] the Turnerian pattern."

2 AGARD, WALTER A. "Classics on the Midwest Frontier." In <u>The Frontier in Perspective</u>. Edited by Walter D. Wyman and Clifton B. Kroeber. Madison: University of Wisconsin Press, pp. 165-83.
   Turner's thesis asserts that the Midwest frontier had relinquished its European past in view of more original development. Suggests, however, that the "classics" of Greece and Rome, though by no means great, did play a contributing role to the development of the Midwest. "As we examine the evidence furnished by architecture, education, and the churches, libraries, and press, we find that they [the classics] provided intellectual and artistic nourishment for the pioneers."

3 ALLEN, H.C. "F.J. Turner and the Frontier in American History." In <u>British Essays in American History</u>. Edited by H.C. Allen and C.P. Hill. New York: St. Martin's Press, pp. 145-66.
   Presents Turner as "perhaps the most influential figure in American historiography." Praises him for having seen "clearly that what American history needed was far less emphasis on heredity and far more stress on environment." After briefly assessing the "influences upon Turner," Allen underscores the fact that "his influence extended far beyond academic circles, for he had a direct effect upon Wilson and . . . Theodore Roosevelt and an indirect effect upon a whole generation of his countrymen." Defends Turner and rejects the historiography critical of Turner's thesis. Reprinted: 1966.1.

119

1957

4 BILLINGTON, RAY ALLEN. "Turner and the Frontier Hypothesis."
   Westerners Brand Book (Chicago) 14 (November):65-67, 71-72.
      Outlines Turner's frontier thesis and discusses the validity
of some of the criticisms leveled at it. In the political arena
and elsewhere, however, "practical applications of the frontier
hypothesis and its demonstrated influence on the nation's development suggest that its critics have been unable to destroy its
effectiveness as a key to the understanding of American history."

5 BOARDMAN, EUGENE P. "Chinese Mandarins and Western Traders:
   The Effect of the Frontier in Chinese History." In The Frontier in Perspective. Edited by Walker D. Wyman and Clifton B.
   Kroeber. Madison: University of Wisconsin Press, pp. 95-110.
      Despite the criticism of Turner's thesis, two major themes
are important: the influence of the frontier on attitudes and
institutions and the factor of environment. These themes are
used in examining the Chinese frontier. Concludes that, converse
to the American frontier experience, the Chinese frontier proved
to be an impediment, "delaying necessary change and handicapping
their twentieth-century reach for adequacy."

6 BURLINGAME, ROGER. "Morality on the Frontier." In The American Conscience. New York: Alfred A. Knopf, pp. 205-17.
      Subscribes to Turner's assumption that the frontier environ-
ment freed men from the restraints of the established East.

7 BURT, A.L. "If Turner Had Looked at Canada, Australia, and
   New Zealand When He Wrote About the West." In The Frontier in
   Perspective. Edited by Walker D. Wyman and Clifton B. Kroeber.
   Madison: University of Wisconsin Press, pp. 59-77.
      On the surface, the form of the French frontier in America
seems to contradict Turner's thesis, but upon closer examination,
one would find a "surprising confirmation" of it. Claims that it
was "physically impossible" for French feudalism to exist in the
frontier. Also notes that by looking across the globe to British
colonization of Australia and New Zealand, Turner "would have
found a striking contrast that throws a flood of light upon his
thesis."

8 CASSIDY, FREDERICK G. "Language on the American Frontier."
   In The Frontier in Perspective. Edited by Walker D. Wyman and
   Clifton B. Kroeber. Madison: University of Wisconsin Press,
   pp. 185-204.
      The English language has undergone a relatively major trans-
formation during the American experience, which "is the direct
result of what happened on the American frontier."

9 CATTON, BRUCE. "Half-Horse, Half-Alligator." <u>American Heritage</u> 9 (December):109-10.
    "No article of faith has had greater force with us than the one which centers around the era of the great frontier and its part in forming the American character. The precise formulation of this article of faith was probably best undertaken by Frederick Jackson Turner who saw the distinctive quality of American character and institutions as deriving from the frontier experience." Turner's thesis is cited as a prime example of the Americans' need "to create their own traditions" and "legends."

10 GATES, PAUL W. "Frontier Estate Builders and Farm Laborers." In <u>The Frontier in Perspective</u>. Edited by Walker D. Wyman and Clifton B. Kroeber. Madison: University of Wisconsin Press, pp. 143-63.
    Too little attention has been given to farm laborers by western historians. Their numbers were large, and their presence, along with the presence of land speculators, indicates a more complex social arrangement in the Middle West than is generally acknowledged. As a result, "concepts of homogeneity of frontier society, similarity of frontier outlook, common addiction to democratic principles, may well be questioned." Reprinted: 1968.11.

11 HALLOWELL, A. IRVING. "The Backwash of the Frontier: The Impact of the Indian on American Culture." In <u>The Frontier in Perspective</u>. Edited by Walker D. Wyman and Clifton B. Kroeber. Madison: University of Wisconsin Press, pp. 229-58.
    Frederick Jackson Turner and his followers made only passing reference to the influence of the Indian on American culture. However, "it is the Indian's continuing presence throughout our whole colonial and national history that has given many aspects of our culture a special coloring." Reprinted: 1967.7.

12 HOCKETT, HOMER C. "Turner's Vision." <u>Wisconsin Magazine of History</u> 41 (Autumn):53.
    Complains that "most of Turner's critics seem not to know that he wrote anything except 'The Significance of the Frontier.'" They miss the important fact that "his last essays show" a "broadening of view."

13 LERNER, MAX. "American History as Extended Genesis." In <u>America as a Civilization: Life and Thought in the United States Today</u>. New York: Simon & Schuster, pp. 35-39.
    Although Turner's frontier thesis had many "blandishments, it could not have had its impact without a core of validity. Turner had a deep insight into the conditions under which the crucial American institutions were shaped." Turner's "insight" is explored.

1957

14 _____ . "Why Was America a Success?" In America as a Civilization: Life and Thought in the United States. New York:
Simon & Schuster, pp. 28-35.
Develops the generalization that "one of the most interesting
efforts to explain American success was the Turner theory of the
moving frontier."

15 LOBANOV-ROSTOVSKY, A. "Russian Expansion in the Far East in
the Light of the Turner Hypothesis." In The Frontier in Perspective. Edited by Walker D. Wyman and Clifton B. Kroeber.
Madison: University of Wisconsin Press, pp. 79-94.
Turner's frontier hypothesis is applicable to the Russian
frontier. If the Cossacks of Russia are compared with the American pioneers, striking similarities can be found. The starting
points and the basic goals of each are the same, and the phases
or waves of migration are nearly identical. The main difference,
however, was that "Turner did not have to face . . . the existence
of two parallel, expanding, and competing frontiers" in his examination of America. Reprinted: 1967.12.

16 MACKENDRICK, PAUL L. "Roman Colonization and the Frontier Hypothesis." In The Frontier in Perspective. Edited by Walker
D. Wyman and Clifton B. Kroeber. Madison: University of Wisconsin Press, pp. 3-19.
Looks at the expansion of the Roman empire "through the
eyes of Frederick Jackson Turner," and finds it "a salutary and
refreshing experience." Finds many similarities, and finds the
differences to be equally instructive, differences that "might
not have been observed if Turner had not pointed the way."

17 MALIN, JAMES C. "On the Nature of Local History." Wisconsin
Magazine of History 40 (Summer):227-30.
Argues that history needs to be written "from the bottom
up" instead of from the top down, with sound evidence and tangible
support. Valid history is not "a popularized and emasculated
product . . . dressed in artificial 'literary' terms"; rather, it
"challenges the intellectual capacity of the author and the reader
both in form and substance." Implicit here is a critique of
Turner.

18 MOORE, ARTHUR K. The Frontier Mind: A Cultural Analysis of
the Kentucky Frontiersman. Lexington: University of Kentucky
Press, 264 pp., passim.
"Turner's widely applauded interpretation" of the frontier
"is selective, uncritical, and lacking in rear vision." Turner
was wrong when he assumed that "men in a state of nature could
. . . create an adequate culture virtually from nothing" or when
he "tended to slight the continuing influence on the emigrants of

some of the noblest concepts of the enlightenment." Instead of
producing a superior American culture as Turner argued, the frontier experience produced a culture inferior to its European
counterpart. Traces most of the desirable characteristics of the
Kentucky frontier back to the eastern seaboard or to Europe. Reprinted: 1981; New York: McGraw-Hill, 1963.

19 NADEL, GEORGE. Australia's Colonial Culture: Ideas, Men and
    Institutions in Mid-Nineteenth Century Eastern Australia.
    Melbourne: F.C. Cheshire, 304 pp., passim.
        Rejects the Turnerian focus upon the agrarian, frontier
    origins of national characteristics and emphasizes the urban
    origin of cultural characteristics of New South Wales.

20 NEUMARK, S. DANIEL. Economic Influences on the South African
    Frontier, 1652-1836. Food Research Institute, miscellaneous
    publication 12. Stanford: Stanford University Press, 196 pp.,
    passim.
        Argues that the part of the Turner thesis that credited the
    frontier with stimulating democracy, self-sufficient households,
    and independent individualism does not hold true for South Africa.
    The frontier economy of South Africa was an "exchange economy"
    deeply dependent upon the outside world. Concludes that "in this
    respect the South African frontier was not unique and bears com-
    parison with frontier expansion in America." Finds that "as in
    the Americas . . . , the impelling force of expansion in South
    Africa came largely from the world outside the frontier-form . . .
    trading centers" rather than from the intrinsic pull of the fron-
    tier as Turner suggested.

21 REYNOLDS, ROBERT L. "The Mediterranean Frontiers, 1000-1400."
    In The Frontier in Perspective. Edited by Walker D. Wyman and
    Clifton B. Kroeber. Madison: University of Wisconsin Press,
    pp. 21-34.
        Several of the factors present in the frontier experience
    of America were also present in the European expansion into the
    Mediterranean area, namely, motivation by lack of opportunity,
    population pressure, and the frontier evolution. Also examines
    the frontier from a vantage point virtually ignored by Turner,
    that of those who are being advanced upon rather than those who
    are advancing.

22 SMITH, HENRY NASH. "Mark Twain as an Interpreter of the Far
    West: The Structure of Roughing It." In The Frontier in Per-
    spective. Edited by Walker D. Wyman and Clifton B. Kroeber.
    Madison: University of Wisconsin Press, pp. 205-28.
        Roughing It is divided into two major sections: the tender-
    foot's experience in the far western frontier and his return to

1957

urban life after the frontier initiation. Twain contributes to
the mythologizing of the frontier, and his "emotion underlies the
belief that the basic virtues of the American character and American institutions are derived from the frontier past. . . ."

23 TINGLEY, DONALD F. Review of The Frontier Mind, A Cultural
   Analysis of the Kentucky Frontiersman, by Arthur K. Moore.
   Illinois State Historical Society, Journal 1 (Winter):434-35.
       "Professor Moore seems to assume that all historians are
   dedicated to the ideas of social evolution as propounded by
   Frederick Jackson Turner." Furthermore, he "distorts the Turner
   thesis."

24 TREADGOLD, DONALD W. The Great Siberian Migration: Government
   and Peasant in Resettlement from Emancipation to the First
   World War. Princeton, N.J.: Princeton University Press, 278
   pp.
       Expanded version of 1952.16; reprinted: Westport, Conn.:
   Greenwood Press, 1976.

25 WEBB, WALTER PRESCOTT. "The Western World Frontier." In The
   Frontier in Perspective. Edited by Walker D. Wyman and Clifton
   B. Kroeber. Madison: University of Wisconsin Press, pp. 111-
   26.
       Argues that Turner's thesis is valid not only for America
   but for the world. Groups all of the "little frontiers," of
   which the American frontier is a part, into the "Great Frontier"
   of world history and applies the frontier thesis to it.

26 WINTHER, OSCAR O. "The Frontier Hypothesis and the Historian."
   Social Education 21 (November):294-98.
       Surveys social-science textbooks identifying the varied
   ways in which Turner's ideas are presented in them. Includes
   textbooks on the primary, secondary, and college levels. Concludes that in spite of the growing criticism of Turner's views,
   "historians are as one in recognizing the potency and originality
   of Turner's ideas."

27 WYMAN, WALKER D., and CLIFTON B. KROEBER. Introduction to The
   Frontier in Perspective. Madison: University of Wisconsin
   Press, pp. xiii-xx.
       Introduces the thirteen essays that follow. "The signifi-
   cance of Turner's propositions is that they have been so widely
   held as assumptions about the American past. It is now time to
   reconsider the frontier in the prospective of world history. . . ."

28 ZAVALA, SILVIO. "The Frontiers of Hispanic America." Translated by Clifton B. Kroeber. In The Frontier in Perspective.

Edited by Walker D. Wyman and Clifton B. Kroeber. Madison: University of Wisconsin Press, pp. 35-58.
Doubts that the Turner thesis applies to the Spanish-Mexican experience, but suggests that the evidence is not all in for a conclusive statement.

1958

1 BARTLETT, RICHARD A. "Freedom and the Frontier: A Pertinent Re-examination." Mid-America 40 (July):131-38.
Turner's thesis is still valuable today in giving historical direction and in helping "to understand ourselves," especially as it relates to the concept of freedom. Freedom on the frontier never meant license; "always there were a few restrictions, always there was the recognized moral law, even if it was not enforced." Today, however, "the frontier freedoms are being crushed by the insecurity of modern society." Suggests that Americans need to regain the "sense of confidence" and the "spirit of freedom" that flourished on the frontier.

2 BILLINGTON, RAY ALLEN. The American Frontier. Service Center for Teachers of History, publication no. 8. Washington, D.C.: Service Center for Teachers of History, 32 pp.
Claims that "for more than half a century the most useful--and controversial--concept employed in interpreting American history has been the 'frontier hypothesis.'" The pamphlet includes sections entitled: "Criticisms of the Frontier Hypothesis," "Turner the Historian," "The Frontier Hypothesis Today," "Expansion of the Frontier Hypothesis," and "The Frontier and Modern Society." Reprinted: 1967.2; expanded: 1971.5.

3 _____. "The Garden of the World: Fact and Fiction." In The Heritage of the Middle West. Edited by John J. Murray. Norman: University of Oklahoma Press, pp. 27-53.
Develops the idea that two frontiers have existed "throughout America's" history; "one was a frontier of fact . . . the other was a frontier of myth." Americans have been as influenced by what they have "believed the frontier to be as . . . by what the frontier actually was."

4 _____. "How the Frontier Shaped the American Character." American Heritage 9 (April):4-9, 86-89.
Observes that "historians have labored . . . to answer the famous question posed by Hector St. John de Crèvecoeur in the eighteenth century: 'what then is the American, this new man?' . . . the most widely accepted--and bitterly disputed--answer was advanced by . . . Frederick Jackson Turner in 1893." This article

1958

attempts to answer two questions: "How has it [Turner's frontier theory] fared" in the "battle of words" surrouding it? "Is it still a valid key to the meaning of American history?" Reprinted: 1966.6.

5 BILLINGTON, RAY A[LLEN]. Introduction to "Some Aspects of Turner's Thought." Agricultural History 32 (October):250.
      Outlines the historiography of the Turner thesis from 1893 to 1958. Introduces papers by Norman J. Simler (see 1958.25) and Gilman Ostrander (see 1958.18).

6 BINGHAM, EDWIN R. Review of The Frontier Mind: A Cultural Analysis of the Kentucky Frontiersman, by Arthur K. Moore. Oregon Historical Quarterly 59 (December):349-50.
      While making it "clear that he has joined the ranks of Frederick Jackson Turner critics," Moore's "Kentuckian who emerges from this book . . . supports Turner's" views. Furthermore "Moore seems insufficiently aware of the modifications made in the Turner thesis by the last generation of interpreters of the American West."

7 BOGUE, ALLAN. "The Iowa Claim Clubs: Symbol and Substance." Mississippi Valley Historical Review 45 (September):231-53.
      Analyzes "the frontier claim club as an illustration of social interaction in newly formed frontier groups." At times, the claim clubs were protective of individual settlers, and at other times, they acted as "the vehicle of men who sought simply to capitalize on priority. . . ." Abridged version reprinted: 1970.5.

8 _____. "Pioneer Farming and Innovation." Iowa Journal of History 56 (January):1-36.
      Lends support to the part of the Turner thesis that attri- buted inventions to the frontier environment. Presents a case study of one county in Iowa.

9 CARMONY, DONALD F. Review of The Frontier in Perspective, edited by Walker D. Wyman and Clifton B. Kroeber. Indiana Magazine of History 54 (December):397-98.
      Although "the editors urged the authors to take the Turner thesis . . . as a reference point, . . . this volume . . . does not come to grips with Turner's ideas."

10 COLEMAN, PETER. "The New Zealand Frontier and the Turner Thesis." Pacific Historical Review 27 (August):221-37.
      "The central weakness of the Turner thesis . . . is that it assumes that so long as there is an abundance of space, certain conditions in society will be produced." Asserts that "the

1958

important factor to be considered is not space but rather the
preconceptions of those who" peopled the frontier. Men and their
ideas were more basic than the environment in the creation of
frontier culture in New Zealand.

11 CRAVEN, AVERY. Introduction to The United States, 1830-1850:
    The Nation and Its Sections, by Frederick Jackson Turner.
    Gloucester, Mass.: Peter Smith, pp. v-ix.
      Traces the development of Turner's mind prior to the com-
pletion of this work, which "extended over a period of some
fifteen years."

12 ELLIOT, CLAUDE. Review of The Frontier in Perspective, edited
    by Walker D. Wyman and Clifton B. Kroeber. Southwestern His-
    torical Quarterly 62 (July):130-32.
      Turner "precipitated a great debate which has continued to
the present. . . . It is kept so constantly before everyone that
a little doggerel seems justified: Oh, Turner, Turner, Turner,
please excuse the slur, Oh why, why, why, did you write that
thesis fur?"

13 GRESSLEY, GENE M. "The Turner Thesis--A Problem in Historiog-
    raphy." Agricultural History 32 (October):227-49.
      Attempts to explain the rise of the "frontier school" in
American historiography and traces the emergence of criticism
after 1930. Underscores the voluminous interpretations and the
variety of ways in which Turner's thesis has been exploited. Reprinted: 1968.13.

14 HANCOCK, WILLIAM KEITH. "Trek." Economic History Review, 2d
    ser. 10 (April):331-39.
      Examines two conflicting analyses concerning the South
African frontier.

15 HAYES, CARLTON J.H. "The American Frontier--Frontier of What?"
    In Literature for Our Time. 3d ed. Edited by Harlow O. Waite
    and Benjamin P. Atkinson. New York: Holt, pp. 833-42.
      Reprint of 1946.6; reprinted: Freeport, N.Y.: Books for
Libraries Press, 1970.

16 MALIN, JAMES C. Review of The Frontier in Perspective, edited
    by Walker D. Wyman and Clifton B. Kroeber. Oregon Historical
    Quarterly 59 (June):164-65.
      Complains that although this volume was done in honor of
Lyman C. Draper, the "pervasive theme is the 'frontier' and
Frederick Jackson Turner--Draper being mentioned only in the
preface."

1958

17 MILLER, JAMES E. "My Antonia: A Frontier Drama of Time."
    American Quarterly 10 (Winter):476-84.
        Suggests that Willa Cather's "My Antonia exemplifies superbly
    Turner's concept of the recurring cultural evolution on the fron-
    tier."

18 OSTRANDER, GILMAN M. "Turner and the Germ Theory." Agricul-
    tural History 32 (October):258-61.
        Attempts to document the generalization that "Turner's fron-
    tier thesis was based upon" the contemporary assumption "that
    political habits are determined by innate racial attributes."
    Suggests that "the Turnerian hypothesis concerning the frontier
    origins of American democracy has remained possible only by the
    implicit retention of . . . old and no longer reputable racial
    assumptions." Reprinted: 1968.38.

19 ROBINSON, ELWYN B. "Theodore Roosevelt: Amateur Historian."
    North Dakota History 25 (January):5-13.
        Explores the importance of the relationship between
    Roosevelt and Turner and in the process assesses the latter as
    "easily the brightest star of the rising generation of professional
    historians."

20 ROSTOW, WALT WHITMAN. "The American National Style." Daedelus
    87 (Spring):110-44.
        Draws upon Turner's thesis in an effort to capture the es-
    sence of what he calls "the American National Style."

21 SELLERS, CHARLES GRIER, Jr. "Andrew Jackson versus the His-
    torians." Mississippi Valley Historical Review 44 (March):
    615-34.
        Links Turner with the progressive historians who use the
    concepts of Jacksonian Democracy as a major focus for historical
    interpretation and as a central theme in the definition of the
    American experience.

22 _____. Jacksonian Democracy. Service Center for Teachers of
    History, publication no. 9. Washington, D.C.: Service Center
    for Teachers of History, 18 pp., passim.
        Without challenging Turner's dominance in the historiography
    of Westward expansion, Sellers believes that "Turner's real sig-
    nificance lies less in his controversial frontier thesis than in
    his influence as leader of the massive shift of American histo-
    riography to a pro-democratic orientation." Underscores his in-
    fluence upon the historiography of Jacksonian democracy.

23 SHANNON, FRED A. "To the Editor." Agricultural History 32
    (October):257.

1958

Refutation of Norman J. Simler's article (see 1958.25) supporting Turner's safety-valve theory.

24 SHARP, PAUL. "From Poverty to Prosperity." In The Heritage
    of the Middle West. Edited by John J. Murry. Norman: University of Oklahoma Press, pp. 54-72.
        Uses the Turner thesis to explain the economic success of
    the Middle West as well as the impact of that success upon midwestern culture.

25 SIMLER, NORMAN J. "The Safety-Valve Doctrine Re-evaluated."
    Agricultural History 32 (October):250-57.
        Reviews briefly the controversy regarding Turner's safety-valve concept with the objective of lending "some credence to
    what appears to be a thoroughly discredited doctrine." Reprinted:
    1968.46.

26 STEVENS, HARRY R. The Middle West. Service Center for
    Teachers of History, publication no. 12. Washington, D.C.:
    Service Center for Teachers of History, 25 pp., passim.
        Assesses the place of Turner and his influence upon the
    historiography of the Middle West.

27 STROUT, CUSHING. The Pragmatic Revolt in American History:
    Carl Becker and Charles Beard. New Haven: Yale University
    Press, pp. 17-26, 46, 65, 72, 87, 99, 122.
        Turner's "philosophical ideas . . . anticipate both the
    relativism and antiformalism later developed by Becker and
    Beard." Turner should be better known as one of the first advocates of the "New History" and for his insistence upon "multiple
    hypothesis" rather than for his frontier thesis. Reprinted:
    Cornell University Press, 1966; Westport, Conn.: Greenwood Press,
    1980.

28 WADE, RICHARD C. "Urban Life in Western America, 1790-1830."
    American Historical Review 64 (October):14-30.
        Argues that instead of the "rural regions" Turner had emphasized, "the towns were [really] the spearheads of the American
    frontier. . . ." Reprinted: 1969.33.

29 WALTON, JOHN. Review of The Frontier in Perspective, edited
    by Walker D. Wyman and Clifton B. Kroeber. Maryland Historical
    Magazine 53 (March):81-83.
        A "sympathetic but cautious" treatment of the Turner thesis;
    serves to demonstrate the high level of interest in Turner's
    ideas.

1958

30 WARD, RUSSEL B. The Australian Legend. Melbourne and New
   York: Oxford University Press, 262 pp., passim.
       Tests the Turner thesis by using it as a model for the
   study of the Australian frontier. Unlike Turner's individualistic
   American frontiersman, the Australian frontiersman was "much more
   collectivist in outlook" and more inclined to form a pastoral
   proletariat than to become an individualistic farmer. The
   Australian experience did not produce a Turnerian form of democracy.

                              1959

1 ALLEN, H.C. Bush and Backwoods: A Comparison of the Frontier
   in Australia and the United States. Sydney: Angus &
   Robertson, 153 pp., passim.
       Objective is to "look . . . at the way in which Frederick
   Jackson Turner's frontier thesis might be broadly applied to
   another continent and society than the North American" in order
   to test "the validity of the frontier hypothesis itself." Concludes that "the effects of the frontier in Australia are certainly such as to justify . . . the Turner doctrine." Reprinted:
   Westport, Conn.: Greenwood Press, 1975.

2 ANON. "Pulitzer Prizes in History, 1917-1959." Wisconsin
   Magazine of History 43 (Winter):106-7.
       Turner is listed as one of three curators of the Historical
   Society of Wisconsin to win the Pulitzer Prize for history.

3 BAILYN, BERNARD. "Politics and Social Structure in Virginia."
   In Seventeenth-Century America: Essays in Colonial History.
   Edited by James M. Smith. Chapel Hill: University of North
   Carolina Press, pp. 90-115.
       Documents the Turnerian generalization that the American
   frontier produced democracy through a study of the frontier in
   Virginia during the seventeenth century. Reprinted: New York:
   Norton, 1972; Westport, Conn.: Greenwood Press, 1980.

4 BREWER, WILLIAM M. "The Historiography of Frederick Jackson
   Turner." Journal of Negro History 44 (July):240-59.
       Relates Turner's life and personality to his work and to
   the development of his frontier thesis. Turner did not deny the
   validity of other possible theories; in fact, he foreshadowed
   many. Turner chose the role of the West because he was convinced
   it would be "inspiring and revealing"; his "supreme purpose was
   to reveal the varied and many sided patterns of American history
   and tradition as revealed in the study of the frontier and section."

5   CARROLL, JOHN ALEXANDER. "Dedication to Frederick Jackson
     Turner." Arizona and the West 1 (Spring):5-6.
     Dedicates this first issue of Arizona and the West to
Turner. Comments on Turner's broad influence and states that "he
still throws a light we cannot ignore."

6   CAUGHEY, JOHN W. "The American West: Frontier and Regions."
     Arizona and the West 1 (Spring):7-12.
     The American West has two faces: the first is the mythic
frontier, an "avenue for adventure and escape"; the second is
the West as a section, as a "region differing from the rest of
the nation. . . ." Asserts in a Turnerian tone that the latter
has received far less attention than is deserved and that there
are significant advantages for considering the West, in both its
past and present states, as a unique section.

7   _____. "Toward an Understanding of the West." Utah Historical
     Quarterly 27 (January):7-24.
     Comments on the history and development of the West as a
region, and discusses significant differences between it and the
East.

8   CONSTANTINE, ROBERT. Review of The Urban Frontier: The Rise
     of Western Cities, 1790-1830, by Richard C. Wade. Indiana
     Magazine of History 55 (December):401-2.
     "The Turner thesis has been a summa for three generations
of American historians" and has "inspired countless monographs
dealing with the frontier." This work is the most recent evidence that the Turner thesis continues to inspire solid research.

9   CUNLIFFE, MARCUS. "The West." In The Nation Takes Shape:
     1789-1837. Chicago History of American Civilization Series,
     edited by Daniel J. Boorstin. Chicago: University of Chicago
     Press, pp. 70-95.
     Subscribes to Turner's theory that the frontier experience
"held a profound significance for Americans," but modifies his
safety-valve concept by pointing out that the "lure of the West
. . . was apt to raise inordinate hopes and then inevitably lead
to disappointment."

10   CURTI, MERLE, with assistance from ROBERT DANIEL SHAW
     LIVERMORE, Jr., JOSEPH VAN HISE, and MARGARET W. CURTI. The
     Making of an American Frontier Community: A Case of Democracy
     in a Frontier County. Stanford: Stanford University Press,
     483 pp., passim.
     Attempts to test the validity of Turner's assumption that
"the ready accessibility of free or almost free land promoted
economic equality and that this was followed by political

1959

equality." The approach involves "combining long-accepted
methods of historical investigation with certain quantitative
methods used in the social sciences." The authors come to the
conclusion that their study "lends support to . . . the main implications of Turner's thesis about the frontier and democracy."
The study is based upon the view that while there is little need
for more analysis of Turner's general theories there is a pressing
need for "careful study of particular frontier areas in this
light of the investigator's interpretation of Turner's theory"
that "free land promoted economic eqaulity and that this was
followed by political equality." Trempealean County, Wisconsin,
is the locality under study. Pages 442-48 reprinted: 1966.12;
85-113 reprinted: 1969.8; reprinted: 1969.

11 DEGLER, CARL N. Out of Our Past: The Forces That Shaped
    Modern America. New York: Harper & Row, 404 pp., passim.
        Claims that American historiography "has not been the same"
since Turner delivered his famous frontier thesis. Turner's
argument that the settling of new land was a larger force in
shaping the character of American people and institutions than
was the European heritage is the most influential aspect of the
frontier hypothesis. Concludes that even in the face of its most
adverse criticism, Turner's thesis still contains much "to be
salvaged. . . ." Revised: 1970.

12 FORBES, JACK D. "The Indian in the West: A Challenge for
    Historians." Arizona and the West 1 (Autumn):206-15.
        "Unfortunately for the Indian, Turner's otherwise compre-
hensive thinking did not duly consider the role of the native"
for "his own studies were concerned exclusively with the white
intruder." In the typical Turnerian treatment, which has dominated
the historiography of the West, "the Indian is clearly not a part
of this frontier. He is, rather, a part of the environment on
which the frontier acts." Argues that the "Indian also had a
frontier" and "this Indian frontier surely is a part of the American frontier."

13 GERHARD, DIETRICH. "The Frontier in Comparative View." Com-
    parative Studies in Society and History, An International
    Quarterly 1 (March):205-29.
        Because "Turner's concept of the frontier as the central
theme in American history has proved to be one of the most formative forces in the development of American historiography," his
suggestion that the significance of the frontier "in the formation of other societies ought to be investigated" warrants a response. Reexamines the Turner thesis in light of the frontier
experiences of Canada, Australia, South Africa, Germany, and
Russia.

1959

14 GOETZMAN, WILLIAM H. Army Exploration in the American West,
    1803-1863. New Haven: Yale University Press, 509 pp., passim.
    "The missing archtype" in existing histories of frontier
    expansion "is the United States Army's Topographical Engineer,"
    who is presented as one of the best examples of the Turnerian
    view of the "western frontier as a struggle between the individual
    and the wilderness environment." Reprinted: 1965; University of
    Nebraska Press, 1979.

15 GULLEY, J.L.M. "The Turnerian Frontier: A Study in the Migra-
    tion of Ideas." Tijdschrift voor Economische en Sociale
    Geografie 50 (March-April):65-72; (May):81-91.
        Underscores the international diffusion of Turner's frontier
    thesis. Includes an analysis of his ideas and the school of his-
    toriography, which has been built upon the foundation laid by
    Turner.

16 HURWITZ, HOWARD L. "Frontier Theory--Shadow or Substance?"
    Senior Scholastic, Teacher's Edition 75 (7 October):17T-19T.
        Summarizes Turner's frontier thesis and briefly examines its
    critics and defenders.

17 HUTCHINSON, WILLIAM T. "Unite to Divide; Divide to Unite:
    The Shaping of American Federalism." Mississippi Valley His-
    torical Review 46 (June):3-18.
        Argues that, in the present, "The strength of the nation no
    longer hinges upon its capacity for territorial growth." But the
    widening frontier and the option for territorial expansion was of
    singular importance in the development of the Union. Discusses
    how this ability to expand "helped to determine the nature of
    early American federalism. . . ."

18 JOSEPHY, ALVIN M., Jr. "Conquest of a Continent." In The
    American Heritage Book of the Pioneer Spirit. Edited by
    Richard M. Ketchum et al. New York: American Heritage Pub-
    lishing Co., pp. 311-36.
        The frontier is treated within a Turnerian framework; opens
    with an emphasis upon a "series of frontiers" and concludes with
    "the disappearance of America's . . . frontier."

19 JOSEPHY, ALVIN M., Jr., PETER ZYON, and FRANCIS RUSSELL.
    "Interpreting the Frontier." In The American Heritage Book of
    the Pioneer Spirit. Edited by Richard M. Ketchum et al. New
    York: American Heritage Publishing Co., pp. 370-71.
        The most exciting event that took place at "Chicago's
    Columbian Exposition in 1893" was not the demonstration of the
    latest mechanical inventions; it was "when . . . Turner . . .
    read a paper, 'The Significance of the Frontier in American His-
    tory.'"

1959

20 KRISTOF, K.D. "The Nature of Boundaries and Frontier."
    Association of American Geographers, Annals 49 (September):
    269-82.
        Attempts to differentiate between "frontiers," such as the
    Turnerian concept of frontier, and "boundaries." International
    and comparative in approach.

21 MEAD, W.R. "Frontier Themes in Finland." Geography 44, no.
    205 (July):145-56.
        Shows that Turner's depiction of the American frontier as
    attractive to settlers does not coincide with the Finnish ex-
    perience. The Finnish frontier was so unattractive that leaders
    had to devise ways to stem the tide of "undue migration to urban
    areas."

22 MURPHY, GEORGE G.S., and ARNOLD ZELLNER. "Sequential Growth,
    the Labor-Safety-Valve Doctrine and the Development of Ameri-
    can Unionism." Journal of Economic History 19 (September):
    402-21.
        "This paper attempts to present an up-to-date version of
    the labor-safety-valve doctrine which has its roots in Turner's
    work." Without "the American frontier process . . . the process
    of sequential growth could not have taken place." And since the
    latter stimulated the entire economy, which in turn made the
    Turnerian safety valve a reality, one can conclude "that there is
    substantial evidence for the truth of the safety-valve doctrine."
    Reprinted: 1968.36.

23 NEVINS, ALLEN. "The Strenuous Life." In The American Heritage
    Book of the Pioneer Spirit. Edited by Richard M. Ketchum et
    al. New York: American Heritage Publishing Co., pp. 353-85.
        Includes a section entitled "Interpreting the Frontier,"
    which credits Turner with having challenged the leaders of his
    era to look for new frontiers to replace the original agrarian
    frontier.

24 ROBINSON, ELWYN B. "The Themes of North Dakota History."
    North Dakota History 26 (Winter):5-24.
        "Turner's themes of frontier history are seen in the history
    of the Dakota frontier" for all "who think about the western
    country have been influenced by the writings of Turner."

25 RUNDELL, WALTER, Jr. "Concepts of the 'Frontier' and the
    'West.'" Arizona and the West 1 (Spring):13-41.
        Examines "the various historical concepts that have grown
    out of the twin terms, 'Frontier' and 'West.'" Defines the terms
    and discusses the concepts of "Free Land" and the "Safety-Valve."
    Examines the idea of a "World Frontier" and analyzes the frontier

1959

as an agent of democracy, nationalism, and isolation. Identifies the "Character of the Westerner" and concludes with a discussion of the impact of "Geographic Determinism."

26 ____. "Interpretations of the American West." Arizona and the West 3 (Spring):69-88; 3 (Summer):148-68.
    Presents an annotated bibliography of writings on the American West and on the frontier. Comments that articles written on Turner's thesis or which are influenced by Turner "have prominent roles in this assessment."

27 STEENSMA, ROBERT. "Rölvaag and Turner's Frontier Thesis." North Dakota Quarterly 27 (Autumn):100-104.
    O.E. Rölvaag's Giants in the Earth "shows clearly the working of the [frontier] process described by Turner." Per Hansa, the main character, is the "prototype" of Turner's pioneer, and his wife, Beret, symbolizes the pioneer who is unable to measure up to the demands of the frontier. Rölvaag's description of the evolution of Plains communities also matches Turner's concepts.

28 WADE, RICHARD C. The Urban Frontier: The Rise of Western Cities, 1790-1830. Cambridge, Mass.: Harvard University Press, 360 pp., passim.
    Does not specifically mention Turner, but clearly argues against Turner's frontier thesis by maintaining that "towns were the spearheads of the frontier." Examines pioneer life in early Pittsburgh, Cincinnati, Lexington, Louisville, and St. Louis and analyzes their roles in the development of the frontier.

29 WEBB, WALTER PRESCOTT. "History as High Adventure." American Historical Review 64 (January):265-81.
    While acknowledging that his thesis shares much in common with Turner's, Webb insists that he formulated it independently of Turner and his disciples.

30 WILLIAMS, GEORGE HUNTSTON. "The Wilderness and Paradise in the History of the Church." Church History 28 (March):3-24.
    Comments in a vein similar to Turner's that the wilderness has played a substantial role in the biblical interpretation of the Christian movement. It has served as both a garden and a desert, a place of refuge and an expression of the wrath of God.

31 WINKS, ROBIN W. "Changing Interpretations." In Recent Trends and New Literature in Canadian History. Service Center for Teachers of History, publication no. 19. Washington, D.C.: Service Center for Teachers of History, pp. 6-14.
    Assesses the influence of the Turner school upon the writing of Canadian history.

1960

1960

1 ANON. "Report of the Council." Annual Meeting, 1960, of the
Massachusetts Historical Society. In <u>Massachusetts Historical
Society, Proceedings</u> 72 (October 1957-December 1960):491-96.
Turner is included in a list of nineteen famous historians.

2 BENSON, LEE. <u>Turner and Beard: American Historical Writing
Reconsidered</u>. New York: Free Press, 241 pp.
"In recent decades a tendency has developed to view
Frederick Jackson Turner and Charles A. Beard as though their
seminal ideas derived from, and represented, radically different
theories of history. This book challenges that view and argues
that their surface differences should not obscure their fundamental similarities. Searching for an overarching scheme that
would help them comprehend and summarize American experience,
Turner and Beard both drew upon European models. Both adopted
eclective approaches that inconsistently combined concepts taken
from the 'economic interpretation of history' and from economic
determinism. Consequently, they both presented theses that are
ambiguous and self-contradictory." The body of the book includes
articles published earlier in <u>Agricultural History</u> (see 1950.2,
1951.2). Reprinted: Westport, Conn.: Greenwood Press, 1980.

3 BERTHOFF, ROWLAND. "The American Social Order: A Conservative
Hypothesis." <u>American Historical Review</u> 65 (April):495-526.
Develops the thesis that the "westward movement, which since
Frederick Jackson Turner's time has figured as a special field
claiming fundamental importance, had better be considered as only
one of a number of kinds of physical and social movements."

4 BILLINGTON, RAY ALLEN. "The American Frontier Thesis."
<u>Huntington Library Quarterly</u> 23 (May):201-16.
Originally an address delivered on Founder's Day, 29
February 1960, at the Henry E. Huntington Library and Art Gallery.
The author celebrates Henry E. Huntington's birth and the insti-
tution he founded by associating them with the "man responsible
for" a "revolution in historical interpretation, Frederick
Jackson Turner."

5 _____. "The West of Frederick Jackson Turner." <u>Nebraska His-
tory</u> 41 (December):261-79.
Summarizes Turner's ideas and answers his critics, who "increased in number and virulence after Turner's death in 1932."
Concludes that "no single interpretation of American history . . .
is more meaningful today than the 'frontier hypothesis' enunciated
by Frederick Jackson Turner."

1960

6　BILLINGTON, RAY ALLEN, and WILBUR R. JACOBS.　"The Frederick
　　Jackson Turner Papers in the Huntington Library."　Arizona and
　　the West 2 (Spring):73-77.
　　　　A "brief appraisal" of Turner's "correspondence, research
notes, and allied materials" available to scholars at the Huntington Library, San Marino, California.

7　BOGUE, ALLEN G.　"Social Theory and the Pioneer."　Agricultural
　　History 34 (January):21-34.
　　　　Examines the frontier from the perspectives of several
major behavioral scientists.　Analyzes, among other aspects, the
elements of pioneer individualism, social cooperation, and political participation on the frontier.　Reprinted:　1968.8.

8　CARROLL, JOHN ALEXANDER.　Introduction to The Significance of
　　the Frontier in American History.　El Paso, Tex.:　Academic
　　Reprints, pp. i-iv.
　　　　"By any measurement . . . Turner's . . . 'frontier essay'
must be judged a classic in historical literature because it
transports elegantly and almost lyrically a compelling idea."

9　CARTER, HARVEY L.　"The Far West in Relation to the Turner
　　Hypothesis."　In The Far West in American History.　Service
　　Center for Teachers of History, publication no. 26.　New York:
　　Macmillan, pp. 3-4.
　　　　Summarizes Turner's thesis and concludes that his major
contribution was his emphasis upon the "differences between Amer-
icans and their . . . European ancestors."

10　COLEMAN, PETER J.　"Beard, McDonald, and Economic Determinism
　　in American Historiography."　Business History Review 34
　　(Spring):113-21.
　　　　Argues that "the Turners and the Beards began with an idea
which allowed them to impose an imaginative synthesis upon American History before a problem had been adequately investigated.
. . ."　Turner and his followers are especially criticized because they too readily accepted a thesis that resulted from a
"premature and irresponsible synthesis."　The Turners and the
Beards have done a "disservice" to the historical profession by
"enticing scholars into fruitless or meaningless investigations,"
and leaving other, more important questions virtually untouched.

11　GATES, PAUL W.　"Farm Management Practices."　In The Farmer's
　　Age:　Agriculture 1815-1860.　The Economic History of the
　　United States Series, vol. 3.　New York:　Holt, Rinehart &
　　Winston, pp. 138-44.
　　　　Argues that "pioneering in the new cotton areas of the West
was something very different from the process described by
Turner . . . and others of the 'frontier' school of historians."

1960

12 GOETZMAN, WILLIAM H. "The West and the American Age of Ex-
    ploration." Arizona and the West 2 (Autumn):265-78.
        Raises the "possibility that this [Turnerian] experience of
    the American West was characteristic of the whole of America
    rather than just a part of it. . . . Viewed in this way, the ex-
    perience in the American West seems somewhat less than unique."
    Pleads for a breaking away "from the old Turnerian tyranny which
    has failed to satisfy us . . . but which is still too valuable
    emotionally to part with completely." Abridged version reprinted:
    1970.15.

13 HEILBRONER, ROBERT L. "The Impasse of American Optimism."
    American Scholar 29 (Winter):13-20.
        Argues, in a vein similar to Turner, that American optimism
    has emerged and grown because of separation from Europe and Euro-
    pean disillusionment and because of a "huge and virtually uncon-
    tested continent" filled with an abundant wealth of resources.
    Finds, however, that in the present, this "optimism blinds us to
    a central reality of our historical situation. . . ."

14 JACOBS, WILBUR R. Review of The Making of an American Com-
    munity, A Case Study of Democracy in a Frontier County, by
    Merle Curti. Arizona and the West 2 (Autumn):294-99.
        Turner was interdisciplinary in his study of history and
    therefore it should not be surprising that Professor Curti's
    study verifies Turner's frontier thesis by utilizing "the objec-
    tive quantitative method of the social scientist."

15 JOHANSEN, DOROTHY O., and EARL POMEROY. Review of The Making
    of an American Community: A Case Study of Democracy in a
    Frontier County, by Merle Curti. Oregon Historical Quarterly
    61 (September):343-47.
        "It appears that Merle Curti and his associates have as-
    sumed that quantitative techniques are more objective than the
    historian's insights, and supplying them, have found that their
    study . . . 'lends support to what we believe are the main im-
    plications of Turner's thesis about the frontier and democracy."

16 KLINGBERG, FRANK J. "Memoirs of Frank J. Klingberg." His-
    torical Magazine of the Protestant Episcopal Church 29 (June):
    106-38.
        While discussing education received at Wisconsin, writes
    that students of Turner would watch "for the gleam in his eyes.
    His eyes sparkled about twice in an hour. Then we sat up and
    took notes."

1960

17 McKITRICK, ERIC L., and STANLEY ELKINS. "Institutions in
    Motion." American Quarterly 12 (Summer):188-97.
        Meant to be read as a corollary to their "A Meaning for
    Turner's Thesis" (see 1954.10). Turner's hypotheses are not
    meant to be adopted without hesitation, but rather, they are to
    be used as starting points for other investigations. Turner is
    used to analyze the Americanization of institutions through (1)
    the great strains put upon them as they are transported into the
    New World, and (2) the necessary portability, which is essential
    to their survival. Reprinted: 1968.33.

18 MEINIG, D.G. "Commentary to Walter Prescott Webb's 'Geographi-
    cal-Historical Concepts in American History.'" Association of
    American Geographers, Annals 50 (March):95-96.
        Categorizes the fundamental geographic elements in Turner's
    theory and concludes that "Turner was a true geographical rather
    than an environmental determinist."

19 MIKESELL, MARVIN W. "Comparative Studies in Frontier History."
    Association of American Geographers, Annals 50 (March):62-74.
        Calls for a comparative approach in the study of frontiers
    because "without the perspective afforded by knowledge of develop-
    ments in foreign areas, it is not possible to interpret the sig-
    nificance of the American frontier." Considers "Canada, Australia,
    and South Africa" as the nations to which scholars should "look
    for fruitful comparisons." Condensed: 1968.35.

20 PIERSON, GEORGE W. "Afterthoughts on the Frontier." New
    England Social Studies Bulletin 18:5-6.
        Contends that the Turner thesis is oversimplified and has
    limited validity: "It takes in too few men, too few institutions,
    and too few American traits." Analyzes why it has gained such
    popularity and notes that it should not be abandoned, "but amended
    and expanded to take in the entire American experience."

21 POMEROY, EARL. "Old Lamps for New: The Cultural Lag in
    Pacific Coast Historiography." Arizona and the West 2 (Summer):
    107-26.
        Argues that Pacific Coast historiography has become ironi-
    cally old fashioned, "out of touch with contemporary scholarship
    and with the contemporary world." Asserts that part of the prob-
    lem lies with western historians, including Turner, who have
    stressed differences between the past and the present, "by offer-
    ing escape rather than solution. . . ."

22 SMITH, PAGE. "Academic History." In The Historian and His-
    tory. New York: Alfred A. Knopf, pp. 138-64.
        Develops the idea that we "can best understand the Turner

1960

thesis as the declaration of independence of that part of the
United States which lay west of the Mississippi." Reprinted:
1964.

23 ____. "The Professionals: History and the 'Social Sciences.'"
In The Historian and History. New York: Alfred A. Knopf, pp.
110-37.
    "Turner's enormously influential account of the effect of
the frontier in American history is an excellent example" of a
school of history that explains "cultural differences on the
basis of soil and climate." Reprinted: 1964.

24 STRICKLAND, REX W. The Turner Thesis and the Dry World. El
Paso: Texas Western Press, 16 pp.
    Critical of the Turner thesis for having "emphasized the
effect of environment to the neglect of the biological and cultural heritage of his pioneers" and for having been too theoretical
simply "chanting the paean of free land and democracy." Tests
the validity of the Turner thesis by studying the "arid Southwest"
and concludes that "there seems to be little of the Turnerian
pattern in the settlement of the arid border."

25 THUAITE, FRANK. "Reflections on Boorstin's America." Journal
of Modern History 32 (December):371-75.
    Daniel Boorstin is credited with having formulated "the
first major re-interpretation of American history . . . since
Turner." Like Turner, "his purpose is to get at the essentially
American quality of life."

26 VAN ALSTYNE, R.W. "Manifest Destiny and Empire, 1820-1870."
In The Rising American Empire. London: Oxford, Basil &
Blackwell, pp. 100-23.
    Develops the idea that there "is a highly conventionalized
picture of the United States advancing in a single direction westward . . . until 1890, when it is said to have been extinguished.
But this picture of 'the westward movement' as a methodical advance from coast to coast is fictitious" for it is "a simplified
version of the famous frontier hypothesis of Frederick Jackson
Turner."

27 VANCE, MAURICE M. Charles Richard Van Hise: Scientist Progressive. Madison: State Historical Society of Wisconsin,
pp. 60-62, 69-70, 72, 74-75, 163-64.
    Discusses the personal and intellectual relationship be-
tween Turner the historian and Van Hise the geologist. Turner
was instrumental in getting Van Hise named as the president of
the University of Wisconsin.

1960

28 VEYSEY, LAURENCE R. "Myth and Reality in Approaching American
    Regionalism." American Quarterly 12 (Spring):31-43.
       Calls Turner one of the leading authorities on "regional
    distinctions within America."

29 WALTERS, EVERETT. "Populism: Its Significance in American
    History." In Essays in American Historiography: Papers Pre-
    sented in Honor of Allen Nevins. Edited by Donald Sheehan and
    Harold C. Syrett. New York: Columbia University Press, pp.
    217-30.
       Identifies Turner and his school of historiography as one
    of "two main categories" in the interpretation of populism. Sum-
    marizes the Turnerian interpretation of populism.

30 WARD, JOHN W. "Individualism Today." Yale Review 49 (Spring):
    380-92.
       Discusses Turner's concept of individualism in light of
    Emerson, Jackson, and evangelical revivalism. "Turner represents
    a culmination in an attempt to self-understand, . . . and the
    theme of beginning over again by taking one's way out of society
    and beginning anew is central to his interpretation of American
    history." Asserts that Turner was concerned with the problem of
    preserving "the importance of the individual in the context of an
    increasingly impersonal and organized society." Notes that this
    "is still our problem today."

31 WELTER, RUSH. "The Frontier West as Image of American Society:
    Conservative Attitudes before the Civil War." Mississippi
    Valley Historical Review 46 (March):593-614.
       Explores an aspect of the frontier that Turner ignored by
    analyzing the views of "conservative eastern spokesmen for Amer-
    ican institutions" regarding the American West. Modifies Turner's
    safety-valve doctrine by suggesting that "it is plausible to
    argue that by appealing to the economic promise implicit in
    western settlement conservative spokesmen helped to divert demo-
    cratic discontent in the East into harmless channels."

32 WILLIAMSON, CHILTON. "Suffrage in the New West." In American
    Suffrage from Property to Democracy, 1760-1860. Princeton:
    Princeton University Press, pp. 208-22.
       Argues that although "Turner implied that a major motive
    for suffrage reform in the east was the prevention of a drain of
    population to the west, . . . the facts of seaboard suffrage re-
    form do not support this thesis."

33 WISH, HARVEY. "Turner and the Moving Frontier." In The Amer-
    ican Historian: A Social-Intellectual History of the Writing
    of the American Past. New York: Oxford University Press, pp.
    181-208.

1960

Traces the development of Turner's career in an attempt to explain why "no man shaped twentieth-century histories of the United States as much as Turner did."

34 WOODWARD, C. VANN. "The Age of Reinterpretation." American Historical Review 66 (October):1-19.
Theorizes that "free security," i.e., military security provided by natural barrier--the Atlantic and Pacific Oceans and the Arctic ice cap--was as significant in American history as the "free land" emphasized by Turner in the frontier thesis. Discusses the dramatic effect of the end of this "free security."

<u>1961</u>

1 BARITZ, LOREN. "The Idea of the West." American Historical Review 66 (April):618-40.
Presents a brief history of the mythic west, particularly as it relates to America. Cites a long "list of sages . . . stretching at least from Horace to Horace Greeley," including, among others, Columbus, Amerigo Vespucci, Henry Hudson, Samuel Sewell, and Henry David Thoreau. Does not specifically mention Turner, but does indicate the mythic proportions the West has played in occidental thought.

2 BENSON, LEE. "Some Crude Generalizations about American Voting Behavior." In The Concept of Jacksonian Democracy: New York as a Test Case. Princeton: Princeton University Press, pp. 271-78.
Credits Turner with having been one of only two historians who provided a "set of interrelated principles to guide researchers attempting to organize the data of American voting behavior" but concludes that his approach is no longer credible. Undertakes to formulate an "integrated theory" to supersede Turner's antiquated one. Reprinted: 1964.1.

3 BILLINGTON, RAY ALLEN. "Introduction: Frederick Jackson Turner--Universal Historian." In Frontier and Section: Selected Essays of Frederick Jackson Turner. Edited by Ray Allen Billington. Classics in History Series. Englewood Cliffs, N.J.: Prentice-Hall, pp. 1-9.
"The essays in this volume have been selected to show Frederick Jackson Turner in his true light, not simply as the father of the 'frontier' and 'sectional' interpretations of American history, but as a scholar whose interests were universal and whose views were as modern as tomorrow."

1961

4 BLEGEN, THEODORE C. "The Saga of the Immigrant." In <u>Immigra-</u>
   <u>tion and American History: Essays in Honor of Theodore C.</u>
   <u>Blegen</u>. Edited by Henry Steele Commager. Minneapolis: University of Minnesota Press, pp. 139-52.
        Reprint of 1961.5.

5 _____. "The Saga of the Immigrant." In <u>Research Opportunities</u>
   <u>in American Cultural History</u>. Edited by John Francis McDermott.
   Lexington: University of Kentucky Press, pp. 66-80.
        Acknowledges that recent immigration historiography contends
   "that the frontier hypothesis of Turner by no means explained the
   diversity in American customs . . . or revealed the full complexity
   of American culture." Believes, however, that Turner foreshadowed
   later developments in immigration history. Reprinted: 1961.4.

6 BURKHART, J.A. "The Turner Thesis: A Historian's Controversy."
   In <u>Wisconsin Witness to Frederick Jackson Turner</u>. Edited by
   O. Lawrence Burnette, Jr. Madison: State Historical Society
   of Wisconsin, pp. 160-73.
        Reprint of 1947.6.

7 BURNETTE, O. LAWRENCE, Jr. Introduction to <u>Wisconsin Witness</u>
   <u>to Frederick Jackson Turner: A Collection of Essays on the</u>
   <u>Historian and the Thesis</u>. Madison: State Historical Society
   of Wisconsin, pp. xi-xvi.
        Presents a brief biographical and intellectual sketch of
   Turner. Introduces the essays that follow, all but one of which
   were published in the <u>Wisconsin Magazine of History</u>.

8 CRAVEN, AVERY. "Frederick Jackson Turner, Historian." In
   <u>Wisconsin Witness to Frederick Jackson Turner</u>. Edited by O.
   Lawrence Burnette, Jr. Madison: State Historical Society of
   Wisconsin, pp. 100-16.
        Reprint of 1942.7.

9 CRUDEN, ROBERT. "Rhodes and the Writing of History." In
   <u>James Ford Rhodes: The Man, the Historian, and his Work</u>.
   Cleveland: Press of Western Reserve University, pp. 225-41.
        "[Rhodes] showed no understanding at all, either in corres-
   pondence of his work, or the epoch-making achievements of
   Frederick Jackson Turner."

10 CURTI, MERLE E. "Frederick Jackson Turner." In <u>Wisconsin</u>
   <u>Witness to Frederick Jackson Turner</u>. Edited by O. Lawrence
   Burnette, Jr. Madison: State Historical Society of Wisconsin,
   pp. 175-204.
        Reprint of 1949.4.

143

1961

11 DOWNS, ROBERT B. "The Great Wide Open Spaces: Frederick
    Jackson Turner's The Significance of the Frontier in American
    History." In Famous Books Since 1492. New York: Barnes &
    Noble, pp. 334-36.
        Summarizes Turner's frontier thesis and briefly comments on
    its critics.

12 FISH, CARL RUSSELL. "The Frontier a World Problem." In Wis-
    consin Witness to Frederick Jackson Turner. Edited by O.
    Lawrence Burnette, Jr. Madison: State Historical Society of
    Wisconsin, pp. 3-23.
        Reprint of 1917.3.

13 GRANT, CHARLES S. Democracy in the Connecticut Frontier Town
    of Kent. Columbia Studies in the Social Sciences, no. 601.
    New York: Columbia University Press, 227 pp., passim.
        Analyzes Turner's "frontier process" in the small community
    of Kent, Connecticut, during the eighteenth century. Concludes
    that the general assumptions advanced by Turner and his disciples
    regarding the frontier process are not validated by the history
    of Kent, Connecticut.

14 KREY, A.C. "My Reminiscences of Frederick Jackson Turner."
    Arizona and the West 3 (Winter):377-81.
        Recalls experiences as an undergraduate and as a graduate
    student under Turner's tutelage. Turner's course on the history
    of the West was composed of "brilliant lectures" during the first
    three weeks and during the final three weeks but the intervening
    days were "meticulous" and "dreary." Comments on Turner's pro-
    found interest in his teaching and in his students.

15 LEE, EVERETT S. "The Turner Thesis Re-examined." American
    Quarterly 13 (Spring):77-83.
        The Turner thesis has been hotly contested (in many ways
    justly so) but it "still commands credence" because "in emphasiz-
    ing the frontier" it opened up doors for "a more general theory
    of migration." Argues that migration, not the frontier, was the
    real "safety valve" and that a study of the influence of migra-
    tion, following Turner's lead, would reveal much concerning Amer-
    ican democracy, American character, and American civilization.
    Reprinted: 1966.22, 1968.27, 1968.28; abridged version reprinted:
    1970.21.

16 LOTTICK, KENNETH V. "The Western Reserve and the Frontier
    Thesis." Ohio Historical Quarterly 70 (January):45-57.
        Whether Turner's "geographical determinism" applies gener-
    ally is a debatable point, but in western New York and in Con-
    necticut's Western Reserve, it does not apply. Argues that these

areas were much more heavily influenced, both socially and psychologically, from eastern institutions and customs.

17 McAVOY, THOMAS T., ed. "What Is the Midwestern Mind?" In The
    Midwest: Myth or Reality? Notre Dame, Ind.: University of
    Notre Dame Press, pp. 53-72.
        Argues that "there has been too much of Frederick Jackson
    Turner in evaluations of the Midwest." Finds that the midwestern
    mind is original, but this is not due to "the irrational element"
    of "the region," but to the make-up of its inhabitants. Analyzes
    the midwestern mind and develops the influences that affected it.

18 MALIN, JAMES C. "On the Nature of the History of Geographical
    Area, with Special Reference to the Western United States."
    In The Grassland of North America: Prolegomena to Its History.
    4th printing. Lawrence, Kans.: James C. Malin, pp. 471-86.
        Argues against the Turnerian analysis of the Great Plains.
    Turner begins the study of the West with the Anglo-American dis-
    placement of the Indians and concludes it with the passing of the
    frontier in 1890. A full study of the geographical region would
    take into account "its geological history, its ecological history,
    and the history of human culture since the beginning of occupancy
    by primitive men," and the study would continue throughout the
    present time. New issues and reappraisals of cultural values
    would then be necessitated. Reprinted: Gloucester, Mass.:
    Peter Smith, 1967.

19 MOOD, FULMER. "Little Known Fragments of Turner's Writings."
    In Wisconsin Witness to Frederick Jackson Turner. Edited by
    O. Lawrence Burnette, Jr. Madison: State Historical Society
    of Wisconsin, pp. 86-99.
        Reprint of 1940.14.

20 NETTLES, CURTIS. "Frederick Jackson Turner and the New Deal."
    In Wisconsin Witness to Frederick Jackson Turner. Edited by
    O. Lawrence Burnette, Jr. Madison: State Historical Society
    of Wisconsin, pp. 45-53.
        Reprint of 1934.13.

21 PIERSON, GEORGE WILSON. "American Historians and the Frontier
    Hypothesis (I and II)." In Wisconsin Witness to Frederick
    Jackson Turner. Edited by O. Lawrence Burnette, Jr. Madison:
    State Historical Society of Wisconsin, pp. 118-59.
        Reprint of 1942.16, 1942.17.

22 SANFORD, CHARLES L. The Quest for Paradise: Europe and the
    American Moral Immigration. Urbana: University of Illinois
    Press, 282 pp., passim.

1961

"My work, as it has appeared chapter by chapter in published articles, has frequently been compared with that of Henry Nash Smith. His first book, <u>Virgin Land</u> (1950), attempted to place Frederick Jackson Turner's frontier hypothesis within an intellectual tradition. I am concerned with something rather different, which is to define the intellectual tradition to which both the 'philosophers of primitivism' and the 'trailblazers of progress' have subscribed." Attempts to explain the appeal of the ideas which have come to be associated with Turner.

23 SCHAFER, JOSEPH. "Some Facts Bearing on the Safety-Valve Theory." In <u>Wisconsin Witness to Frederick Jackson Turner</u>. Edited by O. Lawrence Burnette, Jr. Madison: State Historical Society of Wisconsin, pp. 67-84.
Reprint of 1936.14.

24 _____. "Turner's Frontier Philosophy." In <u>Wisconsin Witness to Frederick Jackson Turner</u>. Edited by O. Lawrence Burnette, Jr. Madison: State Historical Society of Wisconsin, pp. 25-43.
Reprint of 1933.21.

25 SKINNER, CONSTANCE LINDSAY. "Notes Concerning My Correspondence with Frederick Jackson Turner." In <u>Wisconsin Witness to Frederick Jackson Turner</u>. Edited by O. Lawrence Burnette, Jr. Madison: State Historical Society of Wisconsin, pp. 55-67.
Reprint of 1935.21.

26 STECKLER, GERALD G. "North Dakota Versus Frederick Jackson Turner." <u>North Dakota History</u> 28 (Winter):33-43.
Attempts to test the validity of the Turner thesis "against the frontier history . . . of North Dakota." Concludes that "striking similarities and just as striking dissimilarities emerge from a comparison of North Dakota's frontier history and Frederick Jackson Turner's six stages of frontier development," but in the final analysis "much of his generalization has been vindicated."

27 VAN EVERY, DALE. <u>Forth to the Wilderness: The First American Frontier, 1754-1774</u>. New York: William Morrow, 369 pp., passim.
Turner's theories are tested in the eighteenth-century milieu and found to be as valid for the late colonial era as Turner believed they were for the nineteenth century. Includes an introduction by Ray A. Billington.

28 WALKER, ROBERT H. "The Poets Interpret the Western Frontier." <u>Mississippi Valley Historical Review</u> 47 (March):619-35.
Western poets were in general agreement with Turner's

conception that the stages of the frontier, "commencing with the
primitive, would encourage the improvement of American characteristics and institutions."

29 WELTER, RUSH. "The Frontier West as Image of American Society,
    1776-1860." Pacific Northwest Quarterly 52 (January):1-6.
        Examines the influence of the frontier upon American thought
    prior to the late nineteenth century when "Turner somehow gathered
    together in his writings many of the perspectives in which Ameri-
    cans of fifty or seventy-five years before him had seen the West."
    Challenges the originality of Turner's thesis but acknowledges
    the genius of the thesis in that it articulated the "images of the
    the frontier West" which "embodied a wide range of historic Amer-
    ican attitudes."

30 WILKINS, BURLEIGH TAYLOR. Carl Becker: A Biographical Study
    in American Intellectual History. Cambridge, Mass.: MIT
    Press and Harvard University Press, 246 pp., passim.
        Turner is depicted as Becker's "great teacher." Includes a
    chapter entitled "How Becker Decided to Become a Professor of
    History: The Example of Frederick Jackson Turner" (pp. 36-48).

31 WILLIAMS, WILLIAM APPLEMAN. The Contours of American History.
    Cleveland: World Publishing Company, 513 pp., passim.
        Explores the relationship between Turner's frontier thesis
    and American imperialism. Reprinted: Chicago: Quadrangle
    Books, 1966; New York: New Viewpoints, 1973.

32 WINTHER, OSCAR O., ed. A Classified Bibliography of the Peri-
    odical Literature of the Trans-Mississippi West, 1811-1957.
    2d ed. Bloomington: Indiana University Press, 626 pp.,
    passim.
        Expands the list of 3,500 articles on western history in
    the first edition (1942) to 9,000 articles. As in the first
    edition, many of these articles deal with Turner and his theories.
    Includes a section entitled "Frederick Jackson Turner and the
    Frontier Hypothesis," which includes thirty-nine entries. Re-
    vised version of 1942.20; revised: 1972.

33 WRIGHT, JOHN K. "Daniel Coit Gilman, Geographer and Historian."
    Geographical Review 51 (July):381-99.
        Turner is mentioned as one of "three distinguished histo-
    rians who took their doctorates at Johns Hopkins in President
    Gilman's time" who would later "influence the development of
    Geographical studies in this county in a variety of ways. . . ."

<u>1962</u>

1 BILLINGTON, RAY ALLEN. Foreword to <u>The Frontier in American</u>
   <u>History</u>, by Frederick Jackson Turner. New York: Holt,
   Rinehart & Winston, pp. vii–xviii.
       Summarizes Turner's views and attempts to explain the
   appeal of his ideas.

2 _____. Foreword to <u>Rise of the New West, 1819–1829</u>, by
   Frederick Jackson Turner. New York: Collier Books, pp. 7–20.
       Analyzes the relationship between Albert Bushnell Hart, the
   editor, and Frederick Jackson Turner, the author, during the production of this volume. Finds, through an examination of their
   correspondence, that the writing of the book was painful and
   arduous, and without Hart's persistent prodding, the book never
   would have been completed.

3 _____. "Frederick Jackson Turner Comes to Harvard." <u>Massa-</u>
   <u>chusetts Historical Society, Proceedings</u> 74 (January–December):
   51–83.
       An attempt to cast light upon the "universally misunder-
   stood" move of "Turner from the University of Wisconsin to Harvard
   University." Disagreement over the "right of faculty members in
   state–supported institutions to engage in pure research" is
   identified as the reason that Turner left the University of Wisconsin.

4 _____. "Introduction: The Santa Fe Conference and the Writing
   of Western History." In <u>Probing the American West, Papers</u>
   <u>from the Santa Fe Conference</u>. Edited by K. Ross Toole et al.
   First Conference on the History of Western America. Santa Fe:
   Museum of New Mexico Press, pp. 1–16.
       The Santa Fe conference was a success because although
   Turner had been "subjected to scathing criticism . . . for thirty
   years after 1929," by the early 1960s "time was ripe for a revival of interest in western studies." Traces the development of
   Turnerian historiography.

5 _____. "Young Fred Turner." <u>Wisconsin Magazine of History</u> 46
   (Autumn):38–52.
       Explores the early years of Turner's life in an attempt to
   explain why he was able to formulate such an original concept as
   the frontier thesis so early in his career. The focus is upon
   Portage, Wisconsin, the frontier town in which Turner was born
   and raised. Argues that the basic assumptions involved in his
   thesis were already formulated prior to his graduate training in
   history at Johns Hopkins University.

1962

6 BURTON, DAVID H. "The Influence of the American West on the
   Imperialist Philosophy of Theodore Roosevelt." Arizona and
   the West 4 (Spring):5-26.
        Argues that Roosevelt was greatly influenced by Turner's
   views and like Turner believed that "the great feature of American history was the settlement of the 'vast and fertile vacant
   spaces' of the frontier."

7 COLEMAN, PETER J. "Restless Grant County: Americans on the
   Move." Wisconsin Magazine of History 46 (Autumn):16-20.
        Credits Turner with having been one of the first historians
   to emphasize the import of "population mobility in shaping the
   nation's development and spirit." Reprinted: 1969.7.

8 FORBES, JACK D. "Frontiers in American History." Journal of
   the West 1 (July):63-73.
        "To the Turnerians . . . the Frontier consisted solely in
   Anglo-Americans" to the exclusion of "those groups, such as the
   Indians, who opposed the expansion of the Anglo-Americans."
   Forbes rejects this "approach to frontier history" because it "is
   essentially one-sided and ethnocentric." In its place Forbes
   proposes the following definition: "A frontier is an instance of
   dynamic interaction between human beings and involves such processes as acculturation, assimilation, miscegenation, race prejudice, conquest, imperialism and colonization."

9 GARA, LARRY. A Short History of Wisconsin. Madison: State
   Historical Society of Wisconsin, pp. 9, 175-77.
        Turner is presented as one of the state's foremost leaders
   and credited with having "inspired more discussion and controversy than any other scholarly writing in the field of American
   history."

10 HAEGER, JOHN D. "The American Fur Company and the Chicago of
   1812-1835." Illinois State Historical Society, Journal 61
   (Summer):117-39.
        Contends that Turner laid the groundwork for "romantic il-
   lusions" about "the fur trade" and undertakes to dispel these
   illusions.

11 HAWGOOD, JOHN A. "British Interest in the History of Western
   America." In Probing the American West, Papers from the Santa
   Fe Conference. Edited by K. Ross Toole et al. First Conference on the History of Western America. Santa Fe: Museum
   of New Mexico Press, pp. 175-84.
        Suggests that Turner was deeply indebted to the British
   scholar James Bryce for his "frontier hypothesis."

1962

12 HOLLINGSWORTH, J. ROGERS. "Consensus and Continuity in Recent American Historical Writing." South Atlantic Quarterly 61 (Winter):40-50.
    After World War II, historical writing became more sedate, more "middle of the road." The Progressive influence became blurred, and "the triumvirate of Frederick Jackson Turner, Charles Beard, and Vernon Parrington no longer exercised a persuasive influence on the writing of American history." The themes of conflict had lost their importance. Looks forward to the sixties where "themes of conflict and diversity will probably receive greater emphasis in historical writing. . . ."

13 JOHNSON, GEORGE W. "The Frontier behind Frank Norris' McTeague." Huntington Library Quarterly 26 (November):91-104.
    "The loss of the frontier . . . which has come to represent a Great Divide in American Culture" and which "became manifest in . . . a new historiography [Turner's] of American uniqueness . . . was of the greatest imaginative import to one of the period's major . . . writers, Frank Norris."

14 LATTIMORE, OWEN D. "The Frontier in History." In Studies in Frontier History: Collected Papers, 1928-1958. London: Oxford University Press, pp. 469-91.
    Study of Chinese frontiers which attempts a "comparison of the significance of frontiers in history as a whole." Concludes that an international study of frontiers reveals that Turner's basic "argument . . . will not stand up. . . . When he thought he saw what the frontier did to society, he was really seeing what society did to the frontier." Reprinted: 1968.26.

15 _____. "Inner Asian Frontiers: Chinese and Russian Margins of Expansion." In Studies in Frontier History: Collected Papers, 1928-1958. London: Oxford University Press, pp. 134-59.
    Contrasts the Asian and American frontiers.

16 LEE, LAWRENCE B. "The Homestead Act: Vision and Reality." Utah Historical Quarterly 30 (Summer):215-34.
    Analyzes the differences between western and eastern conceptions of the Homestead Act. Also analyzes the differences between Mormon homesteading and homesteading in the rest of the western frontier.

17 LYON, WILLIAM H. "The Third Generation and the Frontier Hypothesis." Arizona and the West 4 (Spring):45-50.
    "When the promoters of the [Turner] hypothesis in the first generation were guilty of vagueness in definition, the critics of the second generation were guilty of dogmatism." States several

1962

proposals which the third generation, comprised of the historians who reapproved the frontier thesis, should consider: (1) that vagueness should be corrected with clear terminology, (2) that historians should stop dwelling on the "end of an era" ideas, (3) "that a significant heritage had to be brought to the American frontier for it to operate as it did," and (4) that historians should look at the westward movement through individuals rather than through institutions.

18 MORGAN, NEIL. "The Great Westward Tilt." Saturday Review 65 (20 October):40-42, 64-67.
     Paints a word picture of the West of the early 1960s that is Turnerian in tone: the West is the most dynamic segment of the nation symbolizing growth, mobility, individuality, freedom, and material prosperity.

19 MORSE, RICHARD M. "Some Characteristics of Latin American Urban History." American Historical Review 67 (January):317-38.
     Rejects Turner's frontier thesis as too "localized and culture-bound" as well as too rural to be a "fruitful hypothesis for a comparative history of the Americas."

20 NEVINS, ALLEN. "The Food of the Gods." In The State Universities and Democracy. Urbana: University of Illinois Press, pp. 69-109.
     Suggests "that Frederick Jackson Turner's essay . . . on the significance of the frontier did more for the world reputation of Wisconsin [University] than all the feats of the College of Agriculture" and other similar "professional training" programs.

21 PEARCE, T.M. "The 'Other' Frontiers of the American West." Arizona and the West 4 (Summer):105-12.
     "The 'American frontier' as described by Turner and explored by his many disciples has had its intellectual limits--and the result has been that the human forces on the frontiers other than the Anglo-American have been inadequately studied or completely overlooked." Attempts to broaden the Turnerian concept of the frontier by stressing the multifaceted dimensions of the frontier and the role of ethnic groups as reflected in literary sources.

22 PIERSON, GEORGE W. "The M-Factor in American History." American Quarterly 14 (Summer):275-89.
     After reviewing the demise of the Turner thesis, Pierson asks: "If the frontier [as defined by Turner] did not produce the effects ascribed to it, what did?" His answer to this question is "the M-factor: the factor of movement, migration, mobility."

1962

23 POMEROY, EARL. "The Changing West." In <u>The Reconstruction of</u>
    <u>American History</u>. Edited by John Higham. London: Hutchinson,
    pp. 64-81.
        "The popularity and proportions of Western studies seem to
    follow in large part on the influence of one historian, Frederick
    Jackson Turner. . . . Most of the elder statesmen have acknowledged
    themselves his disciples or felt obliged to explain why they were
    not. . . . Before Turner, western history did not even appear in
    the colleges' curricula." Explores Turner's contribution by
    underscoring his methodology, his view of the role of the West in
    the development of the United States, the appeal of his frontier
    thesis, the growth of western history as a field of study, and
    the emergence of Turner's critics after his death in 1932. In-
    cludes a brief historiographical sketch of frontier history.

24 POTTER, DAVID M. "The Quest for the National Character." In
    <u>The Reconstruction of American History</u>. Edited by John Higham.
    London: Hutchinson, pp. 197-220.
        Credits Turner with having concentrated the "diffused
    agrarian ideal into a sharp frontier focus" and for having "penned
    a major contribution to the literature of national character."
    Elaborates at length on the following generalization: "A signif-
    icant but . . . unnoticed aspect of Turner's treatment is the
    fact that, in his quest to discover the traits of the American
    character, he relied for proof not upon descriptive evidence that
    given traits actually prevailed, but upon the argument that given
    conditions in the environment would necessarily cause the develop-
    ment of certain traits."

25 RUNDELL, WALTER, Jr. "The West as an Operatic Setting." In
    <u>Probing the American West, Papers from the Santa Fe Conference</u>.
    Edited by K. Ross Toole et al. First Conference on the His-
    tory of Western America. Santa Fe: Museum of New Mexico
    Press, pp. 49-61.
        Studies the emerging image of the West in the East by
    analyzing selected operas of the twentieth century. Underscores
    the fact that the "most popular of all operas, Bizet's <u>Carmen</u>,
    pays tribute to Turner's 'safety-valve concept.'" Concludes by
    suggesting that if "we might translate Turner's hypothesis to the
    operatic field, we could say that when a native school of opera
    develops, the most characteristically American of operas will be
    those with western settings."

26 SCHMIDT, LOUIS BERNARD. "Dedication to Everett E. Edwards."
    <u>Arizona and the West</u> 4 (Summer):99-103.
        Edwards studied as a graduate student at Harvard under
    Turner, and from him learned the importance of economic and social
    aspects of the development of agriculture in the United States.

1962

27 VON NARDOFF, ELLEN. "The American Frontier as a Safety Valve--
    The Life, Death, Reincarnation and Justification of a Theory."
    Agricultural History 36 (July):123-42.
        The safety-valve theory predated Turner. "By mentioning
    the safety valve . . . he [Turner]" simply "accorded historical
    respectability to what had previously been a bit of classical
    economics" for "over a century of American economic development."
    Decries the tendency among historians to assume "that the in-
    vention of safety-valvism was largely Turner's doing." Reprinted:
    1966.35.

28 WARD, JOHN WILLIAM. "The Age of the Common Man." In The Re-
    construction of American History. Edited by John Higham.
    London: Hutchinson, pp. 82-97.
        Argues that "in Turner's dramatization of history, the Old
    World fell easily into the role of the evil and corrupt villain.
    The hero was, of course, the new man created by a new environ-
    ment." Explores this aspect of Turner's thought and concludes
    that "Turner could never decide if the twin American ideals of
    social equality and individual freedom could survive the passing
    of the frontier."

29 WHEELER, WAYNE. "Frontiers, Americanization, and Romantic
    Pluralism." MidContinent American Studies Journal 3 (Fall):
    27-41.
        Consists of "a sociologist's reflections on the Turner
    thesis." Attempts to use Weber's "ideal-type method . . . to
    develop an abbreviated ideal-type statement of some of the ele-
    ments in the concept 'frontier.'"

30 WINTHER, OSCAR O. "The Frontier Hypothesis and the Historian."
    Social Education 22 (November):294-98.
        Assesses Turner's impact upon historical scholarship and
    social science studies in the public schools, and reviews some of
    the literature on Turner. Concludes with a call for a revision
    of the Turner thesis: "The time . . . has come to consider, not
    just the impact of frontier environment upon the West and the
    East, but to consider . . . the influence of the East upon the
    West down to the present day."

31 WISH, HARVEY. "Frederick Jackson Turner (1861-1932) and the
    Frontier Thesis." In American Historians: A Selection. New
    York: Oxford University Press, pp. 282-84.
        Introduces "The Significance of History" and "The Signif-
    icance of the Frontier in American History." Cites Turner's
    influence.

1963

1 BILLINGTON, RAY ALLEN. "The Frontier in American Thought and Character." In The New World Looks at Its History: Proceedings of the Second International Congress of Historians of the United States and Mexico (1958). Edited by Archibald R. Lewis and Thomas F. McGann. Austin: University of Texas Press for the Institute of Latin American Studies of the University of Texas, pp. 77-94.
Billington's thesis is that "since the enunciation of Frederick Jackson Turner's 'frontier hypothesis' sixty-five years ago historians have generally agreed that many of the unique features of American thought and character can be ascribed to the nation's pioneering experience." Also deals with "why . . . the traits and institutions" of America "differ from those of other frontier countries whose evolution has been roughly similar."

2 _____. "The New Western Social Order and the Synthesis of Western Scholarship." In The American West: An Appraisal. Edited by Robert G. Ferris. Second Conference on the History of the American West. Santa Fe: Museum of New Mexico Press, pp. 3-12.
Analyzes the rise in popularity and sophistication of western history, and discusses the role Turner played in this trend. Argues, however, that the "meaningless quibbling" among Turnerians "must cease" because it serves only to narrow the audience of western history rather than making it palatable to a wider audience.

3 _____. "Why Some Historians Rarely Write History: A Case Study of Frederick Jackson Turner." Mississippi Valley Historical Review 50 (June):3-27.
Turner's failure to publish more than "twenty-six major articles" in spite of the fact that he "desperately wanted to write" is examined in light of the broader issue of why many historians publish so little. Despite the offer of advances and royalties from numerous publishers, Turner was "intellectually, emotionally, and physically . . . incapable of the sustained effort needed to complete a major scholarly volume." He instead spent his time preparing for his classes which served as a "pleasant escape from the agonies of writing."

4 BLEGEN, THEODORE C. "Education Moves Ahead." In Minnesota: A History of the State. Minneapolis: University of Minnesota Press, pp. 409-30.
"There is need of a new Turner to formulate an interpretation comparable in importance with the 'frontier hypothesis'" that would identify "education as a major force in the shaping of the nation."

1963

5   BOGUE, ALLAN G.   "The People Come."   In From Prairie to Corn
    Belt: Farming on the Illinois and Iowa Prairies in the Nine-
    teenth Century.   Chicago: University of Chicago Press, pp. 8-
    28.
        Qualifies the "Turnerian formula" regarding the "three-
    stage" development of agricultural settlement.

6   GOETZMANN, WILLIAM H.   "The Mountain Man as Jacksonian Man."
    American Quarterly 15 (Spring):402-15.
        Challenges the Turnerian emphasis upon the influence of the
    frontier by arguing that even the mountain men were not solely
    conditioned by the frontier environment. Mountain men were more
    interested in and influenced by eastern civilization than by the
    frontier environment.

7   HANCOCK, Sir KEITH.   "The Moving Metropolis."   In The New
    World Looks at Its History: Proceedings of the Second Inter-
    national Congress of Historians of the United States and
    Mexico (1958).   Edited by Archibald R. Lewis and Thomas F.
    McGann.   Austin: University of Texas Press, for the Institute
    of Latin American Studies of the University of Texas, pp. 135-
    41.
        Compares and contrasts Walter Prescott Webb's ideas with
    those of Turner.

8   HARPER, NORMAN D.   "The Rural and Urban Frontier."   Historical
    Studies, Australia and New Zealand 10 (May):401-21.
        Originally an address to the Australian and New Zealand
    Association for the Advancement of Science, August 1962. Suggests
    that Turner's "focal point for a study of the interaction of
    people and environment as frontier and section . . . could well
    be town rather than the agrarian frontier."

9   HARTZ, LOUIS.   "American Historiography and Comparative Anal-
    ysis: Further Reflections."   Comparative Studies in Society
    and History 5 (July):365-77.
        Criticizes the nationalist historiography of Turner, and of
    Beard and Parrington who follow, for collapsing into subjectivism
    and fragmentation. Discusses a comparative approach that will
    eliminate American provincialism and turn American history into
    world history. This "will link us to humanity, not through the
    discovery of superior virtue but through the discovery of a com-
    mon dilemma: the conservation of the cultural fragment and the
    challenges it encounters."

10   _____.   "The Rise of the Democratic Idea."   In Paths of Ameri-
    can Thought.   Edited by Arthur M. Schlesinger, Jr., and Morton
    White.   Boston: Houghton Mifflin, pp. 37-70.

1963

Modifies Turner's assertion that democracy was a product of
the frontier environment by arguing that the "American democratic
success" was based on the wider European context from which the
American experience was extracted. Agrees with Turner that "the
liberal idea could not have flourished so successfully unless
there had been an open place to put it," but traces the "liberal
tradition" back to Europe rather than to Turner's frontier.

11 HINE, ROBERT, and EDWIN R. BINGHAM, eds. The Frontier Experi-
    ence: Readings in the Trans-Mississippi West. Belmont,
    Calif.: Wadsworth Publishing Co., 418 pp., passim.
        "The themes and Hypotheses of this book of readings are
    based on two" of Turner's "'intellectual traits,'" namely, "the
    individualistic and the innovative threads of frontier experience,
    versus the cooperative and the traditional threads." The overall
    aim of the collection is to help the reader answer the question:
    "What was the nature of the frontier experience and how did it
    relate to those parts of the American character called individual-
    ism, cooperation, innovation, tradition?" Body of the work is a
    collection of primary and secondary selections including four of
    Turner's writings.

12 HOGAN, WILLIAM R. "Comment: Fallacies in the Turner Thesis."
    In The New World Looks at Its History: Proceedings of the
    Second International Congress of Historians of the United
    States and Mexico (1958). Edited by Archibald R. Lewis and
    Thomas F. McGann. Austin: University of Texas Press for the
    Institute of Latin American Studies of the University of Texas,
    pp. 127-31.
        Critical of the "disciples" of Turner, who have become "a
    priesthood" dedicated to making Turner's ideas an "orthodox gos-
    pel." This "gospel" has "become the predominant United States
    view of its own past."

13 KARP, ABRAHAM J. "What's American about American Jewish His-
    tory: The Religious Scene." American Jewish Historical Quar-
    terly 52 (June):283-94.
        Argues that the "Turner thesis . . . is a most useful con-
    cept in the understanding of certain aspects of American Jewish
    religious history."

14 LaFEBER, WALTER. "Frederick Jackson Turner and the American
    Frontier." In The New Empire: An Interpretation of American
    Expansion, 1860-1898. Ithaca, N.Y.: Cornell University
    Press, pp. 63-72.
        Explores the interrelationships between Turner's ideas and
    the psychology of American imperialism; concludes that "Turner
    . . . provided the key to understanding American foreign policy

in the first half of the twentieth century." Turner influenced
leaders of the stature of Theodore Roosevelt and Woodrow Wilson.

15 LEHMER, DONALD J. "The Second Frontier: The Spanish." In
    The American West: An Appraisal. Edited by Robert G. Ferris.
    Second Conference on the History of the American West. Santa
    Fe: Museum of New Mexico Press, pp. 141-50.
        Provides a Turnerian analysis of the Spanish-American fron-
    tier, and compares it to the Anglo-American frontier. Finds sig-
    nificant cultural and environmental differences between the two,
    but notes that the pattern of settlement is strikingly similar
    and that between them, "the two frontiers gave North America its
    European heritage."

16 LERNER, ROBERT E. "Turner and the Revolt Against E.A. Freeman."
    Arizona and the West 5 (Summer):101-8.
        "In many respects he [Turner] was following in the path of
    the English historians then in revolt against the influence of
    Edward Augustus Freeman, the medievalist whose dictum 'history is
    past politics'" was the dominant approach among historians of
    Turner's era. Concludes that "Turner's revolt against Freeman
    . . . suggests that Turner's thesis was part of a wide, inter-
    continental trend."

17 LOWER, ARTHUR R.M. "Professor Webb and 'The Great Frontier'
    Thesis." In The New World Looks at Its History: Proceedings
    of the Second International Congress of Historians of the
    United States and Mexico (1958). Edited by Archibald R. Lewis
    and Thomas F. McGann. Austin: University of Texas Press, Pub-
    lished for the Institute of Latin American Studies of the Uni-
    versity of Texas, pp. 142-54.
        "Frederick Jackson Turner," although "dead, yet speaketh"
    through disciples like Walter Prescott Webb, who in his book The
    Great Frontier attempts to "complete the work of the master."
    The main body of the article is a critique of Webb's thesis as
    well as that of his master.

18 LYND, STAUGHTON. "On Turner, Beard and Slavery." Journal of
    Negro History 48 (October):235-50.
        "The thesis of this essay is that the significance of
    slavery in American history has been obscured partly because the
    twin giants of modern American historiography, Frederick Jackson
    Turner and Charles Beard, systematically minimized its importance."
    More explicitly, "Turner . . . attempted to shift attention from
    slavery to the frontier." Turner was never able to fit the
    "Southwestern frontier with its plantation pioneers" into his
    thesis because in that part of the West "the effect of frontier
    life was to coarsen and brutalize the peculiar institution, not
    to humanize it." Reprinted: 1967.14, 1968.31.

1963

19 McCARTHY, KIERAN, ed. "Inter-American Notes." Americas 19
    (January):315-23.
       Announcement of efforts on the part of the Publications
    Committee of the Inter-American Academy to make "Frederick
    Jackson Turner's great thesis, The Frontier in American History,
    available in Spanish."

20 NASH, GERALD D. "Research in Western Economic History--Prob-
    lems and Opportunities." In The American West: An Appraisal.
    Edited by Robert G. Ferris. Second Conference on the History
    of the American West. Santa Fe: Museum of New Mexico Press,
    pp. 61-69.
       Points out those areas of western history that have been
    neglected. Argues that Turner's impact came not only from his
    "mental brilliance" and "superlative imagination," but also from
    "the relevance of his ideas to his own time." Present historians
    need to devote their attention to the contemporary importance of
    the historical issues which they raise.

21 NEWCOMER, LEE NATHANIEL. "Frederick Jackson Turner and His
    Meaning for Today." Social Education 27 (May):244-48.
       Summarizes Turner's life, teaching style, and historical
    methodology. Calls "'The Significance of the frontier in American
    history' . . . probably the most influential single piece of
    writing in American historiography . . . an historiographical
    Declaration of Independence."

22 PAUL, RODMAN WILSON. Mining Frontiers of the Far West, 1848-
    1880. New York: Holt, Rinehart & Winston, 235 pp., passim.
       "When Frederick Jackson Turner wrote his classic essay on
    'The Significance of the Frontier in American History'" he "rec-
    ognized that mining booms were an explosive force" but he failed
    to "recognize how thoroughly a mining boom disrupted the regular
    advance that he thought he had discerned in earlier 'Wests.'" In
    his treatment of the impact of the mining frontier as "in so many
    of his writings, Turner was suggestive rather than specific."
    This monograph is an attempt to fill this gap in Turnerian his-
    toriography. Concludes that Turner's description of the mining
    frontier must be modified: "There was never a single mining fron-
    tier, nor a frontier line. Mining development was not that
    orderly. Rather, there were many mining frontiers, not necessarily
    contiguous in place or time."

23 RENSHAW, PATRICK. "Frontier and Freedom." Quarterly Review
    301 (April):123-31.
       Briefly explains Turner's frontier thesis; examines its in-
    fluence and presents criticisms of it. Concludes by showing the
    relationship between democracy and the frontier.

1964

24 RUNDELL, WALTER, Jr. "A Dedication to the Memory of Walter
    Prescott Webb, 1888-1963." Arizona and the West 5 (Spring):
    1-3.
        Having been influenced by Turner, Webb "set out to apply on
    a global basis the frontier hypothesis with which Turner had so
    eloquently interpreted the American West."

25 SIMONSON, HAROLD P. Introduction to The Significance of the
    Frontier in American History, by Frederick Jackson Turner.
    Milestones of Thought Series, edited by Hans Kohn and Sidney
    Hook. New York: Frederick Ungar, pp. 1-24.
        Underscores Turner's supreme importance in American histo-
    riography, outlines his career, summarizes his thesis, and reviews
    the work of "critics" who have attacked him.

26 SUSMAN, WARREN I. "The Useless Past: American Intellectuals
    and the Frontier Thesis: 1910-1930." Bucknell Review 11
    (March):1-20.
        Deals with the revolt of certain intellectuals of the period
    against the "American pioneering experience" as interpreted by
    the Turnerian school of historiography. "What rendered the fron-
    tier experience useless" in the view of these intellectuals "was
    the uses to which that past had been put."

                              1964

1 BENSON, LEE. "Some Generalizations About American Voting Behavior." In American History and the Social Sciences. Edited
   by Edward N. Saveth. Glencoe, Ill.: Free Press, pp. 295-
   300.
       Reprint of 1961.2.

2 BERKHOFER, ROBERT F., Jr. "Space, Time, Culture and the New
   Frontier." Agricultural History 38 (January):21-30.
       The purpose of this study is to "show how dependent Turner
   was upon contemporary thought, and how the American frontier
   should be viewed in the new perspective afforded by modern social
   theory." Concludes that the frontier should be "viewed not as an
   area demanding innovation," as Turner suggested, but "as an opportunity for the proliferation of old institutions." Abridged
   version reprinted: 1970.1.

3 BILLINGTON, RAY ALLEN. "Frederick Jackson Turner and the
   Interpretation of American History." California Social Science
   Review 3 (February):7-16.
       Insists that Turner's "frontier hypothesis" should be
   taught in public schools "as one--but only one--of the valid

1964

interpretations of the American past." Cites evidence of a revival of interest in Turner's thesis "among professional historians" and reviews the published evidence of this interest.
Goes on to argue that Turner's "manuscripts exonerate their
author of the two most serious charges levied against him: that
he was a monocausationist, and that he believed in geographic
determinism."

4 _____. "Manuscripts and the Biographer." Manuscripts 16
(Summer):30-35.
   Finds that Turner's manuscripts present an image of himself
that differs markedly from the image projected to the world. Con-
trary to his public image, Turner suffered from ill health, he
had an oversized ego, and he found classroom hours to be dis-
tasteful. Turner's notes also indicate that, far from being a
"monocausationist," he subscribed to a theory of multiple causation.

5 BLEGEN, THEODORE C. "Frederick Jackson Turner and the Kensington Puzzle." Minnesota History 39 (Winter):133-40.
   The Kensington Rune Stone would, if authentic, indicate
that Nordic voyagers, prior to the time of Columbus, explored the
interior of the North American continent. Gisle Bothne, the
linguistic authority chosen to investigate the stone, wrote to
Turner in 1910 asking for advice. Turner replied declining to
offer a personal judgment of the stone's authenticity, but he did
offer suggestions for the investigating procedure. Bothne did
not make his receipt of the letter known publicly, and though he
may have incorporated some of the suggestions, he never referred
to his correspondence with Turner. Turner's letter is presented
here in full.

6 DAVIS, W.N., Jr. "Will the West Survive as a Field in American
History? A Survey Report." Mississippi Valley Historical Review 50 (March):672-85.
   Report on the status of course offerings in western history
at American colleges and universities. Nineteen of the 285 re-
spondents surveyed "specifically . . . urge a departure from the
Turnerian approach" to the study of western history. Concludes
that the "ideas of Turner and the pre-Turnerians are still dominant, but such is the force . . . of the anti-, un-, and non-
Turnerian groups that it would appear only a matter of time until
they attain majority status."

7 ELKINS, STANLEY, and ERIC McKITRICK. "Turner Thesis: Predictive Model." In American History and the Social Sciences.
Edited by Edward N. Saveth. New York: Collier-Macmillan, pp.
379-99.
   Reprint of 1954.9.

1964

8   FRYKMAN, GEORGE A.   "Thought toward a Philosophy of Northwest
    History." Idaho Yesterdays 8 (Fall):26-32.
        Argues that regional and local historical studies, espe-
    cially in the Pacfic Northwest, need to be revised and recon-
    structed before they become meaningless and antiquarian. Examines
    the trends in historiography from the frontier thesis to David
    Potter's theory of abundance.

9   HARTZ, LOUIS. "The Making of the Fragment Tradition." In The
    Founding of New Societies: Studies in the History of the
    United States, Latin America, South Africa, Canada, and Aus-
    tralia. New York: Harcourt, Brace, pp. 6-10.
        Turner placed too much emphasis upon the "open land of the
    frontier." Furthermore, "Turner, like the average American,
    'cannot see' Europe," and as a result he failed to see that the
    American drama is an extension of the European drama.

10 HICKS, JOHN D. "The Personal Factor in the Writing of History."
    Pacific Northwest Quarterly 55 (July):97-104.
        "While most writers of history are seemingly at pains to
    conceal the personal influences that have shaped their thought,
    there are a few notable exceptions." Turner is cited as one such
    exception.

11 JACOBS, WILBUR R. "Frederick Jackson Turner." American West
    1 (Winter):32-35, 78-79.
        Sympathizes with Turner's difficulty in writing for publica-
    tion and ascertains that this difficulty occurred because (1) his
    work was original and independent and there were no background
    materials for him to draw upon and (2) the objects of his investi-
    gations were exceedingly dense and complex. Goes on to explain
    Turner's views of history and of the West as a process. Reprinted:
    1965.12.

12 _____. "Frederick Jackson Turner's Notes on the Westward
    Movement, California, and the Far West. Introduced and Edited
    by Wilbur R. Jacobs." Southern California Quarterly 46 (June):
    161-68.
        Introduction and Turner's notes deal with Turner's contribu-
    tion to the Henry E. Huntington Library in San Marino, California,
    as well as his response to the opportunities for research from
    1927 until his death.

13 JACOBS, WILBUR R., ed. The Paxton Riots and the Frontier
    Theory. Chicago: Rand McNally, 51 pp., passim.
        Examines the Paxton riots of the late colonial era in light
    of Turner's frontier thesis.

1964

14 KLOSE, NELSON. A Concise Guide to the American Frontier.
    Lincoln: University of Nebraska Press, 269 pp., passim.
        Synopsis of "various main subjects of frontier history."
    Topical approach includes the "Theory of the Frontier," "Regional
    Frontier," "Problems and Features of the Frontier," and "Leading
    Types of Frontiers." Under the heading "The Frontier Hypothesis,
    or Turner Thesis," Turner's views are summarized. General ap-
    proach is Turnerian. Includes a thorough bibliography (pp. 201-
    256) as well as a list of historical journals dealing with fron-
    tier history.

15 LABOR, EARLE. "A Dedication to the Memory of Jack London."
    Arizona and the West 6 (Summer):93-96.
        London was a child of the frontier, and his was the last
    generation to enjoy the freedom and the drive that "Turner defined
    as the American intellect derived from the frontier experience."

16 LITTLEFIELD, HENRY M. "Has the Safety Valve Come Back to
    Life?" Agricultural History 38 (January):47-49.
        "Nardoff has not revitalized the safety valve theory" as
    claimed in her article (see 1962.27), for "it remains entombed in
    the grave dug for it by Goodrich and Davison, Shannon, and Kane
    twenty-five years ago" (see 1935.13, 1940.11, 1945.14).

17 MARTIN, CURTIS. "Impact of the West on American Government
    and Politics." Colorado Quarterly 13 (Summer):51-69.
        The myth of Turner's "self-sufficient and self-reliant
    West" put aside, attempts to examine what the West was "really
    like," especially in its influence upon American government and
    politics. Finds that the West was much more heavily influenced
    by the East than vice-versa, and "government had a greater impact
    upon the West than the West had upon government." Argues that
    "the myth of the individualistic, isolated, self-sufficient
    Westerner is largely that--a myth."

18 MIYAKAWA, T. SCOTT. Protestants and Pioneers: Individualism
    and Conformity on the American Frontier. Chicago: University
    of Chicago Press, pp. 7-8, 21, 130, 202, 224-40, passim.
        "The larger Protestant denominations," which played a major
    role in the West, were not composed of "lone individuals in an
    atomistic society" as Turner's view of the frontier would neces-
    sitate, but were in fact "members of disciplined groups and an
    increasingly organized society." Concludes that a study of de-
    nominationalism in the West challenges the validity of Turner's
    views about the connection between the frontier and nationalism,
    individualism, the reversion to a primitive state and the alleged
    rejection of the "seaboard and Old World Culture." Excerpt re-
    printed: 1970.24.

1964

19 ODUM, HOWARD W. "From Sectionalism to Regionalism." In <u>Folk,</u>
     <u>Region, and Society: Selected Papers of Howard W. Odum.</u>
     Edited by Katharine Jocher et al. Chapel Hill: University of
     North Carolina Press, pp. 175-91.
        Without denying that sectionalism as defined by Turner has
been an accurate description of our nation in the past, Odum calls
for a new regionalism that will encourage national unity to replace the Turnerian style sectionalism.

20 _____. "The Implications and Meanings of Regionalism." In
     <u>Folk, Region, and Society: Selected Papers of Howard W. Odum.</u>
     Edited by Katharine Jocher et al. Chapel Hill: University of
     North Carolina Press, pp. 143-74.
        The author's purpose is to summarize "Professor Turner's
portraiture of the nation as a series of sections" in order to
underscore the "fundamental difference between sectionalism and
regionalism."

21 PIERSON, GEORGE W. "The Restless Temper." <u>American Historical</u>
     <u>Review</u> 69 (July):969-89.
        Suggests that the bountiful supply of frontier resources
and the accompanying mobility generated undesirable American cultural characteristics rather than the desirable ones the Turnerian
interpretation underscored. Traces his interest in "the consequences of mobility" to his earlier "re-examination of Turner's
frontier hypothesis."

22 POMEROY, EARL. "Comments on 'Space, Time, Culture and the New
     Frontier." <u>Agricultural History</u> 38 (January):31-33.
        Comments on Robert Berkhofer's article in the same journal
(see 1964.2). Turner's principles should not be adopted wholeheartedly, but by the same token, his methodology and the construction of his thesis are too important to be ignored. Turner
is not as dogmatic or as narrow as his critics claim; in fact,
"Turner was not a Turnerian" in the same way that his followers
or in the way that Turnerian thought has been criticized.

23 _____. "What Remains of the West?" <u>Utah Historical Quarterly</u>
     35 (Winter):37-55.
        Examines population statistics for the rate of growth in
the West. Finds many similarities with patterns of settling in
the East, but notes, more interestingly, that the large growth
rate of the West should make it "especially hard to believe the
announcement that the frontier was gone was not premature."

1964

24 POTTER, DAVID M. "American Women and the American Character."
    In American Character and Culture: Some Twentieth Century
    Perspectives. Edited by John A. Hague. DeLand, Fla.: Everett
    Edwards Press, pp. 65-84.
        Qualifies Turner's frontier thesis: "If we accept Turner's
    own assumption that economic opportunity is what matters, and
    that the frontier was significant as the context within which
    economic opportunity occurred, then we must observe that for
    American women, . . . opportunity began . . . where the frontier
    left off."

25 SIMONSON, HAROLD P. "Frederick Jackson Turner: Frontier His-
    tory as Art." Antioch Review 24 (Summer):201-11.
        Argues that Turner's fame rests as much on his literary
    skill as upon the appeal of the frontier thesis itself. "His
    essays are in fact what the English romantic DeQuincy would have
    called 'Literature of power.'" Through his frontier symbol and
    imagery, Turner "captured the emotions and visions of an entire
    nation."

26 SUSMAN, WARREN I. "History and the American Intellectual:
    Uses of a Usable Past." American Quarterly 16, part 2, sup-
    plement (Summer):243-55.
        "The genius of Turner was essentially" that he "took a
    major American myth and made it effective history." The net re-
    sult of Turner's "kind of history was . . . an ideology . . .
    which was to become in part the official American ideology" and
    as a result Turner's ideas have been "adapted to many ends in the
    America of the Twentieth century" and have triggered a "wide-
    scale public debate." Reprinted: 1968.48.

27 TINDALL, GEORGE B. "Mythology: A New Frontier in Southern
    History." In The Idea of the South: Pursuit of A Central
    Theme. Edited by Frank E. Vandiver. William Marsh Rice Uni-
    versity Semicentennial Publications. Chicago: University of
    Chicago Press, pp. 1-15.
        Draws an analogy between Turner's frontier thesis and
    scholarly attempts to find a "central theme" in southern history.
    Concludes that "the quest for the central theme, like Turner's
    frontier thesis, becomes absorbed willy-nilly into the process of
    myth making."

28 WRIGHT, LOUIS B. "Culture and Anarchy on the Frontier." In
    Literary Views: Critical and Historical Essays. Edited by
    Carroll Camden. William Marsh Rice University Semicentennial
    Publications. Chicago: University of Chicago Press, pp. 131-
    43.
        Criticizes the chaotic elements of the frontier (those

elements that presumably emerged in the frontier society) and
praises those pioneers who brought traditional, cultured values
with them to the new environment. "These were the people who
struggled to reproduce the best of the older civilizations they
had left." Shows the relevance of this study to contemporary
social problems. "Upon intelligent and cultivated citizens rests
the heavy responsibility of saving society from the chaos of the
cheap and tawdry."

1965

1 BABCOCK, C. MERTON. The American Frontier: A Social and
  Literary Record. New York: Holt, Rinehart & Winston, pp. 1-
  19, 29-42 passim.
    Introduction is Turnerian and Turner's "The Significance of
the Frontier in American History" is included. Structurally
divided into twelve parts and includes forty-nine selections of
Frontier literature.

2 BILLINGTON, RAY ALLEN. The Frontier and American Culture.
  California Library Association, Keepsake no 7. Fairfax,
  Calif.: Mallette Dean, artist and printer, 26 pp.
    Addresses the question whether "America's . . . frontiers-
men . . . succumbed to barbarism or perpetuated the culture they
had known in the East." Acknowledges that pioneers were "determined to transfer the cultural institutions of their homelands to
their new communities," but concludes that environmental factors
"doomed all efforts to build in the West patent-office models of
eastern civilization." The West was a "land where imported cultural patterns were modified to conform to the unique conditions"
of the West. Reprinted: 1977.4.

3 BONNER, JAMES C. "Plantation and Farm: The Agricultural
  South." In Writing Southern History: Essays in Historiography
  in Honor of Fletcher M. Green. Edited by Arthur S. Link and
  Rembert W. Patrick. Baton Rouge: Louisiana State University
  Press, pp. 147-74.
    Credits Turner with stimulating scholarly "interest in the
history of agriculture in the United States" and asserts that "no
discussion of the historiography of the plantation and farm would
be complete without a consideration of the Turner frontier thesis."

4 DAVIS, ALLEN F. "The American Historian vs. the City." Social
  Studies 56 (March):91-96.
    In an attempt to explain the anti-urban bias of American
historians, Davis identifies Turner and the school of historiography which he founded as a major factor.

1965

5 EVANOFF, ALEXANDER. "The Turner Thesis and Mormon Beginnings
   in New York and Utah." Utah Historical Quarterly 33 (Spring):
   157-73.
       Utilizes the "Turner thesis . . . to determine: Whether
   Mormon faith was of frontier origin, and whether or not it ap-
   pealed mostly to non-frontier people." Concludes that the
   "Mormon response to environment would seem to be in accord with
   Turner's expectations."

6 FARRELL, RICHARD T. Review of Frontier: American Literature
   and the American West, by Edwin Fussell. Indiana Magazine of
   History 61 (September):263-64.
       Fussell is criticized for having failed to analyze more
   thoroughly the "Turner thesis" in light of his own "frontier
   metaphor" thesis.

7 FUSSELL, EDWIN S. Frontier: American Literature and the
   American West. Princeton, N.J.: Princeton University Press,
   450 pp., passim.
       Accepts Turner's interpretation of American history as
   authoritative and draws upon his writings to provide the historical
   backdrop for his analysis of frontier literature.

8 GOING, ALLEN J. "The Agrarian Revolt." In Writing Southern
   History: Essays in Historiography in Honor of Fletcher M.
   Green. Edited by Arthur S. Link and Rembert W. Patrick.
   Baton Rouge: Louisiana State University Press, pp. 362-83.
       Identifies "Turner's seminal ideas," especially those that
   stimulated "interest in sectional history," as having "prompted
   an outburst of writings on the South."

9 HICKS, JOHN D. "My Nine Years at Nebraska." Nebraska History
   46 (March):1-27.
       Acknowledges Turner's influence upon his life and scholar-
   ship.

10 HIGHAM, JOHN. "The Reorientation of American Culture in the
   1890s." In The Origins of Modern Consciousness. Edited by
   Horace John Weiss. Detroit: Wayne State University Press,
   pp. 25-48.
       Identifies William James, Frederick Jackson Turner and
   Frank Lloyd Wright as the three leaders of the 1890s who best
   exemplify the pragmatic revolt of the late nineteenth century.
   Turner's writings called for a "revolt against the eastern,
   European-oriented view of American history that prevailed. . . .
   Turner inaugurated a broadly economic interpretation of American
   history" and thereby was a "great leavening and liberating"
   leader within the historical profession.

11 HIGHAM, JOHN, with LEONARD KRIEGER and FELIX GILBERT. "The
    Rise of Progressive History." In History. Englewood Cliffs,
    N.J.: Prentice-Hall, pp. 171-82.
       Turner is presented as "the first and most influential" of
    the "progressive historians."

12 JACOBS, WILBUR R. "Frederick Jackson Turner." In Turner,
    Bolton, and Webb: Three Historians of the American Frontier.
    Seattle: University of Washington Press, pp. 3-39.
       Reprint of 1964.11.

13 _____. Frederick Jackson Turner's Legacy: Unpublished Writings
    in American History. San Marino, Calif.: Huntington Library,
    217 pp.
       A collection of Turner's personal papers, which "reveal the
    interesting story of his formative period, the influence of his
    teachers and associates, and the kind of books and pamphlets he
    read." In addition, the "pieces published for the first time in
    this volume give us an expanded view of the seminal character of
    his research and writings and show how Turner's fascination with
    the present was linked with his study of the past." Describes in
    the introduction (pp. 1-42) the Huntington collection of Turner's
    papers, examines "Turner's formative years," identifies contem-
    poraries who influenced Turner, briefly addresses Turner's in-
    ability to publish, and summarizes his famous frontier thesis.
    Revised: 1969.14.

14 McMILLAN, MALCOLM C. "Jeffersonian Democracy and the Origins
    of Sectionalism." In Writing Southern History: Essays in
    Historiography in Honor of Fletcher M. Green. Edited by
    Arthur S. Link and Rembert W. Patrick. Baton Rouge: Louisiana
    State University Press, pp. 91-124.
       Assesses Turner's contribution to the growth of "a certain
    aura" that came to characterize "Jeffersonianism" within American
    historiography.

15 MERRENS, H. ROY. "Historical Geography and Early American
    History." William and Mary Quarterly 22 (October):529-48.
       There are three major areas of concern in historical geog-
    raphy: the spatial tradition; area studies, or the choreographic
    tradition; and the man-land tradition. Examines these traditions
    in twentieth-century contributions to early American history.
    Though Turner did not deal directly with early American history,
    he did influence those who did.

16 MILES, EDWIN A. "The Jacksonian Era." In Writing Southern
    History: Essays in Historiography in Honor of Fletcher M.
    Green. Edited by Arthur S. Link and Rembert W. Patrick.

1965

Baton Rouge: Louisiana State University Press, pp. 125-46.
Generalizes that "Turner was highly influential in shaping both the manner in which historians considered the role of the South in the Jacksonian period and also the way in which they treated southern state politics of that era."

17 NOBLE, DAVID W. Historians Against History: The Frontier Thesis and the National Covenant in American Historical Writing Since 1830. Minneapolis: University of Minnesota Press, 197 pp.
Explores the complex relationship between the American concept of "covenant" and Turner's frontier thesis. Chapter three is entitled "Frederick Jackson Turner: The Machine and the Loss of the Covenant." Concludes that "Turner . . . failed to find the intellectual formula to preserve the Jeffersonian Covenant in the new urban-industrial society of the late nineteenth-century America."

18 SEABERG, STANLEY, and WILLIAM MULHAIR. "High School Students Test the Frontier Thesis." Social Education 29 (May):279-80.
Describes a project where high-school students applied the frontier concept to a statistical analysis (derived through questionnaires) to the Santa Clara Valley in California.

19 STRATTON, DAVID H. "The Dilemma of American Elbowroom." Pacific Northwest Quarterly 56 (January):30-35.
American historiography has been written within a "main stream of optimism . . . associated with the benefits of American land space" which reached its apex in the "Gospel of the West according to Frederick Jackson Turner." Includes an analysis of "Turner's 'Space Concept of History.'"

20 WARD, JOHN WILLIAM. "Cleric or Critic? The Intellectual in the University." American Scholar 35 (Winter):101-13.
Compares Turner's interpretation of the American experience with that of Nathaniel Shaler. Suggests that while Turner makes the West "stand for the moment of rebirth and life-giving simplicity," Shaler views it as the place of "undeveloped beginnings, the rude and primitive start of a process."

21 WHITE, MORTON. Foundations of Historical Knowledge. New York: Harper & Row, pp. 61-66 passim, 84.
Cites Turner as one of the examples of historians "who are influenced by a simple-minded regularism. . . ." Reprinted: 1969.

22 WOOLFOLK, GEORGE R. "Turner's Safety-Valve and Free Negro
    Westward Migration." Journal of Negro History 50 (July):185-
    97.
        Cites several objections to Turner's safety-valve theory
and attempts to "reopen [it] to a definitive and realistic investigation" by examining its validity in relation to free Negro migration to Texas before the Civil War. Reprinted: 1965.23, 1968.53.

23 _____. "Turner's Safety-Valve and Free Westward Migration."
    Pacific Northwest Quarterly 56 (July):125-30.
        Reprint of 1965.22.

                               1966

1 ALLEN, H.C. "The Thesis Upheld." In The Frontier Thesis:
   Valid Interpretation of American History? Edited by Ray Allen
   Billington. American Problems Series, edited by Oscar Handlin.
   New York: Holt, pp. 107-18.
       Reprint of 1957.3.

2 BARNHART, JOHN D. "American Democracy Distinguished from
   Democracy in General." In The Frontier Thesis: Valid Inter-
   pretation of American History? Edited by Ray Allen Billington.
   American Problems Series, edited by Oscar Handlin. New York:
   Holt, pp. 69-74.
       Reprint of 1953.2. Pages 224-35 of Barnhart's Valley of
Democracy: The Frontier Versus the Plantation in the Valley,
1775-1818 are presented here. Reprinted: 1977.

3 BECKMAN, ALAN C. "Hidden Themes in the Frontier Thesis: An
   Application of Psychoanalysis to Historiography." Comparative
   Studies in Society and History 8 (April):361-82.
       Uses "psychoanalytic understanding in an attempt to shed
light upon . . . the frontier thesis of Frederick Jackson Turner."
Discusses the mythic and anthropomorphic content of the frontier
thesis and concludes that its great popularity "has been due to
the fact that it symbolically depicted a universal wish-drama of
childhood. . . . " Also presents a brief psychoanalytic explanation for how and why Turner arrived at his formulation.

4 BILLINGTON, RAY ALLEN. America's Frontier Heritage. Histories
   of the American Frontier. New York: Holt, Rinehart & Winston,
   302 pp.
       Most complete and authoritative restatement of the Turner
thesis. By utilizing contemporary social science, Billington defines the frontier "as the process through which the socioeconomic-
political experiences and standards of individuals were altered

1966

by an envrionment where a low man-land ratio and the presence of untapped natural resources provided an unusual opportunity for individual self-improvement." While reaffirming Turner's assertion that the American character can not be explained without an understanding of the impact of the frontier experience, Billington is careful to disassociate himself from those who point to the frontier as the only source of American character. Chapter 7, "The Frontier in American Thought and Character," pp. 139-57, is reprinted: 1972.5.

5 _____. "The Frontier and the Teaching of American History." In The Westward Movement and Historical Involvement of the Americas in the Pacific Basin; Conference Proceedings. Edited by Theodore C. Hinckley. San Jose, Calif.: History Department, San Jose State College, pp. 29-41.
   Laments the lack of "courses in the history of the American frontier" in public schools. Argues that students would gain an appreciation of America as a "land of opportunity for the downtrodden" and would discover the importance of migration and the uniqueness of the United States if they studied the history of the frontier from a Turnerian perspective. Summarizes Turner's views in a sympathetic tone.

6 _____. "How the Frontier Shaped the American Character: Turner's Frontier Thesis." In The Craft of American History. Vol. 1. Edited by Abraham S. Eisenstadt. New York: Harper Torchbooks, pp. 135-48.
   Reprint of 1958.4.

7 _____. Introduction to Frederick Jackson Turner's "The Significance of the Frontier in American History." In An American Primer. Edited by Daniel Boorstin. Chicago: University of Chicago Press, pp. 522-23.
   Places Turner's essay in its historical setting.

8 BITTON, DAVIS. "A Re-evaluation of the 'Turner Thesis and Mormon Beginnings. . . .'" Utah Historical Quarterly 34 (Fall):326-33.
   Argues that Professor Evanoff's article (see 1965.5) constitutes "a misreading of Mormon history" in order "to draw unwarranted conclusions as to the validity of the frontier thesis." Attacks the Turner thesis as too simplistic.

9 CARTER, HARVEY L. "A Dedication to the Memory of Archie Butler Hurlburt." Arizona and the West 8 (Spring):1-6.
   Comments on Hurlburt's cordial relationship with Turner. Both shared much in common intellectually, and Hurlburt "did as much as Turner himself to explain and amplify" the frontier thesis.

1966

10 COLEMAN, WILLIAM. "Science and Symbol in the Turner Frontier
    Hypothesis." American Historical Review 72 (October):22-49.
        Turner was greatly influenced by contemporary scientific
    thought. His thesis was "a variation on the post-Darwinian
    evolutionary themes." The "metaphor of the social organism pro-
    vided the central theme of the frontier hypothesis," which was
    borrowed from the biological sciences. Behind the "ideas leading
    to the enunciation of the Frontier thesis" lay "two broader
    themes . . . : the triumph of natural science and a popular
    democracy related to the myth of the forest and the American
    West."

11 CROWE, CHARLES. "The Emergence of Progressive History."
    Journal of the History of Ideas 27 (January-March):109-24.
        Examines the major progressive historians, Turner, Beard,
    Parrington, and Becker, and discusses their influence. Compares
    their methodology to the methods of philosophical pragmatism.
    They ascribe to epistemological relativism, evolutionary develop-
    ment, and utility.

12 CURTI, MERLE. "The Impact of the Frontier: A Case Study."
    In The Frontier Thesis: Valid Interpretation of American His-
    tory? Edited by Ray Allen Billington. American Problems
    Series, edited by Oscar Handlin. New York: Holt, pp. 75-79.
        Reprint of 1959.10. Pages 442-48 of Curti's The Making of
    an American Community: A Case Study of Democracy in a Frontier
    County are presented here. Reprinted: Melbourne, Fla.: Krieger,
    1977.

13 DUNBAR, WILLIS F. "Frontiersmanship in Michigan." Michigan
    History 50 (June):97-110.
        Opens with an analytical review of the "revisionist" crit-
    icism of the "practitioners of the art of frontiersmanship" ac-
    cording to the doctrines of Turner. Sees the Turner thesis as
    useful in the study of Michigan history.

14 FITE, GILBERT C. "Daydreams and Nightmares: The Late Nine-
    teenth-Century Agricultural Frontiers." Agricultural History
    40 (October):285-93.
        Explores the fact that "thousands of people helped to con-
    quer the frontier, but thousands more were conquered by it."
    Instead of benefiting from the frontier envrionment in a Turnerian
    fashion, "thousands of agricultural pioneers" found that "grim
    realities turned their daydreams into nightmares."

1966

15 GATES, PAUL W. "Ulysses Prentiss Hedrick: Horticulturist and
    Historian." New York History 47 (July):219-47.
        Credits Turner with being one of three prominent early
    twentieth-century historians most responsible for stimulating
    interest in agricultural history.

16 GOODRICH, CARTER, and SOL DAVISON. "The Wage-Earner in the
    Westward Movement." In Pivotal Interpretations of American
    History. Vol. 1. Edited by Carl N. Degler. New York: Harper
    & Row, pp. 115-58.
        Reprint of 1935.13, 1936.3.

17 GRESSLEY, GENE M., ed. Preface to The American West: A Re-
    orientation. University of Wyoming Publications, vol. 32.
    Laramie: University of Wisconsin Press, pp. v-xiv.
        Attributes the unwillingness of specialists in western his-
    tory "to re-evaluate . . . their own historiography" to their
    "pre-occupation with the envrionmental-radical theories of
    Frederick Jackson Turner, which has straight-jacketed the con-
    ceptual outlook of Western historians for two generations."

18 HINCKLEY, THEODORE C. Introduction to The Westward Movement
    and Historical Involvement of the Americas in the Pacific
    Basin; Conference Proceedings. Edited by Theodore C. Hinckley.
    San Jose, Calif.: History Department, San Jose State College,
    pp. vii-xii.
        Introduces five studies on the "Pacific Basin in ferment,"
    noting that they have a "Turnerian flavor." They deal with the
    western boundary of the frontier, the mining frontiers, the
    teaching of frontier history in schools, the role of railroads in
    frontier expansion, and secondary literature on the westward
    movement respectively.

19 HOFSTADTER, RICHARD. "The Thesis Disputed." In The Frontier
    Thesis: Valid Interpretation of American History? Edited by
    Ray Allen Billington. American Problems Series, edited by
    Oscar Handlin. New York: Holt, pp. 100-106.
        Reprint of 1941.11; reprinted: Melbourne, Fla.: Krieger,
    1977.

20 JURICEK, JOHN T. "American Usage of the Word 'Frontier' from
    Colonial Times to Frederick Jackson Turner." American Philo-
    sophical Society, Proceedings 110 (18 February):10-34.
        "This paper is an attempt to provide an accurate sketch of
    the history of the American usage of 'frontier' before the present
    century." In addition, "the implications . . . for 'frontier'
    historiography will be explored" in order to understand "Turner's
    mistaken views."

21 LEACH, DOUGLAS EDWARD. The Northern Colonial Frontier, 1607-
    1763. Histories of the American Frontier, edited by Ray Allen
    Billington. New York: Holt, 266 pp., passim.
        Acknowledges that "years ago Frederick Jackson Turner . . .
    went over much the same ground that we have explored in this
    volume." While confirming some aspects of Turner's thesis, this
    study proves that "much of the evidence that Turner gathered on
    the colonial frontier was exceptional rather than typical, selected
    for the very reason that it did seem to sustain his hypothesis."
    Argues that "transplated European culture" had a great or greater
    impact upon the colonial way of life as did the frontier environ-
    ment.

22 LEE, EVERETT S. "Mobility a Strong Influence." In The Fron-
    tier Thesis: Valid Interpretation of American History?
    Edited by Ray Allen Billington. American Problems Series,
    edited by Oscar Handlin. New York: Holt, pp. 90-95.
        Reprint of 1961.15; reprinted: Melbourne, Fla.: Krieger,
    1977.

23 MONAGHAN, JAY. "Did Expansion of the Traditional American
    West Stop at the Pacific?" In The Westward Movement and His-
    torical Involvement of the Americas in the Pacific Basin; Con-
    ference Proceedings. Edited by Theodore C. Hinckley. San
    Jose, Calif.: History Department, San Jose State College,
    pp. 1-16.
        Views his subject as "somewhat akin to the Turner hypothe-
    sis."

24 MORGAN, DALE L. "The Fur Trade and Its Historians." American
    West 3 (Spring):28-35, 92-93.
        Claims that Hiram Martin Chittenden "may have made a funda-
    mentally more useful contribution to western history than either
    [Frederick Jackson] Turner or [Walter Prescott] Webb." His epi-
    sodic commentary, The North American Fur Trade of the Far West,
    "influenced nearly everything written about the history of the
    West in the first half of the nineteenth century. . . ." Re-
    printed: 1966.25.

25 _____. "The Fur Trade and Its Historians." Minnesota History
    40 (Winter):151-56.
        Reprint of 1966.24.

26 NYE, RUSSEL B. "America and the Individual." In This Almost
    Chosen People: Essays in the History of American Ideas. East
    Lansing: Michigan State University Press, pp. 208-55.
        A "major source of American individualism was the continued
    renewal of the frontier. . . . As Frederick Jackson Turner pointed

1966

out in his famous essay in 1893, the frontier instilled an 'intense individualism' in the national character." Credits Turner
with having "brilliantly synthesized the individualist tradition
and the frontier experience."

27 PAUL, RODMAN WILSON. "Mining Frontiers in the Americas and
    the British Commonwealths." In The Westward Movement and His-
    torical Involvement of the Americas in the Pacific Basin; Con-
    ference Proceedings. Edited by Theodore C. Hinckley. San
    Jose, Calif.: History Department, San Jose State College, pp.
    17-28.
        Tests Turner's "generalizations concerning the role of
mining in the pioneer phase of the Americas and the British Com-
monwealths of the Pacific Basin" and finds them in need of modifi-
cation.

28 PIERSON, GEORGE W. "Turner's Views Challenged." In The Fron-
    tier Thesis: Valid Interpretation of American History?
    Edited by Ray Allen Billington. American Problems Series,
    edited by Oscar Handlin. New York: Holt, pp. 31-40.
        Reprint of 1940.15. Final two-thirds of the article are
presented here. Reprinted: Melbourne, Fla.: Krieger, 1977.

29 POMEROY, EARL. "The Significance of Continuity." In The Fron-
    tier Thesis: Valid Interpretation of American History?
    Edited by Ray Allen Billington. American Problems Series,
    edited by Oscar Handlin. New York: Holt, pp. 80-89.
        Reprint (with omissions) of 1955.21; reprinted: Melbourne,
Fla.: Krieger, 1977.

30 POTTER, DAVID M. "The Role of Abundance." In The Frontier
    Thesis: Valid Interpretation of American History? Edited by
    Ray Allen Billington. American Problems Series, edited by
    Oscar Handlin. New York: Holt, pp. 96-99.
        Reprint of 1954.21. Pages 154-60 of Potter's People of
Plenty are presented here. Reprinted: Melbourne, Fla.: Krieger,
1977.

31 RICHARDS, JAMES O. "Local History and Parochial History."
    Filson Club History Quarterly 40 (April):144-58.
        Presents Arthur K. Moore's The Frontier Mind as a "prime
example" of excellent local history; its merit lay in the author's
ability to relate what was happening on the Kentucky frontier to
the broader development of western culture and in its challenge
to the "prevailing view" of frontier history, which is "substan-
tially that of Frederick Jackson Turner."

1966

32 SCHAPSMEIR, EDWARD, and FREDERICK SCHAPSMEIR. "Theodore
    Roosevelt's Cowboy Years." Journal of the West 5 (July):398-
    408.
        Argues that Roosevelt rather than Turner should be credited
    for having first recognized the significance of the West.

33 SHANNON, FRED A. "Not Even an Indirect Safety Valve Attracting
    Eastern Farmers." In The Frontier Thesis: Valid Interpreta-
    tion of American History? Edited by Ray Allen Billington.
    American Problems Series, edited by Oscar Handlin. New York:
    Holt, pp. 41-50.
        Reprint of 1945.14; reprinted: Melbourne, Fla.: Krieger,
    1977.

34 SMITH, PAGE. The Historian and History. New York: Knopf,
    pp. 111, 149-50, 186, 216.
        Turner's thesis was naturally appealing: "it was, nonethe-
    less, a myth . . . [and] it closed the eyes of most historians to
    any facts which did not conform to it."

35 VON NARDOFF, ELLEN. "A Resources and Sociopsychological
    Safety Valve." In The Frontier Thesis: Valid Interpretation
    of American History? Edited by Ray Allen Billington. American
    Problems Series, edited by Oscar Handlin. New York: Holt,
    pp. 51-62.
        Reprint of 1962.27; reprinted: Melbourne, Fla.: Krieger, 1977.

36 WHITE, LYNN, Jr. "The Legacy of the Middle Ages in the Ameri-
    can Wild West." American West 3 (Spring):72-79, 95.
        Argues in an anti-Turnerian fashion that the frontier ex-
    perience was neither unique nor an entirely new, innovative re-
    sponse to a novel environment. Instead, most of the frontiers-
    men's responses were extensions of medieval traditions and medieval
    inventiveness. Concludes that "to comprehend ourselves as Ameri-
    cans we must recover, and relate ourselves to our deeper past,
    the Middle Ages."

37 WILKINSON, BUD. "Our Remaining Frontier." Great Plains Jour-
    nal 6 (Fall):1-7.
        "The great historian, Frederick Jackson Turner" is cited as
    the authority who demonstrated that "'what the Mediterranean was
    to the Greeks, the retreating frontier has been to the United
    States.'" Presents a popularized version of Turner's assumptions
    regarding the significance of the West.

38 YOUNG, J.M.R. "Australia's Pacific Frontier." Historical
    Studies: Australia and New Zealand 12 (October):373-88.
        The Turnerian approach to the study of "'the frontier' in

1966

Australian history," which has implied a "comparison with the
United States" experience, has obscured an important difference:
the American frontier lay in one direction only whereas "for
Australia there have always been two frontiers."

<u>1967</u>

1 BALDWIN, DONALD N. "Wilderness: Concept and Challenge."
<u>Colorado Magazine</u> 44 (Summer):224-40.
Finds that "just as Frederick Jackson Turner in 1893 had
been disturbed by the foreseeable consequences of the closing of
the frontier, there were some in the post-World War I period who
found the rapid diminution in the amount of wilderness land
alarming" and worked for its preservation.

2 BILLINGTON, RAY ALLEN. "The American Frontier." In <u>Beyond
the Frontier</u>. Edited by Paul Bohannan and Fred Plog. American
Museum Sourcebooks in Anthropology. Garden City, N.Y.:
Natural History Press, pp. 3-24.
Reprint of 1958.2.

3 BRAGDON, HENRY WILKINSON. <u>Woodrow Wilson: The Academic
Years</u>. Cambridge, Mass.: Belknap Press of Harvard University,
pp. 103, 178, 185, 188-89, 193-94, 219, 226-27, 233, 236, 239-
43, 453.
Underscores the extensive interaction between Turner and
Wilson as well as their mutual admiration.

4 CULMSEE, CARLTON. "The Frontier: Hardy Perennial." <u>Utah
Historical Quarterly</u> 35 (Summer):228-35.
Although scholars in the Turnerian tradition have assumed
that the frontier opportunity is a thing of the past, Americans
still see the frontier opportunity as alive "because there is an
enduring physical basis" for it.

5 DEGLER, CARL N. "The Economic Revolution: The West, Farmers
and Industrial Workers." In <u>The Age of the Economic Revolution, 1876-1900</u>. Scott Foresman American History Series.
Glenview, Ill.: Scott Foresman, pp. 57-94.
Applies a Turnerian analysis to the discussion of the settling of the far-western frontier. Claims that, "In a sense the
history of the United States is the story of the frontier. . . ."
Notes the differences between the frontiers of the Midwest and
the Far West. Reprinted: 1977; pp. 58-68 reprinted: 1970.11.

6 DUNHAM, HAROLD H. Review of <u>America's Frontier Heritage</u>, by
    Ray Allen Billington. <u>Colorado Magazine</u> 44 (Fall):351-54.
       Calls for a moratorium on any further rehashing of Turner's
    thesis; let Billington's work be the final word on Turner, for
    historians have more important things to do than perpetuate a
    fruitless discussion of Turner's ideas.

7 HALLOWELL, A. IRVING. "The Backwash of the Frontier: The Im-
    pact of the Indian on American Culture." In <u>Beyond the Fron-</u>
    <u>tier</u>. Edited by Paul Bohannan and Fred Plog. American Museum
    Sourcebooks in Anthropology. Garden City, N.Y.: Natural His-
    tory Press, pp. 319-45.
       Reprint of 1957.11.

8 HAWGOOD, JOHN A. "The End of the West? Twentieth-Century
    Frontiers." In <u>America's Western Frontiers: The Exploration</u>
    <u>and Settlement of the Trans-Mississippi West</u>. New York:
    Alfred A. Knopf, pp. 384-412.
       Traces the ebb and flow of popular and scholarly reaction
    to Turner's hypothesis from 1893 to the present from a pro-
    Turnerian point of view.

9 HICKS, JIMMIE. "The Frontier and American Law." <u>Great Plains</u>
    <u>Journal</u> 6 (Spring):53-67.
       "Turner sought to call attention to the influences of the
    frontier process on the shaping of American institutions. . . .
    The purpose of this essay is to discuss some of these influences
    . . . on the shaping of American Law."

10 JACOBS, WILBUR R. <u>The Paxton Riots and the Frontier Thesis</u>.
    Chicago: Rand McNally, 51 pp., passim.
       Examines the Paxton riots of the late colonial era in light
    of Turner's frontier thesis.

11 JONES, ARCHIE H. "Cops, Robbers, Heroes and Anti-Heroines:
    The American Need to Create." <u>Journal of Popular Culture</u> 1
    (Fall):114-27.
       Calls Turner the "patron saint" of American historians.
    "He expressed in scholarly terms another version of the myth that
    Buffalo Bill embodied." Discusses the development and evolution
    of the American hero from Buffalo Bill to the present day and in-
    cludes an analysis of Turner's role in this "national myth."

12 LOBANOV-ROSTOVSKY, A. "Russian Expansion in the Far East."
    In <u>Beyond the Frontier</u>. Edited by Paul Bohannan and Fred Plog.
    American Museum Sourcebooks in Anthropology. Garden City, N.Y.:
    Natural History Press, pp. 87-101.
       Reprint of 1957.15.

1967

13 LORD, CLIFFORD L., and CARL UBBELOHDE. <u>Clio's Servant: The</u>
    <u>State Historical Society of Wisconsin, 1846-1954</u>. Madison:
    State Historical Society of Wisconsin, 598 pp., passim.
        Documents Turner's extensive involvement in the State His-
    torical Society of Wisconsin.

14 LYND, STAUGHTON. "On Turner, Beard, and Slavery." In <u>Class</u>
    <u>Conflict, Slavery, and the United States Constitution</u>.
    Indianapolis: Bobbs-Merrill, pp. 135-52.
        Reprint of 1963.19.

15 McDERMOTT, JOI FRANCIS. "The Frontier Re-examined." In <u>The</u>
    <u>Frontier Re-examined</u>. Urbana: University of Illinois Press,
    pp. 3-13.
        Argues against the Turner thesis by claiming that "men of
    capital and enterprise" led the movement into the frontier and
    stresses the "prime importance of business" on the frontier. Em-
    phasizes the role of the town and city in frontier development.

16 MARTORELLA, PETER H. "Carl Becker and Secondary Social
    Studies." <u>Social Studies</u> 58 (October):194-99.
        Stresses Turner's profound influence upon Carl Becker the
    teacher and educational theorist.

17 MAYER, ARNO J. "Historical Thought and American Foreign
    Policy in the Era of the First World War." In <u>The Historian</u>
    <u>and the Diplomat: The Role of History and Historians in</u>
    <u>Foreign Policy</u>. Edited by Francis L. Loewenheim. New York:
    Harper & Row, pp. 73-90.
        Links Turner with Veblen, Robinson, Beard, and Becker as
    the only social scientists who "had the necessary historical
    imagination to study [World War I] and its consequences in the
    light of world history." Claims that all five thought and wrote
    "in keen awareness" of Marxist theories, although Turner was per-
    haps the most politically moderate. Turner's "International
    Political Parties in a Durable League of Nations" is presented in
    the appendix, pp. 203-8.

18 NEVINS, ALLAN. "The Old History and the New." In <u>The Art of</u>
    <u>History: Two Lectures</u>, by Allan Nevins and Catherine Drinker
    Bowen. Washington, D.C.: Published for the Library of Con-
    gress by the Gertrude Clarke Whitehall Poetry and Literature
    Fund, pp. 1-19.
        Turner is identified as one of "three historians who have
    made the deepest impression in recent times . . . through pro-
    vocative new ideas broadly . . . related to the social studies."

1967

19 PAUL, RODMAN. "The Mormons as a Theme in Western Historical
    Writing." Journal of American History 54 (December):511-23.
        Urges historians to break out of the confines of the
    Turnerian approach to western history and focus upon "some of the
    major topics" with the objective of discerning "a new synthesis
    of western history as a whole."

20 POTTER, DAVID M. "Depletion and Renewal in Southern History."
    In Perspectives on the South: Agenda for Research. Edited by
    Edgar T. Thompson. Durham, N.C.: Duke University Press, pp.
    75-89.
        Argues that the nature of southern history changed when
    historians such as Turner reformulated the concept of "section"
    as an important factor in American history. Turner's interpreta-
    tion broadened the scope of regional studies in general and
    southern history in particular.

21 SOSIN, JACK M. The Revolutionary Frontier, 1763-1783. His-
    tories of the American Frontier Series, edited by Ray Allen
    Billington. New York: Holt, Rinehart & Winston, 241 pp.,
    passim.
        Accepts the truism that it "was the trans-Appalachian region
    Frederick Jackson Turner had in mind when he posed his famous
    frontier thesis." "Turner's thesis on the significance of the
    transmontane frontier and his analysis of the contribution of the
    Old West are two themes for investigation."

22 TUTTLE, WILLIAM M. "Forerunners of Frederick Jackson Turner:
    Nineteenth-Century British Conservatives and the Frontier
    Thesis." Agricultural History 41 (July):219-27.
        "Several decades before Turner . . . enunciated" his famous
    essay concerning the frontier, "English writers and conservative
    politicians had formulated a frontier thesis to explain American
    institutions." No attempt is made to prove that Turner was aware
    of these English writers or that he was in any way directly in-
    fluenced by their views.

23 VORPAHL, BEN M. "Presbyterianism and the Frontier Hypothesis:
    Tradition and Modification in the American Garden." Presby-
    terian Historical Society, Journal 45 (September):180-92.
        The Presbyterian church constitutes, "in some ways at least,
    a kind of exception to the frontier hypothesis advanced by
    Frederick Jackson Turner." The church did not stand in awe of the
    vast amount of space in the frontier and, subsequently, was not
    greatly influenced by environmental factors; the Presbyterians
    were already more democratic than the nation of which they were a
    part, and they brought to the frontier a creed which would mold
    the frontier far more than the frontier would mold it.

1968

1968

1 ANDERSON, JACK. "Frederick Jackson Turner and Urbanization."
   Journal of Popular Culture 2 (Fall):292-98.
       In his later essays, "Turner reveals an attitude towards
   urbanization that bears a striking resemblance to that held
   earlier by Thomas Jefferson." Turner lamented the rise of large
   urban centers because they necessitated a shift from a "competa-
   tive individualism" to a "new collectivism," which would rely on
   strong government controls. Turner also resented the large in-
   flux of immigrants from southeastern Europe because "they carried
   their national self-consciousness with them" and rejected the
   "melting-pot" ideal.

2 BATMAN, RICHARD DALE. "The California Political Frontier:
   Democratic or Bureaucratic?" Journal of the West 7 (October):
   461-70.
       Examines Turner's contention that political structures on
   the frontier were much more democratic and allowed broader opportunities than in the East. Studies the men who rose to political prominence in California, and argues that those who attained
   high office did so because of a lack of a strong political elite.
   But the cross section of these politicians is not as democratic
   as one might expect; the great majority were lawyers or were already politically experienced; and once in office, they created
   and sustained a political elite similar to that of the East.
   Concludes that "the American West was in reality producing the
   politician's dream--a frontier where opportunities were far more
   bureaucratic than democratic."

3 BILLINGTON, RAY ALLEN. "Frederick Jackson Turner Visits New
   England: 1887." New England Quarterly 41 (September):409-36.
       Describes Turner's six-week visit to New England. Presents
   Turner's letters to his family written during his vacation.

4 _____. "Frontiers." In The Comparative Approach to American
   History. Edited by C. Vann Woodward. New York: Basic Books,
   pp. 75-90.
       Though Turner is not mentioned in the text, the tone is
   clearly Turnerian. Claims that the frontier experience in America
   was unique; other nations that experienced a frontier past (notably
   Latin America, Canada, Australia, and Siberia) had physical or
   cultural differences that created a significant alteration of the
   influence of the frontier on social development. Discusses how
   the American frontier influenced the spread of democratic spirit,
   the growth of materialist values, and the belief in upward
   mobility.

1968

5 _____. "The Origins of Harvard's Mormon Collection." Arizona and the West 10 (Autumn):211-24.
    Discusses the awkward circumstances that plagued Harvard's attempt to purchase a 2,700-volume collection on Mormonism, and notes Frederick Jackson Turner's involvement in the enterprise.

6 _____. "Turner, Frederick Jackson." International Encyclopedia of the Social Sciences. Edited by David L. Sills. New York: Macmillan, 16:168-69.
    A brief biographical sketch and summary of Turner's ideas. Assesses Turner's contribution to history as a field of study. Includes a brief bibliography.

7 BOATRIGHT, MODY C. "The Myth of Frontier Individualism." In Turner and the Sociology of the Frontier. Edited by Richard Hofstadter and Seymour Martin Lipset. New York: Basic Books, pp. 43-64.
    Reprint of 1941.3.

8 BOGUE, ALLAN G. "Social Theory and the Pioneer." In Turner and the Sociology of the Frontier. Edited by Richard Hofstadter and Seymour Martin Lipset. New York: Basic Books, pp. 73-99.
    Reprint of 1960.7.

9 ELKINS, STANLEY, and ERIC McKITRICK. "A Meaning for Turner's Frontier: Democracy in the Old Northwest." In Turner and the Sociology of the Frontier. Edited by Richard Hofstadter and Seymour Martin Lipset. New York: Basic Books, pp. 120-51.
    Reprint of 1954.9.

10 FORBES, JACK D. "Frontiers in American History and the Role of the Frontier Historian." Ethnohistory 15 (Spring):203-35.
    The concept of "frontier" used by Turner and his later interpreters has been "one-sided and ethnocentric. It is . . . looking at an inter-group contact situation entirely from the point of view of one of the interested participants." Argues that valid social science yields a "social science" definition that characterizes the "frontier as an inter-group contact situation."

11 GATES, PAUL W. "Frontier Estate Builders and Farm Laborers." In Turner and the Sociology of the Frontier. Edited by Richard Hofstadter and Seymour Martin Lipset. New York: Basic Books, pp. 100-119.
    Reprint of 1957.10.

1968

12 GIBSON, ARREL M. "America's Frontier Heritage: A Review
    Essay." Civil War History 14 (September):250-58.
        Reviews Ray Allen Billington's book America's Frontier
    Heritage. Applauds Billington's renewal of the Turner thesis and
    claims that "his national revisionist treatment of the subject
    will perhaps mitigate the Turner controversy." Believes, along
    with Billington, that Turner belongs in the historiographic per-
    spective as "a pioneer, breaking new ground."

13 GRESSLEY, GENE M. "The Turner Thesis--A Problem in Historiog-
    raphy." In American Themes: Essays in Historiography. Edited
    by Frank Otto Gatell and Allen Weinstein. New York: Oxford
    University Press, pp. 261-90.
        Reprint of 1958.13.

14 HAMILTON, W.B. "The Transmission of English Law to the Fron-
    tier of America." South Atlantic Quarterly 67 (Spring):243-64.
        Surveys the development of law on the frontier and finds
    that Turner's hypothesis that political institutions in America
    evolved in response to the frontier is invalid. American law was
    neither unique nor original, but instead was drawn from English
    precedents; "English law was transported to America where it was
    received and took root."

15 HARTSHORNE, THOMAS L. The Distorted Image: Changing Concep-
    tions of the American Character Since Turner. Cleveland: The
    Press of Case Western Reserve University, 226 pp.
        "Chronologically, the study will be confined to the twen-
    tieth century, or, more precisely, to the period following the
    publication of Turner's essay on the frontier. Because of its
    simplicity, clarity, and cogency, Turner's essay has become the
    prototype of the national-character study. This inquiry begins
    with Turner and may be regarded as a survey of attempts to dis-
    cover an alternative to the frontier thesis." Contains an anno-
    tated bibliography of cited sources.

16 HICKS, JOHN D. My Life with History: An Autobiography.
    Lincoln: University of Nebraska Press, 366 pp., passim.
        Refers to himself as a "dedicated Turnerian." Entire auto-
    biography reflects this orientation.

17 HIGHAM, JOHN. "The Old Frontier." New York Review of Books
    25 (April):10-14.
        Comments on Turner's thesis and its critics. Asserts that
    the Turner thesis has not died because there was nothing else to
    replace it; "critics . . . had less success in giving an alterna-
    tive explanation of what was unique about American history and
    the American character." Examines some more recent studies of

the West that also deal with the frontier thesis. Expanded: 1970.17.

18 HOFSTADTER, RICHARD. Introduction to <u>Turner and the Sociology</u> <u>of the Frontier</u>. Edited by Richard Hofstadter and Seymour Martin Lipset. New York: Basic Books, pp. 3-8.
    Outlines the major elements of Turner's frontier thesis and introduces the articles that follow, showing their relationship to that thesis. Claims that "Turner was probably the first American historian" to understand the "repetitive sociological and economic processes that have refashioned men and institutions in the American environment." Views Turner's frontier thesis as a part of a broader "cultural revolt . . . against the cultural dominance of the East. . . ."

19 _____. <u>The Progressive Historians: Turner, Beard, Parrington</u>. New York: Alfred A. Knopf, pp. 3-164, 167-498, passim.
    Analyzes historical writing before Turner and discusses Turner's impact on the historical profession. Turner was a product of the "Western Revolt" and he incorporated this ideology into his own historical outlook. Comments on the political import of the frontier thesis and of Turner's sectional theories, especially as they relate to the development of American democracy. Argues against critics by maintaining that "much of the Turner thesis can be salvaged. . . ." Reprinted: New York: Vintage Books, 1970; University of Chicago Press, 1978.

20 HOOVER, DWIGHT W., ed. "The Historians Blinded." In <u>Under-</u> <u>standing Negro History</u>. Chicago: Quadrangle Books, pp. 93-94.
    "Frederick Jackson Turner and Charles A. Beard quite possibly have had more influence upon members of the historical profession than anyone else in the twentieth century."

21 JACOBS, WILBUR R. <u>The Historical World of Frederick Jackson</u> <u>Turner with Selections from His Correspondence</u>. New Haven: Yale University Press, 289 pp.
    "More than one-hundred-and-fifty odd letters excerpted or given in full in this book have been selected from several thousand letters that Turner wrote. . . . I have . . . attempted to include the letters of intrinsic value--those in which Turner states his beliefs, talks about himself, or discusses some aspect of his own character. . . . Through the letters and connecting commentary I have tried to present a portrait of the man himself, one drawn mainly by Turner's own words." Includes a bibliographical section, discussing the Turner Collection at the Henry E. Huntington Library. Reprinted: 1970.

1968

22 _____. "Turner's Methodology: Multiple Working Hypotheses or Ruling Theory?" Journal of American History 54 (March):853-63.
   Examines the "extent to which Turner . . . adopted" geologist Thomas C. Chamberlin's "idea of multiple hypotheses."

23 _____. "Wider Frontiers--Questions of War and Conflict in American History: The Strange Solution by Frederick Jackson Turner." California Historical Society Quarterly 47 (September):219-36.
   This is a "detailed analysis of conflict" as illustrated "through special reference to the word of a man who has exercised an incalculable influence on contemporary studies, Frederick Jackson Turner." Praises "Turner's ideas concerning ways for keeping conflict in America at a minimum." Depicts Turner as one who wished to resolve international conflict through a "community of nations" rather than through violence.

24 KESSELMEN, STEVEN. "The Frontier Thesis and the Great Depression." Journal of the History of Ideas 29 (April):253-68.
   Analyzes the intellectual connections between the frontier theory and the New Deal. "The Turner thesis fitted [the New Deal] like a glove. The New Deal rejected the past; it saw itself as a new beginning; and the Turner thesis let it, for if there was one thing that the Turner thesis told you about past American history, it was that it was over." Distinguishes four "economic 'frontiers'" other than the land frontier; the "technological frontier," the "production frontier," the "organizational frontier," and the "population, or fertility, frontier."

25 LAMAR, HOWARD R. "Historical Relevance and the American West." Ventures 8 (Fall):62-70.
   While "Turner's frontier hypothesis" was "the most pervasive and popular historical explanation of American history between 1900 and 1930" it later became "useless as a guide for the present" because it "implied that a discontinuity existed between America's rural past and its urban-industrial present."

26 LATTIMORE, OWEN D. "The Frontier in History." In Theory in Anthropology. Edited by Robert A. Manners and David Kaplan. Chicago: Aldine Publishing Co., pp. 374-86.
   Reprint of 1962.14.

27 LEE, EVERETT S. "The Turner Thesis Re-examined." In The American Experience: Approaches to the Study of the United States. Edited by Hennig Cohen. Boston: Houghton Mifflin, pp. 64-71.
   Reprint of 1961.15.

28 _____. "The Turner Thesis Re-examined." In Turner and the
Sociology of the Frontier. Edited by Richard Hofstadter and
Seymour Martin Lipset. New York: Basic Books, pp. 65-72.
   Reprint of 1961.15.

29 LIPSET, SEYMOUR MARTIN. "The 'Newness' of the New Nation."
In The Comparative Approach to American History. Edited by C.
Vann Woodward. New York: Basic Books, pp. 62-74.
   Evaluates the impact of Turner's "frontier hypothesis"
upon comparative studies of frontiers in "other pioneer settle-
ment countries."

30 _____. "The Turner Thesis in Comparative Perspective: An
Introduction." In Turner and the Sociology of the Frontier.
Edited by Richard Hofstadter and Seymour Martin Lipset. New
York: Basic Books, pp. 9-14.
   Briefly compares the American frontier with other frontiers
(namely, in Canada, Australia, and Brazil) and examines signifi-
cant differences among them.

31 LYND, STAUGHTON. "On Turner, Beard and Slavery." In Under-
standing Negro History. Edited by Dwight W. Hoover. Chicago:
Quadrangle Books, pp. 106-20.
   Reprint of 1963.18.

32 McCLUGGAGE, ROBERT W. Review of Frederick Jackson Turner's
Legacy: Un-published Writings in American History, edited by
Wilbur R. Jacobs. Illinois State Historical Society, Journal
41 (Winter):495-97.
   Complains that this selection from the "'thirty-four bulging
file-cabinet drawers' of lectures" does not, as the editor claims,
constitute the "Turner legacy," nor does it "'mirror' Turner's
concerns 'as a historian and teacher.'"

33 McKITRICK, EARL L., and STANLEY ELKINS. "Institutions in
Motion." In The American Experience: Approaches to the Study
of the United States. Edited by Hennig Cohen. Boston:
Houghton Mifflin, pp. 280-89.
   Reprint of 1960.17.

34 MARSHALL, LYNN L., and SEYMORE DRESCHER. "American Historians
and Tocqueville's Democracy." Journal of American History 55
(September):512-32.
   Turner "found no use for Tocqueville," yet he could have
"because his intellectual prowess in some ways approached that of
Tocqueville in the Democracy."

1968

35 MIKESELL, MARVIN W. "Comparative Studies in Frontier History."
    In Turner and the Sociology of the Frontier. Edited by
    Richard Hofstadter and Seymour Martin Lipset. New York:
    Basic Books, pp. 152-71.
        Condensed version of 1960.19.

36 MURPHY, GEORGE G.S., and ARNOLD ZELLNER. "Sequential Growth,
    the Labor-Safety-Valve Doctrine, and the Development of Ameri-
    can Unionism." In Turner and the Sociology of the Frontier.
    New York: Basic Books, pp. 201-24.
        Reprint of 1959.22.

37 OSBORN, GEORGE C. Woodrow Wilson: The Early Years. Baton
    Rouge: Louisiana State University Press, pp. 165, 189-91,
    235, 277-79.
        Documents the close ties between Wilson and Turner as well
    as Wilson's attempt to convince Turner to join the faculty at
    Princeton University.

38 OSTRANDER, GILMAN M. "Turner and the Germ Theory." In Intel-
    lectual History in America; vol. 2, From Darwin to Neibuhr.
    Edited by Cushing Strout. New York: Harper & Row, pp. 39-46.
        Reprint of 1958.18.

39 PARKER, WILLIAM N. "American Economic Growth: Its Historiog-
    raphy in the Twentieth Century." Ventures 8 (Fall):71-82.
        "American Economic History has grown up as a subject of
    study and research under the shadow . . . of two very large . . .
    oaks--Frederick Jackson Turner and Charles A. Beard." Compares
    Turner's thought with that of Beard.

40 PIERSON, GEORGE WILSON. "The Frontier and American Institu-
    tions: A Criticism of the Turner Theory." In Turner and the
    Sociology of the Frontier. Edited by Richard Hofstadter and
    Seymour Martin Lipset. New York: Basic Books, pp. 15-42.
        Reprint of 1942.18.

41 PIERSON, GEORGE W. "Mobility." In The Comparative Approach
    to American History. Edited by C. Vann Woodward. New York:
    Basic Books, pp. 106-20.
        Attributes his own interest in mobility in American history
    to a "dissatisfaction with Frederick Jackson Turner's frontier
    hypothesis."

42 POTTER, DAVID. The South and the Sectional Conflict. Baton
    Rouge: Louisiana State University Press, pp. 60, 147, 160-61,
    178-79, 190.
        Notes that Turner was the first historian to stress

1968

distinctively American factors. Claims that it is "an error to
suppose that writers on Lincoln preceded Turner in grasping [the
frontier] thesis. . . . But it is certainly a significant fact
that even before the Turner interpretation . . . they began to
replace Lincoln the saintly Emancipator with Lincoln the robust
Frontiersman."

43 RISCHIN, MOSES. "Beyond the Great Divide: Immigration and
the Last Frontier." Journal of American History 55 (June):
42-53.
The Far West merits "national and international attention"
and demands "fresh and imaginative research." Discusses the
interrelationships of immigration, internal migration, and far
western regionalism.

44 ROLLE, ANDREW F. The Immigrant Upraised: Italian Adventures
and Colonists in an Expanding America. Norman: University of
Oklahoma Press, pp. 4, 6, 28-30, 100.
Comments that although Turner did not emphasize the role of
the immigrant in the settling of the frontier, it is evident that
it was a factor in his analysis. Turner's treatment of immigrants
is positive, but notes that he "showed occasional ethnic preju-
dices. . . ." A foreword by Ray Allen Billington is also included (pp. vii-x).

45 SHANNON, FRED A. "A Post-Mortem on the Labor-Safety-Valve
Theory." In Turner and the Sociology of the Frontier. Edited
by Richard Hofstadter and Seymour Martin Lipset. New York:
Basic Books, pp. 172-86.
Reprint of 1945.14.

46 SIMLER, NORMAN J. "The Safety-Valve Doctrine Re-evaluated."
In Turner and the Sociology of the Frontier. Edited by
Richard Hofstadter and Seymour Martin Lipset. New York:
Basic Books, pp. 187-200.
Reprint of 1958.25.

47 SIMONSON, HAROLD P. "The Closed Frontier and American Tragedy."
Texas Quarterly 11 (Spring):56-69.
Turner's frontier thesis brought history into a deeper
level of the human spirit—myth. His announcement of the closed
frontier, however, significantly suggests the tragic "end of the
Edenian myth and the illusion it fostered." This theme is used
to examine various social and cultural perplexities in nineteenth-
and twentieth-century America.

1968

48 SUSMAN, WARREN I. "History and the American Intellectual
    Uses of a Useable Past." In The American Experience. Edited
    by Hennig Cohen. Boston: Houghton Mifflin, pp. 84-105.
        Reprint of 1964.26.

49 VANCE, RUPERT B. "Region: Regionalism in the United States."
    International Encyclopedia of the Social Sciences. Edited by
    David L. Sills. New York: Macmillan, 13:377-81.
        Credits Turner with having been the American historian most
    responsible for developing the concept of regionalism.

50 WADE, RICHARD C. "Urbanization." In The Comparative Approach
    to American History. Edited by C. Vann Woodward. New York:
    Basic Books, pp. 186-205.
        Acknowledges that "Frederick Jackson Turner was the his-
    torian most responsible" for the "poetic vision" of the frontier
    as the key to understanding American history. Identifies Turner's
    thesis as a major source of the distorted view of the role of the
    city in American history.

51 WILLIAMS, BURTON J. "The Platte, the Plains, and the Peak:
    Grand Theory and Local History." Great Plains Journal 8
    (Fall):1-15.
        Contrasts Turner's view of the Great Plains frontier with
    the views of Albert D. Richardson, Horace Greeley, John J.
    Ingalls, and Henry Villard. Turner praised the frontier way of
    life while the others wrote in pejorative terms. Argues that
    Turner "was searching for universals, not so much to explain
    American history, but rather to demolish a host of other explana-
    tions of which he personally disapproved." Reprinted: 1973.34.

52 WOODWARD, C. VANN, ed. "The Comparability of American History."
    In The Comparative Approach to American History. New York:
    Basic Books, pp. 3-17.
        Assesses the place of Turner's "famous . . . Frontier
    Thesis" within the field of comparative history.

53 WOOLFOLK, GEORGE R. "Turner's Safety Valve and Free Negro
    Westward Migration." In Understanding Negro History. Edited
    by Dwight W. Hoover. Chicago: Quadrangle Books, pp. 189-99.
        Reprint of 1965.22.

1969

1 BARTLETT, RICHARD A. Review of The Historical World of
   Frederick Jackson Turner, with Selections from His Correspon-
   dence, edited by Wilbur R. Jacobs. Michigan History 53
   (Summer):158-60.

"Turner's importance is often only half understood" because too little emphasis is placed upon "his career as a teacher. For he was a master trainer of historians."

2 BENSON, LEE. "The Historian as Myth-maker: Turner and the Closed Frontier." In The Frontier in American Development: Essays in Honor of Paul Wallace Green. Edited by David M. Ellis. Ithaca, N.Y.: Cornell University Press, pp. 3-19.
    Contends that Turner "functioned as a myth-maker when he popularized Achille Loria's 'free land' theory of history and applied it to America in the form of the 'frontier thesis.'" Critically examines the "Loria-Turner thesis" and discusses its impact and influence. Also argues against Ray Allen Billington's attempt to resurrect the frontier thesis in "the form of a myth of the psychological closed frontier."

3 BESTOR, ARTHUR E. "Patent-Office Models of the Good Society: Some Relationships between Social Reform and Westward Expansion." In The Old Northwest: Studies in Regional History, 1787-1910. Edited by Harry N. Scheiber. Lincoln: University of Nebraska Press, pp. 68-92.
    Reprint of 1953.4.

4 BILLINGTON, RAY ALLEN. "Frederick Jackson Turner and Logan's 'National Summer School,' 1924." Utah Historical Quarterly 37 (Summer):307-36.
    Discusses Turner's participation in the "National Summer School" sponsored by the Utah Agricultural College. Uses Turner's letters to his wife as a way of presenting his day to day activities while in Utah, both in the classroom and at the fishing streams.

5 BILLINGTON, RAY A[LLEN]. "Frederick Jackson Turner and Walter Prescott Webb: Frontier Historians." In Essays on the American West. Edited by Harold M. Hollingsworth and Sandra L. Myres. Austin: University of Texas Press, pp. 89-114.
    Asks: "Why do we rightly acclaim Frederick Jackson Turner and Walter Prescott Webb as the greatest historians of the American frontier?" Responds by suggesting that their greatness lay in their ability to formulate "challenging hypotheses" that "stimulated more constructive effort on the part of scholars than any other interpretations of American history." Both scholars were products of their frontier environments and were "merely translating into theory a world with which they were all too familiar."

1969

6 BOGUE, ALLEN G. "Senators, Sectionalism, and the 'Western' Measures of the Republican Party." In The Frontier in American Development: Essays in Honor of Paul Wallace Gates. Ithaca, N.Y.: Cornell University Press, pp. 20-46.
Cites Turner as the established authority on the relationship between sectionalism and congressional politics.

7 COLEMAN, PETER J. "Restless Grant County: Americans on the Move." In The Old Northwest: Studies in Regional History, 1787-1910. Edited by Harry N. Scheiber. Lincoln: University of Nebraska Press, pp. 279-87.
Reprint of 1962.7.

8 CURTI, MERLE. "Social Relationships in Trempealeau County." In The Old Northwest: Studies in Regional History, 1787-1910. Edited by Harry N. Scheiber. Lincoln: University of Nebraska Press, pp. 93-130.
Reprint of 1959.10 (pp. 85-113).

9 DAVIS, CALVIN DeARMOND. "The Frederick Jackson Turner Census: Its Indiana Memorial." Indiana Magazine of History 65 (December):268-82.
Frederick Jackson Turner is primarily responsible for the fame of the 1890 census. The background of this census and superintendent Porter's role in the census are discussed. The body of this work examines the erection of a monument near Greenburg, Indiana, marking the center of the population of America based on the data of the 1890 census.

10 DONALD, DAVID. "The Grand Theme of American Historical Writing." Journal of Historical Studies 2 (Autumn):186-201.
After examining major historians who have succeeded in writing general histories, Donald looks "at one of even greater talents who failed: Frederick Jackson Turner." Finds that much of his work is "among the most discerning analyses ever written of nineteenth-century American society," but his attempt to complete a comprehensive statement was a failure.

11 FRITZ, HENRY E. "Nationalistic Response to Frontier Expansion." Mid-America 51 (October):227-43.
Documents the formation of the frontier mythology, relates this mythology to manifest destiny, provides evidence "that territorial expansion and the frontier West had a more direct and pervasive impact upon the entire nation than Frederick J. Turner understood," and presents parallels between Turner's thesis and the frontier myths of the Jacksonian era. Argues in a Turnerian tone that "the frontier gave a powerful impetus to national democratic aspirations."

12 GREEN, FLETCHER MELVIN. "Resurgent Southern Sectionalism,
    1933-1955." In Democracy in the Old South and Other Essays.
    Edited by J. Isaac Copeland. Nashville: Vanderbilt University
    Press, pp. 288-306.
       Reprint of 1956.5.

13 HUTCHINSON, C. ALAN. "The California Frontier." In Frontier
    Settlement in Mexican California: The Hijar-Pardres Colony,
    and Its Origins, 1769-1835. New Haven: Yale University Press,
    pp. 393-402.
       A central point of the article is that "California under
    Mexico does not appear to have been a frontier in the same sense
    that Turner used the term."

14 JACOBS, WILBUR R. America's Great Frontiers and Sections:
    Frederick Jackson Turner's Unpublished Essays. Lincoln: Uni-
    versity of Nebraska Press, 217 pp.
       Revised version of 1965.13.

15 _____. "British-Colonial Attitudes and Policies toward the
    Indian in the American Colonies." In Attitudes of Colonial
    Powers Toward the American Indian. Edited by Howard Peckham
    and Charles Gipson. Salt Lake City: University of Utah Press,
    pp. 81-106.
       The tendency to glorify the actions of frontiersmen "owes
    much to the frontier thesis of Frederick Jackson Turner who
    tended to ignore minority groups, especially the Indians." Argues
    that the Indian side of American colonial history needs to be re-
    examined.

16 JACOBS, WILBUR [R.]. "Frederick Jackson Turner's Views on
    International Politics, War, and Peace." Australian National
    University Historical Journal, no. 6 (November):10-15.
       Analyzes Turner's contention, formulated in the context of
    World War I, that the "powerful rivalries that developed between
    all the sections . . . greatly resembled the complex rivalries of
    European nations." Also looks at his suggestion that "if American
    political parties were the political cement that held American
    sections together" it should be reasonable to believe that "inter-
    national political parties" could play a role "in preventing
    international conflict."

17 KERNEK, STERLING. "Pierson versus Turner: A Commentary of
    the Frontier Controversy." Historical Studies 14 (October):3-
    18.
       Defends Turner's thesis in the face of the "adverse criti-
    cism" of G.W. Pierson. Pierson's primary criticisms were directed
    at Turner's "imprecise definitions" and "hazy rhetoric," and

1969

Pierson rejected the frontier hypothesis because of its contra-
dictions, fallacies, and "untenable concepts." These criticisms
are themselves, however, "confused" and "overestimated." Concludes that "considerable confusion could be avoided if critics
would first consider Turner's aim and keep in mind the comparative
framework which gives the frontier hypothesis some plausibility."

18 KOELSCH, WILLIAM A. "The Historical Geography of Harlan H.
Barrows." Association of American Geographers, Annals 59
(December):632-51.
       Frederick Jackson Turner and Ellen Churchill Semple were
"the two most important intellectual influences" on Barrows's
course on historical geography in the United States. The
"Turnerian Revolution," which linked culture to environment and
history to the natural sciences, helped shape Barrows's interest
in "the relations of earth conditions and resources to American
development."

19 LAMAR, HOWARD R. "Frederick Jackson Turner." In Pastmasters:
Some Essays on American Historians. Edited by Marcus Cunliffe
and Robin W. Winks. New York: Harper & Row, pp. 74-109.
       Shifts the focal point from the frontier thesis to Turner
the man. Discusses Turner's role as a noted historian and sensitive teacher. Also examines his methods, his view of history,
and his impact on American historical thought. Presents a penetrating analysis of Turner the individual. Reprinted: 1975;
Westport, Conn.: Greenwood Press, 1979.

20 LIEBER, TODD. "The Significance of the Frontier in the
Writing of Antebellum Southern History." Mississippi Quarterly
22 (Fall):337-54.
       Looks at several southern historians (most notably U.B.
Phillips, Verner W. Crane, William E. Dodd, Avery O. Craven, and
Thomas P. Abernethy) and analyzes the influence of Turner's frontier thesis on their interpretations of the history of the South.
Finds that Turner's thesis has been utilized, but other historical
approaches that are more uniquely southern (for example, "either
climate, the presence of Negroes, or the Plantation system") are
"of greater value."

21 McCURDY, FRANCIS LEA. Stump, Bar and Pulpit: Speechmaking on
the Missouri Frontier. Columbia: University of Missouri
Press, 218 pp., passim.
       Acknowledges that the "interpretations of the frontier . . .
proved especially helpful" in the research and writing of this
work and that this was especially true of "essays on the Turner
thesis." Concludes that frontier rhetoric articulated the "vague
feelings and undefined values" of the frontier, and when these

values are woven into a broader picture the result is something
similar to Turner's frontier democracy. The frontier produced
not only democracy of a Turnerian variety but orators as well to
popularize and articulate it.

22 MEADE, ROBERT O. "The Atlantic and the Frontier." In The
    Atlantic: Essays in American-European Cultural History. New
    York: New York University Press, pp. 27-55.
        "Without denying the validity of much of the famous 'fron-
    tier thesis,' the point I would stress is that America remained
    Europe's frontier."

23 MERK, FREDERICK. Foreword to The Frontier in American Develop-
    ment: Essays in Honor of Paul Wallace Gates. Edited by David
    M. Ellis. Ithaca, N.Y.: Cornell University Press, pp. ix-
    xxx.
        "In 1893, Frederick Jackson Turner read his essay that was
    destined to become famous and to draw the notice of the academic
    world to the meaning of the frontier process. . . . Its generaliza-
    tions have become a battleground for American historians and for
    historians of frontiers on other continents."

24 NASH, LEE M. "Scott of the Oregonian: The Editor as His-
    torian." Oregon Historical Quarterly 60 (September):197-232.
        Study of Oregon's famous editor, frontiersman, popularizer
    of history, and creator of "his personal tailor-to-Oregon 'fron-
    tier thesis.'" Examines the influence of "University of Oregon
    Professor Frederick G. Young . . . , who was a student and ex-
    ponent of the original frontier thesis of Frederick Jackson
    Turner," upon Scott's thinking.

25 NELSON, ANNE K., and HART M. NELSON. "Family Articles in
    Frontier Newspapers: An Examination of One Aspect of Turner's
    Frontier Thesis." Journal of Marriage and the Family 31
    (November):644-49.
        An examination of miscellaneous literary columns in Nash-
    ville newspapers for the years 1801, 1811, and 1821 reveals that
    "the newspaper was not particularly responsive to the frontier
    situation and thus tended to reflect the values of the seaboard
    civilization." Concludes that "the Turner thesis may be more
    applicable to political than to social institutions."

26 POLE, J.R. "Daniel J. Boorstin." In Pastmasters: Some
    Essays on American Historians. Edited by Marcus Cunliffe and
    Robin W. Winks. New York: Harper & Row, pp. 210-38.
        "Boorstin draws on more than one tradition the earliest
    being Frederick Jackson Turner's. The emphasis is on what was
    new, unexpected, and what Americans owed . . . to the land . . . .

1969

But these themes are far more varied and complex than Turner's.
Where Turner's primary emphasis was on democracy and public institutions, Boorstin's is on the whole experience of a growing
community, on the style and quality of life it lived." Reprinted:
1975; Westport, Conn.: Greenwood Press, 1979.

27 POTTER, JIM. "Some British Reflections on Turner and the
    Frontier." Wisconsin Magazine of History 53 (Winter):98-107.
        In Britain, Turner is "perhaps the best known of all Amer-
    ican historians," partly because his approach to the social sci-
    ences insists "upon the essential unity of all the social sci-
    ences." Examines the economic and demographic effects of the
    frontier on American development. Reprinted: 1976.10.

28 SAUM, LEWIS O. "Pat Donan's West and the End of the Age of
    Hate." Pacific Northwest Quarterly 60 (April):66-76.
        Argues that the "West provided an emotional outlet for the
    American nation," but acknowledges that this kind of safety-valve
    is more difficult to document than the Turnerian economic safety-
    valve concept. Implies that the West supplied an emotional and
    ideological release mechanism for many easterners.

29 SCHEIBER, HARRY N., ed. "Government and Politics." In The
    Old Northwest: Studies in Regional History, 1787-1910.
    Lincoln: University of Nebraska Press, pp. 291-95.
        Introduces the four articles in this section of the book by
    emphasizing how they modify or challenge the "Turnerian tradition."

30 _____. "Pioneer Period: Early Institutions and Problems."
    In The Old Northwest: Studies in Regional History, 1787-1910.
    Lincoln: University of Nebraska Press, pp. 3-5.
        Rejects the "central theme in . . . Turner's writings that
    all frontier regions had the same egalitarian, democratizing
    effects."

31 _____. "Preface: On the Concepts of 'Regionalism' and 'Fron-
    tier.'" In The Old Northwest: Studies in Regional History,
    1787-1910. Lincoln: University of Nebraska Press, pp. vii-
    xix.
        Challenges Turnerian assumptions regarding the uniqueness
    and significance of the frontier. Includes a summary of Turner's
    ideas and concludes with a plea to eliminate "from the definition
    of 'frontier' . . . normative concepts" that Turner and his fol-
    lowers attached to the term "frontier."

32 SCHEIBER, HARRY N. "Turner's Legacy and the Search for a Re-
    orientation of Western History: A Review Essay." New Mexico
    Historical Review 44 (July):231-48.

     Breaks Turner's thesis into two major assumptions and five
major hypotheses in an attempt to understand "what went wrong."
Finds that the most important problem is the lack of empirical
evidence to support Turner's claim that the interaction between
culture and environment was similar in each successive frontier.
Examines where the field of western history presently lies, and
claims that until "basic conceptual issues are settled . . . the
failure of the Turner legacy leaves history of the West a subject
in quest of a purpose."

33 THOMPSON, ROGER. "The Frontier in American History." In The
    Golden Door: A History of the United States of America (1607-
    1945). London: Allman & Son, pp. 233-38.
       "In 1893 . . . Turner" formulated "the most influential
single piece of historical writing ever done in the United States."
Summarizes Turner's views and reviews the literature critical of
the Turner thesis.

34 WADE, RICHARD C. "Urban Life in Western America, 1790-1830."
    In The Old Northwest: Studies in Regional History, 1787-1910.
    Edited by Harry Scheiber. Lincoln: University of Nebraska
    Press, pp. 229-48.
       Reprint of 1958.28.

35 WILLIAMS, BURTON J. "The Twentieth Century American West:
    The Old versus the New." Rocky Mountain Social Science Jour-
    nal 6 (October):163-67.
       "If the historian can free himself from the ruling theory
of the Turner tradition, new vistas open up affording virtually
unlimited opportunity in the realm of Western historiography."
The past needs to be dealt with more fully and less impartially,
and the significance of events in the West since 1890 needs to be
incorporated and developed.

36 WILLIAMS, WILLIAM APPLEMAN. The Roots of the Modern American
    Empire: A Study of the Growth and Shaping of Social Con-
    sciousness in a Marketplace Society. New York: Random House,
    pp. xii-xvi; 545 pp., passim.
       Discusses the influence of expansionism on the development
of American foreign policy and American social thought. Comments
on the influence of Turner's frontier thesis: the expansionist
themes in the frontier thesis have been quickly paved over by
most historians, but these themes are significant and deserve
"very serious attention." Argues that the expansionist, imperial
foreign policy was "formulated in industrial times" and was
directed toward economic objectives. Reprinted: New York:
Vintage Books, 1970.

1969

37 WINTHER, OSCAR O. "A Dedication to the Memory of Robert
    Carlton Clark, 1877-1939." Arizona and the West 11 (Spring):
    1-4.
        Turner highly recommended Clark when he applied for a posi-
    tion at the University of Oregon. Clark was a product of the
    "Bolton and Turner schools of Western American history."

38 WISHART, DAVID J., ANDREW WARREN, and ROBERT H. STODDARD. "An
    Attempted Definition of a Frontier Using a Wave Length Analogy."
    Rocky Mountain Social Science Journal 6 (April):73-81.
        Examines several past definitions of "frontier" (including
    Turner's) and finds them to be full of complications. Argues
    that a more dynamic definition is needed since the frontier it-
    self is a dynamic condition. Presents a definition based on a
    wave theory analogous to the "wave, or succession of waves, of
    people moving westward."

39 WITT, GRACE. "The Bad Man as Hipster: Norman Mailer's Use of
    Frontier Metaphor." Western American Literature 4 (Fall):203-
    17.
        Mailer's "'Western' hero" is very similar to Turner's
    typical frontiersman. Like Turner, Mailer contends that we
    "'have used up our frontier.'"

40 YOUNG, MARY. "Congress Looks West: Liberal Ideology and Pub-
    lic Land Policy in the Nineteenth Century." In The Frontier
    in American Development: Essays in Honor of Paul Wallace
    Gates. Edited by David M. Ellis. Ithaca, N.Y.: Cornell Uni-
    versity Press, pp. 74-112.
        The Turnerian tradition of historiography identifies the
    "developing frontier" as having "always served Americans as a
    metaphor of their nation's unique potentialities." Young modi-
    fies Turner's safety-valve concept by arguing that the "frontier
    was a safety valve of liberalism."

                              1970

1 BERKHOFER, ROBERT F., Jr. "Space, Time, Culture and the New
   Frontier." In The West of the American People. Edited by
   Allan G. Bogue, Thomas D. Phillips, and James E. Wright.
   Itasca, Ill.: Peacock Publishers, pp. 30-35.
       Abridged version of 1964.2.

2 BILLINGTON, RAY ALLEN, ed. "Dear Lady": The Letters of
   Frederick Jackson Turner and Alice Forbes Perkins Hooper,
   1910-1932. San Marino, Calif.: Huntington Library, 487 pp.
       In the seventy-seven-page introduction, Billington explains

1970

the significance of the friendship and correspondence between
Turner and Mrs. Hooper. The letters "written by Turner offer an
intimate glimpse into the true character of the man and reveal an
intellectual breadth, a catholicity of interest." Turner's personal opinions on a wide range of subjects are documented in this
rich collection. Includes approximately three hundred letters.

3 BILLINGTON, RAY ALLEN. "The Frontier and I." Western Historical Quarterly 1 (January):4-20.
        In Billington's words, this is a "personal account of my
love affair with Western history" in which the author answers the
question: "How did I become interested in frontier history?"
The focus is upon an autohistoriographical analysis of America's
Frontier Heritage (1966.4), which "was designed not only to en-
lighten, but to convert." Billington considers this work to be
his major contribution to that body of historical scholarship
dedicated to the restoration of "Turner and his theories . . . to
their proper place in historiography." Although he designed this
book to proselytize, he acknowledges that neither the "general
public" nor the "social science-oriented historians" were recep-
tive in his plea to "restore Turner and his theories to their
rightful place in interpreting the past."

4 BLEDSTEIN, BURTON J. "Frederick Jackson Turner: A Note on
   the Intellectual and the Professional." Wisconsin Magazine of
   History 54 (Autumn):50-55.
        Turner has been criticized for being a nineteenth-century
romantic, but his thesis deserves to be reconsidered because of
its reflexive nature, which makes it particularly relevant to the
twentieth century. "Turner penetrated the problems of identity,
confidence, melancholy, and maturity in American society." Turner
was a spokesman for America's democratic institutions, and his
thesis "implied that American history would defy Marx's prediction." His thesis may renew faith in the progressive liberal
tradition.

5 BOGUE, ALLAN G. "The Iowa Claim Clubs: Symbol and Substance."
   In The West of the American People. Edited by Allan G. Bogue,
   Thomas D. Phillips, and James E. Wright. Itasca, Ill.: Pea-
   cock Publishers, pp. 195-201.
        Abridged version of 1958.7.

6 BOGUE, ALLAN G., THOMAS D. PHILLIPS, and JAMES E. WRIGHT, eds.
   The West of the American People. Itasca, Ill.: Peacock Publishers, pp. 3-4, 285-92, 517-25.
        Notes the influence of Frederick Jackson Turner upon western
history and examines the Turnerian model.

1970

7   BOYLE, THOMAS E.   "Frederick Jackson Turner and Thomas Wolfe:
    The Frontier as History and as Literature." Western American
    Literature 4 (Winter):273-85.
        Presents evidence which suggests that "an examination of
    the image of the West in the fiction of Thomas Wolfe provides
    remarkable parallels to the Turner thesis and significant dif-
    ferences as well." Finds that Turner's thesis is limited and
    that "Wolfe's treatment of the frontier provides an intelligible
    meaning of the American past, and affirms an open viable attitude
    toward the future."

8   CARELESS, J.M.S.   "Urban Liberalism and the Clear Grits."   In
    The Frontier Thesis and the Canadas. Edited by Michael S.
    Cross. Toronto: Copp Clark, pp. 152-57.
        Reprint of 1948.3.

9   CRAVEN, AVERY. "Some Historians I Have Known." Maryland His-
    torian 1 (Spring):1-11.
        Examines relationships with several teachers and colleagues,
    and notes that Frederick Jackson Turner was the "most stimulating
    and inspiring professor" at Harvard. Comments on Turner's "crys-
    tal clear honesty and genuine modesty" and discusses his enthu-
    siasm for discovery.

10 CROSS, MICHAEL S., ed.   The Frontier Thesis and the Canadas:
    The Debate on the Impact of the Canadian Environment. Toronto:
    Copp Clark, 188 pp.
        Presents articles and documents relevant to the application
    or the critique of the application of the frontier thesis to the
    study of Canadian history. Notes in the introduction (pp. 1-7)
    that "evidence of the frontier approach is to be discovered in
    the writings of a great many historians, many of whom would take
    umbrage at having this fact drawn to their attention."

11 DEGLER, CARL N. "The Challege of the Far West." In The
    Sweep of American History. Vol. 2. Edited by Robert R. Jones
    and Gustav L. Seligmann, Jr. New York: John Wiley, pp. 109-
    21.
        Reprint of 1967.5 (pp. 58-68); reprinted: 1974.

12 ELKINS, STANLEY, and ERIC McKITRICK. "A Meaning for Turner's
    Frontier. . . ." In The West of the American People. Edited
    by Allan G. Bogue, Thomas D. Phillips, and James E. Wright.
    Itasca, Ill.: Peacock Publishers, pp. 26-30.
        Abridged version of 1954.9.

1970

13 ELKINS, STANLEY, and ERIC McKITRICK. "Social Scientists Defend Turner." In The Frontier Thesis and the Canadas. Edited
by Michael S. Cross. Toronto: Copp Clark, pp. 161-65.
Reprint of 1954.9.

14 FRANTZ, JOE B. "Western Impact on the Nation." Western Historical Quarterly 1 (July):249-64.
Presents a lighthearted yet profound analysis of the history
of the West and its influence. Concludes that "the West's message to the world and to the nation is the message of the old
prospector always looking for one more stake, always dreaming of
rich veins that never run out, always more interested in moving
hopefully than intelligently."

15 GOETZMANN, WILLIAM H. "The West and the American Age of Ex-
ploration." In The West of the American People. Edited by
Allan G. Bogue, Thomas D. Phillips, and James E. Wright.
Itasca, Ill.: Peacock Publishers, pp. 70-75.
Abridged version of 1960.12.

16 HICKS, JOHN D. "The People's Party in Minnesota." In The
West of the American People. Edited by Allan G. Bogue,
Thomas D. Phillips, and James E. Wright. Itasca, Ill.: Pea-
cock Publishers, pp. 462-65.
Abridged version of 1924.6.

17 HIGHAM, JOHN. "The Divided Legacy of Frederick Jackson
Turner." In Writing American History; Essays on Modern
Scholarship. Bloomington: Indiana University Press, pp. 118-
29.
Expanded version of 1968.17.

18 HOFSTADTER, RICHARD. "The Frontier Thesis Under Attack." In
The Frontier Thesis and the Canadas. Edited by Michael S.
Cross. Toronto: Copp Clark, pp. 23-28.
Reprint of 1949.11.

19 JACOBS, WILBUR R. "Frontiersmen, Fur Traders, and Other Var-
mints; An Ecological Appraisal of the Frontier in American
History." American Historical Association Newsletter 3:5-11.
Charges that the Turnerian school of historiography fails
to acknowledge the destructive impact of the frontier experience
upon the physical environment.

20 ____. "The Many-Sided Frederick Jackson Turner." Western
Historical Quarterly 1 (October):363-72.
Analyzes the broad range of Turner's vision, examining both
"his versatility and the multiplicity of his concerns." Looks at

1970

the influence Turner exercised upon the historical profession and also discusses his attitudes toward international problems.

21 LEE, EVERETT S. "The Turner Thesis Re-examined." In The West of the American People. Edited by Allan G. Bogue, Thomas D. Phillips, and James E. Wright. Itasca, Ill.: Peacock Publishers, pp. 21-25.
    Abridged version of 1961.15.

22 LOWER, A.R.M. "The Natures of Canadian and American Democracy Compared." In The Frontier Thesis and the Canadas. Edited by Michael S. Cross. Toronto: Copp Clark, pp. 129-33.
    Reprint of 1930.11.

23 McDOUGALL, JOHN L. "The Frontier School and Canadian History." In The Frontier Thesis and the Canadas. Edited by Michael S. Cross. Toronto: Copp Clark, pp. 35-38.
    Reprint of 1929.7.

24 MIYAKAWA, T. SCOTT. "The Heritage of the Popular Denominations." In The West of the American People. Edited by Allan G. Bogue, Thomas D. Phillips, and James E. Wright. Itasca, Ill.: Peacock Publishers, pp. 511-16.
    Abridged version of 1964.18.

25 NASH, RODERICK. "The State of Environmental History." In The State of American History. Edited by Herbert J. Bass. Chicago: Quadrangle Books, pp. 249-60.
    Credits Turner with having founded a school of environmental history that emphasized the interrelationship between man's environment and his thought. Turner's "investigation of the frontier . . . launched American environmental history."

26 SHARP, PAUL F. "Three Frontiers: Some Comparative Studies of Canadian, American and Australian Settlement." In The West of the American People. Edited by Allan G. Bogue, Thomas D. Phillips, and James E. Wright. Itasca, Ill.: Peacock Publishers, pp. 15-20.
    Abridged version of 1955.22.

27 SIMONSON, HAROLD P. The Closed Frontier: Studies in American Literary Tragedy. New York: Holt, 160 pp., passim.
    Argues that "the closed frontier [serves] as the metaphor for American tragedy. . . ." Applies this concept to a study of American literature. Includes a chapter entitled "Frederick Jackson Turner: Frontier History as Symbol," where it is argued that Turner's literary style and poetic language are central to the frontier hypothesis.

1970

28 SMITH, HENRY NASH. "Consciousness and Social Order: The
   Themes of Transcendence in the Leatherstocking Tales."
   Western American Literature 5 (Fall):177-94.
      Frederick Jackson Turner, in writing of the frontier and
the pioneer, has implied a transcendence of past experience and
circumstances, "a ritual death and rebirth." Argues that
"Turner's interpretation makes all American history a constantly
renewed process of transcendence. . . ." Uses this transcendental
concept in evaluating Natty Bumppo and the Leatherstocking Tales.

29 SOLWAY, CLIFFORD. "Turning History Upside Down." Saturday
   Review, 20 June, pp. 13-15, 62-64.
      Traces the roots of the new left interpretation of American
history back to Turner.

30 SPACKMAN, S.G.F. "The Frontier and Reform in the United
   States." Historical Journal 13 (June):333-39.
      Reviews the Turnerian influence on seven different books.
Concludes that "in spite of all the knocks it has taken, the
frontier hypothesis remains profoundly true, though in a way that
Frederick Jackson Turner never comprehended."

31 STAVRIANOS, L.S. "A Frontierist Interpretation of the Re-
   bellions of 1837." In The Frontier Thesis and the Canadas.
   Edited by Michael S. Cross. Toronto: Copp Clark, pp. 135-40.
   Reprint of 1938.16.

32 VECOLI, RUDOLPH J. "Ethnicity: A Neglected Dimension of
   American History." In The State of American History. Edited
   by Herbert J. Bass. Chicago: Quadrangle Books, pp. 70-88.
      Generalizes that the "historians who established immigra-
tion history as a field of study after World War I were . . .
Turnerians" who had "a profound confidence in the power of the
New World to transform human nature." As a result they focused
upon how the American environment transformed the immigrant rather
than an emphasis upon ethnic factors.

33 WADE, RICHARD C. "An Agenda for Urban History." In The State
   of American History. Edited by Herbert J. Bass. Chicago:
   Quadrangle Books, pp. 43-69.
      Because "Frederick Jackson Turner and Charles A. Beard . . .
commanded the strategic heights of historical writing for more
than two generations," the study of urban history has been
greatly slighted.

1970

34 YOUNG, MARY. "The West and American Cultural Identity: Old
    Themes and New Variations." Western Historical Quarterly 1
    (April):137-60.
        Identifies "Turner's 1893 thesis" as the most well known
    "essay in cultural self-consciousness" that revisionist historians
    have attacked as a major "source of false historical self-con-
    sciousness which impedes Americans in attempts to cope with
    present problems." Reviews recent contributions of American
    studies scholars to the understanding of the role of the West on
    our nation's cultural identity. Treats the "myth-critics, Henry
    Nash Smith, Alfred K. Moore, and Charles L. Sanford," as a study
    in "the projection of particular myths onto frontier experience,"
    which "created a cultural predisposition to primitivism that out-
    lasted the frontier as much as Turner's egalitarianism and democ-
    racy were to outlast the reinforcing conditions of the frontier
    environment."

                              1971

1 AMBROSIUS, LLOYD E. "Turner's Frontier Thesis and the Modern
   American Empire." Civil War History 17 (December):332-39.
        Review of William Appleman Williams's The Roots of the
   Modern American Empire (see 1969.35). Williams employs the
   Turner thesis in analyzing the American Empire, but he gives the
   thesis a "Beardian twist" by relying too heavily on an economic
   interpretation. By ignoring the cultural influences inherent in
   the frontier thesis, "Williams failed to offer a persuasive interpretation of the nineteenth-century origins of twentieth-century
   American foreign relations."

2 ATHEARN, ROBERT G. "A Dedication to the Memory of Colin
   Brummitt Goodykoontz, 1885-1958." Arizona and the West 13
   (Autumn):217-20.
        Comments on Goodykoontz's relation to Turner as a graduate
   student under his tutelage at Harvard.

3 BANNON, JOHN FRANCIS. "Herbert Eugene Bolton--Western Historian." Western Historical Quarterly 2 (July):261-82.
        Identifies Turner as the scholar who was most responsible
   for attracting Bolton, who became "one of America's most distinguished historians" in his own right, into the field of history.

4 BERQUIST, GOODWIN F., Jr. "The Rhetorical Heritage of
   Frederick Jackson Turner." Wisconsin Academy of Sciences,
   Arts and Letters, Transactions 59 (May):23-32.
        Discusses Turner's training in rhetoric. Examines his
   parental influence, Professor Frankenburger's instruction, and
   his classroom expertise.

5   BILLINGTON, RAY ALLEN. "The American Frontier Thesis: Attack
and Defense." American Historical Association Pamphlets, no.
101. Richmond, Va.: William Byrd Press, 58 pp.
Expanded version of 1958.2.

6   _____. "Frederick Jackson Turner and the Closing of the Frontier." In Essays in Western History in Honor of Professor T.A.
Larson. Edited by Roger Daniels. Laramie: University of
Wyoming Publications, vol. 37 (October):45-56.
Comments on Malthusian "Alarmists" who, with the announcement of the closing of the frontier, sensationally predicted vast
overpopulation and dwindling food supplies. Turner, though "too
wise a man to succumb completely to this tide of propaganda,"
made his own exaggerated calculations of the world's future,
which were, in many ways, similar to the alarmists' predictions.
Turner lamented that the frontier values of individualism would
be inadequate to the demands that the twentieth century would
present.

7   _____. "Frederick Jackson Turner, Non-Western Historian."
Wisconsin Academy of Sciences, Arts, and Letters, Transactions
59 (May):7-21.
Answers Turner's critics by claiming that Turner was an
historian whose views were modern and whose techniques were far
in advance of his time. His theories were not monocausationalist,
but relied upon a theory of multiple causation. He was "a pioneer in the interdisciplinary approach to research." Discusses
Turner's use of geography, statistics, sociology, and economics
in his historical investigations.

8   _____. The Genesis of the Frontier Thesis: A Study in Historical Creativity. San Marino, Calif.: Huntington Library,
315 pp.
"The author's purpose in this book is to retrace the young
historian's thinking as the frontier thesis evolved in his mind."
The volume is divided into three descriptive sections: (1) "The
Years of Preparation, 1885-1892"; (2) "Formulating the Thesis,
1842-1893"; and (3) "Frederick Jackson Turner Remembers." The
last section focuses upon Turner's correspondence, in which he
"tries, at a much later date, to recall the genesis of the frontier thesis." Concludes that "Turner's recollections of his
early years were usually wrong in detail as they were in recon-
structing the overall pattern" of his frontier thesis.

9   CRAVEN, AVERY. "A History Still Unwritten." Western Historical Quarterly 2 (October):377-83.
Autobiographical summation of Craven's career, depicting
his indebtedness to Frederick Jackson Turner. Analyzes conversa-

1971

tions with Turner while both were at the Huntington Library and
notes that Turner "resented having to spend his time at the
library trying to write a book." Also comments on Turner's historical vision and his own relationship to that vision.

10 CURTI, MERLE. Review of "Dear Lady": The Letters of Frederick
    Jackson Turner and Alice Forbes Perkins Hooper 1910-1932,
    edited by Ray A. Billington. Journal of American History 58
    (September):488-90.
        "The letters supplement our knowledge of Turner as a member
of this historical profession and as a human being." They reveal
his views on historians and history, on political issues, and on
America's involvement in world affairs.

11 EVANS, PAUL D. "The Frontier in American Development: A Re-
    view." New York History 52 (January):51-61.
        Reviews The Frontier in American Development: Essays in
Honor of Paul Wallace Gates, edited by David M. Ellis, commenting
in particular on Lee Benson's essay "The Historian as Mythmaker:
Turner and the Closed Frontier." Finds several of Benson's
criticisms to be too harsh. Notes that Turner was "the least
pretentious and most modest of men"; he wrote with "devotion" and
with "imagination."

12 FERRISS, WILLIAM H. "The Pragmatic Definition of History."
    Southern Humanities Review 5 (Spring):182-95.
        Traces the New Left historiography, which emerged in the
1960s, back to Turner.

13 FISHER, JAMES A. "The Political Development of the Black Com-
    munity in California, 1850-1950." California Historical Quar-
    terly 50 (September):256-66.
        Thesis: "Frederick Jackson Turner's interpretation of the
significance of the West . . . did not depict the reality faced
by black people in the West" because they did not experience
"'individualism, economic equality, freedom to rise [and] democracy.'"

14 HOOVER, HERBERT T. "John Milton Leeper: Pioneer Farmer."
    Nebraska History 52 (Spring):31-44.
        Presents a narrative description of a Nebraska pioneer
family that closely matches Turner's description of the "pioneer
farmer."

15 JACOBS, WILBUR R. "Colonial Origins of the United States:
    Turnerian View." Pacific Historical Review 49 (February):21-
    37.
        Summarizes criticisms of Turner and his application of the

frontier thesis to colonial America, and concludes that such
criticisms "of his over-simplified approach are not entirely
borne out by examination of the evidence. . . . Turner was anything but a one-theory man. . . ." Turner used multiple hypotheses in discussing historical causation, and his approach to
colonial America is actually rich and complex.

16 _____. "The Fatal Confrontation: Early Native-White Relations on the Frontiers of Australia, New Guinea, and America--
A Comparative Study." Pacific Historical Review 40 (August):
283-309.
    Compares problems faced by natives after the "alien inva-
sion," especially as they relate to use of land. Concludes that
Turner's frontier theory "is evidence of the historians' concern
for the development of white civilization and the exploitation of
the land." The frontier thesis reflects the unsympathetic attitude toward native peoples, treating them "as if they were some
kind of geographical obstacle to the westward movement of whites."

17 LARSEN, LAWRENCE H., and ROBERT L. BRANYAN. "The Development
of an Urban Civilization on the Frontier of the American
West." Societas 1 (Winter):33-50.
    "By the decade of the 1880s the cities of the Great West,
despite the mythology fostered by numerous pulp magazines and
dime authors, simply were not frontier outposts. As the United
States became a nation of cities, the physical characteristics of
western urban centers differed little from their eastern counterparts."

18 LUEBKE, FREDERICK C. "Ethnic Group Settlement on the Great
Plains." Western Historical Quarterly 8 (October):405-30.
    The settlers of the great plains are generally regarded as
a homogeneous group, and little significance has been given to
the importance of ethnic factors. Examines the role of immigrants
in the settling of the plains and discusses the push-pull factors
that brought them there.

19 SMITH, DUANE A. "Colorado's Urban-Mining Safety Valve."
Colorado Magazine 48 (Fall):299-318.
    Finds that, at least in Colorado, the safety valve "was
both urban and frontier at the same time. . . ." It did not
operate in the same way that Turner interpreted it, but neither
did it operate as his critics have charged.

20 TUMA, ELIAS H. Economic History and the Social Sciences.
Berkeley: University of California Press, pp. 82, 93-217
passim.
    Compares methodological problems of eight contributors to

1971

economic history: Marx, Weber, Pirenne, John Chapman, Turner,
Eli F. Heckscher, Paul Mantoux, and Robert Cameron. Turner is
part of "the interpretive school" and is interdisciplinary in
scope, and he criticizes economists and others who formulate
theories of the present but who resort to history for illustrations. Turner's own methodology, however, is inadequate. He
does not produce evidence or criteria for his assertions, his
contributions lack data evidence, and his arguments are supported
by opinion. "In general, Turner is satisfied with qualitative
measurements such as 'important,' 'significant,' or 'influential'
with no documentation."

21 WINKS, ROBIN W. The Myth of the American Frontier: Its
    Relevance to America, Canada and Australia. Leicester, England:
    Leicester University Press, 39 pp.
        Emphasizes the influence of Turner and his interpreters
    upon the way in which Americans have viewed their frontier ex-
    perience. Identifies some weaknesses of Turner's views. Explores
    the results of the exportation of the "myth of the Frontier" to
    other nations.

1972

1 BELL, ROBERT GALEN. "James C. Malin and the Grasslands of
   North America." Agricultural History 46 (July):414-24.
       Comments on Malin's analysis of the "closed-space fatalism"
   of Turner's frontier hypothesis.

2 BENSON, LEE. "The Historian as Mythmaker: Turner and the
   Closed Frontier." In Toward the Scientific Study of History,
   Selected Essays. Philadelphia: Lippincott, pp. 175-89.
       Turner "functioned as a mythmaker" when he borrowed "Achille
   Loria's 'free land' theory of history and applied it to America
   in the form of the 'frontier thesis.'" It is no longer enough to
   discuss the validity or invalidity of the thesis because its influence and scope have grown too broadly; the frontier thesis now
   fits "the 'sociological' definition of 'myth.'"

3 BERGER, CARL C. "Internationalism, Continentalism, and the
   Writing of History: Comments on the Carnegie Series on the
   Relations of Canada and the United States." In The Influence
   of The United States on Canadian Development: Eleven Case
   Studies. Edited by Richard A. Preston. Duke University Com-
   monwealth--Studies Center, no. 40. Durham, N.C.: Duke University Press, pp. 32-54.
       Assesses the influence of the Turner thesis upon Canadian
   historiography.

1972

4 BILLINGTON, RAY ALLEN. "Frederick Jackson Turner: The Image and the Man." Western Historical Quarterly 3 (April):137-52.
Turner is generally discussed in terms of his academic contributions and influences and has become somewhat of a legend; however, underneath this exterior he is a sensitive, warm, and fallible human being. This latter side is examined here. Turner's extravagant appetites, which kept him in financial trouble, are discussed, and his sense of social equality also is analyzed. Notes further that Turner was not the dynamic teacher he is heralded as being; rather, many of his undergraduates failed to become inspired and were bored by his presentations. Nevertheless, Turner is remembered as "a warm, attractive, kindly mortal who was liked as well as respected by his contemporaries."

5 _____. "Frontier Democracy: Social Aspects." In The Turner Thesis: Concerning the Role of the Frontier in American History. 3d ed. Edited by George Rogers Clark. Problems in American Civilization Series. Boston: D.C. Heath, pp. 160-84. Reprint of 1966.4.

6 BLOOM, JO TICE. "Cumberland Gap versus South Pass: The East or West in Frontier History." Western Historical Quarterly 3 (April):153-67.
Examines the problems associated with the terms "frontier" and "West." Turner used the terms interchangeably and broadly, but since then they have been narrowed in scope. Argues for a return to broader approaches and wider horizons. Historians need to explore the "cis-Missouri West" as well as the "trans-Missouri," and areas of study ignored in the past need to be incorporated more fully. Asserts that "it is time for western historians to begin writing with maturity the history of the 350 years of the American frontier."

7 CARPENTER, RONALD H. "The Rhetorical Genius of Style in the 'Frontier Hypothesis' of Frederick Jackson Turner." Southern Speech Communication Journal 37 (Spring):233-48.
In formulating the frontier thesis, and in the actual writing of it, Turner employed a rhetorical approach which was meant to be hortatory and evocative rather than scientific or epistemological. "Turner was a rhetor in the classical sense of the word," and he used individualistic syntax, amplification, alliteration, and other rhetorical devices for his "suasory design." A brief analysis of the evolution of Turner's rhetorical style is presented.

8 CLARK, THOMAS D. "The Heritage of the Frontier." West Virginia History 34 (October):1-17.
From the perspective of the twentieth century, the signifi-

1972

cance of the frontier experience lies in its wastefulness and
despoliation of resources rather than in its yield of a Turnerian
version of American democracy.

9 FELDMAN, EGAL. "The American City: From George Bancroft to
   Charles A. Beard." Societas 2 (Spring):121-42.
      Examines twelve "American general historians whose writing
   appeared between the 1830s and the 1930s, that is, prior to the
   decade in which American historians 'discovered' the city."
   Turner was the first of this group to ask questions regarding the
   "rise of cities." Half of Turner's references to cities deal
   with economic development, and he paid only slight attention to
   other dimensions of urban growth.

10 GRESSLEY, GENE M. West by East: The American West in the
    Gilded Age. Charles Redd Monographs in Western History, no.
    1. Provo, Utah: Brigham Young University Press, 54 pp.,
    passim.
       "Where are the Turners of today, with their horizon-sweeping
    theses, whereby all complexities appear to fall neatly into in-
    telligent pattern? We would propose that we know both too little
    and too much of the history of the West to be long ensnared by
    the simplicity of an all-embracing explanation like Turner's."

11 JACOBS, WILBUR R. Dispossessing the American Indian: Indians
    and Whites on the Colonial Frontier. New York: Scribner's,
    pp. 20-26, 149-50, 152, 183, 184.
       Argues that Turner and other frontier historians have pre-
    sented a "one-sided view of the fur trade in American history,"
    and Turner helped shape the myths that made heroes out of the
    early exploiters of the American continent. The rest of this
    volume purports "to throw light on the ecology of the frontier
    and on the shadowy history of early native-white relations. . . ."

12 KAMMEN, MICHAEL. "The Old World and the New, Pari Passu." In
    People of Paradox: An Inquiry Concerning the Origins of Amer-
    ican Civilization. New York: Alfred A. Knopf, pp. 14-30.
       Challenges those historians who have been "inoculated with
    the serum of environmentalism, from Turner to Boorstin" and have
    rejected any "suggestion that things European might long survive
    the . . . transforming powers" of the North American continent.

13 KLEIN, MILTON M. "New York in the American Colonies: A New
    Look." New York History 53 (April):132-56.
       Credits Turner with having been one of the first historians
    to underscore the importance of "the Middle Atlantic area" in
    "initiating the American tradition."

1972

14 LEWIS, MERRILL E. "The Art of Frederick Jackson Turner: The
    Histories." Huntington Library Quarterly 35 (May):241-55.
        Indicates Turner's lack of respect for traditional narra-
    tive history and discusses Turner's attempt to synthesize narra-
    tive and analytical approaches. Turner wrote of the "dramatic
    conflict between sections and nation" instead of exaggerating
    conflicts between individuals, but he does utilize individuals as
    "representative men," standing as "voices or spokesmen" for the
    region they epitomize. Introduces the article with a discussion
    of Turner's response to Theodore Roosevelt's The Winning of the
    West.

15 LOEWENBERG, BERT JAMES. "Herbert Baxter Adams and American
    Historical Craftsmanship." In American History in American
    Thought: Christopher Columbus to Henry Adams. New York:
    Simon & Schuster, pp. 363-79.
        Argues that Adams's "restriction of the study of American
    institutions to the Atlantic seaboard led to the intellectual
    rebellion of Frederick Jackson Turner." Furthermore, the "re-
    bellion of Frederick Jackson Turner led to a search for the Amer-
    ican origins of American institutions in the American West."

16 MASTERSON, JAMES R., and JOYCE E. EBERLY. Writings on American
    History, 1960. Washington, D.C.: United States Government
    Printing Office, compiled by the National Historical Publica-
    tions Commission, 367 pp.
        Cites ten publications that are important in understanding
    Turner's ideas and contribution as a historian.

17 MEINIG, D.W. "American Wests: Preface to a Geographical
    Interpretation." Association of American Geographers, Annals
    62 (June):159-84.
        American geographers have given very little attention to
    the importance of sectional studies. Suggests that much can be
    learned about the West by examing it as a section composed of
    other smaller sections, and a model is presented for such a
    study. This model has even wider applications because it allows
    for an understanding of the interrelationships of sections as
    well as an indication of their differences.

18 NASH, RODERICK. "American Environmental History: A New
    Teaching Frontier." Pacific Historical Review 41 (August):
    362-72.
        Presents an outline for a course on "American environmental
    history," and gives "a bow to Frederick Jackson Turner" for his
    synthesis of environmental and historical relationships.

1972

19 NICHOLS, DAVID A. "Civilization Over Savage; Frederick
    Jackson Turner and the Indian." <u>South Dakota History</u> 2 (Fall):
    383-405.
        Analyzes Turner's view of the role of the Indian in American
    history. Turner was not unaware of the Indian, but he felt that
    the influence of Indian culture on American development was insig-
    nificant. To Turner, "the Indian was part of the landscape";
    Turner believed that "the Indian was important only insofar as he
    contributed to the 'environment' of the frontier--<u>the pioneer's
    environment</u>." Also comments on Turner's rejection of the germ
    theory: Turner "never denied the European origins of the 'germs'
    that were planted in the American environment. He simply wanted
    to shift attention to the environment."

20 TUCKER, FRANK H. "East Meets West: Woodrow Wilson in 1894."
    <u>Colorado Magazine</u> 49 (Spring):109-15.
        Finds significance in President Woodrow Wilson discovering
    the West through travel in the same year that his friend
    "Frederick Jackson Turner . . . read his famous paper 'The Sig-
    nificance of the Frontier in American History.'"

21 WRIGHT, LOUIS B., and ELAINE W. FOWLER, eds. "Conclusion: A
    Nation in Motion." In <u>The Moving Frontier: North America as
    Seen Through the Eyes of Its Pioneer Discoverers</u>. The Great
    Explorers Series, edited by Evelyn Stephansson. New York:
    Delacorte Press, pp. 333-35.
        Summarizes Turner's ideas regarding the frontier influence
    upon American development and accepts his views, as modified in
    recent historiography, as the most convincing explanation of cer-
    tain characteristics of American culture.

1973

1 BAILEY, THOMAS A. "The Mythology of the West." In <u>Probing
    America's Past: A Critical Examination of Major Myths and
    Misconceptions</u>. Vol. 1. Lexington: D.C. Heath, pp. 232-47.
        Deals briefly with the validity of Turner's safety-valve
    concept, the originality of his thesis, and the impact of his
    thesis upon historiography.

2 BENSON, LEE. "The Historical Background of Turner's Frontier
    Essay." In <u>American History in Honor of James C. Malin</u>.
    Edited by Burton J. Williams. Lawrence, Kans.: Coronado
    Press, pp. 22-71.
        Reprint of 1951.2.

1973

3 BILLINGTON, RAY ALLEN. <u>Frederick Jackson Turner: Historian,</u>
<u>Scholar, Teacher</u>. New York: Oxford University Press, 599 pp.
    In the words of the author, this is "a full-length portrait
of the man [Turner] and his ideas." A monumental biography
authored by Turner's most authoritative interpreter. Includes a
fifteen-page bibliography.

4 _____. "Tempest in Clio's Teapot: The American Historical
Association's Rebellion of 1915." <u>American Historical Review</u>
78 (April):348-69.
    Analyzes the revolt against the American Historical Associa-
tion's governing body by a small group of "insurgents" arguing
for democratic reforms in the association and for association
control of the <u>American Historical Review</u>. Turner was a member
of the governing council, and he and J. Franklin Jameson were
singled out as two "self-seeking" bureaucrats who "must be ousted
before reform was possible." Turner took a middle-of-the-road
stance on these reforms, and the author comments on his role in
the "rebellion."

5 BOGUE, ALLAN G. "Frederick Jackson Turner: Historian,
Scholar, Teacher." <u>Pacific Northwest Quarterly</u> 64 (October):
175-77.
    Review of Ray Allen Billington's biography of Turner (see
1973.3). Claims that the book is "industrially researched" and
"charmingly written," but because of its obvious biases, it does
not adequately answer several important questions relating to
Turner and the development of the frontier thesis.

6 _____. "The People Come." In <u>Patterns and Perspectives in</u>
<u>Iowa History</u>. Edited by Dorothy Schwieder. Ames: Iowa
State University Press, pp. 83-103.
    Reprint of 1963.6.

7 BOSTERT, RUSSELL H., and JOHN A. DeNOVO. "Samuel Flagg Bemis."
<u>Massachusetts Historical Society, Proceedings</u> 85:117-29.
    Credits Turner with having instilled in Bemis "a lasting
appreciation of the West's influence on American development."
Explores the influence of Turner's thesis upon Bemis's treatment
of diplomatic history.

8 CRAVENS, HAMILTON. "The Genesis of the Frontier Thesis."
<u>Pacific Northwest Quarterly</u> 64 (July):119.
    A review of Ray Allen Billington's <u>A Genesis of the Frontier</u>
<u>Thesis: A Study in Historical Creativity</u> in which Billington is
praised for having made "a substantial contribution to Turnerians"
by "making sense of Turner's rather chaotic notes and jottings--
even in underlinings in his books."

1973

9 CROSS, ROBERT D. "How Historians Have Looked at Immigrants to
   the United States." International Migration Review 7 (Spring):
   4-13.
        Analyzes the views historians have held toward immigration,
   ranging from extreme prejudice to open encouragement. Turner re-
   duced the influence that immigrant values had on the development
   of American culture and stressed instead "the supreme importance
   of the American environment."

10 DEUTSCH, HERMAN J. "Pacific Northwest History in Some World
    Perspectives." Pacific Northwest Quarterly 64 (January):1-7.
        "With some exceptions, scholarship in the field of American
   history during the past century has been postulated upon two
   well-known . . . hypotheses, namely, the germ theory which ac-
   cented the European heritage and the frontier hypothesis which
   emphasized the impact of the American environment." This article
   is an analysis of these two theories of history.

11 DOOLITTLE, GRAYDON. "Culture and Environment on the Cumberland
    Frontier." Papers in Anthropology (University of Oklahoma) 14
    (Spring):31-43.
        Considers the Turnerian perspective of the frontier to be
   wanting. Applies a cultural-ecological analysis to the pioneer
   situation in order to determine influences on social change and
   to find those factors that "provide links back to the mother
   cultures."

12 EIGENHEER, RICHARD. "The Frontier Hypothesis and Related
    Spatial Concepts." California Geographer 14:55-69.
        Reviews those propositions within the Turner thesis that
   are spatial in nature. Looks at Turner's theory of successive
   stages, the frontier as a "cultural hearth," regional variations,
   and the frontier as a "closed world." Examines both the advocates
   and the critics of these propositions. Claims that the Turner
   thesis, though not completely satisfactory, could serve as "a
   starting point for a geographic study of the processes of settlement."

13 GOTTMANN, JEAN. "Crossroads and Frontiers Amid Modern Fluidity:
    The Shifting Demands of Territory." In The Significance of
    Territory. Charlottesville: University Press of Virginia,
    pp. 123-58.
        Places Turner's ideas concerning the American frontier
   within the international "concept of territory."

14 GUGLER, STEVEN K. "The Philippine Frontier." Papers in
    Anthropology (University of Oklahoma) 14 (Spring):53-68.
        Finds that "there are major differences" between the Turner
    thesis and the Philippine frontier experience.

15 HAWKINS, HOMER C. "Trends in Black Migration from 1863 to
    1960." Phylon 34 (June):140-52.
        Notes that "the motivational content of the Turner thesis
    . . . serves to explain" black migration to parts of the frontier
    during the period from 1863 to 1900.

16 HEALE, M.J. "The Role of the Frontier in Jacksonian Politics:
    David Crockett and the Myth of Self-Made Man." Western His-
    torical Quarterly 4 (October):405-23.
        Finds, contrary to Turner, that the rise of the West "was
    in large part the product, and not the cause, of the egalitarian
    democracy of the Jacksonian era." Analyzes the reality and myth
    of David Crockett in light of this argument.

17 HINE, ROBERT V. The American West: An Interpretive History.
    Boston: Little, Brown, 371 pp., passim.
        Although revisionist in tone, the frontier experience is
    treated within a Turnerian framework. Ascribes great influence
    to Turner and his ideas and explains the "acceptance of Turner's
    thesis" as a result of "the remarkable accuracy of his predic-
    tions" and because he made the "frontier theory" a "part of Amer-
    ican intellectual history."

18 HUTSON, JAMES H. "Benjamin Franklin and the West." Western
    Historical Quarterly 4 (October):425-34.
        Analyzes Franklin's view of the influence of the frontier
    in shaping the American character, and compares this view to
    Turner's.

19 JACOBS, WILBUR R. "The Indian and the Frontier in American
    History--A Need for Revision." Western Historical Quarterly
    4 (January):43-56.
        Argues that American frontier history, especially history
    that follows the "Turnerian theme of progress," needs to be re-
    vised to incorporate the Indian point of view.

20 LAMAR, HOWARD R. "Persistent Frontier: The West in the
    Twentieth Century." Western Historical Quarterly 4 (January):
    5-25.
        The West is still as significant as when Turner wrote, and
    given new historical methods, contains several productive fron-
    tiers for western historians. Revisionist history has made many
    inroads toward an understanding of America's past, and several of

1973

these are applicable to the West, most notably: multi-racial
studies, trade themes, family studies, and studies of ideological
themes, "Saddle up your typewriters, ladies and gentlemen, it is
time to ride herd on these new frontiers."

21 LANTZEFF, GEORGE V., and RICHARD A. PIERCE. "Conclusions."
   In Eastward To Empire: Exploration and Conquest on the Russian Open Frontier to 1750. Montreal: McGill-Queen's University Press, pp. 221-30.
       Elaborates upon the generalization that "certain . . .
   aspects of . . . F.J. Turner's famous hypothesis concerning the
   influence of the frontier upon the development of the United
   States . . . do seem applicable to Russia."

22 LEE, ROBERT EDSON. "Politics and Society in Sioux City, 1859."
   In Patterns and Perspectives in Iowa History. Edited by
   Dorothy Schwieder. Ames: Iowa State University Press, pp.
   161-74.
       Challenges the Turnerian generalizations regarding the re-
   lationship between the frontier and "equality of opportunity,
   . . . individualism, . . . idealism," and "the absence of social
   castes."

23 McAVOY, THOMAS T. "What Is the Midwestern Mind?" In Patterns
   and Perspectives in Iowa History. Edited by Dorothy Schwieder.
   Ames: Iowa State University Press, pp. 5-24.
       "There has been too much of Frederick Jackson Turner in
   evaluations of the Midwest" and as a result histories of the
   region have overemphasized environment. Dismisses the "frontier
   thesis" as a "bit of American romanticism." Reprint of 1961.17.

24 NASH, GERALD D. The American West in the Twentieth Century:
   A Short History of an Urban Oasis. Englewood Cliffs, N.J.:
   Prentice-Hall, 312 pp., passim.
       "Thanks to Frederick Jackson Turner and his devoted band of
   disciples over the last severnty-five years, we know much more
   about the West before 1890 than thereafter. . . . But it can be
   argued that the frontier hypothesis of Frederick Jackson Turner
   is not very applicable . . . to an understanding of the American
   West after 1890. . . . The dynamic forces that shaped western
   development after 1890 were somewhat different from those described by Turner."

25 NORDSTROM, CARL. Frontier Elements in a Hudson River Village.
   National University Publications, Series in American Studies,
   edited by James P. Shenton. Port Washington, N.Y.: Kennikat
   Press, 199 pp., passim.
       "In this work . . . the frontier thesis of Frederick Jackson

Turner . . . is first developed as an ideal type and then . . .
tested through a close study of economic and social relations
in . . . Nyack, New York." Formulates "an ideal-type model of
the frontier . . . constructed out of material mined from Turner's
work as well as from that of his advocates and critics." In
method and conclusions this "study is concerned primarily with
events and subsequent transformations in an American locality as
they are illuminated by the frontier thesis and only incidentally
with an abstract set of definitions referring to that thesis."

26 PIERSON, GEORGE W. The Moving Americans. New York: Alfred
    A. Knopf, 290 pp., passim.
        This book was in part a result of a "fascination with
Frederick Jackson Turner's 'frontier hypothesis'" and at the same
time a "growing dissatisfaction with his materialism--particularly
with his concentration on 'free land' or the explanation or causal
factor in Americanization." Rejects Turner's theory as explaining
"far too much by far too little" and advances what he calls "the
'M-factor' in American history" to explain the effects Turner
attributed to the frontier.

27 POTTER, DAVID M. "Abundance and the Turner Thesis." In His-
    tory and American Society: Essays of David M. Potter. Edited
    by Don E. Fehrenbacher. New York: Oxford University Press,
    pp. 109-34.
        Reprint of 1954.21.

28 _____. "The Quest for the National Character." In History
    and American Society: Essays of David M. Potter. Edited by
    Don E. Fehrenbacher. New York: Oxford University Press, pp.
    228-55.
        Reprint of 1962.24.

29 ROBBINS, WILLIAM. "Community Conflict in Roseburg, Oregon,
    1870-1885." Journal of the West 12 (October):618-32.
        Argues against the consensus view of frontier history using
the community of Roseburg, Oregon, as a case study.

30 SMITH, ALICE E. The History of Wisconsin. Vol. 1, From Ex-
    ploration to Statehood. Madison: State Historical Society of
    Wisconsin, pp. 412-15, 574.
        Summarizes the historiography of the Turner school and
generalizes that many of its "conclusions" are in harmony with
"Wisconsin's nature-born historian of the frontier," who asserted
that "the harsh realities of existence . . . had stripped the
frontiersmen of their European culture and transformed them into
a people strong in . . . individualism."

1973

31 STARR, RAYMOND. "The Great Frontier Thesis as a Framework for
    the American History Survey in Secondary Schools." History
    Teacher 6 (February):227-32.
        Presents an outline utilizing Walter Prescott Webb's "Great
    Frontier Thesis" as a vehicle for organizing "an inquiry-oriented
    United States history course." Although Turner is not mentioned,
    much of the presentation and many of the questions are clearly
    Turnerian in flavor.

32 STEFFEN, JEROME O. "Some Observations on the Turner Thesis:
    A Polemic." Papers in Anthropology (University of Oklahoma)
    14 (Spring):16-30.
        Places Turner in his historiographic context. Contends
    that Turner should not be discarded "in a blanket fashion, for in
    his hypothesis he did manage to capture the essence of American
    development." Agrees with critics that Turner's thesis does not
    apply to the mining and ranching frontiers of the trans-Mississippi
    West, but argues that "if the environmental circumstances of the
    two frontiers are considered, there is no valid reason why the
    Turner thesis should even be tested in these areas."

33 WELLS, ROBIN F. "Frontier Systems as a Sociocultural Type."
    Papers in Anthropology (University of Oklahoma) 14 (Spring):
    6-15.
        Argues, following the influence of Turner, Webb, and others,
    that "the study of frontier systems is the very substance of
    socio-cultural history." Analyzes the characteristics of frontier
    systems. Concludes, in a Turnerian tone, that the "history of
    the world . . . has been in a large measure the history of ever-
    widening expansions followed by the ebb of a succession of
    ethnological frontiers."

34 WILLIAMS, BURTON J., ed. "The Platte, the Plains and the
    Peak: Grand Theory and Local History." In Essays in American
    History in Honor of James C. Malin. Lawrence, Kans.: Coronado
    Press, pp. 221-38.
        Reprint of 1968.51.

35 WILLIAMS, WILLIAM APPLEMAN. "The Frontier Thesis and American
    Foreign Policy." In History as a Way of Learning. New York:
    New Viewpoints, pp. 135-57.
        Reprint of 1955.25.

36 WISE, GENE. American Historical Explanations: A Strategy for
    Grounded Inquiry. Homewood, Ill.: Dorsey Press, 370 pp.,
    passim.
        Uses Turner as a case study for examining the problem of
    "paradigm strain," where "mind . . . becomes unreliable as a

guide to one's world of experience." Turner's progressivism suffers from the dilemma of contradiction: he asserts, on the one hand, that American democracy flourished because of the frontier, yet he also notes that the frontier has passed which should indicate that democracy has also passed. Examines this dilemma and the stress it causes on Turner's outlook.

37 WOOD, CHARLES L. "C.D. Perry: Clark County Farmer and Rancher, 1884-1908." Kansas Historical Quarterly 39 (Winter): 449-77.
Turner's "'safety-valve' for the discontented and depressed masses of the East" cannot be substantiated by the history of Clark County, Kansas. In fact "in this instance Turner's safety-valve thesis was reversed. Easterners tended to migrate to Clark County . . . during times of prosperity, and then retraced their steps to the East when they encountered a depression."

38 ZELINSKY, WILBUR. The Cultural Geography of the United States. Englewood Cliffs, N.J.: Prentice-Hall, pp. 33-35, 37.
Argues that an intermediate position between Turner's critics and his proponents needs to be realized. As the declaration of an important state of mind, the Turner thesis "is valid and useful. But if we wish to discover how American culture really developed, we must turn elsewhere."

1974

1 BARTLETT, RICHARD A. The New Country: A Social History of the American Frontier, 1776-1800. New York: Oxford University Press, 487 pp., passim.
Views the westward movement, "not as a myriad of incidents, but as a great sweep Westward, unbroken, inevitable, of epic proportions." Discusses the social factors which inspired and which resulted from this "rapid" and "inevitable" sweep.

2 BOLT, CHRISTINE. "Return of the Native: Some Reflections on the History of American Indians." Journal of American Studies 8 (August):247-59.
Discusses the inadequacies of the treatment of Indians by white historians. Finds Turner and his disciples, among others, to be "disappointing" in their analysis of the influence of the Indian on American civilization.

3 BURT, JESSE. Review of Frederick Jackson Turner: Historian, Scholar, Teacher, by Ray Allen Billington. Tennessee Historical Quarterly 33 (Summer):234-35.
"Turner's high position in American thought was given

1974

impeccable endorsement in the supplement to the 7th edition of
Subject Headings Used in the Dictionary Catalogs of the Library
of Congress. . . . Turner perhaps uniquely among American historians . . . was given his 'L C call number,' which . . . shows
the significance of his work."

4 CAUGHEY, JOHN W. "The Insignificance of the Frontier in American History or 'Once Upon a Time There Was an American West.'"
   Western Historical Quarterly 5 (January):5-16.
      Presents a quantitative analysis of historical material
covering the West, and laments that only a relatively small
amount of time is spent on the West after 1890. Western historians
should break out of the "self-imposed imprisonment in the early
and antique West" and bring the history up to date. The significance of the West has "too long been clouded by our obsession
with the frontier."

5 COHEN, BRONWEN J. "Nativism and Western Myth: The Influence
   of Nativist Ideas on the American Self-Image." Journal of
   American Studies 8 (April):23-39.
      Examines the impact of immigration and the hostility toward
immigrants on the development of the western myth. The western
myth was a product of the growing nationalism in America.
Turner's relationship to this nationalism is explored.

6 CONTENT, ROBIN. "The Emergence of the American Professor."
   History of Education Quarterly 14 (Fall):430-34.
      Review of Ray Allen Billington's Frederick Jackson Turner:
Historian, Scholar, Teacher. Argues that Turner's lack of publication "cannot necessarily be blamed on the demands of teaching."
His teaching of graduate students was excellent, but "he was not
particularly popular with undergraduates and his public service
had a slight tinge of crass commercialism. . . ." One comes away
from this biography with "increased respect" for Turner, however,
and one wishes there were more biographies of university professors.

7 COOPER, JOHN MILTON, Jr., ed. "Frederick Jackson Turner and
   the Wisconsin Idea: A Recently Discovered Letter." Wisconsin
   Magazine of History 57 (Summer):310-12.
      Turner is lauded as "the most distinguished and influential
mind produced by the institution [University of Wisconsin] and
the state." Includes one of Turner's obscure letters which deals
with his traumatic departure from the University of Wisconsin in
1910.

1974

8 CUNLIFFE, MARCUS. "New World, Old World: The Historical
   Antithesis." In Lessons from America: An Exploration.
   Edited by Richard Rose. New York: John Wiley, pp. 19-45.
       "Some scholars . . . emphasize dissimilarity: discontinuity
   in Time, the effect of environment. . . . This was the intent of
   Frederick Jackson Turner." This aspect of Turner's thesis is ex-
   plored throughout the article.

9 _____. "The Two or More Worlds of Willa Cather." In The Art
   of Willa Cather. Edited by Bernice Slote and Virginia
   Faulkner. Lincoln: University of Nebraska Press, pp. 21-42.
       Though in all probability Turner and Cather never read each
   other, there are many parallels in their work. This relationship
   is examined in detail.

10 ELAZAR, DANIEL J. "Land Space and Civil Society in America."
    Western Historical Quarterly 5 (July):261-84.
        A study of "Turner's . . . point that land and its use has
    had particular social and political implications for American
    society." Concludes that Turner's contention that "land has been
    used as a major guarantor of the liberties of Americans" is still
    valid.

11 ELKINS, STANLEY, and ERIC McKITRICK, eds. "Richard Hofstadter:
    A Progress." In The Hofstadter Aegis: A Memorial. New York:
    Alfred A. Knopf, pp. 300-67 passim.
        Includes a brief assessment of Hofstadter's treatment of
    Turner and his place in historiography.

12 HOLLON, WILLIAM EUGENE. "Melting Pot or Pressure Cooker?" In
    Frontier Violence: Another Look. New York: Oxford Univer-
    sity Press, pp. 16-35.
        "In 1893 . . . Frederick Jackson Turner revolutionized the
    teaching of American history with the hypothesis that our fron-
    tiers were the most potent force in molding the character of the
    American people. Most scholars today still accept the basic
    premise of the Turner thesis. Even so, it would seem from the
    scattered events herein examined that the proclivity for violence
    in the American character was well developed long before large
    numbers of settlers were ready to move into the . . . far west."

13 HOLTGRIEVE, DONALD G. "Frederick Jackson Turner as a Region-
    alist." Professional Geographer 26 (May):159-65.
        Discusses and acclaims Turner's sectional ideas. Defends
    Turner against critics who claimed he was an environmental deter-
    minist: Turner "went to great lengths to emphasize that he was
    not a determinist of any sort." Defines Turner's use of "region"
    and relates it to his "multiple working-hypothesis methodology."

1974

14 HUBBELL, JOHN T. Review of <u>Frederick Jackson Turner: Historian, Scholar, Teacher</u>, by Ray Allen Billington. <u>Maryland Historical Magazine</u> 69 (Summer):237-40.
    "Frederick Jackson Turner is probably the most written-about, if not the most read, American historian" because "American historians harbor a particular interest in Turner, who, because he charted new areas of interpretation and research invites criticism."

15 LARSON, T.A. "Women's Role in American West." <u>Montana: The Magazine of Western History</u> 24 (Summer):2-11.
    "Frederick Jackson Turner set the pattern" of assigning "small significance" to women in "his famous essay 'The Significance of the Frontier in American History,'" and all those who have followed in his footsteps have remained true to his precedent.

16 LUCKINGHAM, BRADFORD. "The City in the Westward Movement--A Bibliographical Note." <u>Western Historical Quarterly</u> 5 (July): 295-306.
    Turner recognized that the role of the city in the westward movement had been neglected, and he indicated that historians needed to pay more attention to this dimension. Only a few scholars have followed his advice, and "selected themes from their work are the subject of this bibliographical essay."

17 McZACHLAN, JAMES. "American Colleges and the Transmission of Culture: The Case of the Mugwumps." In <u>The Hofstadter Aegis: A Memorial</u>. Edited by Stanley Elkins and Eric McKitrick. New York: Alfred A. Knopf, pp. 184-206.
    Discusses Turner's possible influence upon "public affairs" with special focus upon his alleged influence upon Franklin D. Roosevelt.

18 NACKMAN, MARK E. "Anglo-American Migrants to the West: Men of Broken Fortunes? The Case of Texas, 1821-46." <u>Western Historical Quarterly</u> 5 (October):441-55.
    Discusses push-pull factors leading to Anglo-American migration to Texas. Most were "misfits," "debtors," and other social "delinquents." Turner's safety-valve theory may be discredited, but "Turner may have been right in another way: Men in dire financial straits or those in trouble with the law <u>did</u> go west, not so much for new opportunity as to flee the hounding creditor or sheriff."

19 NELSON, HOWARD J. "Town Founding and the American Frontier."
    <u>Association of Pacific Coast Geographers Yearbook</u> 36:7-23.
        Examines two views of the relationship between town founding
and the frontier: that of Frederick Jackson Turner and Ray A.
Billington, who argue that towns developed slowly by accretion;
and that of Richard C. Wade, who argues that towns were "planted
far in advance of the line of settlement." Finds, through evidence on the founding of 168 cities, that there is little support
for Wade's theory that towns were "spearheads" holding the land
for future settlers. Neither is there enough support for Turner's
conceptions. "Growth of towns to urban status may have been
characteristic of a final 'urban frontier,' but town founding in
itself was not."

20 NICHOLAS, H.G. "The Relevance of Tocqueville." In <u>Lessons
    From America: An Exploration</u>. Edited by Richard Rose. New
    York: John Wiley, pp. 46-66.
        Alexis de Tocqueville was not a precursor of Turner and his
frontier thesis as some historians have argued.

21 PRISCO, SALVATORE. "A Note on John Barrett's China Policy."
    <u>Pacific Historian</u> 18 (Summer):47-54.
        Theorizes that John Barrett "carried Frederick Jackson
Turner's frontier thesis to the shores of Asia."

22 ROBINSON, W. STITT. <u>The Southern Colonial Frontier, 1607-
    1763</u>. Histories of the American Frontier, edited by Ray Allen
    Billington and Howard Lamar. Albuquerque: University of New
    Mexico Press, 293 pp., passim.
        Argues that because "Turner was most interested in the ex-
pansion to the piedmont and back country beyond the fall line" he
failed to understand that his frontier thesis was as relevant for
the colonial era as it was for later periods of American history.
This synthesis of the colonial frontier process provides convincing evidence that "European institutions on the first Atlantic
frontier were subjected to some of the same reforging" that characterized Turner's version of the nineteenth-century American
frontier.

23 SCHROEDER, FRED E.H. "The Development of the Super-Ego on the
    American Frontier." <u>Soundings</u> 57 (Summer):189-205.
        Compares Turner and Freud. Analyzes the frontier from
Freud's perspective of the "six characteristics of civilization,"
concentrating on the second stage, "regulation of social relationships." This second stage is the movement from selfish individualism to the super-ego, or "group conscience," and there emerged
"a new and historically unique super-ego which has developed out
of the shared guilt and primal sin [egotism and selfishness] of

1974

frontier." Also explores the "Americanization" of immigrants in this process.

24 SIEVERS, RODNEY M. "The Lost World of Daniel Boorstin." Maryland Historical Magazine 69 (Fall):293-99.
    The environmentalism in Daniel J. Boorstin's writings "has quite properly prompted some scholars to compare Boorstin's work with that of the most famous environmental historian--Frederick Jackson Turner."

25 SMITH, DAVID C. "The Logging Frontier." Journal of Frontier History 18 (October):96-106.
    Presents an analysis of one aspect of the frontier about which "neither Turner, his followers, nor even his detractors have had much to say." Argues that more research needs to be done, especially in regard to the influence of the East on the logging frontier and vice versa, and in regard to the character types who were involved in this frontier.

26 TOLL, WILLIAM. "W.E.B. DuBois and Frederick Jackson Turner: The Unveiling and Preemption of America's 'Inner History.'" Pacific Northwest Quarterly 65 (April):66-78.
    Examines reasons why "Turner's insights and techniques received professional attention and those of his black professional contemporary, William Edward Burghardt DuBois, did not. . . ." Turner's view was broader and more comprehensive; DuBois produced a "narrow literature" that focused on social problems of minority groups. Argues that historians need to incorporate the tensions contained in this latter view in order to present a more complete synthesis of American history.

27 WEBER, R. DAVID. "Socioeconomic Change in Racine, 1850-1880." Journal of the West 13 (July):98-108.
    Agrees with Turner that the West was a "land of opportunity" and finds that this frontier egalitarianism existed in the urban areas of the American West as well as in the rural areas.

28 WILKINS, ROBERT P. "A Dedication to the Memory of Orin G. Libby, 1864-1952." Arizona and the West 16 (Summer):107-10.
    Libby studied under Turner at Wisconsin, and he learned and incorporated Turner's eclectic method. He taught at Wisconsin after completing his Ph.D., but because his field was already occupied and his relations with Turner became "strained," he "was forced to look for another position. He never forgave Turner."

29 WOODRESS, JAMES. "Willa Cather: American Experience and
European Tradition." In The Art of Willa Cather. Edited by
Bernice Slote and Virginia Faulkner. Lincoln: University of
Nebraska Press, pp. 43-62.
Notes that Cather's novels are regarded as "the fictional
counterparts of the Turner thesis."

1975

1 BAKER, STEWART A. "Strict Scrutiny of Right to Travel." UCLA
Law Review 22 (July):1129-60.
Argues, following Turner, that "travel is near the heart of
the American experience." Attempts "to determine how the right
of travel can be made more predictable and principled" in the
American courts, and suggests the "the Burger Court is wisely--
though not always consistently--limiting the right."

2 BENNETT, JAMES D. Frederick Jackson Turner. Twayne's United
States Author Series. Boston: Twayne, 138 pp.
"The attempt . . . has been to bring together in this book
the major ideas which Turner expressed and some of the reactions
which these ideas stimulated. An additional attempt has been
made to present information about Turner the man and the teacher
because this is vital in understanding his impact upon the study
and teaching of United States history." The chapters are entitled "Frederick Jackson Turner," "The Frontier Thesis," "The
Sectional Hypothesis," "Criticisms of the Frontier Thesis,"
"Turner and American Historiography."

3 BLEGEN, THEODORE C. "Education Moves Ahead." In Minnesota:
A History of the State. Minneapolis: University of Minnesota
Press, pp. 409-30.
Reprint of 1963.4.

4 CALDWELL, RICHARD G. "Right to Travel and Community Growth
Controls." Harvard Journal on Legislation 12:244-80.
Argues that "'Right to travel' is a misnomer. What is at
issue is a right of resettlement. . . ." Turner's frontier has
passed, but the same sentiment that induced pioneers to migrate
is still operative today. Right to travel should not be re-
stricted; rather, "a way must be found to balance, on a case by
case basis, the private interest in residential mobility and the
public interest in planned growth."

1975

5 CARPENTER, RONALD H. "The Stylistic Identification of
   Frederick Jackson Turner with Robert M. LaFollette: A Psychologically Oriented Analysis of Language Behavior." Wisconsin
   Academy of Sciences, Arts and Letters, Transactions 63:102-15.
       Because Turner's "Frontier Thesis is a rhetorically founded
   discourse," there is a need for a "psychological model that helps
   clarify how and why Turner" was more a rhetorician than an historian. Concludes that Turner's model was based upon his "emula-
   tion for and imitation of Robert M. LaFollette's style in discourse."

6 GRAAF, LAWRENCE B. "Recognition, Racism, and Reflections on
   the Writing of Western Black History." Pacific Historical Review 44 (February):22-51.
       Surveys the recent literature on the migration of blacks
   into the trans-Mississippi West during the period 1890 to the
   Second World War. Finds that the history of blacks, though im-
   proving, is sadly incomplete. Blames part of the "blindness of
   many earlier scholars to ethnic history . . . to their infatua-
   tion with the ideas of Frederick Jackson Turner."

7 FIDLER, DOUGLAS K., GEORGE CORONEOS, and MICHAEL TAMBURRO.
   "Frederick Jackson Turner, the Revisionists, and Sport Historiography." Journal of Sport History 2 (Spring):41-49.
       Investigates Turner's safety-valve theory and "its effect
   on subsequent theories of the importance of sport." Sport has
   been proclaimed the "new safety valve" by several historians upon
   the announcement of the closing of the frontier.

8 FLINK, JAMES J. The Car Culture. Cambridge, Mass.: MIT
   Press, 260 pp., passim.
       "The frontier, as defined by Turner, offered Americans a
   unique form of geographic and social mobility that centrally influenced the development of nineteenth-century American institutions and values. But in 1893 neither Turner nor anyone else
   foresaw that a new form of mobility was to become even more significant in shaping the lifeways of twentieth-century Americans.
   Six motor vehicles were displayed at the 1893 Columbia Exposition
   [where Turner read his paper]. . . . Auto mobility was rapidly to
   develop into a force with a deeper and broader influence than
   Turner's frontier."

9 GIBSON, ARRELL M., ed. Frontier Historian: The Life and Work
   of Edward Everett Dale. With introductory essays by Arrell M.
   Gibson, Angie Debe, and John S. Ezell. Norman: University of
   Oklahoma Press, 367 pp., passim.
       Turner's influence upon Dale is evident throughout this
   volume. Includes a section entitled "Memories of Frederick

Jackson Turner," first published in the Mississippi Valley Historical Review, 1943.4.

10 GOTTMANN, JEAN. "Evolution of the Concept of Territory."
    Social Science Information 14, no. 3/4:29-47.
        Analyzes the relationship between territory ("a portion of
    geographical space that coincides with the spatial extent of a
    government's jurisdiction") and political power. Finds, as
    Turner concluded before, that "the concept of territory with its
    material and psychological components is a psychosomatic device
    needed to preserve the freedom and variety of separate communities
    in an interdependent accessible space."

11 MATHEWS, ROBIN. "Susanna Moodie, Pink Toryism, and 19th Cen-
    tury Ideas of Canadian Identity." Journal of Canadian Studies
    10 (August):3-15.
        Moodie, a nineteenth-century immigrant to Canada and an
    accomplished writer, would have disagreed with Turner's "descent
    into barbarism." She rejected "the individualism of the Yankee"
    and, as a pink Tory, disagreed with "the supremacy of the indiv-
    idual. She combined a sense of the past and a sense of community
    with a clear sense of what needed to be changed." But she could
    not see that "Canadians of wealth would become the office clerks
    of U.S. expansionism. . . ."

12 MILLER, ORLANDO W. The Frontier in Alaska and the Matanuska
    Colony. New Haven: Yale University Press, pp. 3-6, 217.
        While resisting the temptation to pile "up references to
    the large and important additions to the literature on the fron-
    tier and Frederick Jackson Turner that have appeared since 1965,"
    Miller couches his study within the Turnerian tradition.

13 MOSS, RICHARD J. "Jackson Democracy: A Note on the Origins
    and Growth of the Term." Tennessee Historical Quarterly 34
    (Summer):145-53.
        In "Turner's hands, the term Jacksonian democracy became an
    almost mystical force."

14 PETERSON, RICHARD H. "The Frontier Thesis and Social Mobility
    on the Mining Frontier." Pacific Historical Review 44
    (February):52-67.
        Analyzes statistical evidence concerning prominent mining
    leaders and bonanza kings, evidence such as national and ethnic
    origins, parents' financial status, and education, and finds data
    that corroborate Turner's claim that the frontier offered vertical
    social mobility. "Although the mining frontier, like the rest of
    the nation, practiced radical and ethnic discrimination, it was
    evidently more democratic than the older, more settled areas of

1975

the country in extending opportunities for outstanding industrial
success."

15 RICHARDS, KENT D. "A Dedication to the Memory of Edmond S.
    Meany, 1862-1935." Arizona and the West 17 (Autumn):201-4.
        "Turner reinforced Meany's interest in statistical data,
    which derived from his days as a press agent, and introduced him
    to proper historical methodology."

16 STEEL, THOMAS. "Right to Travel and Exclusionary Zoning."
    Hastings Law Journal 26 (January):849-74.
        Turner is footnoted as a source that "may be cited in sup-
    port of the historical importance of free travel as an individual
    liberty."

17 STERNSHER, BERNARD. "America Since the 1890s." In Consensus,
    Conflict, and American Historians. Bloomington: Indiana Uni-
    versity Press, pp. 275-81.
        Discusses the Turnerian origins of the New Left school of
    historiography, which emerged in the 1960s.

18 _____. "A False Dichotomy." In Consensus, Conflict, and
    American Historians. Bloomington: Indiana University Press,
    pp. 353-69.
        Deals with the fragmentation of Turner's frontier thesis as
    a result of comparative studies of frontiers in countries like
    Canada and Australia.

19 STROUT, CUSHING. Review of Frederick Jackson Turner: His-
    torian, Scholar, Teacher, by R.A. Billington. History and
    Theory 13, no. 3:315-25.
        Praises Billington's book, but complains that it bends over
    backwards to rationalize Turner's lack of publication. Tries to
    put this view of Turner into its proper perspective through a
    better psychological understanding than Billington has presented.

20 WEINRYB, ELAZAR. "Justification of a Causal Thesis: An
    Analysis of the Controversies Over the Theses of Pirenne,
    Turner, and Weber." History and Theory 14, no. 1:32-56.
        Presents a philosophical framework for a justification of
    Turner's causal thesis; argues against Morton White's criticism
    (see 1965.21) reflecting singular causal statements like Turner's
    by stating that "if there are faulty, questionable patterns of
    criticism, then there are, perhaps, also right and justified
    ones." The identification of legitimate means of causal state-
    ments will help justify the concept of historical causation.
    Proceeds in the attempt to justify Turner's causal thesis through
    "a theoretical redescription of the effect phenomenon" and by re-
    formulating the basic principles of the theory.

1976

21 WELTER, RUSH. "The Frontier West as Image of American Society."
    In The Mind of America, 1820-1860. New York: Columbia Uni-
    versity Press, pp. 298-328.
        For most Americans of the early nineteenth century, the
West was more an "imagined phenomenon" than a historical reality
and this view of the "West that Americans embraced was essentially"
similar to the West depicted in Turner's thesis.

1976

1 ALLISON, CLINTON B. "Intellectual and Educational Attitudes
   in Old Northwest: Picture Painted by Travelers to Frontier."
   Journal of Thought 11 (April):110-20.
        The views of Frederick Jackson Turner and Ellwood P.
Cubberly toward the frontier and the frontiersman were not just
based upon their own biases; "their views on intellectual and
educational activity on the frontier were congruent with the observations of literate travelers to the West."

2 BILLINGTON, RAY ALLEN. "Cowboys, Indians, and the Land of
   Promise: The World Image of the American Frontier." In Proceedings of the Fourteenth International Congress of Historical
   Sciences. New York: Arno Press, pp. 79-99.
        Examines some of the myths of the frontier West in America
and analyzes the influence of this image in America and abroad.
Finds that parts of the frontier myth are still active in contemporary society. Reprinted: 1977.3.

3 BINGHAM, EDWIN R. "A Dedication to the Memory of Dan Elbert
   Clark, 1884-1956." Arizona and the West 18 (Summer):107-10.
        Comments on Clark's textbook The West in American History.
Notes that Clark agreed with Turner's assumption that the frontier
had ended by the turn of the twentieth century.

4 FRANTZ, J.B. "Frontier in American History: Frederick Jackson
   Turner." Social Science Quarterly 57 (June):230-33.
        Reviews the importance and significance of Turner's frontier
thesis. Criticizes Turner's attackers for being "pot-shotters,"
but admits to having a "quarrel with Turner" for his extremely
Anglo-American tone, which today would be branded "WASP-ish."
Applauds Turner, nevertheless, for his insight and his tenacity.

5 FURMAN, NECAH STEWART. "W.P. Webb: Idea Man and Seminarian."
   In Walter Prescott Webb: His Life and Impact. Albuquerque:
   University of New Mexico Press, pp. 101-24.
        Although "critics . . . condemned" Webb's "work as an exten-
sion of the Turner thesis" Webb himself "felt no obligation to
the frontier historian."

1976

6 GOETZMAN, WILLIAM H. "Times American Adventures: American
   Historians and Their Writing since 1776." Social Science
   Quarterly 57 (June):2-48.
        Analyzes the various stages of American historical writing.
   Claims that Turner is "the prime example" of the "best scientific
   history" because he understood the necessity for a hypothesis.
   "With Turner scientific history in America had come of age."

7 JACKSON, W. TURRENTINE. "Australians and the Comparative
   Frontier." In The Walter Prescott Webb Memorial Lectures:
   Essays on Walter Prescott Webb. Edited by Kenneth R. Philp
   and Elliott West. Austin: University of Texas Press, pp. 17-
   51.
        Discusses the influence of Webb and Turner on the writing
   of frontier history in Australia. Argues that there are major
   differences between Australian and American frontiers, but these
   do not deny the importance of the frontier on Australian development. Includes a bibliographic essay on the frontier theme in
   Australian history.

8 LEWIS, MERRILL. "Language, Literature, Rhetoric, and the
   Shaping of the Historical Imagination of Frederick Jackson
   Turner." Pacific Historical Review 45 (August):399-424.
        Turner has been criticized for incorporating poetic or
   literary elements in his writings, but these are often used
   rhetorically. Discusses the development of Turner's style and
   shows the influence of literature on his approach to historical
   investigation, an influence first instilled by his teacher William
   Allen.

9 LOEWENBERG, ROBERT J. "Jason Zee, Reform and the Historical
   Past." In Equality on the Oregon Frontier; Jason Zee and the
   Methodist Mission, 1834-43. Seattle: University of Washington Press, pp. 36-77.
        Criticizes the tendency in the historiography of American
   Methodism to assent to "Turner's view that democracy grows or is
   affected in positive ways through contact with the frontier."
   Concludes that the treatment of concepts like "democracy, equality,
   and liberty" is a study in "normative faits accomplis instead of
   explanations."

10 POTTER, JIM. "Some British Reflections on Turner and the
    Frontier." In American History--British Historians: A Cross-
    Cultural Approach to the American Experience. Edited by David
    H. Burton. Chicago: Nelson-Hall, pp. 127-48.
         Reprint of 1969.27.

11 PUTNAM, JACKSON K. "The Turner Thesis and the Westward Move-
    ment: A Reappraisal." Western Historical Quarterly 7
    (October):377-404.
        Summarizes Turner's hypotheses and claims that Turner has
    outlasted his critics because he was "remarkably, even madden-
    ingly, flexible in his opinions. . . ." Examines several major
    criticisms from the point of view of Turner's flexibility; es-
    pecially important are Turner's "excessive environmentalism," the
    "selective migration thesis," the argument of "'culture' versus
    'nature,'" the safety-valve thesis, and the "Protestant thesis."
    Claims that historians need to pay more attention to the "sym-
    bolic frontier" and that "a new Turner . . . is needed to make
    the westward movement as relevant for the present generation as
    Turner did for his."

12 WIECZYNSKI, JOSEPH L. The Russian Frontier: The Impact of
    Borderlands upon The Course of Early Russian History. Char-
    lottesville: University Press of Virginia, 108 pp., passim.
        Summarizes Turner's frontier thesis in the first chapter,
    entitled "The Frontier Hypothesis," and accepts a modified ver-
    sion of it as a valid theoretical construct for the study of
    Russian history. Develops the thesis that only one European
    nation fits the "Turnerian mold as well as, or perhaps better,
    than, America. That nation, which both Turner and Webb ignored
    in their writings, was Russia."

                              1977

1 BERCUSON, DAVID J. "Labor Radicalism and Western Industrial
   Frontier, 1897-1919." Canadian Historical Review 58 (June):
   154-75.
        The frontier of Frederick Jackson Turner has been called "a
   great leveler," a place where class distinctions were broken down
   and men were more nearly equal. The Canadian industrial frontier,
   however, was far from being a leveler. For immigrants moving
   into the Canadian West, opportunities for social and economic advancement were almost nonexistent and there were major divisions
   between classes. As a result, radical thought and radical action
   were precipitated on several levels. The frontier itself acted
   as the primary stimulus for class consciousness and radical
   activity in the Canadian West.

2 BILLINGTON, RAY ALLEN. "The American Frontiersman." In America's Frontier Culture. College Station: Texas A & M University Press, pp. 19-50.
        Reprint of 1954.4.

1977

3 _____. "Cowboys, Indians, and the Land of Promise." In American Frontier Culture. College Station: Texas A & M University Press, pp. 74-97.
   Reprint of 1976.2.

4 _____. "The Frontier and American Culture." In American
Frontier Culture. College Station: Texas A & M University
Press, pp. 51-73.
   Reprint of 1965.2.

5 CARPENTER, RONALD H. "Frederick Jackson Turner and the
Rhetorical Impact of the Frontier Thesis." Quarterly Journal
of Speech 63 (April):117-29.
   Examines the rhetorical impact of Turner's thesis upon the
"national psychology." Turner wrote primarily for purposes of
persuasion, and he definitely succeeded, but the effect of the
frontier thesis went farther than this. "A statement intended to
alter the course of American historiography became instead the
rhetorical source of a mythic, national self-conception."

6 _____. "Style in Discourse as an Index of Frederick Jackson
Turner's Historical Creativity: Conceptual Antecedents of the
Frontier Thesis in His "American Colonization." Huntington
Library Quarterly 40 (May):269-77.
   Attempts to modify Ray Billington's analysis of "the moment
of illumination" of Turner's frontier thesis by examining significant changes in Turner's rhetorical style. Through an analysis
of key changes in wording and phrasing and through the interpretation of prominent analogies, Carpenter finds that Turner anticipated his frontier thesis in his address on "American Colonization" in 1891 and that the final polishing of this address "may
have been the pivotal event" in the construction of the frontier
hypothesis.

7 HAGUE, HARLAN. "Eden Ravished: Land, Pioneer Attitudes, and
Conservation." American West 14 (May/June):30-33, 65-69.
   In writing the frontier thesis, Turner failed to detect one
of the most important themes that had "an immense impact" on the
development of the American character: "this was the belief that
the resources of the West were inexhaustible. Farmers, miners,
and cattlemen all believed that the West was a great cornucopia
which could not be used up, and the country's resources were
vastly exploited." This exploitation led to excessive waste, and
here "the Turner thesis is most meaningful, for the belief in the
inexhaustibility of resources in the West generated the unique
American acceptance of waste as the fundamental tenet of a life-
style." Hopefully, Americans are learning the need for conservation for both aesthetic and utilitarian purposes.

1977

8   HAUPTMAN, LAWRENCE M.   "Mythologizing Westward Expansion:
    Schoolbooks and the Image of the American Frontier Before
    Turner."   Western Historical Quarterly 8 (July):269-82.
        Schoolbooks, ranging from first-grade readers to college
    texts, emphasized the lure of the frontier for more than one
    hundred years before Turner's thesis. Discusses schoolbook
    treatment of the following: the inevitability of continental
    expansion, prejudicial treatment of Indians, the notion of the
    frontier as "safety-valve," and the description of the West as
    "Arcadia."

9   HUDSON, JOHN C.   "Theory and Methodology in Comparative Fron-
    tier Studies."   In The Frontier: Comparative Studies.   Edited
    by David Harry Miller and Jerome O. Steffen. Norman: Univer-
    sity of Oklahoma Press, pp. 11-31.
        "Comparative Frontier Studies were first suggested in 1904
    by the inventer of the frontier, Frederick Jackson Turner. . . .
    Although the literature is not abundant and is scattered through
    books and journals whose publication spans more than seventy
    years, it seems that there is an inherent appeal in comparative
    frontier research that has transcended criticism of the frontier
    thesis itself. This is important since the original purpose . . .
    has been to 'test' Turner's thesis. Tests of the frontier thesis
    have been no less but scarcely more successful than tests of the
    Holy Scriptures, yet this has not discouraged those who would
    attempt to perform such tests. The words of Frederick Jackson
    Turner are as stimulating, aggravating, and worthy of discussion
    today as they were seventy-five years ago." In the body of the
    article itself Hudson attempts to "outline methodologies that
    overlap frontier research [Turnerian in approach] and to organize
    the relevant concepts into a few heuristic models of the frontier
    process."

10 HUGINS, WALTER.   "American History in Comparative Perspective."
    Journal of American Studies 11 (April):27-44.
        Turnerian "scholars have been satisfied to test the validity
    of Turner's thesis in his own terms" rather than to conduct more
    promising comparative studies based upon "comparative methodology."

11 JACKSON, W. TURRENTINE.   Foreword to American Frontier Culture,
    by Ray Allen Billington. College Station: Texas A & M Uni-
    versity Press, pp. 11-15.
        Discusses the intellectual relationship between Billington
    and Turner.

1977

12 KNOPF, EDWARD. "Untarnishing the Dream: Mobility, Opportunity,
    and Order in Modern America." Journal of Social History 11
    (Winter):206-27.
        Enters into the debate between historians such as Turner
    who argue that mobility and movement were sources of freedom and
    opportunity and historians who complain that movement was a re-
    sult of confusion and uncertainty. Examines the community of
    Chelsea, Massachusetts, and finds more evidence for the former.

13 LEACOCK, ROBERT A., and HAROLD I. SHARLIN. "Nature of Physics
    and History: Cross-discipline Inquiry." American Journal of
    Physics 45 (February):146-53.
        Describes a cross-disciplinary course that examines the
    similarity and interrelationship between physics and history.
    The theories and methodologies of historians Turner and Beard are
    examined alongside those of the physicists Brahe, Kepler, and
    Newton with the intent of "illuminating" the nature of both
    "physics and history." Turner is selected because of his signifi-
    cance, his use of "large generalizations or theories," and the
    abundance of material on his theory. One of the impacts of the
    class is the resulting appreciation that historians "such as
    Turner, Beard, and Hofstadter must formulate and construct
    theoretical structures not entirely unlike those in . . . sci-
    entific disciplines."

14 LEWIS, ROBERT. "Frontier and Civilization in the Thought of
    Frederick Law Olmstead." American Quarterly 29 (Fall):285-403.
        Olmstead viewed the influence of the frontier on American
    civilization from a position opposite to that of Turner. He
    argued that the frontier was a negative force, propelling America
    backwards into a "new barbarism." He was convinced that "'fron-
    tierism' was a grave threat to the future of the United States"
    and he advocated more "civilized" forms of social progress and
    social control.

15 McCARTHY, MICHAEL. "Africa and the American West." Journal
    of American Studies 11 (August):187-201.
        Africa has held many of the same implications as the fron-
    tier West for many Americans. "In one sense, the American exper-
    ience in Africa, from the late nineteenth to the early part of
    the twentieth century, might serve to exemplify and to verify the
    deep-rootedness of the idea of 'the West' in American life."

16 MILLER, DAVID HARRY, and JEROME O. STEFFEN. Introduction to
    The Frontier: Comparative Studies. Edited by David Harry
    Miller and Jerome O. Steffen. Norman: University of Oklahoma
    Press, pp. 3-10.
        "Discussion of the possibilities of comparative frontier

studies among historians generally involves the implicit assumption that the frontier theories commonly identified with Frederick Jackson Turner offer a sufficient theoretical base." Central to the criteria used to select the thirteen articles included in this volume is the assumption that "the application of Turnerian frontier notions to other forntiers often proves . . . to be unproductive."

17 MILLER, DAVID HARRY, and WILLIAM W. SAVAGE, Jr. Introduction to <u>The Character and Influence of the Indian Trade in Wisconsin: A Study of the Trading Post as an Institution</u>, by Frederick Jackson Turner and edited by David Harry Miller and William W. Savage, Jr. Norman: University of Oklahoma Press, pp. vii-xxxiv.

Attempts to explain why "Turner has consistently been pointed out by professional historians themselves as one of the very few major American historians." Argues that "Turner . . . anticipated all of the major ideas of the New Historians." Explains the significance of Turner's Ph.D. dissertation, which is here reprinted.

18 OSBORNE, BRIAN S. "Frontier Settlement in Eastern Ontario in the Nineteenth Century: A Study in Changing Perceptions of Land Opportunity." In <u>The Frontier: Comparative Studies</u>. Edited by David Harry Miller and Jerome O. Steffen. Norman: University of Oklahoma Press, pp. 201-25.

The controlling idea of the article is the following Turnerian assumption: "Indeed, it could be argued that the settlers on the frontier [eastern Ontario] experienced a recapitulation of the general social development from the state of 'barbarism' to that of 'civilization' a recapitulation which was often unique to each specific region."

19 RILEY, GLENDA. "Images of the Frontierswoman: Iowa as a Case Study." <u>Western Historical Quarterly</u> 8 (April):189-202.

To Turner the frontier was conquered by men while "women were an invisible or perhaps non-existent force," and this attitude is predominant in the writing of western history. Discusses several reasons for this oversight and attempts to correct the error. Analyzes four possible typologies of western men: (1) the Calamity Jane, (2) the sex object, (3) the frontier suffragist, and (4) the "saint in the sunbonnet."

20 ROBBINS, WILLIAM G. "The Conquest of the American West: History as Eulogy." <u>Indian Historian</u> 10 (Winter):7-13.

American western historians have viewed the Indian and the white treatment of Indians through "the dominant values of America's imperial system."

1977

21 ROGIN, MICHAEL. "Nature as Politics and Nature as Romance."
    Political Theory 5 (February):5-30.
        Argues that "the romance of nature . . . plays a powerful
    role in the political tradition itself." Notes the influence of
    the frontier on national identity. Comments on the ideas of con-
    temporary social scientists, Benjamin Franklin, and Karl Marx in
    relation to the theme of nature and politics, and examines "the
    two dominant images of natural virtue in the history of American
    politics--pastoral harmony and wilderness regeneration."

22 SMITH, JAMES CHARLES. Review of Transformation of American
    Law, 1780-1860, by Morton J. White. Wisconsin Law Review
    4:1253-76.
        Observes in a footnote that "the American frontier may have
    helped to stimulate the development of instrumentalism" in Amer-
    ican law. The frontier spirit may have been responsible for the
    rejection of outdated legal institutions, replacing them with
    innovative forms.

23 STAVE, BRUCE M. "A Conversation with Bayrd Still." Journal
    of Urban History 3 (May):323-60.
        Presents a stimulating interview concerning the function of
    urban history. Bayrd Still comments that Turner did not fully
    understand or appreciate the relationship of urban development
    to the westward movement. Turner saw the city as "a product of
    the nation's frontier expansion" and not as an "integral part"
    of the process.

24 TYLER, S. LYMAN. "Americana Collections Reflect Our Con-
    tinuing Fascination with the Frontier and the West." Western
    Historical Quarterly 8 (October):443-54.
        In examining the collection of western memorabilia, dis-
    cusses collection of books, art, and original manuscripts. The
    collection and holding of such items represent a good investment
    because their value will continue to escalate.

25 TYRRELL, WILLIAM BLAKE. "Star Trek as Myth and Television as
    Mythmaker." Journal of Popular Culture 10 (Spring):711-19.
        Compares Star Trek to the myth of the western frontier.
    The influence of Turner on the western myth is noted.

                              1978

1   BILLINGTON, RAY ALLEN. Review of The Character and Influence
    of the Indian Trade in Wisconsin: A Study of the Trading Post
    as an Institution, by Frederick Jackson Turner, edited by
    David H. Miller and William W. Savage. Journal of American

1978

History 64 (March):1096-97.
   Turner's doctoral dissertation is given new significance by
the editors.

2 BINGHAM, EDWIN R. Review of The Character and Influence of
   the Indian Trade in Wisconsin: A Study of the Trading Post as
   an Institution, by Frederick Jackson Turner, edited by David
   H. Miller and William W. Savage, Jr. Western Historical Quarterly 9 (April):214-15.
      Criticizes the editors' introduction: "not only [do they]
inflate the significance of Turner's dissertation, but they fail
to clarify their historiographical position."

3 DEVENEAU, GUS. "Frontier in Recent African History." International Journal of African Historical Studies 11, no. 1:63-85.
      The concept of the frontier, especially as articulated by
Frederick Jackson Turner, is the most useful tool toward examining
African society today. Compares African, Asian, and European
aspects of the frontier.

4 ELLSWORTH, S. GEORGE. "The Alexander James Portrait of
   Frederick Jackson Turner." Western Historical Quarterly 9
   (July):277-80.
      Discusses the making of the portrait of Turner that hangs
in the History Seminar Room of the Harvard Library.

5 HENNESSY, ALISTAIR. "The Frontier in Latin American History."
   In The Frontier in Latin American History. Histories of the
   American Frontier Series, edited by Ray Allen Billington and
   Howard R. Lamar. Albuquerque: University of New Mexico Press,
   pp. 6-27.
      Attempts to explain why Turner's thesis has been viewed
"with a jaundiced eye" by scholars in Latin America. Acknowledges,
however, that "Latin Americans have seen some relevance in
Turner's view." Documents the differences between the frontier
experience of the United States and the frontier in Latin America.
Attributes the appeal of Turner's thesis to "its mythic force and
its ability to provide a legitimating . . . nationalist ideology,"
and concludes that Latin America had "No frontier experience
which could provide the basis for a nationalist myth."

6 JACOBS, WILBUR R. "The Great Despoliation: Environmental
   Themes in American Frontier History." Pacific Historical
   Review 47 (February):1-26.
      Discusses the negative impact of modern civilization upon
the ecological environment of the frontier. Cites the influence
of Francis Walker (Superintendent of the Census, 1870, 1880, and
1890) on Turner and argues that "Walker as well as Turner stressed

1978

a theory of frontier progress and growth, which in time came to
mean the commercialization and conquest of nature." Far ahead of
Turner in terms of understanding environmental impact were two
other critics from Wisconsin: Thorstein Veblen and John Muir.

7 KNEE, STUART F. "Roosevelt and Turner: Awakening in the
   West." Journal of the West 17 (April):105-12.
      Discusses the personal and intellectual relationship between
Turner and Theodore Roosevelt. Both ascribed to a Darwinian
methodology, emphatically endorsing "evolution, struggle, conquest and race superiority. . . ." Turner, however, looked back-
wards to a romantic, agrarian past, while Roosevelt looked forward
to a progressive future where "the frontier experience would take
and adjust to the twentieth century environment."

8 MELBIN, MURRAY. "Night as Frontier." American Sociological
   Review 43 (February):3-22.
      With the end of the land frontier in 1890, the search for
new frontiers has increased. One such frontier is the frontier
of time; time, like space, can be occupied by humans. Presents
the hypothesis that "night is a frontier, that expansion into the
dark hours is a continuation of the geographic migration across
the face of the earth." Compares wakeful activity in contemporary
Boston to the geographic expansion of the frontier west, and uses
a methodology similar to Frederick Jackson Turner's in examining
the evidence.

9 PAUL, RODMAN W. "Frederick Merk, Teacher and Scholar: A
   Tribute." Western Historical Quarterly 9 (April):141-48.
      Summarizes Turner's and Merk's personal and professional
relationship, and discusses their similarities and differences.
Comments that Merk was regarded as a greater teacher.

10 WILLIAMS, JOHN ALEXANDER. "A New Look at an Old Field."
    Western Historical Quarterly 9 (July):281-96.
      Attempts to "clarify the place of state history with re-
spect to local, urban, and regional history. . . ." Comments on
Turner's relationship to state history, and analyzes the contributions several of Turner's students have made in this field.

11 WILLIS, MORRIS W. "Sequential Frontiers: The Californian and
    Victorian Experience, 1850-1900." Western Historical Quarterly
    9 (October):483-94.
      Finds many parallels between the Californian and Australian
frontiers. Both were remote areas; both contained a dynamic
interplay between an urban metropolis (San Francisco and Melbourne)
and its hinterland; and both were large mining areas. Also analyzes the effects of abundance of land mixed with a scarcity of
labor.

1979

1 BETTS, RAYMOND F. "Immense Dimensions: The Impact of the
   American West on Late Nineteenth-Century European Thought
   about Expansion." Western Historical Quarterly 10 (April):
   149-65.
       The vastness of the American frontier created a new "meta-
   physics of space" among European economic and political commenta-
   tors, and it served as an inspiration to European expansion into
   Africa. This European vision of America was bifocal: "On the
   higher plane, the farther scene of the energetic extension of Old
   World Civilization in an unusual geographical situation; on the
   lower plane, the more immediate scene of the internal colonization of the Great Plains."

2 MATTSON, VERNON E. "Frederick Jackson Turner: A Study in
   Misplaced Priorities?" Nevada Historical Society Quarterly 22
   (Summer):100-14.
       Laments that little research has been done on Turner as a
   teacher. Turner did not forsake publishing because of "misplaced
   priorities"; instead evidence indicates that both as an academic
   administrator and as a scholar, "teaching was given the highest
   priority," and Turner was actively committed to "excellence in
   the classroom." "Turner believed that an institution of high
   learning had to distinguish itself first in instructional excellence as a requisite before becoming a research center."

3 POLE, JACK R. Paths to the American Past. New York: Oxford
   University Press, pp. 267-68, 276, 285, 288-89, 293-94, 300,
   313, 314.
       Notes Turner's relativism and describes him as a geoeconomic
   determinist.

4 PROCTOR, BEN. "A Dedication to the Memory of Frederick Merk
   1887-1977." Arizona and the West 21 (Winter):313-16.
       Turner had already left Wisconsin by the time Frederick
   Merk enrolled there, but Merk followed him to Harvard in order to
   study western history under him for the Ph.D. When Turner retired
   from Harvard in 1924, Merk took over teaching History 17, "History
   of the West."

5 RAITZ, KARL B. "Themes in the Cultural Geography of European
   Ethnic Groups in the United States." Geographical Review 69
   (January):79-94.
       Examines some of the literature regarding European ethnic
   groups in America. Analyzes the problems of acculturation and
   assimilation of immigrants into the mainstream of American life
   and examines the effects of the cultural and environmental factors.

1979

6   REPS, JOHN WILLIAM. Cities of the American West: A History
    of Frontier Urban Planning. Princeton, N.J.: Princeton Uni-
    versity Press, pp. ix-xi; 667-70.
        Describes the evolution of Turner's frontier thesis and dis-
    putes it by arguing that the majority of towns preceded rather
    than followed the advance of farming and ranching on the American
    frontier.

7   STEINER, MICHAEL C. "The Significance of Turner's Sectional
    Thesis." Western Historical Quarterly 10 (October):437-66.
        Contends that the sectional thesis, not the frontier thesis,
    was Turner's primary concern, and argues that more detailed
    studies should be directed at the concept of sectionalism. Pre-
    sents biographical and intellectual sources for Turner's theories.
    Especially notes the influence of Josiah Royce. Concludes that
    the society must become more aware of environmental concerns and
    that we should "open our eyes to the value of Turner's sectional
    concepts."

8   TEMPERLEY, HOWARD. "Frontierism, Capital, and the American
    Loyalists in Canada." Journal of American Studies 13 (April):
    5-27.
        Compares Turner's thesis to the experiences of American
    loyalists who migrated to Canada and finds that, at first sight,
    they "seem to meet Turner's requirements more precisely" than
    most American frontier communities. One defect of the Turner
    thesis as applied to Canada is that it takes no account of the
    influence of capital. Loyalists were able to draw on two sources
    of finance: compensation for losses sustained in the war and
    military pensions. This alters, in some respects, their frontier
    heritage.

                            1980

1   ALLEN, GAY WILSON. "How Emerson, Thoreau, and Whitman Viewed
    the Frontier." In Toward a New American Literary History:
    Essays in Honor of Arlin Turner. Edited by Louis J. Budd et
    al. Durham, N.C.: Duke University Press, pp. 111-28.
        Both Emerson and Thoreau agreed in spirit with what is now
    regarded as Turner's "spirit of the Frontier," but both were also
    antagonistic to the reality of the westward movement because of
    its inherent exploitation and because of the base nature of the
    common frontiersman. Whitman applauds the westward migration
    both in spirit and in actuality, and he praises the frontier's
    democratic nature.

1980

2 BLOCK, ROBERT H. "Frederick Jackson Turner and the American
   Geography." Association of American Geographers, Annals 70
   (March):31-42.
       Analyzes the reciprocal bonds that connected Turner with
   American geography, and examines Turner's use of "environment,
   evolution, and cartography." Turner was actively involved with
   the community of geographers, and several of the individual relationships are discussed, most notably those of C.R. Van Hine,
   Ellen Semple, and Isaiah Bowman. Turner left an important legacy
   to speculative geographic thought.

3 DEGLER, CARL N. "Remaking American History." Journal of American History 67 (June):7-25.
       Portrays Turner as the only Progressive historian who could
   accurately be described as an exceptionalist, concerned with the
   differences rather than the similarities between America and
   Europe. Analyzes the shifts in attitude toward American excep-
   tionalism in historical scholarship since World War II.

4 DeLORME, RONALD L. "Westward the Bureaucrats: Government
   Officials on the Washington and Oregon Frontiers." Arizona
   and the West 22 (Autumn):223-36.
       Includes government bureaucrats in the progression of "suc-
   cessive waves" initially described by Turner.

5 GOODIN, ROBERT, and JOHN DRYZEK. "Rational Participation:
   The Politics of Relative Power." British Journal of Political
   Science 10 (July):273-92.
       Sets out to prove that political nonparticipation is not
   necessarily a negative condition of apathy. It is a rational
   response for many citizens to "regard political participation as
   a waste of time." Plugs the frontier hypothesis into the "rational
   participation model," and finds a link between frontier equality
   (or inequality) and the democratic structure.

6 JENSEN, RICHARD. "On Modernizing Frederick Jackson Turner:
   The Historiography of Regionalism." Western Historical Quarterly 11 (July):307-22.
       Complains that Turnerian evaluations of sections has focused
   upon what is "unique" rather than upon what is "important."
   Applies this critique to the history of education, political culture, economic development, and conflicts between North and South.
   Finds that the Turnerians are "more successful in the realm of
   demographic history," but notes that, except in a few cases, they
   ignore the role of women and children. Argues that regional historians should use the approach of modernization, which "subsumes
   and synthesizes earlier, more awkward formulations. . . ."

1980

7 KEARL, J.R., CLAYNE L. POPE, and LARRY T. WIMMER. "Household
Wealth in a Settlement Economy: Utah, 1850-1870." Journal of
Economic History 40 (September):477-96.
Notes, as Turner suggested, that the frontier was a "leveling
influence" but finds that wealth distribution changed with the
progression of the frontier society. Examines this change in the
development of society in Utah.

8 LAWSON, RICHARD. "Towards Demythologizing the Australian
Legend—Turner Frontier Thesis and the Australian Experience."
Journal of Social History 13 (Summer):577-87.
Argues against Russell Ward's theory of the "bush ethos"
inspired by Turner's frontier thesis (see 1958.30). Urban roots
are far more important in analyzing the history of Australia.

9 LIVINGSTONE, D.A., and R.T. HARRISON. "The Frontier: Metaphor, Myth, and Model." Professional Geographer 32 (May):127-
32.
Discusses the "potency of the frontier as both metaphor and
myth" and examines the "pervasive influence" of the frontier
spirit on American society. Presents a model for the "image of
the frontier outpost. . . ."

10 NASH, GERALD D. "The Census of 1890 and the Closing of the
Frontier." Pacific Northwest Quarterly 71 (July):98-100.
Questions Turner's "periodization of the American West" by
challenging his belief that the census of 1890 constituted a
turning point in American history. Raises serious doubt about
the professional competence of Robert P. Porter, the superintendent who issued the census. Turner and those who have followed
his lead accepted as fact the census report of 1890 when in
reality it was "impressionistic" and in error.

11 SCHULTE, STEVEN C. "American Indian Historiography and the
Myth of the Origins of the Plains Wars." Nebraska History 61
(Fall):437-46.
Laments that the history of the Plains wars have been in-
adequately studied and inaccurately analyzed because of the
tendency to view Indian events only as they relate to white expansion, a tendency that began with Turner's frontier thesis.

12 SHARPLESS, JOHN B. "Population Redistribution in the American
Past: Empirical Generalizations and Theoretical Perspectives."
Social Science Quarterly 61 (December):401-17.
Although Turner underscored migration as a major force in
American history, he failed to deal with population redistribu-
tion per se.

1981

13 STEFFEN, JEROME O. <u>Comparative Frontiers: A Proposal for the</u>
    <u>American West</u>. Norman: University of Oklahoma Press, 139 pp.
        Develops the following thesis: "Turner's hypothesis, in a
    rudimentary and perhaps unwitting manner, anticipated some of the
    concerns of present-day social scientists. Turner's assumption
    that frontier environments dominated the frontiersmen, though
    oversimplified and too deterministic, is the essential foundation
    of cultural ecology, an interest which holds significant place
    in modern anthropology and geography. Furthermore, . . . Turner
    instinctively . . . anticipated the work of social psychologists
    influenced by Freud and of those sociologists who stress the im-
    portance of role playing."

14 TURNER, JAMES. "Understanding the Populists." <u>Journal of</u>
    <u>American History</u> 67 (September):354-73.
        Offers a "subtle remodeling" of the Turner thesis by arguing
    that while Populism was spawned on the frontier, it grew out of
    the need for connections and interdependence rather than from
    individualism and self-reliance.

15 WILLIAMS, BURTON J. "A Dedication to the Memory of James C.
    Malin, 1893-1979." <u>Arizona and the West</u> 22 (Autumn):207-10.
        Comments that Malin challenged Turner's frontier hypothesis
    and, in particular, his safety-valve theory.

                                <u>1981</u>

1 ALLEN, DAVID GRAYSON. <u>In English Ways: The Movement of So-</u>
   <u>cieties and the Transferal of English Local Law and Custom to</u>
   <u>Massachusetts Bay in the Seventeenth Century</u>. Chapel Hill:
   University of North Carolina Press, 312 pp.
       Examines five Puritan Massachusetts communities (Rowley,
   Hingham, Newbury, Ipswich, and Watertown) and finds that, con-
   trary to the Turner thesis, the "most vital functions [of] New
   England local institutions were adapted from the English backgrounds of each town's inhabitants."

2 BOGUE, ALLAN G. "Numerical and Normal Analysis in United
   States History." <u>Journal of Interdisciplinary History</u> 12
   (Summer):137-75.
       Asserts that although Turner insightfully suggested that
   the "method of the statistician as well as that of the critic of
   evidence is absolutely essential" if historians are going to
   understand American history, even historians within the Turnerian
   tradition have not taken Turner's call for numerical analysis
   seriously.

1981

3 BURCHELL, R.A. "The Character and Function of a Pioneer
   Elite: Rural California, 1848-1880." Journal of American
   Studies 15 (December):377-89.
        Turner's theory that the frontier was populated by a suc-
   cession of waves, moving from the "pioneer" to the "emigrant" to
   the "men of capital and enterprise" does not work in an examination of the history of the settlement of California. Here, the
   Californian elite were involved in all three groups, not just in
   the last. Goes on to describe the early pattern of power in
   California.

4 CARPENTER, RONALD H. "Carl Becker and the Epigrammatic Force
   of Style in History." Communication Monographs 48 (December):
   318-39.
        Underscores Turner's influence on Becker's rhetorical
   literary style. "Turner himself was a rhetorical stylist" and he
   "demanded similar rhetorical flair" from Becker. Concludes that
   Becker's essay "Kansas" had as much rhetorical power as Turner's
   famous "Significance of the Frontier in America."

5 EBNER, MICHAEL H. "Urban History: Retrospect and Prospect."
   Journal of American History 68 (June):69-84.
        Comments on the importance of Turner's scholarship on the
   writing of urban history.

6 HUTSON, JAMES H. "Country, Court, and Constitution: Anti-
   federalism and the Historians." William and Mary Quarterly 38
   (July):337-68.
        Argues that "Turner's frontier thesis became one of the
   principle tools for converting Anti-federalists to Democrats"
   despite Turner's refusal to assign virtues like democracy to the
   Anti-federalists. Turner stood in awe of the Constitution and
   its friends.

7 KREYCHE, GERALD F. "The American West: A Philosophical
   Interpretation." Journal of Thought 16, no. 2:11-24.
        Analyzes the development and the mythos of the American
   West according to philosophical theory, and maintains that this
   "thoroughly American experience" is philosophy in "its concretized
   form."

8 LAWSON, MERLIN P., and CHARLES W. STOCKTON. "Desert Myth and
   Climatic Reality." Association of American Geographers, Annals
   71 (December):527-35.
        Re-examines Turner's interpretation of the Great American
   Desert from a climatological perspective. Concludes that scholars
   in the Turnerian tradition have neglected the "possibility of
   climatic variability sufficient enough to justify the disparaging
   accounts of the territory."

1981

9 LEWIS, FRANK D. "Farm Settlement on the Canadian Prairies,
   1898-1911." Journal of Economic History 41 (September):517-
   33.
        Develops a "new interpretation of the Canadian prairie
settlement during the 'wheat boom' period." Presents this thesis
as the latest interpretation within the tradition established by
Turner.

10 McINTOSH, C. BARRON. "One Man's Sequential Land Alienation on
    the Great Plains." Geographical Review 71 (October):427-45.
        Because the study of the "American frontier has long been
dominated by a search for generalizations and abstractions, the
most famous of which is the frontier thesis of Frederick Jackson
Turner," we know very little about the "role of individual
settlers who went westward." Attempts to fill this gap in the
historiography of the frontier by studying the plight of one
Nebraska frontiersman.

11 OPIE, JOHN. "Frederick Jackson Turner, the Old West, and the
    Formation of a National Mythology." Environmental Review 5,
    no. 2:79-91.
        Suggests that "Turner's historical writing is closely re-
lated to the classical narrative myths and historical sagas which
were traditionally used to explain, defend, and predict the
course of a nation's destiny. We have in Turner's work a form of
'sacred history,' containing superpowerful places, extraordinary
heroes, and a crucial sequence of events."

12 PICKENS, DONALD K. "Westward Expansion and the End of American
    Exceptionalism: Sumner, Turner, and Webb." Western Historical
    Quarterly 12 (October):409-18.
        Argues that William Graham Sumner, Frederick Jackson Turner,
and Walter Prescott Webb "shared in the common intellectual tradition of tracing the origins of American uniqueness to westward
expansion."

13 REID, JOHN P. "In English Ways: The Movement of Societies
    and the Transferal of English Local Law and Custom to Massa-
    chusetts Bay in the Seventeenth Century." New York University
    Law Review 56 (October):850-66.
        Presents a survey of the "pioneer" or "frontier" theories
of American legal history and traces their roots to Turner.
Places David Grayson Allen's book In English Ways into this historiographical context and complains that he fails to answer the
question of why, given its English roots, local custom lost its
vitality in America.

1981

14 RICHARDS, KENT D. "In Search of the Pacific Northwest: The
    Historiography of Oregon and Washington." Pacific Historical
    Review 50 (November):415-43.
        Through an examination of the trends in the historical
    interpretations of the Pacific Northwest, finds that Turner had
    a profound influence. Many historians considered the Pacific
    Northwest to be the culmination of Turner's frontier thesis be-
    cause they regarded the region as the last frontier. Argues that
    new directions and rejuvenated interests must be brought to bear
    on this valuable but relatively neglected region.

15 RIDGE, MARTIN. "Ray Allen Billington, 1903-1981: Historian
    of the American Frontier." American West 28 (May/June):22-23.
        A tribute to Ray Allen Billington in which the late
    Billington is presented as "not only Frederick Jackson Turner's
    biographer but . . . a thoroughgoing follower of the Turner
    school of Western historians."

16 RUSH, G.B., E. CHRISTENSEN, and J. MALCOLMSON. "Lament for a
    Nation: The Development of Social Science in Canada." Cana-
    dian Review of Sociology and Anthropology 18 (November):519-44.
        Argues that Canadian historiography has finally moved be-
    yond the influence of Turner's thesis and has achieved "an appro-
    priately Canadian perspective on historical development."

17 SINGH, N. GOPALDATTA. "Nationalism and Westward Expansion in
    America: A Study in Interpretations." Political Science Re-
    view (India) 20:163-71.
        Presents Turner's frontier thesis as the foundation for the
    interpretation of westward expansion and discusses both the posi-
    tive and negative influences it has had on later theorists.

18 STEPHAN, G. EDWARD, and DOUGLAS R. McMULLIN. "Historical Dis-
    tribution of County Seats in the United States: A Review,
    Critique, and Test of the Time-Minimization Theory." American
    Sociological Review 46 (December):907-17.
        Utilizes "time-minimization theory" to critique traditional
    interpretations of the American frontier experience such as
    Turner's.

1982

1 FIELDS, EMMET B. "Another Look at the American Character."
   Soundings 65, no. 1:41-56.
        Argues that even though the development of America has been
   one of continuous change, "the character of the American people
   . . . has remained arguably much the same through all changes."

Finds in the literature of American character two major interpretations: the individualist, which stresses liberty, and the con-
formist, which stresses equality. Examines Turner, Walter
Prescott Webb, and David Potter as examples of the first;
Tocqueville, David Riesman, and William H. Whyte as examples of
the second.

2 FOWERAKER, JOE. "Accumulation and Authoritarianism on the
   Pioneer Frontier of Brazil." Journal of Peasant Studies 10
   (October):95-117.
       Challenges Turner's frontier thesis by asserting that the
nature of a particular capitalistic state (i.e., Brazil) is more
significant in any attempt to understand the frontier experience
of a nation than the geography of the frontier itself.

3 OPIE, JOHN. "Learning to Read the Pioneer Landscape:
   Braudel, Eliade, Turner, and Benton." Great Plains Quarterly
   2 (Winter):20-30.
       Turner's importance lies not in his historical stance but
in his mythic perspective. Turner's objective was to give America a "sacred history," both a usable past and a national myth to
stand "in contrast to the useless and profane present."

4 OREVEC, CHRISTINE. "The Evolutionary Sublime and the Essay of
   Natural History." Communication Monographs 49 (December):215-
   28.
       Argues that the rhetorical foundations of social change can
be found in popular literature as well as in polemical tracts,
and describes the influence of scientific evolutionary theory on
literature and on historical interpretation. Finds that Turner
was a neo-Lamarckian and a spokesman for reform Darwinism, and
that his frontier theory contributed to the growing concern for
environmental conservation in America.

5 SCHAPIRO, MORTON O. "Land Availability and Fertility in the
   United States, 1760-1870." Journal of Economic History 42
   (September):577-600.
       "For Turner, the adverse conditions associated with the
decline in available land in the East did not lead to political,
social, and economic upheaval experienced in a number of other
nations because out-migration from the East to the frontier acted
as a safety-valve for eastern laborers." Argues that the re-
stricting of family size and "the decline in the demand for
children" seems to have served a similar function.

1982

6 WYNN, GRAEME. "Cities of the American West: A Review."
   Progress in Human Geography 6, no. 2:300-303.
       Praises the many illustrations of John W. Reps's book
   Cities of the American West but criticizes the text's lack of
   depth, particularly because the book's reversal of the Turner
   thesis had already been conceded two decades earlier with the
   criticisms of Bayrd Still and Richard Wade.

1983

1 CARPENTER, RONALD H. The Eloquence of Frederick Jackson
   Turner. San Marino, Calif.: Huntington Library, 238 pp.
       A penetrating study of Turner's eloquent style combined
   with his uncommon ability to communicate his ideas to a general
   audience.

Dissertations

1917   *HOCKETT, HOMER C. "Western Influence on American Political Parties to 1825." University of Wisconsin.

1929   *ELLIS, JAMES F. "The Influence of Environment on the Settlement of Missouri." St. Louis University.

1932   *WEBB, WALTER PRESCOTT. "The Great Plains." University of Texas.

1942   *PEFFER, E. LOUISE. "The Closure of the Public Domain." University of California.

1949   *CURETON, MINNIE E. "The History of the Criticisms of the Turner Thesis." Stanford University.

1957   *HILL, LEWIS E. "The Frontier: An Economic Analysis of a Historical Concept." University of Texas.

1965   *HARRIS, FAYE E. "A Frontier Community: The Economic, Social, and Political Development of Keokuk, Iowa, from 1820-1866." University of Iowa.

       *HARTSHORNE, THOMAS L. "Changing Conceptions of the American Character: Alternatives to the Frontier Thesis." University of Wisconsin.

       *HUSTON, ROBERT S. "A.M. Simons and the American Socialist Movement." University of Wisconsin.

1966   *FORD, RICHARD B. "The Frontier in South Africa: A Comparative Study of the Turner Thesis." University of Denver.

1967   *LITTLEFIELD, HENRY MILLER. "Textbooks, Determinism and Turner: The Westward Movement in Secondary School History and Geography Textbooks, 1830-1960." Columbia University.

Dissertations

*SOUTH, ORON P. "Systematics in American Historiography since 1900." Vanderbilt University.

1968   *GRUBER, CAROL S. "Mars and Minerva: World War I and the American Academic Man." Columbia University.

*LEWIS, MERRILL EMBERT. "American Frontier History as Literature: Studies in the Historiography of George Bancroft, Frederick Jackson Turner, and Theodore Roosevelt." University of Utah.

*MAGINNIS, PAUL. "The Social Philosophy of Frederick Jackson Turner." University of Arizona.

Index

Note: this index includes authors, titles, names of people, and a number of subject entries. Although we have attempted to include the major subjects that are prominent in the secondary literature on Turner and his frontier theory, the user of this guide should not presume that all possible subjects have been included. The subjects have been identified by the symbol † in order to aid the reader in his search for a subject heading. Dissertations are indicated by a "D" following the date.

Index

"Age of Reinterpretation, The"
(C.V. Woodward), 1960.34
"Age of the Common Man, The"
(J.W. Ward), 1962.38
†Agrarian ideal and the frontier
thesis, 1962.24
Agrarian Revolt in Western
Canada, The (P.F. Sharp),
1948.12
"Agrarian Revolt, The" (A.J.
Going), 1965.8
Agricultural History (F.A.
Shannon), 1958.23
†Agricultural history and the
frontier thesis, 1965.3;
1966.14, 16
Albion, Robert G., 1932.2
Alexander, Edward P., 1943.1;
1946.2
Alexander, Franz, 1942.2, 3
Alexander, Fred, 1947.2
"Alexander James Portrait of
Frederick Jackson Turner,
The" (S.G. Ellsworth),
1978.4
"Algie Martin Simons and Marxism
in America" (W.A. Glaser),
1954.12
Allen, David Grayson, 1981.1
Allen, Gay Wilson, 1980.1
Allen, H.C., 1957.3; 1959.1;
1966.1
Allison, Clinton B., 1976.1
Almack, John C., 1925.1
Alvord, Clarence W., 1916.1;
1921.1
Ambrosius, Lloyd E., 1971.1
"Amenities as a Factor in Re-
gional Growth" (E.L. Ullman),
1954.23
"America--A Young Civilization?"
(M. Lerner), 1946.8
America and French Culture, 1750-
1848 (H.M. Jones), 1927.12
"America and the Individual"
(R.B. Nye), 1966.26
America as a Civilization: Life
and Thought in the United
States Today (M. Lerner),
1957.13-14
"America as Frontier" (T.H.

Johnson), 1947.10
America Is Different: The
Search for Jewish Identity
(S.E. Rosenberg), 1955.22
America Moves West (R.E. Riegel),
1930.17; reviews of (A.P.
James), 1932.27
"America Since the 1890s" (B.
Steinsher), 1975.17
America: The Story of a Free
People (A. Nevins and H.S.
Commager), 1942.15
American Biographies (W.
Preston), 1940.16
† American Character. See
national character and the
frontier thesis
"American City: From George
Bancroft to Charles A. Beard,
The" (E. Feldman), 1972.9
"American Colleges and the Trans-
mission of Culture: The Case
of the Mugwumps" (J.
McZachlan), 1974.17
American Conscience, The (R.
Burlingame), 1957.6
"American Definition of History:
Turner, An" (F. Stern),
1956.15
"American Democracy and European
Interpreter" (W.E. Lingelbach),
1937.8
"American Democracy and the Fron-
tier" (B.F. Wright, Jr.),
1930.21
"American Democracy Distinguished
from Democracy in General"
(J.D. Barnhart), 1966.2
American Development: Essays in
Honor of Paul Wallace Gates
(F. Merk), 1969.22
"American Economic Growth: Its
Historiography in the Twen-
tieth Century" (W.N. Parker),
1968.39
"American Environmental History:
A New Teaching Frontier" (R.
Nash), 1972.18
"American Evaluations of European
Agriculture" (C.H. Danhof),
1949.6

Index

Index

"City in American Civilization,
The" (A.M. Schlesinger),
1949.18
"City in American History, The"
(A.M. Schlesinger), 1940.17
"City in the Westward Movement--
A Bibliogrpahical Note, The"
(B. Luckingham), 1974.16
"City's Place in Civilization,
The" (C.A. Beard), 1928.1
"Civilization in Transit" (D.R.
Fox), 1927.6
"Civilization Over Savage;
Frederick Jackson Turner and
the Indian" (D.A. Nichols),
1972.19
Clark, Dan Albert, 1937.2;
1942.3
Clark, Robert Carlson, 1932.25;
1969.36
Clark, Samuel D., 1942.6
Clark, Thomas D., 1972.8
"Clarksville Compact of 1785,
The" (S.C. Williams), 1944.11
Class Conflict, Slavery, and the
United States Consitution
(S. Lynd), 1967.14
Classified Bibliography of the
Periodical Literature of the
Trans-Mississippi West, 1811-
1957, A (O. Winther), 1961.32
"Classics on the Midwest Fron-
tier" (W.A. Agard), 1957.2
"Cleric or Critic? The Intellec-
tual in the University" (J.W.
Ward), 1965.20
Clio's Servant: The State His-
torical Society of Wisconsin,
1846-1954 (C.L. Lord and C.
Ubbelohde), 1967.13
"Closed Frontier and American
Tragedy, The" (H.P.
Simonson), 1968.47
Closed Frontier: Studies in
American Literary Tragedy,
The (H.P. Simonson), 1970.27
†Closed-space doctrine, 1944.5-6;
1946.11; 1950.9; 1955.18;
1965.19; 1969.2; 1972.1;
1973.12; 1974.10
†Closing of the frontier, 1902.1;

1909.3; 1919.1; 1925.5; 1926.
5; 1927.9; 1930.15; 1931.1,
16; 1932.20; 1935.4; 1937.2;
1946.2; 1947.14; 1948.12;
1951.5; 1954.19; 1964.23;
1969.2; 1973.12
"Closure of the Public Domain,
The" (E.L. Peffer), 1942D
Cohen, Bronwen J., 1974.5
Coleman, Peter J., 1958.10; 1960.
10; 1962.7; 1964.13
Coleman, William, 1966.10
†Colonial history and the fron-
tier thesis, 1961.27; 1964.13
"Colonial Origins of the United
States: Turnerian View"
(W.R. Jacobs), 1971.15
"Colonial Struggle Against
Barbarism, The" (L.B.
Wright), 1955.26
Colony to Nation: A History of
Canada (A.R.M. Lower), 1946.9
"Colorado's Urban-Mining Safety
Valve" (D.A. Smith), 1971.19
Coman, Katherine, 1912.1
Commager, Henry Steele, 1927.5;
1933.6; 1942.15; 1950.6;
1951.7
"Comment: Fallacies in the
Turner Thesis" (W.R. Hogan),
1963.12
"Comments on 'Space, Time, Cul-
ture and the New Frontier'"
(E. Pomeroy), 1964.22
"Commentary to Walter Prescott
Webb's Geographical-Histori-
cal Concepts in American His-
tory" (D.G. Meinig), 1960.18
Commons, John R., 1918.2
-and Turner, 1954.5
"Communication Revolution, The"
(R.G. Albion), 1932.2
"Community Conflict in Roseburg,
Oregon, 1870-1885" (W.
Robbins), 1973.29
"Comparability of American His-
tory, The" (C.V. Woodward),
1968.52
"Comparative Analysis of Economic
Development in the American
West and South, A" (D.F.
Dowd), 1956.2

257

Index

Index

"Frontier: Hardy Perennial, The" (C. Culmsee), 1967.4

Frontier Historian: The Life and Work of Edward Everett Dale (A.M. Gibson), 1975.9

"Frontier Hypothesis: A Corollary, The" (W.E. Shiels), 1935.20

"Frontier Hypothesis and Related Spatial Concepts" (R. Eigeneer), 1973.12

"Frontier Hypothesis and the Historian, The" (O.O. Winther), 1957.26; 1962.30

"Frontier Hypothesis in Recent Historiography, The" (M. Zaslow), 1948.15

Frontier in Alaska and the Malaniska Colony, The (O.W. Miller), 1975.12

"Frontier in American Development: A Review, The" (P.D. Evans), 1971.11

"Frontier in American History: Frederick Jackson Turner" (J. B. Frantz), 1976.4

Frontier in American History, The (F.J. Turner), reviews of (C. Becker), 1920.1; (C.W. Alvord), 1921.1; (C.A. Beard), 1921.3; 1939.1; (G. Fuller), 1921.5; (A. Johnson), 1921.7; (E.S. Meany), 1921.8; (R. Thompson), 1969.33

"Frontier in American Literature, The" (J.B. Hubbell), 1925.2; (G. Paine), 1928.6

Frontier in American Literature, The (L.L. Lockwood), 1927.8

"Frontier in American Thought and Character, The" (R.A. Billington), 1963.1

"Frontier in Comparative View, The" (D. Gerhard), 1959.13

"Frontier in Hispanic America, The" (V.A. Belaunde), 1923.3

"Frontier in History, The" (O.D. Lattimore), 1962.14; 1968.26

"Frontier in Illinois History, The" (R.A. Billington), 1950.3

Frontier in Latin American History, The (A. Hennessy), 1978.5

"Frontier in Latin American History, The" (A. Hennessy), 1978.5

"Frontier in Recent African History" (G. Deveneau), 1978.3

"Frontier in the History of New France, The" (A.L. Burt), 1940.3

Frontier in Perspective, The (W. D. Wyman and C.B. Kroeber), reviews of (D.F. Carmony), 1958.9; (C. Elliot), 1958.12; (J.C. Malin), 1958.16; (J. Walton), 1958.29

"Frontier in South Africa: A Comparative Study of the Turner Thesis, The" (R.B. Ford), 1966D

"Frontier Influence--a Perspective, The" (J. Frost), 1947.9

"Frontier Land Clubs, or Claim Associations" (B. Shambaugh), 1900.1

"Frontier: Metaphor, Myth, and Model, The" (D.A. Livingstone and R.T. Harrison), 1980.9

Frontier Mind: A Cultural Analysis of the Kentucky Frontiersman, The (A.K. Moore), 1957.18; reviews of (D.F. Tingley), 1957.23; (E. R. Bingham), 1958.6

"Frontier of New England in the Seventeenth and Eighteenth Centuries and Its Significance in American History, The" (S. D. Dodge), 1942.11

"Frontier or the Market?, The" (R. Hofstadter), 1955.15

"Frontier Re-examined, The" (J.F. McDermott), 1967.15

Frontier Re-examined, The (J.F. McDermott), 1967.15

"Frontier School and Canadian History, The" (J.L. McDougall), 1929.6; 1970.23

"Frontier Settlement in Eastern Ontario in the Nineteenth

267

Index

Frost, James, 1947.9
Frykman, George A., 1952.6; 1964.8
Fuller, George N., 1921.5
†Fur trade, 1898.1; 1909.5; 1962.10
"Fur Trade and Its Historians, The" (D.L. Morgan), 1966.24-25
Furman, Necah Stewart, 1976.5
Fussell, Edwin S., 1965.6-7

Gabriel, Ralph Henry, 1929.3; 1940.5
Gara, Larry, 1962.9
"Garden of the World: Fact and Faction, The" (R.A. Billington), 1958.3
Garland, Hamlin, 1919.1; 1923.4
Garraghan, Gilbert J., 1941.8
Garrison, George P., 1906.1
Gates, Paul Wallace, 1936.2; 1942.13; 1957.10; 1960.11; 1966.15; 1968.11
"Generation of Prairie Historiography, A" (E.D. Ross), 1946.15
"Generation of the Frontier Hypothesis: 1893-1932, A" (F. L. Paxson), 1933.16; 1941.12
"Genesis of the Frontier Thesis, The" (H. Cravens), 1973.8
Genesis of the Frontier Thesis: A Study in Historical Creativity, The (R.A. Billington), 1971.8
"Geographical Boundaries" (E.C. Semple), 1911.1
†Geographical determinism. See Envrionmentalism and the frontier thesis
"Geographical Determinists in Canadian History" (A.R.M. Lower), 1939.11
"Geographical Influences in American History" (D. Perkins), 1947.12
"Geographical News: Twenty-second Annual Meeting of the Association of American Geographers" (Anon.), 1926.1

"Geographical Space Concept: Anglo-American New-land Version" (J.C. Malin), 1955.18
†Geography and the frontier thesis, 1903.1; 1922.1, 4; 1941.4; 1946.10; 1947.12; 1960.18; 1961.33; 1965.15; 1969.18; 1972.17; 1973.38; 1975.8; 1980.2, 13
"Geopolitical Conditions of the Evolution of Russian Nationality" (P. Bizzilli), 1930.2
George, Henry, and Turner, 1955.4
Gerhard, Dietrich, 1959.13
†Germ theory, 1955.24; 1958.18; 1968.38; 1972.19; 1973.10
"Ghost of the Frontier, The" (D. L. McMurry), 1936.8
Giants in the Earth (O.E. Rölvaag), 1972.14
Gibson, Arrell M., 1968.12; 1975.9
Gilbert, Felix, 1965.11
Gilman, Daniel Coit, and Turner, 1961.33
Glaser, William A., 1954.12
Goetzman, William H., 1959.14; 1960.12; 1963.6; 1970.15; 1976.6
Going, Allen J., 1965.8
"Going Beyond the Ninety-fifth Meridian" (E. Dick), 1943.6
Golden Day: A Study in American Experience and Culture, The (L. Mumford), 1926.4
Golden Door: A History of the United States of American (1607-1945), The (R. Thompson), 1969.32
Goldman, Eric F., 1940.6
Goodin, Robert, 1980.5
Goodrich, Carter, 1935.13; 1936.3; 1938.8; 1966.16
Goodykoontz, Colin Brummitt, 1971.2
Gorer, Geoffrey, 1955.9
Gottman, Jean, 1973.13; 1975.10
"Government and Politics" (H.N. Scheiber), 1969.29
Graaf, Lawrence B., 1975.6
"Grand Jury on the Frontier, The" (R.D. Younger), 1956.17

Index

Index

Index

Reid, John P., 1981.13

"Reflections on Boorstin's America" (F. Thuaite), 1960.25

"Reflections on the Nature of the Westward Movement" (J.C. Parish), 1930.12-13; 1943.13

"Region: Regionalism in the United States" (R.B. Vance), 1968.49

Regionalism. See Sectionalism and the frontier thesis

"Regionalism" (H. Hintze), 1934.9; (J.H. Shera), 1953.16

"Regionalism, Nationalism, Localism: The Pacific Northwest in American History" (G.A. Frykman), 1952.6

"Regionalism versus Sectionalism in the South's Place in the National Economy" (H.W. Odum), 1934.14

"Regions, Classes, Sections in American History" (W.B. Hesseltine), 1944.3

"Relations Between History and Geography, The" (J.O.M. Broek), 1941.4

"Relevance of Tocqueville, The" (H.G. Nicholas), 1974.20

†Religion and the frontier thesis, 1923.6; 1924.9; 1926.6; 1930.19; 1935.20; 1939.8; 1963.13; 1964.18; 1965.5

Religion in the Development of American Culture (W.W. Sweet), 1952.16

"Remaking American History" (C.N. Degler), 1980.3

"Remarks" (M.L. Hansen), 1934.5

Renshaw, Patrick, 1963.23

"Reorientation of American Culture in the 1890's, The" (J. Higham), 1965.10

"Report of the Council" (Anon.), 1932.17-18; 1960.1

"Report on the Conference on the Relations of Geography to History" (E.E. Sparks), 1908.2

Reps, John William, 1979.6

"Repudiation of the Pioneer, The" (M. Van Doren), 1928.12

"Research in Western Economic History--Problems and Opportunities" (G.D. Nash), 1963.20

"Resources and Sociopsychological Safety Valve, A" (E. VonNardoff), 1966.35

"Restless Grant County: Americans on the Move" (P.J. Coleman), 1962.7; 1969.7

"Restless Temper, The" (G.W. Pierson), 1964.21

"Resurgent Southern Sectionalism, 1933-1955" (F.M. Green), 1969.12

"Retarded Frontier, The" (G. Vincent), 1898.2

"Return of the Native; Some Reflections on the History of American Indians" (C. Bolt), 1974.2

"Revaluation of the Period before the Civil War: Railroads, A" (R.R. Russel), 1928.8

"Revision Article--Frontier and Section: A Turner 'Myth'" (N.D. Harper), 1952.8

Revolutionary Frontier, 1763-1783, The (J.M. Sosin), 1967.21

Revolutionary New England, 1761-1776 (J.T. Adams), 1923.1

Reynolds, Robert L., 1957.21

†Rhetoric and imagery, 1964.25; 1971.4; 1972.7; 1977.5, 7

"Rhetorical Genius of Style in the 'Frontier Hypothesis' of Frederick Jackson Turner, The" (R.H. Carpenter), 1972.7

"Rhetorical Heritage of Frederick Jackson Turner, The" (G.F. Berquist), 1971.4

"Rhodes and the Writing of History" (R. Cruden), 1961.9

Index

W. Johnson, and F.R. Dunn),
1951.1; 1955.3; (J.A.
Carroll), 1960.8; (H.P.
Simonson), 1963.26; (R.A.
Billington), 1966.7
"Significance of the Frontier in
the Writing of Antebellum
Southern History, The" (T.
Lieber), 1969.20
"Significance of the Mississippi
Valley in American Diplomatic
History, 1686-1890, The" (R.
W. Van Alstyne), 1949.22
"Significance of Turner's Sec-
tional Thesis, The" (M.C.
Steiner), 1978.7
Simler, Norman J., 1958.25;
1968.46
Simons, Algie Martin, 1911.2
-and Turner, 1954.12
Simonson, Harold P., 1963.25;
1964.25; 1968.47; 1970.27
Singh, N. Gopaldatta, 1981.17
"Sir John MacDonald and Canadian
Historians" (D.G. Creighton),
1948.4
"Sixth Newberry Library Con-
ference on American Studies,
The" (Anon.), 1955.2
Skinner, Constance Lindsay,
1935.21; 1961.25
†Slavery and the frontier thesis,
1963.18
Smith, Alice E., 1973.30
Smith, Charlotte Watkins, 1956.14
Smith, David C., 1974.25
Smith, Duane A., 1971.19
Smith, Henry Nash, 1950.15;
1951.17; 1957.22; 1961.22;
1970.28
Smith, James Charles, 1977.22
Smith, Page, 1960.22-23; 1966.34
Social Development of Canada: An
Introductory Study with
Selected Documents, The (S.
D. Clark), 1942.6
Social Forces in American History
(A.M. Simons), 1911.2
†Social equality and the fron-
tier, 1962.28
"Social Philosophy of Frederick

Jackson Turner" (P.
Maginnig), 1968D
Social Politics in the United
States (F.E. Haynes), 1924.4
"Social Relationships in
Trempealeau County" (M.
Curti), 1969.8
"Social Scientists Defend Turner"
(S. Elkins and E. McKitrick),
1970.13
†Social Studies and the frontier
thesis, 1967.17-18; 1968.10;
1969.27; 1970.3, 13; 1980.13
"Social Theory and the Pioneer"
(A.G. Bogue), 1960.7; 1968.8
"Socioeconomic Change in Racine,
1850-1880" (R.D. Weber),
1974.27
Solway, Clifford, 1970.29
"Some Aspects of the Frontier in
Canadian History" (W.N.
Sage), 1928.9
"Some Aspects of the Influence of
Social Problems and Ideas
upon the Study and Writing of
History" (C. Becker), 1913.1
"Some Aspects of the Recent His-
tory of American Historiog-
raphy" (H.H. Bellot), 1952.2
"Some Aspects of Turner's
Thought" (R.A. Billington),
1958.5
"Some British Reflections on
Turner and the Frontier" (J.
Potter), 1969.27; 1976.10
"Some Characteristics of Latin
American Urban History" (R.M.
Morse), 1962.19
"Some Consequences of the Urban
Movement in American History"
(W.S. Halt), 1953.12
"Some Considerations on the Fron-
tier Concept of F.J. Turner"
(M. Kane), 1940.11
"Some Crude Generalizations
About American Voting Be-
havior" (L. Benson), 1961.2
"Some Facts Bearing on the
Safety-Valve Theory" (J.
Schafer), 1936.14; 1961.23
"Some Generalizations About

Index

"Turner Thesis and the Westward Movement: A Reappraisal, The" (J.K. Putnam), 1976.11

Turner Thesis: Concerning the Role of the Frontier in American History, The (G.R. Taylor), 1949.21

"Turner Thesis: Criticism and Defense, The" (R.L. Lokken), 1941.10

"Turner Thesis in Comparative Perspective: An Introduction, The" (S.M. Lipset), 1968.30

"Turner Thesis: Predictive Model" (S. Elkins and E. McKitrick), 1964.7

"Turner Thesis Re-examined, The" (E.S. Lee), 1961.15; 1968.27-28; 1970.21

"Turnerian Frontier: A Study in the Migration of Ideas, The" (J.L.M. Gulley), 1959.15

"Turner's America" (J. Schafer), 1934.19

"Turner's Early Writings" (J. Schafer), 1938.15

"Turner's Formative Period" (F. Mood), 1938.13

"Turner's Frontier Philosophy" (J. Schafer), 1933.21; 1961.24

"Turner's Frontier Thesis and the Modern American Empire" (L.E. Ambrosius), 1971.1

"Turner's Legacy and the Search for a Reorientation of Western History: A Review Essay" (H.N. Scheiber), 1969.32

"Turner's Methodology: Multiple Working Hypotheses or Ruling Theory?" (W.R. Jacobs), 1968.22

"Turner's Safety-Valve and Free Negro Westward Migration" (G. R. Woolfolk), 1965.22; 1968.53

"Turner's Safety-Valve Theory" (I. Rabinowitz), 1952.14

"Turner's 'The Frontier in American History'" (C.A. Beard), 1939.2

"Turner's Theory of Social Evolution" (R. Freund), 1945.4

"Turner's Views Challenged" (G.W. Pierson), 1966.28

"Turner's Vision" (H.C. Hockett), 1957.12

"Turning History Upside Down" (C. Solway), 1970.29

"Turnover of Farm Population in Kansas, The" (J.C. Malin), 1935.15

Tuttle, William M., 1967.22

"Twentieth Century American West, The" (B.J. Williams), 1969.35

"Twenty-fourth Annual Meeting of the Mississippi Valley Historical Association, The" (J. W. Oliver), 1931.10

$2500 a Year: From Scarcity to Abundance (M. Ezekiel), 1936.1

"Two or More Worlds of Willa Cather, The" (M. Cunliffe), 1974.9

Tyler, S. Lymann, 1977.24

Tyrrell, William Blake, 1977.25

Ubbelohde, Carl, 1967.13

Ullman, Edward L., 1954.23

"Ulyssess Prentiss Hedrick: Horticulturist and Historian" (P.W. Gates), 1966.15

Understanding Negro History (D.W. Hoover), 1968.20

Understanding the American Past (E.N. Saveth), 1954.23

"Understanding the Populists" (J. Turner), 1980.14

"Unfamiliar Essay by F.J. Turner, The" (F. Mood), 1937.10

†Uniqueness of the American experience, 1912.4; 1966.4; 1969.31; 1980.6

"Unite to Divide; Divide to Unite: The Shaping of American Federalism" (W.T. Hutchinson), 1959.17

"United States, The" (E.M. Hugh-Jones and E.A. Radice), 1936.6

Index

United States: An Experiment in
Democracy, The (C. Becker),
1920.2
United States, 1830-1850: The
Nation and Its Sections, The
(A. Craven), 1958.11
United States, 1830-1850: The
Nation and Its Sections, The
(F.J. Turner), reviews of (J.
D. Barnhart), 1935.1; (R.M.
Robbins), 1935.19; (G.M.
Stephenson), 1935.22; (J.D.
Hicks), 1936.5; (F. Mood),
1951.14; (R. Bardolph),
1952.1
University of Wisconsin, 1848-
1924, The (M. Curti and V.
Carstensen), 1949.5
"Unpublished Papers of F.J.
Turner, The" (T.M. Plaisted),
1943.15
"Untarnishing the Dream:
Mobility, Opportunity and
Order in Modern America" (E.
Knopf), 1977.12
†Urban development and the fron-
tier thesis, 1909.5; 1923.4;
1928.1; 1933.22; 1934.17;
1940.17; 1941.16; 1945.12;
1948.3; 1949.18; 1953.12;
1955.8; 1958.28; 1959.28;
1963.8; 1965.4; 1967.15;
1968.1, 25, 50; 1970.8, 33;
1971.17, 19; 1972.9; 1974.16,
19; 1977.23; 1978.10
Urban Frontier: The Rise of
Western Cities, 1790-1830,
The (R.C. Wade), 1959.28;
review of (R. Constantine),
1959.8
"Urban History: Retrospect and
Prospect" (M.H. Ebner),
1981.5
"Urban Liberalism and the Clear
Grits" (J.M.S. Careless),
1970.8
"Urban Life in Western America,
1790-1830" (R.C. Wade),
1958.28; 1969.34
"Urbanization" (R.C. Wade),
1968.50

"Useless Past: American Intellectuals and the Frontier Thesis:
1910-1930, The" (W.I. Susman),
1963.26
Usher, Ellis B., 1919.5

Valley of Democracy: The Fron-
tier versus the Plantation in
the Ohio Valley, 1775-1818
(F.D. Barnhart), 1953.2; re-
views of (R. Gerguson),
1954.11; (B.E. Hardin),
1954.13
"Valley of the New Democracy, The"
(J. Finley), 1915.3
Van Alstyne, Richard W., 1949.22;
1960.26
VanDerZee, J., 1910.7
Van Doren, Mark, 1928.12
Van Every, Dale, 1961.27
Van Hise, Charles Richard, and
Turner, 1960.27
Vance, Maurice M., 1960.27
Vance, Rupert B., 1931.14;
1968.49
Veblen, Thorstein, 1978.6
Vecoli, Rudolph J., 1970.32
Veysey, Laurence R., 1960.28
Vincent, George E., 1898.2
Virgin Land: The American West
as Symbol and Myth (H.N.
Smith), 1950.15; reviews of
(R. Hofstadter), 1950.7;
"Virginia and the West: An In-
terpretation" (C.W. Alvord),
1916.1
Von Nardoff, Ellen, 1962.27;
1966.35
Vorpahl, Ben M., 1967.23
"Voting Habits in the United
States: A Note on Two Maps"
(J.K. Wright), 1932.40

"W.E.B. DuBois and Frederick
Jackson Turner: The Unveiling
and Preemption of America's
'Inner History'" (W. Toll),
1974.26
"W.P. Webb: Idea Man and Seminarian" (N.S. Furman), 1976.5

Index

"Willa Cather: American Experience and European Tradition" (J. Woodress), 1974.29

"William Graham Sumner and the Frontier" (E.H. Parker), 1956.11

Williams, Burton J., 1968.51; 1969.35; 1973.34; 1980.15

Williams, George Huntston, 1959.30

Williams, John Alexander, 1978.10

Williams, Mary W., 1915.8

Williams, Samuel C., 1944.11

Williams, William Appleman, 1955.26; 1961.31; 1969.36; 1971.1; 1973.35

Williamson, Chilton, 1960.32

Williamson, W.L., 1953.18

Wills, Morris W., 1978.11

Wilson, Charles Morrow, 1931.16

Wilson, Woodrow, 1895.1; 1897.1; 1943.19

-and Turner, 1927.1; 1945.15; 1954.16; 1956.10; 1957.3; 1967.3; 1968.37; 1972.20

"Wilson's First Battle at Princeton: The Chair for Turner" (W.R. Jacobs), 1954.15

Wimmer, Larry T., 1980.7

"Windfalls of the Frontier" (W.P. Webb), 1951.20

Winks, Robin W., 1959.31; 1971.21

"Winners of the Pulitzer Prizes in Literature" (Anon.), 1933.2

Winther, Oscar Osbourn, 1942.20; 1957.26; 1961.32; 1962.30; 1969.37

"Wisconsin: A Constitution of Democracy" (F.L. Paxson), 1918.4

"Wisconsin Historian" (C.L. Becker), 1946.4

Wisconsin River of a Thousand Isles, The (A. Derleth), 1942.8

Wisconsin Witness to Frederick Jackson Turner: A Collection of Essays on the Historian and the Thesis (O.L. Burnette, Jr.), 1961.7

"Wisconsin's Eminence" (L.P. Kellogg), 1938.12

Wise, Gene, 1973.36

Wish, Harvey, 1960.33; 1962.31

Wishart, David J., 1969.38

Witt, Grace, 1969.39

Witke, Carl, 1939.16

Woestmeyer, Ina Faye, 1939.17

Wolfe, Thomas, 1970.7

†Women and the frontier, 1964.24; 1974.15; 1977.19

"Women's Role in American West" (T.A. Larson), 1974.15

Wood, Charles, 1973.37

Woodburn, James A., 1926.7

Woodress, James, 1974.29

"Woodrow Wilson and Frederick Jackson Turner" (G.C. Osborn), 1956.10

Woodrow Wilson: Life and Letters, Princeton, 1890-1910 (R.S. Baker), 1927.1

Woodrow Wilson: The Academic Years (H.W. Bragdon), 1967.3

Woodrow Wilson: The Early Years (G.C. Osborn), 1968.37

"Woodrow Wilson's Opinion of Professor Turner" (W. Wilson), 1943.19

Woodward, C. Vann, 1960.34; 1968.52

Woolfolk, George R., 1965.22-23; 1968.53

Wright, Benjamin F., Jr., 1930.21; 1933.26; 1934.21; 1949.23

Wright, C.W., 1926.8

Wright, Frank Lloyd, and Turner, 1965.10

Wright, John K., 1932.39-40; 1961.33

Wright, Louis B., 1948.14; 1955.26; 1964.28; 1972.21

Writing American History; Essays on Modern Scholarship (J. Higham), 1970.17

Writing of American History (M. Krause), 1953.13

Writing Southern History: Essays in Historiography in Honor of Fletcher M. Green (edited by A. Link and R. Patrick), 1965.3